How Wood
POLLICUT GROUNDS
Foot Path from Chilton to Wootten
CHILTON
A Scale of Chains
Nine to one Inch

COWS & CURATES

The story of the land and livings of Christ Church, Oxford

COWS & CURATES

The story of the land and livings of Christ Church, Oxford

Judith Curthoys

P

PROFILE BOOKS

First published in Great Britain in 2020 by
Profile Books Ltd
29 Cloth Fair
London EC1A 7JQ
www.profilebooks.com

1 3 5 7 9 10 8 6 4 2

A CIP catalogue record for this book is available from the British Library.

ISBN: 978 1 78816 250 0

Text design by Sue Lamble
Typeset in Photina by MacGuru Ltd

Printed and bound in Great Britain by TJ International, Padstow

Contents

	List of illustrations	vii
	Introduction and acknowledgements	xiii
1	Foundation and endowment	1
2	Managing the agricultural estate I: revenue	19
3	Parsons and parsonages: Christ Church's incumbencies	44
4	Managing the agricultural estate II: expansion and improvement	74
5	From tillage to towns: Christ Church's urban estates	113
6	Managing the agricultural estate III: reform	137
7	The right of 'coleing': Christ Church's mining estates	158
8	Managing the agricultural estate IV: the modern period	168
	Appendix 1: Monastic houses suppressed to endow Cardinal College, 1525	189
	Appendix 2: Christ Church's foundation and trust endowment	191
	Appendix 3: Treasurers of Christ Church	204
	Appendix 4: Deans of Christ Church	206
	Conventions and monetary values	207
	Notes	208
	Bibliography	241
	Index	249

Illustrations

Except where otherwise indicated, all illustrations are from the Christ Church Archive and are reproduced by permission of the Governing Body of Christ Church. Abbreviated sources refer to entries in the bibliography on pages 241–7.

Endpapers

Front: A map of Dorton in Buckinghamshire, revised by Richard Davis of Lewknor, surveyor and topographer to George III, from an earlier map, to accompany a written survey and valuation of 1789. (CCA Maps Dorton 1)

Back: Map of Barrets Farm in Shropshire, from John Probert's survey of the Careswell Trust estates in Shropshire and Staffordshire, 1769. (CCA viii.a.53, fol. 10v)

Colour plates

Photographs by Alina Nachescu unless otherwise indicated.

The church of St Laurence, Blackmore, Essex. (Wikicommons)

The chapel at Bradwell Priory in Buckinghamshire. (With thanks to Dr Noël James)

Elizabeth I, by an unknown artist. (By kind permission of the Governing Body of Christ Church)

The strongroom in the Muniment Tower at Magdalen College. (By kind permission of the President and Fellows of Magdalen College, Oxford)

Plan of Oxford Castle, drawn around 1617. (CCA Maps Oxford St George 1)
Canon Thomas Tanner. (By kind permission of the Governing Body of Christ Church)
Maps of Abbots (or College) Wood in South Stoke in 1726 and 1778. (CCA Maps South Stoke 1 and 2)
Map of Binsey by Richard Davis of Lewknor, 1792. (CCA Maps Binsey 2)
Map of Wood Norton, 1757. (CCA Maps Woodnorton 1)
Map of the estate of Wath upon Dearne in 1777. (CCA Maps Wath 1)
Plan of land in Worcester, 1814. (CCA Maps Worcester 5)
Map of Hawkhurst in Kent by Frederick Young, 1818. (CCA Maps Hawkhurst 2)
Benjamin Badcock's huge map of Christ Church's estate in Oxford in 1829. (CCA Maps Oxford 21)
The farm in Kentish Town left to Christ Church by Canon Robert South in 1716; plan of 1832. (CCA Maps Kentish Town 1)
Plan for forty-four villas along the Kentish Town Road, 1833. (CCA Maps Kentish Town 2)
Map of Hillesden, 1847. (CCA xlviii.c.8)
Plan of land sales in Oxford to the Great Western Railway in 1852. (CCA Maps Oxford St Thomas 17)
Section of Badcock's 1829 map showing properties in Fish (or Fisher) Row sold to a local brewer. (CCA Maps Oxford 21)
A page from Badcock's accompanying book presenting his map in small sections. (CCA viii.c.2)
Plans of the land above Radford coalmine, in Somerset, and the workings within it, in 1840. (CCA Maps Midsomer Norton 3 and 4)
Architects' drawing, 1946, for farm labourers' cottages in Elsfield. (CCA Maps Elsfield 4)
Design for cottages at Wragg Marsh Farm, near Spalding, 1947. (CCA Maps Wragg Marsh 1)

Black and white illustrations

Photographs by Alina Nachescu unless otherwise indicated.

Licence to Cardinal Wolsey, dated 10 May 1526, to appropriate certain rectories to Cardinal College. (CCA DP iv.c.2) 2
View of the ruins of Tonbridge Priory in 1735. (Supplied by and used with the kind permission of the Tonbridge Historical Society) 3
Opening page of the bailiffs' book for Cardinal College. (CCA DP iv.c.4) 6
The college seal box. (Photograph by Dave Stumpp) 7
The first membrane of the Charter of Dotation, dated 4 December 1546. (CCA DP vi.c.2) 10
Letter signed by Mary Tudor awarding the parsonage of Tring and Wigginton. (CCA MS Estates 35, fol. 1) 14
Plan of the castle in Wallingford in the early eighteenth century. (CCA Maps Wallingford 1) 15
Notary mark of Thomas Randolph from the Chapter Book, dated 1552. (CCA D&C i.b.1, fol. 20v) 17
Entry in the Book of Evidences for the hamlet of Thrupp, near Daventry. (CCA1.c.3, pp. 774–5) 21
A typical lease, or indenture, for the property in North Nibley from 7 December 1616. (CCA Leases North Nibley 3) 23
Letter sent from Skipton Castle just before it was besieged in 1642. (CCA MS Estates 107, fol. 84r) 29
Map of Chandlings Wood, just outside Oxford, dated 1724. (CCA Maps Chandlings 1) 36
A ninety-nine-year lease from Great Bowden. (CCA Leases Great Bowden A 1) 40
Staverton church and parsonage, photographed in 1868. (CCA xiv.b.2, p. 86) 48
Map showing the huge parish of Kirkham in 1801. (CCA Maps Kirkham 1) 51
Sketch plans of 1813 for an extension to the parsonage house in Kirkham. (CCA xiv.b.2, p. 116) 55

Parsonage at Little Compton built by the Revd Marah in 1857. (CCA Maps Little Compton 1–3) 60
An urban property from the Book of Evidences, showing St Michael's parish in Oxford. (CCA1.c.2, p. 133) 76
A page from the 1494 terrier of the manor of Howard and Stranges in East Walton. (CCA viii.b.54) 77
Title page of the survey of the Careswell Trust estates in Shropshire and Staffordshire, drawn by John Probert in 1769. (CCA viii.a.53, fol. 1r) 100
Map of Sydnall Farm in Shropshire, from Probert's survey. (CCA viii.a.53, fol. 2v) 101
Map of Chadwick in 1764, showing the changes brought about by enclosure. (CCA Maps Chadwick 1) 105
Advertisement in *Jackson's Oxford Journal*, 13 November 1830, announcing the intention to enclose the parish of Benson. 109
St Thomas's parish in Oxford in 1785, soon after the New Road was built. (CCA Maps Oxford St Thomas 4) 117
Poster advertising the sale of building plots in St Thomas's parish in 1872. (CCA Leases St Thomas) 120
Shops in Christ Church's Kentish Town estate, a London suburb, *c.*1900. (CCA MS Estates 46, no. 16) 125
Sketch plan showing the line of the Grand Junction Canal across Christ Church land near Daventry. (CCA Maps Thrupp 1) 130
Plan dated 1610 of Christ Church's only foundation property in London, a single house near the Old Bailey. (CCA Leases St Sepulchre's 4) 133
Sales particulars for the Dean and Chapter's Bostock Trust houses in Windsor. (CCA MS Estates 5, fol. 267) 135
The first page of the printed version of the Christ Church Oxford Act of 1867. (CCA i.a.3) 143
Canon Robert Payne Smith. (© National Portrait Gallery) 144
Auction particulars for Hill Farm in Offenham. (CCA MS Estates 102, fol. 222) 149

Robert Godfrey Faussett. (© National Portrait Gallery) 153
Thomas Vere Bayne. (CCA CR 92/1) 154
Bartholomew Price. (Image by kind permission of the Master, Fellows and Scholars of Pembroke College, Oxford) 155
Lease of 1708 for the right to mine coal on Christ Church land in Somerset. (CCA Leases Midsomer Norton B 1) 160
William 'Strata' Smith; engraving of 1837 by Thomas Anthony Dean, after a portrait by Hugues Fourau. (© National Portrait Gallery) 164
William Buckland, painted by Thomas Phillips. 165
Hill Farm, Elsfield, *c.*1950. (CCA P.TOP.Farms 66) 174
Newspaper report of the fiasco of the distraint order at Elham in 1932. 176
Agricultural labourers' cottages built at Wragg Marsh in 1949. (CCA P.TOP.Farms 55) 182
Cottages in Brize Norton in 1947 before re-thatching. (CCA P.TOP.Farms 106) 182
A Ministry of Works concrete hut in agricultural use by the tenant of College Wood Farm, Woodcote. (CCA P.TOP.Farms 13) 183
Modern farm buildings, *c.*1950, at Manor Farm in Pitchcott. (CCA P.TOP.Farms 95) 183

Location maps

Monastic houses dissolved to fund the college's foundation, and northern estates given for the Dean's stipend. 4
The Henrician endowment. 12
Properties acquired after the foundation from the seventeenth to the twentieth centuries. 96
Christ Church's estate in 2020, showing the number of properties by category in thirteen English counties. (Contains OS data © Crown copyright and database right, 2020) 186

Introduction and acknowledgements

This book is the third volume to grow out of *The Cardinal's College*, my history of Christ Church published in 2012.[1] To include an account of the endowment and the management of the estates, beyond the fact that it happened, would have made that book into a considerable doorstop and would have confused the story it was trying to tell.

Very little has been written about Christ Church's property, except by local historians researching their own 'patch'. Considerable gratitude is due to all those who have used the archive and then shared, with much generosity and enthusiasm, their own vast knowledge of their homes. And two major works have been indispensable: the volumes of the *Victoria County History* and those of the *History of the University of Oxford*, with its chapters on estates and financial management, are invaluable, filling in backgrounds and answering questions. To their editors, many thanks.

David Fletcher, twenty-five years ago, wrote his DPhil thesis on the growth of the use of estates maps from the seventeenth to the early nineteenth centuries – later published as *The Emergence of Estate Maps* – choosing Christ Church's collection as his primary source.[2] Although a book primarily about cartography, it has proved useful time and again. But the archive is rich in material other than its maps that relates to its properties, and it was high time that this lacuna in our published history was filled.

This has been an interesting book to write, creeping out beyond the walls of Christ Church to discover how, sometimes with a very light – almost non-existent – touch and on other occasions with considerable authority, the Dean and Chapter and later the Governing Body ensured that its endowment was managed to ensure the maintenance of its buildings and the education of its students in Oxford. It is very definitely not an account of Christ

Church's financial history; this would take someone with far greater knowledge of accountancy and investment management than I would begin to admit. A companion volume to Professor Robert Neild's fascinating account of the finances of Trinity College, Cambridge, remains to be written. It is instead the story of the administration of the landed estate and the incumbencies – which usually came with land attached – from Wolsey's foundation of Cardinal College in 1525 and the re-foundation by Henry VIII in 1546 until modern times.

Christ Church had an interest, at its foundation, in nearly 200 parishes across England and Wales. These were concentrated in the west of the country, running up from Berkshire and Oxfordshire through the Marches towards Cheshire and Lancashire, but the landholdings stretched from Cornwall to Yorkshire, and Montgomeryshire to Norfolk. I would have loved to include an example from each of these estates, and from those which were either given to Christ Church in trust or purchased, but with such a number to manage it proved difficult. I have, however, tried to draw from as many parts of the country as possible. I can only apologise to those who pick up the book and go straight to the index to find their home if it does not appear.

As with other aspects of Christ Church's history, the recording of its dealings with its tenants and the incumbents of the livings varies from period to period. At some times the concerns were for the management of manors, at others the settlement of entry fines and the division of profits. During the eighteenth and early nineteenth centuries agricultural improvement and industrial development was at the forefront of the Chapter's and the tenants' concerns. By the later years of the nineteenth century, the rise of nonconformity, social issues and the fashion for church restoration fill the pages of correspondence folders and minute books. The calendars of the estates correspondence compiled by Dr E. G. W. Bill from the 1950s have been an invaluable resource as they, and Dr Bill's other notes, have been for my earlier books.

All of these papers are safe and secure in the college's archive, but tracing the history of Christ Church's estates during the twentieth century is not so easy. No volumes of estates correspondence survive in the same form as they do for the period from the foundation to 1900, committee minutes have not been kept in the archive as a matter of course, and reports to the Governing Body by Finance and Estates Committees rarely include any discussion or policy decisions, rather just bald approvals – or disapprovals – of proposals by land agents. The Treasury's files also underwent substantial weeding after the Second World War. To write our modern estates history is, therefore, to attempt a jigsaw puzzle with the fragments of incomplete information needing supplementation from our understanding of land management in the wider world. The second half of the twentieth century, with the increased use of the telephone and then the proliferation of email, will be badly recorded not just at Christ Church but far more widely. We must ensure, for our own benefit and for posterity, that the records of the present century, in whatever format they are created, are better conserved. Without the assistance of Richard Benthall, Treasurer in the 1980s and 1990s, who read the chapter that was to be included in *The Cardinal's College* and made helpful comments then, and Paul Lindon at Savills for his advice on Christ Church's estates management in the modern period, the final chapter of the book would be much the poorer.

As always, Dean Percy has continued his support for my ventures into print. I am privileged to enjoy his friendship and kindness. The present Treasurer, James Lawrie, has also been generous in reading and commenting on the entire text before its submission. His advice and continuing willingness to fund these volumes is gratefully acknowledged.

I could never have begun to write on agricultural history had it not been for Oxford's wonderful Department of Continuing Education and Kellogg College. Over many years of association, these two institutions have enabled me to study part-time archaeology, local history and architectural history to Masters level and beyond. I owe the tutors there – particularly Kate Tiller, Chris Day and Paul Barnwell – more than I can say.

Experts from further afield have also come to my aid. Special mention must go to John Broad, historian of all things estates and agricultural, without whose wisdom and expertise I would be lost, not just in the writing of this book but also in the composition of a dissertation and papers over a period of nearly thirty years. His continued patience is very much appreciated. John Dunbabin, Fellow Emeritus of St Edmund Hall, gave considerable help on the finances of Christ Church, in its crisis years of the late nineteenth century in particular.

As always, my colleague archivists have been supportive providing information and illustrations from their own archives to back up and supplement the evidence of various aspects of estate management at Christ Church. I am especially indebted to Robin Darwall-Smith, archivist of both Jesus and University colleges, who provided reams of fascinating material on topics as far apart as woodland management and the Welsh Tithe War, and to Heidi Clough of the Bodleian Map Room who spent several hours patiently helping me to use map-making software which would otherwise have been beyond me. And then there are my immediate friends and associates at Christ Church, without whom no book would come to fruition: to Alina Nachescu (with the frequent and expert assistance of John Barrett from the Bodleian Library) and Dave Stumpp for their photographic skills, my thanks, and to Sandra Harrison in the Development and Alumni Relations Office, undying gratitude for her cheerfulness and endless labours on my behalf. As for everyone who comes up with ideas for titles and cover illustrations, usually over lunch in the staff dining room, and then who goes out and purchases a copy, I appreciate your interest and your tolerance.

Finally, but definitely not last in the list of those to whom I owe much, is the team at Profile: founder and managing director Andrew Franklin, the design team, the marketing people, and my wonderful copy-editor, Matthew Taylor, but most of all, Paul Forty, who sees me through the whole process from wild idea to celebratory champagne with an iron hand in the softest of velvet gloves. I am fortunate to benefit from such care and expertise.

Judith Curthoys
Christ Church
June 2020

1

Foundation and endowment

In 1525 Thomas Wolsey's intention was to build a college to surpass King's College, Cambridge, in grandeur. Wolsey, famously the son of an Ipswich butcher, was a graduate of Magdalen College, and had a spectacular career rising to become a cardinal, archbishop of York and Lord Chancellor of England. He was King Henry's right-hand man. Education was one of his greatest interests, and he believed that new schools and colleges were the way forward and that declining monastic institutions should be replaced by young and energetic educational establishments.[1] A college of his own foundation in Oxford, fed by a network of new grammar schools across the country, would have seemed a fitting project to achieve his objectives and to leave a lasting impression.

To achieve his purpose, he obtained permission to suppress over twenty monastic houses, mainly in the south-east and East Anglia.[2] Included among them were Bayham Abbey in Sussex, St Peter's in Wolsey's home town of Ipswich, Tonbridge Priory in Kent and St Frideswide's in Oxford. From the temporalities (secular property) belonging to these houses came rental income and court profits from tenements, land and manors. The spiritualities (religious property) included a large number of rectories, which generated not only rental income but also the right to the profitable great tithes, usually of corn and hay. Cardinal College, as it was to be called, would be rich; the income from the monastic houses alone came to more than £2,000 per annum, with a total income of around £2,400.[3]

Licence to Cardinal Wolsey, dated 10 May 1526, to appropriate certain rectories to Cardinal College. The document is on vellum, with a pendant seal attached with white, gold and green silk cords. The initials and miniature of Henry VIII enthroned have been prepared for illumination, but this was never carried out.

The suppression of the monastic houses has traditionally been seen not only as a precursor of the full dissolution of the monasteries a few years later but also as the action of a ruthless man. However, the permission to dissolve these was given to Wolsey by Pope Clement VII; copies of the *bullae* remain in the archive. The houses were often poor and under-staffed, and sometimes the behaviour of their residents was less than spiritual. Usually, the priors and monks or nuns were offered a pension or a transfer to another house. At Thoby (Essex), for example, there were only three men, including the prior, in residence at the time of the suppression, and at Horkesley and Tiptree (Essex) only two.[4] In some cases there was an offer of compensation. At Tonbridge (Kent), for example, Wolsey offered the town a school to replace the priory, which was closed in February 1525. The seven canons were all transferred to other houses, and the Cardinal proposed to found a grammar school for forty boys, with the opportunity for scholarships to Cardinal College. A meeting was held in the town in June 1525, but the response was rather

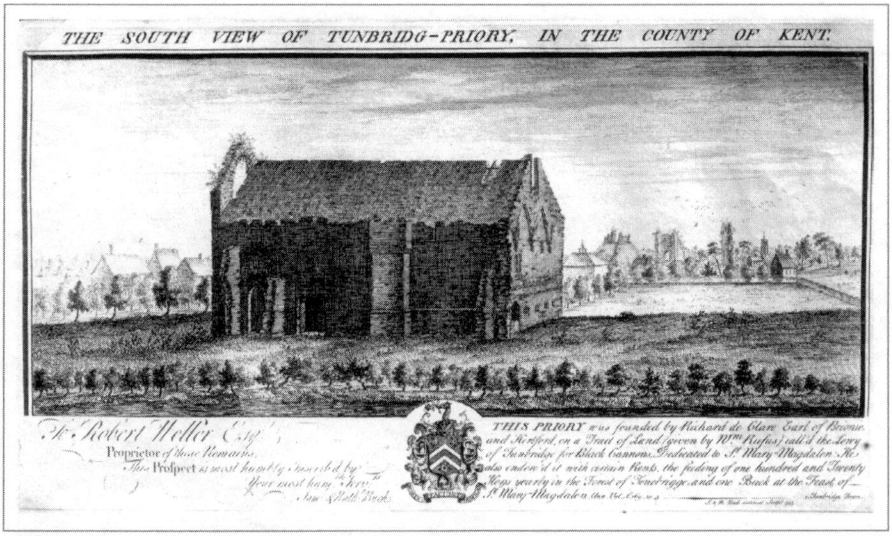

A view of the ruins of Tonbridge Priory in 1735, from Buck's Antiquities, *by Samuel and Nathaniel Buck.*

apathetic, with only sixteen men turning up. Archbishop Warham himself explained the scheme, and the townsmen asked for a few days to consider.[5] When they reported back, having consulted with their neighbours, the men expressed a preference to retain the priory. Needless to say, the priory was not to be re-founded, and so Tonbridge lost out completely.[6]

While the canons of Tonbridge were apparently seemly in their behaviour, the nuns at Littlemore (Oxfordshire) were anything but virtuous. A visitation in 1517 had revealed not only that the prioress had an illegitimate daughter for whose care she had taken some of the monastery's plate, but also that the nuns were inclined to romp with boys in the cloister. There was evidently no dissent at all when Wolsey suggested that Littlemore might be a suitable repression.[7] At Lesnes (Kent), the priory had gained a reputation for fraud, and at Ipswich the monks had failed to provide teaching for local boys.[8]

The dissolutions were not always simple or quick. Rumburgh Priory (Suffolk) had been under the patronage of St Mary's in York for three centuries, and the abbot requested that the priory remain attached to its mother

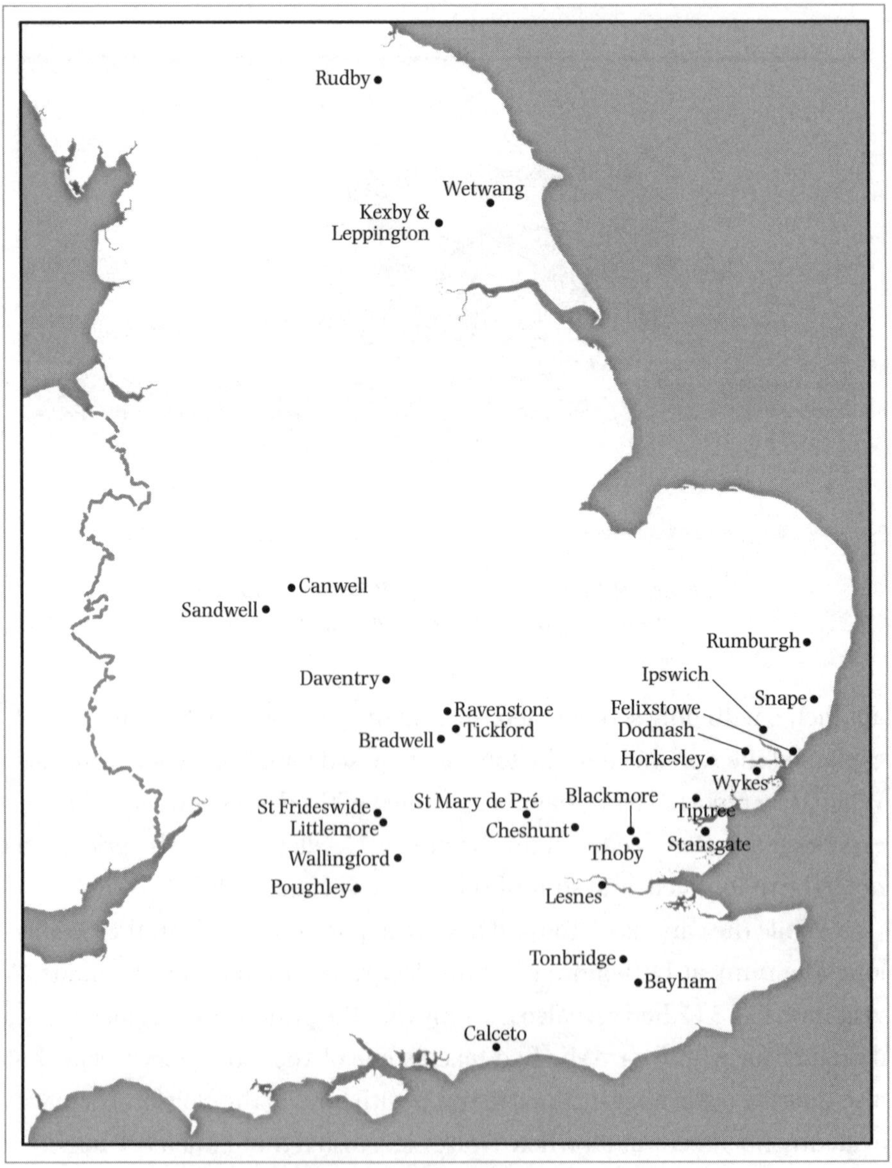

The location of the monastic houses dissolved to fund the foundation of Cardinal College, and of the estates in the north of the country that were given for the Dean's stipend. See Appendix 1 on page 189 for the full list of suppressed houses and their values.

house and offered a princely gift of 300 marks in exchange. It was not to be: a formal release and quitclaim were executed in March 1528.[9] And the inhabitants and neighbours of the abbey at Bayham resisted the closure with an armed force under the leadership of Thomas Towers, who had once been a canon.[10] At Wallingford (Berkshire), the surrender of the priory was made by Prior Geoffrey on 19 April 1525, with Thomas Cromwell – in charge of the building of Cardinal College – as a witness. However, the practical suppression – which usually involved demolition and removal of any valuable materials – was delayed, possibly so that the membership of the new Oxford college would have a residence close to the city. It was not until July 1528 that the site was formally transferred to Wolsey.[11] Another Berkshire house, at Poughley, near Newbury, was also used as temporary accommodation, much to the annoyance of Edward Fetyplace, who believed that he had been granted the property by Cromwell, and had paid 40 shillings to secure it. He complained that goods allegedly belonging to him had been appropriated by the resident scholars either for use there and then or for transport to Oxford.[12]

Statutes were laid down for the administration of the estates, which included a progress by the dean at Easter and a further one in the autumn by one of the senior canons, a means of administration that followed the pattern in medieval monastic houses and in other Oxford and Cambridge colleges.[13] Bishop Fox noted, in the statutes of Corpus Christi College (from which those of Cardinal College were heavily derived), that 'the farther a man is from his estate, the nearer he is to his harm'. Progresses were essential to ensure that estates were being managed properly, to collect rents and other dues – particularly any arrears, and to order or inspect the repair of buildings.[14] A large 'bailiffs' book' was begun which recorded all the income due from the various estates.[15]

Expenses while out and about on college business were refunded but were carefully monitored; claims had to be submitted to the Treasurer within two days of the return home of the dean or the canon or they were forfeit.[16] Accounts were to be maintained accurately and audits held regularly. And in order that the college was always prepared to defend its cause, college writings, evidences and muniments were to be conserved and kept securely

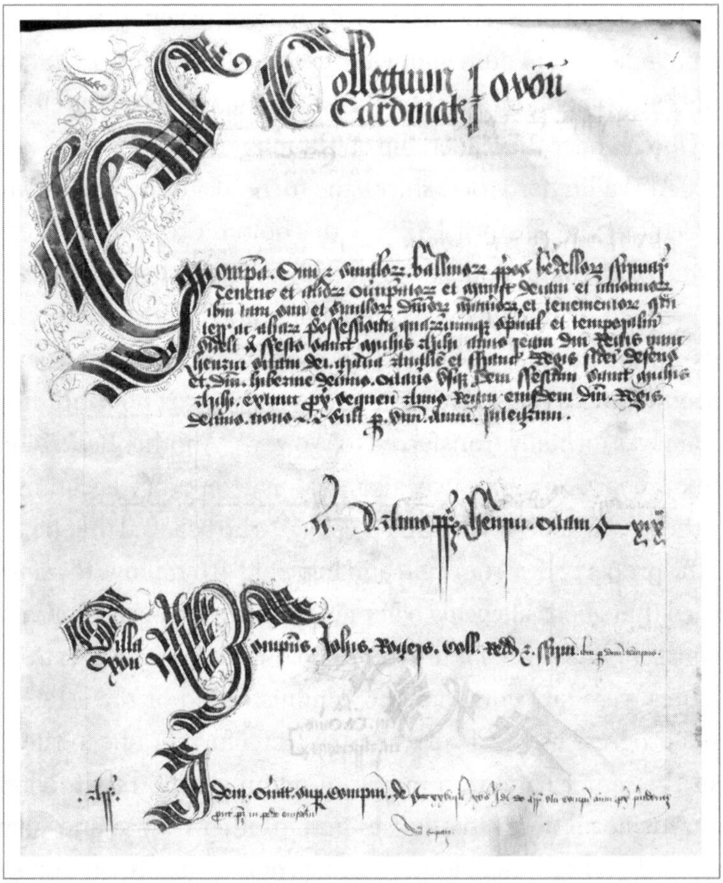

The opening page of the bailiffs' book for Cardinal College, which, had the college survived, would have recorded all the income due from the huge endowment granted by Thomas Wolsey.

in a large chest with three keys, which were to be held by the dean, the sub-dean, and the Censor Theologiae.[17] Estate and account records were to be kept in a divided bookcase. Other chests were to be purchased for the storage of the seal, foundation documents, treasures and money. A register was to be filled in whenever a document or object was removed from the archive.[18] Where these chests and muniment cupboards were to be at Cardinal College is uncertain: possibly in a tower over the main entrance or over the Hall staircase, or even in the turret of the south-west lodgings.[19]

The college seal box, of oak and clad in iron, dates back to the foundation of Christ Church in 1546. The 'Smith' of Abingdon was paid in 1547 for the locks and the keys.

The seal matrix, in its thrice-locked chest, was probably the greatest treasure to be preserved safely. The statutes laid down rules about how it was to be used, who could use it and on what type of documents. As an instrument of validation of college business, it was, and remains, crucial and valuable. Its use was to be in the presence of the majority of the senior canons, and only in the chapel.[20]

No estate or possession was to be alienated, whether it were spiritual – an advowson or rectory – or temporal – physical land or property.[21] Leases – to be made between the dean and canons of the first order on one side, and the lessee on the other – were to be for twenty-one years for estates, and ten years for spiritualities. There would be no subletting without permission. The customs of manorial courts – more than sixty manors were included in Wolsey's endowment to his college – were to be observed. Urban properties could be let for between fifty and sixty years.[22]

All the wealth and the rules for its administration were to come to nothing, however. Within five years, after the fall and then the death of its founder, Cardinal College had ceased to exist, and a large portion of its munificent endowment had been stripped away.[23] The strange collegiate church that was left – King Henry VIII College (formally founded in 1532) – was granted just the land and properties of St Frideswide's Priory, and the lands and revenues of Daventry, Littlemore and Tickford priories.[24] The value was small compared with that of Cardinal College – about £666 per annum, providing a clear income, after salaries and other expenses, of £450. Of course, the canons complained constantly of poverty, but their income was still substantially higher than that of some of its neighbours: Corpus Christi College's income was recorded as around £350 per annum in the *Valor ecclesiasticus* of 1535, and that of University College as a mere £78.[25] The dean was granted the prebend of Wetwang, in Yorkshire, for his income.[26]

Progresses through the college's manors and other properties were demanded by the statutes for the new institution, as they had been for Cardinal College. Preparations were made for audits and annual general meetings, and stipulations were laid down about the length and types of leases, much as before. No papers survive to indicate how the college was administered, but rents must have come in and business must have been conducted; the Court of Augmentation valuation does not suggest that things were in a bad way. Although the income of King Henry VIII College was not small, it was quite insufficient to complete Wolsey's colossal building plans. No attempt was made to build the muniment tower that had been the Cardinal's intention; instead, deeds were to be kept securely in the Chapter House, possibly in the little room between the Chapter House and the old prior's lodgings built by William Tresham.[27] But King Henry VIII College was also short-lived. As soon as the new diocese of Oxford was founded in 1542, its fate was largely sealed.[28] Very shortly, plans were made to move the diocesan seat from Oseney Abbey, on the west side of Oxford, to the old priory church in the centre of town, and for it to be attached to a new college in a unique joint foundation.[29]

Christ Church was, and is, an extraordinary foundation, at once both academic college and diocesan cathedral. From the outset, the dean and eight canons were the governing body with responsibility for the administration of both halves of the establishment, including services in the cathedral – both as college chapel and diocesan seat – the teaching of all students, the board and lodging of both cathedral and academic bodies, and the maintenance of all the buildings and estates. There were to be one hundred Students, of all ages and at all stages of their academic careers, from new undergraduates to some of the most revered and established scholars and clergyman of their day, all funded by the endowment. Almost from the beginning there were fee-paying undergraduates too. In some ways Christ Church was much the same as any other medieval or early modern college except that the graduate Students, some of whom undertook teaching and some of whom remained to do their own research and work towards higher degrees, had no say at all about governance, unlike their colleagues in other colleges who were fellows. Neither, unlike their neighbours, did they receive any benefit from the college or cathedral estates other than their basic stipend except, after 1576, for a portion of the sometimes meagre income from corn rents. The Students were always resentful of their lowly position when compared with their stipendiary colleagues in other colleges, and the discrepancies would cause discontent on numerous occasions through Christ Church's history. In 1641, for example, the Students demanded a share of college windfalls and dividends.[30] They were unsuccessful in their requests and war soon intervened with its devastating impact on college income.[31] And, of course, no other college – not just in Oxford but anywhere – has a cathedral. For centuries, again until the nineteenth century, and to a certain extent because there had been no bishop in the new diocese of Oxford for fifty years or so after its creation, the cathedral barely functioned as more than an enormous college chapel.[32]

A month after the formal foundation of Christ Church on 4 November 1546, the Charter of Dotation – dated 11 December – was signed by the king (or, possibly, as the king was close to death, by one of his senior ministers). This immense document, which extends to nine vellum membranes, each measuring 93 x 58 cm, recorded the grant to Christ Church of a new and lavish endowment of land, livings and manors which would produce an income of £2,200 per annum, more than twice that of its nearest rival.[33] Most of the new endowment, like the old, was derived from confiscated

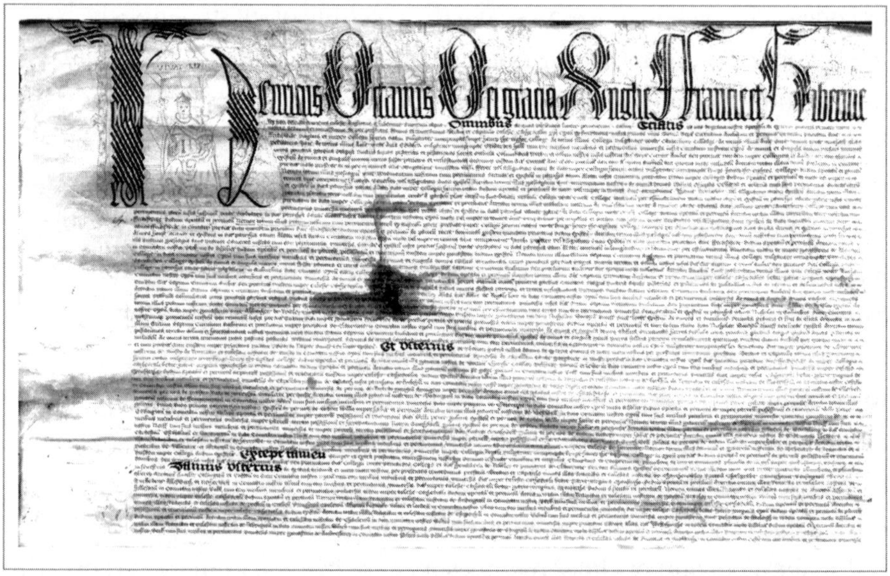

The first membrane of the Charter of Dotation, dated 4 December 1546, in which Henry VIII laid down his endowment for his new college-cum-cathedral.

monastic property by then in the hands of the Court of Augmentations (the court established by Henry VIII in 1536 to manage the revenue generated by the dissolution of the monasteries) and its commissioners. The same small portion of Wolsey's original gift was retained. It was the gift of property from Henry VIII that would produce the revenue for the maintenance of the large and unique establishment.

It is difficult to be precise about the actual quantity of land that Christ Church owned in those early days: as with Cardinal College and other major landowners, much of the college's income derived from profits and tithes and the rental proceeds from rectories and manors, rather than from actual produce or rents of directly managed property. Tenants paid a fixed rent for the tithes and rental income from glebe land and then made as much profit from it as they could. If they improved the land, then the tithes would rise, or they could charge sub-tenants whatever they wished. Fees due to the church could also be paid to the Christ Church tenant. There were, of course, always covenants placed on the lessee which were potentially expensive, not least the responsibility of the rector to maintain the chancel of the parish church. These would, however, be weighed up and costed when the seven-yearly fine was assessed.

Christ Church was given an interest of some sort in around 185 parishes and townships across England and Wales, from Devon to Yorkshire, and from Montgomeryshire to Norfolk. Most were reasonably local: over forty in Oxfordshire, ten in Berkshire, eight in Buckinghamshire and thirteen in Gloucestershire. The focus was Oxfordshire westwards and northwards through the Welsh Marches.[34] It was almost as though Henry VIII had drawn a line down the middle of the country; Christ Church's sister college in Cambridge, Trinity, also founded at the end of 1546 (its Charter of Dotation is dated 24 December), received estates primarily in the east: notably Bedfordshire, Cambridgeshire, Nottinghamshire, Lincolnshire and Yorkshire. Neither college received much property south of the Thames.[35] Both Christ Church and Trinity College received endowments worth well in excess of those of the previously richest colleges in their respective universities.[36]

In spite of its generosity, the Dean and Chapter quibbled over the endowment; the revenues granted were short by £64 0s. 5¾d. The matter was taken to the Court of Augmentations immediately after foundation but was not resolved until the reign of Mary Tudor, when the queen acknowledged the deficiency. This consisted of £29 14s. 1¾d. from property that was granted but not received, £30 6s. 3d. from over-valued property, and the tithes of Shippon manor (Berkshire) which had been granted instead to the Duchy of Cornwall.[37] In recompense, Mary awarded to Christ Church the parsonage of Tring and Wigginton (Hertfordshire).[38]

Christ Church was given no statutes, largely because Henry VIII had died very soon after the foundation of the college, but it is evident that the methods for administration, laid down in the statutes of Cardinal College and King Henry VIII College, were adopted almost wholesale.[39] The Dean and Chapter were the governing body of both college and cathedral (until the mid-nineteenth century) with one canon chosen to be Treasurer, responsible for all the financial administration, domestic and external, including the preparation of the annual audit presented to the Auditor just before

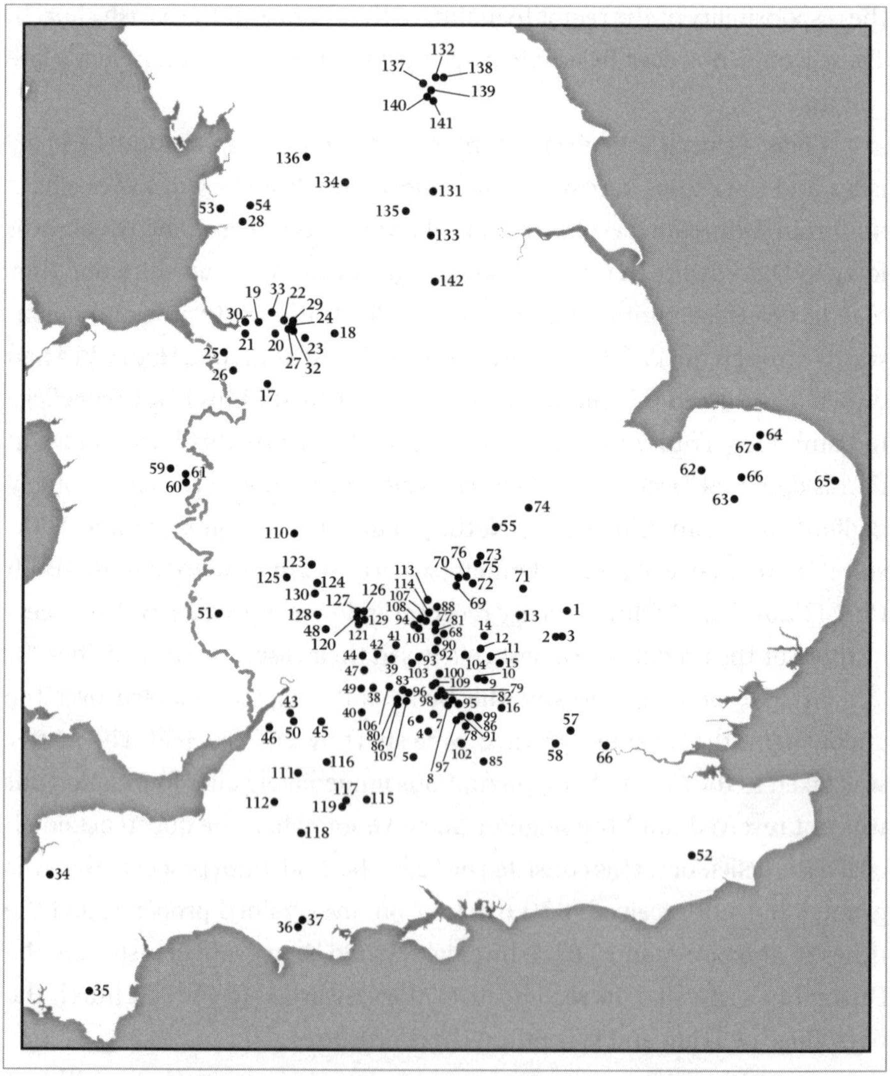

The Henrician endowment. Some properties were actual land, some rectories, advowsons and tithes, others manorial lordships. See key opposite, and also Appendix 2 on page 191 for the complete list.

Key to properties indicated on map

1 Cople
2 Flitton
3 Silsoe
4 Ardington
5 East Garston
6 Lyford
7 Marcham
8 Sandford
9 Ashendon
10 Dorton
11 East Claydon
12 Hillesden
13 Lathbury
14 Maids Moreton
15 North Marston
16 Saunderton
17 Acton
18 Bollington
19 Daresbury
20 Budworth
21 Frodsham
22 High Legh
23 Marthall
24 Mere
25 Newton
26 Hatton
27 Over Tabley
28 Preston
29 Rostherne
30 Runcorn
31 Sudley
32 Tatton
33 Thelwall
34 Great Torrington
35 South Brent
36 Tincleton
37 Tolpuddle
38 Aldsworth
39 Bledington
40 Down Ampney
41 Little Compton
42 Netherswell
43 North Nibley
44 Temple Guiting
45 Tetbury
46 Thornbury
47 Turkdean
48 Twyning
49 Winson
50 Wotton-under-Edge
51 Staunton-on-Wye
52 Hawkhurst
53 Kirkham
54 Whittingham
55 Great Bowden
56 St Sepulchre's
57 Harrow
58 Hillingdon
59 Meifod
60 Welshpool
61 Guilsfield
62 East Walton
63 Saham Toney
64 Swanton Novers
65 Upton
66 Wendling
67 Woodnorton
68 Astrop
69 Badby
70 Daventry
71 Easton Maudit
72 Flore
73 Guilsborough
74 Harringworth
75 Ravensthorpe
76 Thrupp
77 Banbury
78 Benson
79 Binsey
80 Black Bourton
81 Bodicote
82 Botley
83 Brize Norton
84 Cassington
85 Caversham
86 Chalgrove
87 Clanfield
88 Clattercote
89 Cowley
90 Deddington
91 Drayton St Leonard
92 Duns Tew
93 Enstone
94 Epwell
95 Garsington
96 Lew
97 Overy
98 Oxford
99 Pyrton
100 Shipton-on-Cherwell
101 Sibford Gower
102 South Stoke
103 Spelsbury
104 Stratton Audley
105 Weald
106 Westwell
107 Wroxton
108 Balscott
109 Worton
110 Highley
111 Batheaston
112 Midsomer Norton
113 Fenny Compton
114 Shotteswell
115 Charlton
116 Chippenham
117 Easterton
118 Maiden Bradley
119 Market Lavington
120 Aldington
121 Badsey
123 Chadwick
124 Claines
125 Clifton-on-Teme
126 The Littletons
127 Offenham
128 Severn Stoke
129 Wickhamford
130 Worcester
131 Bramham
132 Ellerbeck
133 Featherstone
134 Kildwick
135 Leeds
136 Long Preston
137 Northallerton
138 Osmotherley
139 Thornton-le-Beans
140 Thornton-le-Moor
141 Thornton-le-Street
142 Wath

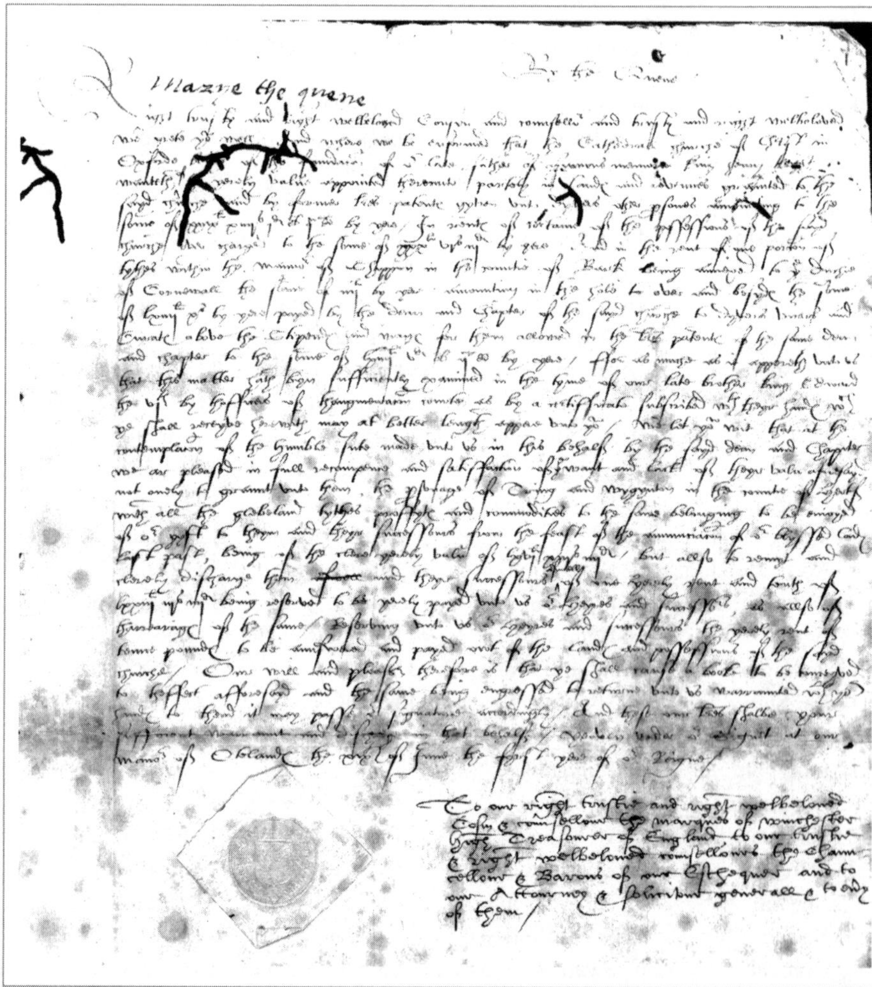
Marye the quene

By the Quene

The letter signed by Mary Tudor, as 'Marye the Quene', righting the shortfall in her father's gift with the award of the parsonage of Tring and Wigginton.

Christmas.[40] It is very likely that the Treasurer was required to sign a bond by which he took responsibility for any debts incurred during his time of office.[41]

From the beginning, according to the first disbursement book, there were also one or two deputies, often Students, rather than canons, who took some of the more everyday functions – such as entering items into

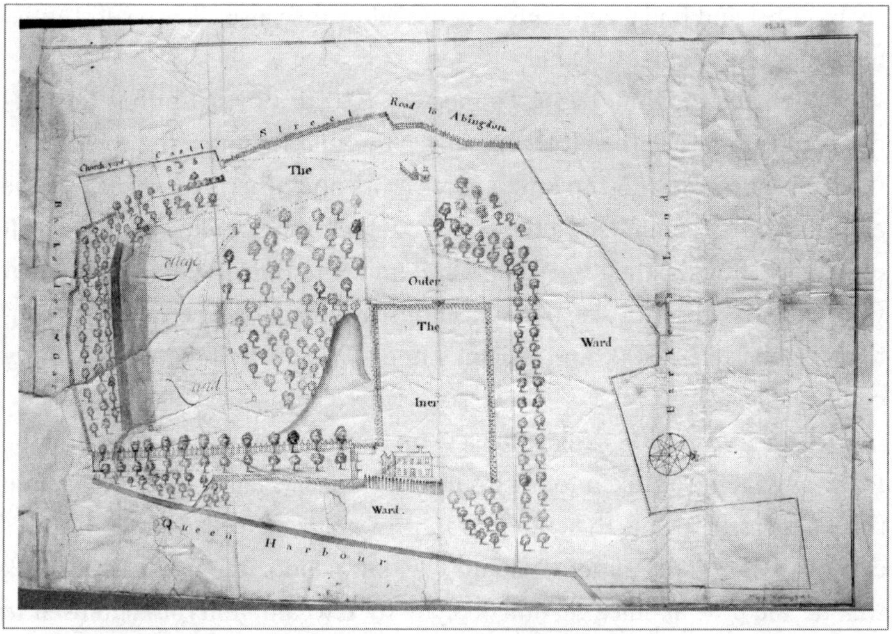

A plan of the castle in Wallingford in the early eighteenth century. The college of St Nicholas, within the castle grounds, was purchased by Christ Church almost immediately after the foundation to be its refuge when plague struck in Oxford.

the receipt books and calculating and demanding rents – from the Treasurer's shoulders. Both men were paid additional stipends for their extra work. The first Treasurer – listed in the disbursement book as the 'high treasurer' – was Alexander Belsyre, soon (in 1557) to be elected as the first president of St John's College, assisted first by Thomas Arderne and then shortly by James Curtoppe and Thomas Francis.[42] One of the first tasks that Belsyre undertook was to seal the purchase of a house, once the College of St Nicholas within the bounds of the medieval castle at Wallingford, which would become Christ Church's refuge in case of plague.[43] Assisting both Treasurer and his deputies was the Chapter Clerk, who, as a lawyer and notary public, drew up leases and kept the Chapter minutes. The role of Auditor was held by the Palmer family for several generations, beginning with Thomas Palmer, who owned property in Hertfordshire and then in South Stoke (Oxfordshire).[44] As Auditor, Palmer was paid £6 13s. 4d. every six months, and had a generous expense allowance as well as a substantial apartment in Chaplains' Quad.[45]

When he died, in 1558, Palmer left £20 to Christ Church towards the completion of either the tower over the main gate or the tower over the Hall stairs, and £50 to buy a silver cross and other ornaments for the church.[46] The remainder of his estate, including his auditorship, was left to his son Thomas, then to William and finally to Barton Palmer. The men were rich; the inventory of William's house in Hertfordshire valued its contents at nearly £2,500, and Barton's house in South Stoke was similarly comfortable.[47]

However, in 1608, a dispute blew up between Dean John King and the Palmers which was taken to the Court of Chancery. Christ Church accused the Palmers of using their auditorship to grow rich at Christ Church's expense. Margaret Palmer, William's widow, said that she did not think that he 'did by that office get and obteyne such wealth and raised himself to such a great state as in the Bill [of Complaint] is supposed'.[48] She stated that William had become wealthy through marriage. The crux of the problem was King's decision to transfer the role of Auditor to his brother Philip; the Palmers felt that the case against them had been brought merely to justify this blatant piece of nepotism. The Palmers, almost needless to say, did not win the battle, and the position was retained by Philip King for some decades until his death, which occurred before the end of his term of office. Like the Palmers before him, Philip left the position to his son, John. During the 1650s King was ousted, to be replaced by a Commonwealth man, Samuel Bedford, who was granted a patent (an exclusive contract) and tried desperately to hang on to it after the Restoration of Charles II. The Dean and Chapter battled equally hard to wrest the patent back from Bedford but in the end were forced to pay the intruder £500 to surrender it. John King stepped back into the lucrative role, but it would appear that he was not the professional that his father had been. In 1678 the Chapter came to a decision. King would be permitted to remain, but all the perquisites that had slowly been added to augment the annual stipend, which was by then £20 10s., were to be taken away: 'All additional allowances [...] of dyet, servants

The notary mark of Thomas Randolph from the Chapter Book, dated 1552. Randolph was a Student of Christ Church, notary public and an ambassador for Elizabeth I.

wages, journeys, soliciting of causes, or anything of the like nature bee for ever vacated and never more bee taken.' The decision was also made that no patent would be granted again but the job be salaried and payments to the Auditor were to be entered into the accounts as they were for all other officers of the House.[49] In 1696, when Roger Altham resigned as Treasurer, the Chapter found themselves in a dilemma concerning the receipt of rents. A circular letter was sent to the absent canons asking for their advice or their approval to appoint James King as receiver in London and John Brooks, the Chapter Clerk, as receiver in Oxford. Brooks and King duly received their letters of attorney just two weeks later. When the Auditor fell ill a few years later, Brooks took on this role too. This arrangement was renewed every year until 1720, when the Chapter Clerk formally absorbed the role of the Auditor.[50]

The administrative functionaries of Christ Church were set very soon after its foundation following, albeit unacknowledged, the statutes of Cardinal College. Receipts and expenses were recorded in annual volumes by quarter; leases and other deeds 'under seal' were copied into ledgers; presentations to college livings were reported in the Chapter minutes; and bonds for large sums of money were signed by an army of bailiffs and senior staff to guarantee loyalty and to secure Christ Church's property against fraud.[51] The bailiffs, with the tenants who paid directly, came annually to the audit, when, having paid their dues, they were treated to a feast.[52] In later years, as banks became more commonplace and colleges acquired accounts, officers were appointed to act as receivers of rents in Oxford and in London. No doubt this would have been much more convenient for the grander tenants, who may well have had properties in the capital as well as in the country.

A system was firmly in place to manage effectively the vast estates to ensure sufficient income to maintain the college and the cathedral in excellent physical, educational and spiritual shape.[53]

2

Managing the agricultural estate I: revenue

Regular income

The primary and regular sources of income for Christ Church were entry fines and rents. In the mid-sixteenth century the tenancies that Christ Church had inherited were long – occasionally up to ninety-nine years – on static 'beneficial' leases, which were the standard form of tenure for large agricultural properties. For generations the property of most colleges, and of many other landed estates, was let on these long leases with a fixed annual rent.[1] Rental income was the foundation on which the colleges managed their affairs, but because the value was fixed, fluctuations caused by outside events made the annual worth of revenues unpredictable.[2]

In order to mitigate this, inflation was managed through a system of entry 'fines'. Theoretically, the entry fine was only due when the lease came up for renewal: on a ninety-nine-year lease this was not, therefore, a lucrative or consistent source of income. In most cases, too, the entry fines were distributed among the dean and canons (a practice also followed in the other colleges and in other institutions, where fines were divided between the heads of houses and their fellows), and so the revenue derived from them was of no help in the daily management of the college.[3] In practice, many agricultural leases were valid for a more manageable twenty-one years and were renewed every seven. On the application of the tenant to renew his lease, the estate was valued and a one-off payment made to the landlord of somewhere between one-and-a-quarter and two-and-a-half times the agreed annual value.[4]

Almost from the date of foundation, inflation began to eat into revenue. Wars, poor harvests, a rapid increase in population, the deliberate debasement of coinage by the government from the mid-1540s into the early 1550s and the influx of silver from the New World via Spain have all been cited as reasons.[5] After the accession of Elizabeth, concern for the financial state of the Oxford and Cambridge colleges, and other similar institutions, increased. In 1571 the twenty-one-year agricultural lease and the forty-year urban lease were fixed by law to help colleges through inflationary periods.[6] More frequent renewals meant more frequent entry fines. The assistance was welcome but presented another problem: that of actually valuing the estates. In order for the Dean and Chapter to maximise their income, valuations had to be accurate.[7] In the later part of the sixteenth century the records of the Court of Augmentations were a useful asset to determine figures for ex-monastic estates, and indeed continued to be used for much longer in some cases; in Daventry (Northamptonshire), for example, the Court's papers were used to settle the value of the estate as late as 1665.[8] But custom and negotiation were the generally accepted ways to determine a price.

Another Elizabethan aid to combat inflation was the Corn Rent Act, passed in 1576. This stipulated that one third of the rent in all the future leases made by Eton College, Westminster School and Oxford and Cambridge colleges had to be 'reserved'. This third portion of the rent was 'index-linked' to the price of grain in the locality. For example, a 10s. rent would be divided so that two-thirds – 6s. 8d. – was paid as a straight money rent and the remaining third in grain. This was usually paid in cash, rather than in kind, but the actual figure of this third fluctuated with the price of wheat, malt or barley at the local market (working with the basic price of wheat in 1550 of 10d. a bushel and for malt of 7½d. per bushel).[9] However, if the cost of grain in Oxford was higher than these standard prices, the value of the reserved rent would rise accordingly.[10] Every quarter, the accounts record a

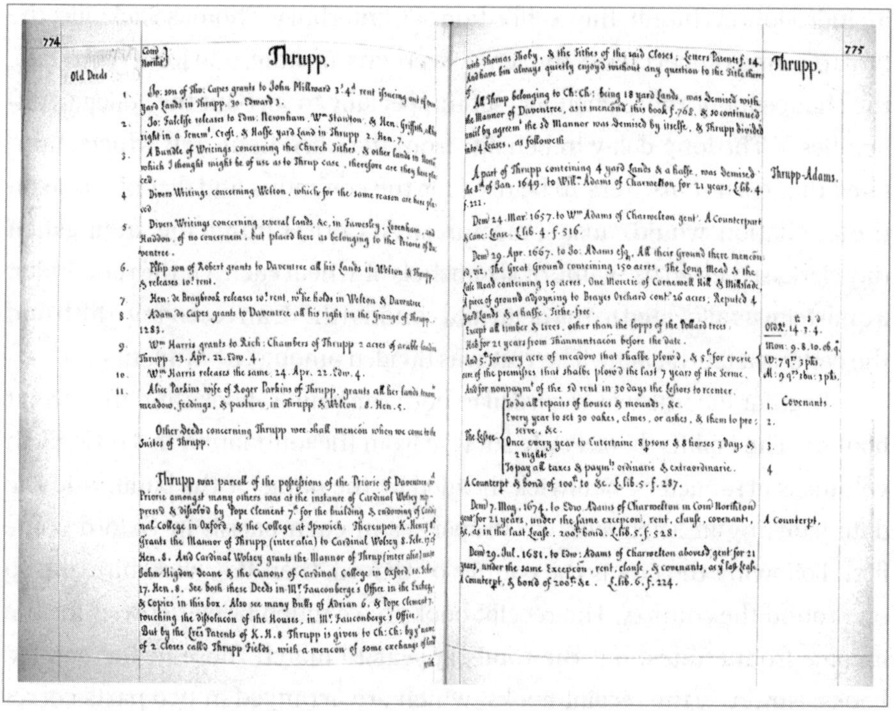

An entry in the Book of Evidences showing the history of the hamlet of Thrupp, near Daventry. The division of the rent into cash and corn (wheat and malt) portions is clear in the right-hand margin.

small payment to the man 'bringing the price of grain'. The Act also made it illegal to make a new lease on a property for which there was still three years to run, providing a little more security for the tenant, who now knew that his rent could not be increased mid-term. The provisions made things better for both parties.[11]

Elizabeth's legislation had different effects in different colleges; All Souls, where urban leases had previously only been issued for twenty years, now found itself suffering from less frequent entry fines. Christ Church, with its incredibly long ninety-nine-year urban leases, which had to be run out before new and shorter terms could be applied, was the last college to benefit from the Corn Rent Act. It was 1630 before it began to see any significant effect, in spite of the best efforts of Elizabeth I's high-powered commission (which included John Whitgift, the archbishop of Canterbury, Thomas Sackville, the lord treasurer, Robert Cecil, the senior secretary of state, and John Fortescue, the chancellor of the exchequer) set up specially to sort out the college's difficulties.[12] The long delay in benefits from the Corn Rent Act, which stipulated that corn rents were to be used for the commons and diet of those on the foundation, would cause some unrest. At Christ Church the singing men (lay clerks) received the value of six bushels of wheat each. Of the remainder, a quarter was allocated to the dean and canons (the dean receiving a fifth and the canons a tenth each). The rest was divided among the Students.

Regular income was recorded in both the bailiffs' books and the receipt books.[13] The bailiffs' books only survive from the foundation to 1633. Each volume is arranged by bailiwick, headed by the name of the bailiff and the date (starting at Michaelmas). Properties in each parish in Oxford come first. Following the city is the county of Oxford, then Warwickshire and so on around the country. The receipt books have much briefer entries for the income from estates, but the totals appear to match those in the bailiffs' books. However, the receipt books, which are arranged in two parts corresponding to the half-yearly rent audits, record income from other sources too. In the years before 1659 many heads of entry occur: decree money is entered until at least 1652; benevolences until 1650; profits of the kitchen appear until 1642, and the sale of skins until 1615; profits of the stable are left out from 1612. Receipt of chamber rents is mentioned in the early years of the seventeenth century, when Peckwater Quad was rebuilt for the first time. With a few exceptions, the price of grain at the two rent audits is stated at the front of the book. From 1866 receipts and disbursements are entered in the same ledger. From 1659 to the end of the series in 1865 the heads of the entries are unchanged, and consist of rents, extraordinary receipts, mulcts (fines for offences) and absences, chamber rents and commons. From 1678 the annual account is balanced at the end of the book.[14]

The structure and clauses of a typical property lease have changed little over centuries, except to become much longer, and show a remarkable uniformity from college to college.[15] An example is that of the tithes and glebe lands of North Nibley (Gloucestershire), leased to John and Thomas

A typical lease, or indenture. This is the lease for the property in North Nibley between the Dean and Chapter and John and Thomas Purnell, clothiers, for twenty-one years from 7 December 1616.

Purnell, clothiers, in 1616.[16] The indenture begins with the date, usually using regnal rather than calendar years so, in this instance: 'the seaventh day of December in the yeares of our Soveraigne Lord James by the grace of God Kinge of England Scotland Fraunce and Ireland defender of the faith etc. That is to say of England Fraunce and Ireland the fourteenth and of Scotland the fiftieth.' The parties signing the lease are listed next, with the Dean and Chapter on one side and the Purnells on the other. The following clause describes the property: 'Tythes of Corne graine hay wolle lamb and woode and all other manner of Tythes', including a parcel of tithes from neighbouring Wotton-under-Edge. After this, the length of the lease (twenty-one years) and the rent due (£11, being £7 6s. 8d. in cash and the remainder as corn rent). The remaining three-quarters of the document consists of covenants, including the obligation to find and pay for a curate, and to allow him the use of the vicarage house alongside the churchyard, to maintain the chancel and to pay all taxes due from the estate.

Management of estates as widely flung as Christ Church's would have been difficult. Progresses were still expected and were conducted from the earliest days. Soon after the foundation, evidence suggests that there was an excursion around all the property given by the Crown, presumably as part of a preliminary check on the extent and condition of Christ Church's new endowment. One visitation took in the parsonages of Batheaston and Midsomer Norton (Somerset), Tolpuddle (Dorset) and East Garston (Berkshire). In Batheaston – where the investigations were doubly important because of an early dispute over ownership of the rectory after the dissolution in 1539 of Bath Abbey, whose property it had been – the vicar was found to have a decent house sitting in a plot of 1½ acres and all the tithes except those of corn, grain and hay; these valuable tithes would have gone to the rector (Christ Church or its principal tenant). At Midsomer Norton, however, the tenant had allowed the barns and the chancel to fall into disrepair, and at East Garston the chancel was in ruins and the parsonage house in a poor condition.[17]

Another similar survey took place in the Midlands. In Great Bowden and Market Harborough (Leicestershire), the three churches were the responsibility of local landowner and Christ Church tenant Robert Styrley (or Strelley), but he had evidently not performed his duties in their maintenance or that of the manor house.[18] The mid-sixteenth-century account suggests that the chancel was on the verge of collapse, with the south side completely lacking the wall-plate which should have been supporting the principal truss. Similarly, the parsonage house was much decayed and ready to fall down. Styrley was to be made to fund the necessary repairs, but he was nowhere to be found at the time of the investigations. It was hard, too, to find an 'honest and mete' priest to be curate; the tithes were low, as most of the inhabitants of Harborough were craftsmen and labourers rather than farmers and 'because every thinge as meate drynke & clothinge is so dere'.[19] Harborough was not a rich living, and the burden of finding a curate who was both capable and willing to live on a low wage was a problem that continued for many years.

Rather than send a canon, two lawyers – James Shallcross and Thomas Dalbeney – were dispatched in 1558 to the Chapter's estate in Montgomeryshire to sort out the non-payment of rent by the tenant of Meifod, William Spenser, who had defaulted from 1546 right the way through to the end of the reign of Edward VI, and then by his widow, Johanne, who had failed to pay throughout the reign of Mary. Altogether, the Dean and Chapter were owed £344 13s. 4d.[20] All Christ Church's leases included details of what was to happen if rent was unpaid; the lease became void and expensive fines had to be paid to re-enter. Careful instructions were given to the Chapter's representative: he was to go to the Red Lion in Shrewsbury and declare that he was there to investigate with the full authority of the Dean and Chapter. He should ask of the local sheriff whether writs had been issued, whether Johanne had assigned the lease, to demand payment and refuse any nonsense that William's debts were nothing to do with her. If Johanne made an offer, which the representative was to encourage, then he should take careful note. The Chapter gave their man the authority to accept £212 plus expenses of £20, which it appears Johanne paid. But three years later there were still issues to be resolved. The Montgomeryshire estate consisted of the rectories, and associated property and tithes, of Meifod, Welshpool and Guilsfield. Records suggest that the three rectories were leased as one and then sublet, and one of the problems with retrieving the lost income was getting all three sub-tenants in one place. The Dean and Chapter, anxious that the '7 or 8 score scholars and students' at Christ Church could not be fed and watered without the regular receipt of rents and dues, took the case to the Council of Wales at Ludlow.[21] Richard Hedley, apparently one of the subtenants, explained to the Council that William Spenser had held the lease but had sublet Meifod and Guilsfield to a Roger Jones and John ap Mores. After William Spenser's death they had hung on to their rents. In her turn, Johanne Spenser, having received letters of administration on her late husband's death, found herself in debt to the Crown to the tune of £460 10s. Paying her rent to Christ Church had become impossible. When Spenser had been sued for the money some years earlier, Jones agreed to pay the £300 to Johanne and to sign a bond with Hedley guaranteeing a payment of £300 to Christ Church. Jones, however, had defaulted for another two years, and now Hedley was stuck with paying the bond on his own. The Council came to a compromise with Hedley, not least, it would appear, because he was the only one of the parties who actually turned up to the hearings.

In 1599 Canon and Treasurer John Weston was charged with taking letters and memoranda from Christ Church to the Lancashire estate of Kirkham to attempt to sort out issues of rent, enclosure and the payment of toll and stallage. The debate over the latter – the levy charged on bringing goods for sale at a market and for the erection of a stall – raged for some years in the Court of the Duchy of Lancaster. Who was to be charged the toll and stallage, and who was entitled to receive it? The plaintiffs – the mayor, burgesses and bailiffs of Kirkham – claimed that they were free of the charge according to the grant of the fair in 1199, whereas the defendants, acting on behalf of the Dean and Chapter, claimed the levy by virtue of a grant of Edward I to the abbey of Vale Royal a century later, in 1296. The Court made its decision that the complainants could have the tolls of the annual five-day fair around the festival of St Luke (18 October) and would be free of payments at all the fairs and markets in Kirkham. The Dean and Chapter (or their lessees) could have the tolls of the five-day fair at the feast of St John in June, the toll of the weekly fairs and the stallage at both the St Luke and St John fairs.[22]

Generally, though, along with most landlords of scattered estates, the Dean and Chapter made little effort to be hands-on administrators all of the time. Only woods retained for timber, local grazing and the estate at Deddington (Oxfordshire), which consisted of a large number of small properties, were managed directly from Oxford. The remainder were leased out, often to noblemen and gentlemen with their own neighbouring landed estates, and were frequently sublet. From the seventeenth century, rather than gallop about the country, the Treasurer often sent a letter to either the tenant or the vicar of the parish with a string of questions about the state of the chancel (if the property was a rectory), the amount and usage of glebe land, the quantity and nature of the tithes received, the state of the parsonage house, whether there was a manor attached and, if so, when the courts were held and what customs of the manor were still maintained.

To all intents and purposes, at least as far as the locals were concerned, their landlords were Christ Church's principal tenants, rather than the Dean and Chapter.[23] It was the principal tenant who managed the estate on a day-to-day, and even year-to-year, basis, arranging sub-leases, building and repairing, receiving some of the tithes and profits of the manor, and taking responsibility for the chancel of the local church.[24]

After the late sixteenth- and early seventeenth-century establishment of routines and the initial run of visitations around the estates to ensure that the Dean and Chapter understood what it owned and how it was administered, things looked reasonably settled. However, it was not to remain that way, and the middle years of the seventeenth century were to cause no end of trouble.

The estates during the Civil War and Commonwealth

The Civil War served to remind the Dean and Chapter of their remoteness from their estates. Samuel Fell, writing on 5 September 1646 in some desperation to Gerard Langbaine, the provost of Queen's College and staunch defender of University privileges, said, 'We are all behouldeng to yu for yr care in the businesse of our rents, we are notoriously abused by our tenents combining with our county committees [...] If we faile here we must laye our keyes under the doore and be gone.'[25] It is not uncommon to find among the correspondence in the archive that rents did not reach the college because of problems of travel during the hostilities. Tenants, particularly those who were further away, or in especially war-torn areas, could find themselves unable to pay, or used the situation as an excuse not to. Some refused to pay rents to intruded Parliamentarian heads of house, and some estates had been sequestered.[26]

Lord Clifford, the fifth Earl of Cumberland, explained his inability to pay the rent on his Yorkshire estate of Long Preston as all his lands were in the hands of the rebels, and the Royalist garrison at Skipton Castle was cut off. 'Wee durst not send five pounds not five miles from the Castle [at Skipton] no way this long tyme, the Rebells haue layen round about us in that manner, they haue come by 3000, one way and as many another to take this Castle but they neuer came within a myle of it for dread of my Lord's ordnance', said the earl's agent, Robert Robotham. Lord Clifford died in 1643, the year after this letter was written, and the estate was inherited by the Earl of Cork, who had married Clifford's daughter Elizabeth. The Dean and Chapter were anxious to receive the rent on the property, but Cork insisted that, willing though he was to pay his dues, he too was unable to get cash through the rebel lines.[27] He wrote to the king asking him to persuade Christ Church not to seek forfeiture of the estate. Charles, who was, of course, resident in Oxford at the time, duly did so, explaining that the earl's inability to pay was occasioned by 'this publique Calamity and Distraction'.[28] The king also issued a general letter to the college tenants, authorising the payment to a designated rent collector, to protect tenants from having to make a dangerous journey to Oxford and to ensure that the Dean and Chapter received their dues.[29] Another tenant in the north, John Egerton, who leased the capital messuage (the house and associated land) in Rostherne (Cheshire), complained that even when times were good the rent took three-quarters of the value of the property, and now war charges were costing the same again.[30] The hostilities had put him in dire straits. In 1651 Egerton was accused of conspiring against the Commonwealth. The bond and sureties that he had to sign to achieve his bail must have dented his finances still further. The Dean and Chapter released him from all covenants of the lease for the remaining eight years of his term.[31]

Rental income fell dramatically during the war years and, as a consequence, so did payments. College finances were dented in other ways too, not least from the expenses of housing the king for four years – Christ Church laid out £600 to receive him in 1642 alone – but also from the loss of fee-paying students and from the 'gifts' of plate and money that they had been expected to make to their royal visitor.[32] Christ Church could afford to pay out only £2,010 of its expected disbursements of £4,227 in the financial year 1643/4.[33] Canons would have felt the pinch too, as entry fines declined as the issuing of leases dropped off during the war years.[34] In fact, the college in its cathedral capacity came close to losing all its land in 1643, when Parliament decided that the estates of all Chapters that had contributed to the royal war effort should be sequestered. The sale of the property of St Paul's Cathedral, including 700 newly built houses in Shadwell (now in Tower Hamlets), for example, raised £152,000 for the war effort.[35] However, Christ

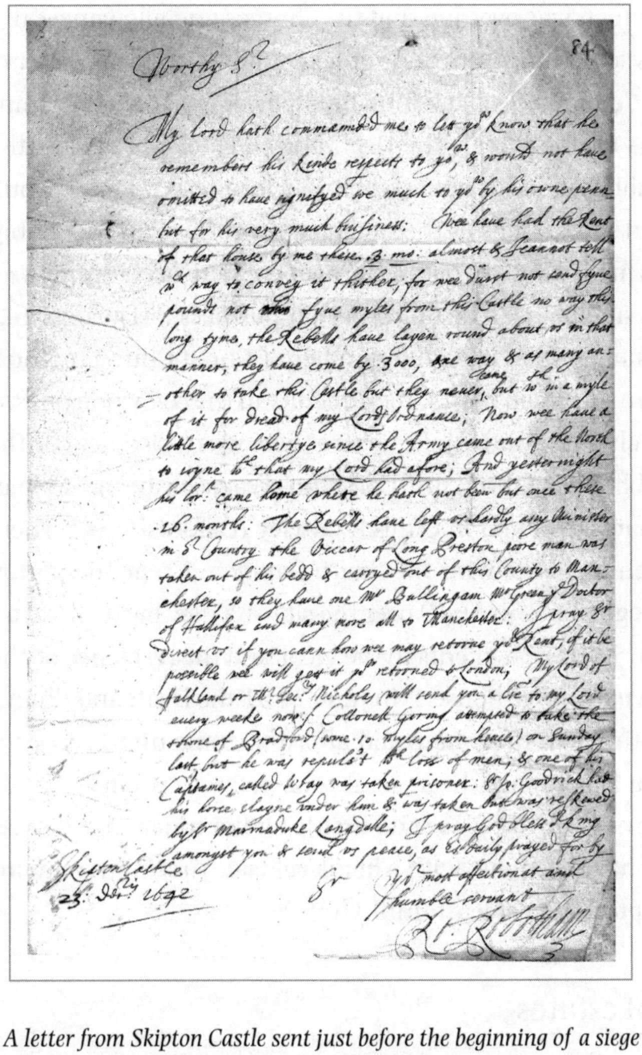
84

Worthy Sr

My lord hath commanded me to let yow know that he
remembers his kinde respects to yow, & would not have
omitted to have signifyed so much to yow by his owne penn
but for his very much businesse: Wee have had the Rent
of that house by me these 3 mo: almost & I cannot tell
wch way to convey it thither, for wee durst not send fyve
pounds not fyve myles from this Castle no way this
long tyme, the Rebells have layen round about vs in that
manner, they have come by 3000, one way & as many another to take this Castle but they never came but wthin a myle
of it for dread of my Lords Ordnance; Now wee have a
little more libertye since the Army came out of the North
to ioyne wth that my Lord had afore; And yesternight
his lop: came home where he hath not been but once these
26 months: The Rebells have left vs hardly any Minister
in or Country the Viccar of Long Preston poore man was
taken out of his bedd & carryed out of this County to Manchester, so they have one Mr Bullingam Mr Green & Doctor
of Hallifax and many more all to Manchester: I pray Sr
direct vs if you can how wee may returne yor Rent, if it be
possible wee will get it yow returned to London; My Lord of
Falkland or Mr Secry Nicholas will send you a lre to my Lord
every weeke now: Collonell Goring attempted to take the
towne of Bradford (some 10 myles from hence) on Sunday
last but he was repuls't wth losse of men; & one of his
Captaines, called Way was taken prisoner: Sr Jo: Goodrick had
his horse slayne under him & was taken but was reskewed
by Sr Marmaduke Langdale; I pray God blesse the King
amongst you & send vs peace, as is daily prayed for by

Skipton Castle
23 Decr 1642

Sr Yor most affectionat and
humble servant
[illegible]

A letter from Skipton Castle sent just before the beginning of a siege that was to last three years. It describes the quite significant difficulties Christ Church's tenant would have in getting his rent to Oxford.

Church was exempted as it was part of the University. As on other occasions before and since, Christ Church was saved by its dual nature.[36]

During the Commonwealth period estates business was soon back to normal; if anything, it was more efficient. In November 1649 Dr Mills, canon Treasurer, was charged with the task of bringing in all the arrears of rents and other payments due from Lady Day 1648 until Michaelmas

1649. So much was overdue that the charges and allowances would not be met unless something were done quickly. Mills was given a letter of attorney under the Common Seal granting him 'power to abate and compound with the tenants for the same'. The Dean and Chapter were evidently confident in Mills's ability, and his honesty; his pay for the extra work would be 'such residue and surplussage of the said revenues profits and advantages to keep and detain in his hands to his own proper use with accompt for a recompense of his care and pains to be taken in that business'.[37] During 1649 to 1651 courts of survey were held in a number of Christ Church manors, perhaps those where there had been some difficulty in the collection or assessment of arrears, including South Stoke, where there was a dispute over the management of Abbots Wood, at Little Compton (Warwickshire), at Maids Moreton (Buckinghamshire) and at Church Cowley (Oxfordshire).[38] There was also a long-running battle with the Smith family in Great Torrington (Devon). This had begun back in 1640 over the site of a new barn, and was picked up again in 1650 over payments to the vicar and the residence of the curate in part of the parsonage house.[39] In June 1651 the Dean and Chapter granted Grace Smith £5 so that she could afford to come up to Oxford to sort out the dispute face to face. Even so, it took years to resolve, Mrs Smith even having the nerve to ask for a scholarship for her son in 1652 – a request that appears to have been met with a blank refusal. Mrs Smith remained a thorn in the Chapter's side at least until 1659.[40]

Manorial estates

Regular visitations were particularly important to estates where the college was manorial lord. Leases often included the requirement to provide bed and board for the visitors and their entourage. The leases of the rectory and a manor in Aldsworth (Gloucestershire), for example, required the housing and entertaining of any preacher sent by the Dean and Chapter, and meat, drink, bedding and stabling for two days and three nights, twice a year, for stewards and receivers, and their servants when they came to collect rents or to view the manor.[41] Similarly, a lease of Swanton Novers (Norfolk) from 1560 included a covenant that the lessee should provide bed and board for up to six officers of the college and their horses for two days and one night every three or four years during the course of the lease.[42] A manuscript in the Bodleian Library details the expenses incurred – mainly the hiring of horses – by Canon Thomas Syddall while he was conducting Christ Church business in Staffordshire and Cheshire in 1553, and papers concerned with the administration of Rostherne in Cheshire include memoranda for the 'progres to be made by Christechurch in to the north' in 1587. Standard questions were laid down to be asked in each of the townships of the estate as well as some very specific queries. The document is also annotated with details of the route taken from Oxfordshire, through Warwickshire and Staffordshire, and then through the estates in both Cheshire and Yorkshire.[43]

As well as rents, the income of dues from the manorial estates was another important source of revenue.[44] Manors were landed estates, held from the king by the manorial lord in return for knight's service. They were governed by the lord through the jurisdiction of a manorial court. Manorial tenants owed service to the lord, which historically had meant working on the demesne land (the lord's property within a manor) for a given number of days each year. During the medieval period male tenants could also have been called on to follow the lord on his military service for the Crown. The portion of the land held by the tenants, which could only be farmed when they were free from duties, was held in villeinage by customary tenure – the feudal system. However, by the sixteenth century, when Christ Church was founded, apart from the need to follow manorial customs in matters such as widows' rights and heriots (a customary fee rather like a death duty), and in its court administration, customary tenure had evolved into copyhold, which, in all practical ways, worked like leasehold except that the deed of admission to a property was 'copied' into the court rolls and the tenant received a copy of the entry.[45]

In many cases, the land farmed by the copyholders, conventional leaseholders and freeholders alike was farmed in large open fields in strips. Access to common land for grazing and general foraging, and to woodland for seasonal feeding of pigs and for woodland products, was included, but the lord usually insisted that tenants had to use his mill, often at inflated prices. Medieval court rolls frequently record complaints about the unscrupulous behaviour of the lord's miller. The lord of the manor could also have rights to the profits of minerals or fishing, for example. While copyholds could be passed from generation to generation, there was an obligation to come to court to be granted the right to take over land and cottage and, needless to say, to pay a heriot to be allowed to enter. Customs of the manor varied from place to place, and there could often be more than one manor associated with a village or parish.

After the Black Death in 1348–9, the manorial system began its slow decline. The huge drop in the population meant that men who had been tied to a manor and service to their lords suddenly found themselves in demand and able to command wages. Large areas of land were also lord-less, and in many places there was the opportunity to consolidate strips in open fields into larger holdings. Of course, that could work the other way too; in places where the lord survived and his tenants perished, gentry or aristocratic control was increased. Villages whose populations were wiped out could be easily demolished and the land turned over to grazing. But manorial courts did not die completely; while the tight management of land and other assets by the calling of regular courts may have been relaxed, copyhold tenure, administered through the courts, survived.

The endowment of Cardinal College included a huge number of manors – about sixty – which would explain why twice-yearly progresses by the Dean and Canons were so vital. The income derived from manorial dues was an important revenue stream. Christ Church had fewer, scattered across the country from Oxfordshire to Yorkshire, but their importance to the income was no less.[46] In Maids Moreton, for example, a court was held at least once every two years from the foundation to the outbreak of the Civil War. A court held on 12 October 1548 included a survey of the manor, and its rolls recorded that there were ten men who owed dues to the manorial lord, five of whom were copyholders. The rents of their small plots – the largest appears to have been only 2 yardlands – varied from just 3 shillings to £1 4s.[47] Apart from the rent of the manor, which was leased to the Auditor, William Palmer, Christ Church reserved to itself the court profits, including the heriots.[48] Historically, a heriot was often a cow or even a horse, but by the early modern period these had been commuted to a money payment, not dissimilar to the entry fine for a conventional leasehold property. In Maids Moreton these were often as high as 46 shillings, a large payment for someone who was, more often than not, little more than a smallholder.[49]

The manor of Deddington was much more complicated. It consisted of 36½ yardlands of leasehold property and 24 yardlands of copyhold land lying scattered throughout the three towns of Deddington, Clifton (to the east) and Hempton (to the west). Clifton Mill, always a valuable asset, formed part of the manor's property along with a portion of the profits of any fairs held in Deddington. It was a valuable estate, which commanded a rent of £52 5s. per annum but was let on very long leases until 1648. After the Restoration, in 1665 Christ Church as lessor, its principal tenant, Sir John Cartwright of Aynho, and all the leaseholders were called together for a meeting.[50] A new arrangement was made by which only the copyholders held their properties from Cartwright. All the leaseholders were, from then on, to take their leases directly from the Dean and Chapter.[51] The division meant that Christ Church now managed, in addition to the head lease with Cartwright, more than fifty individual properties in Deddington. Small wonder that the lease required Cartwright to put up ten men and their horses whenever a progress to the town was needed.

One of the regular covenants in the leases of manorial property required lessees not to convert copyholds into regular leaseholds. The enfranchisement of copyholds would occur in later years as estates were enclosed and under later property legislation, but in the early modern period Christ Church and other landowners were anxious to hold onto the profits that manorial properties provided. If lessees failed to abide by the covenant, Christ Church was quick to act.

In the late 1590s Daventry manor, with all the land and income that went with it, was leased to one Isacke. According to Isacke, the previous tenant, Richard Andrews, had allowed the collection of the small court profits to slip, almost from the beginning of his tenancy in 1547. Isacke was evidently using Andrews' laxity as his own defence: the Dean and Chapter accused Isacke of suppressing the copyholds and turning them into leaseholds, ruining the capital messuage, cutting down all the timber, failing to keep a house for the poor and not paying his rent to Christ Church. Under the standard terms of their leases, the Chapter required that Isacke's tenancy be revoked, and a new lease issued with a fresh entry fine. Isacke was a slippery customer though. At court, he agreed to terms: he would repair the mansion, pay an extra £20 to fund the house for the poor, make good the waste, ensure that the copyholders' rents were subject to proper arbitration and enter into a bond for one thousand marks. He tried to wriggle out of the agreement by 'pollicie', but the Chapter had the law on its side. The Corn Rent Act gave them the perfect excuse to draw up a new twenty-one-year agreement. It took two years for the case to be settled, but in the end Isacke and Thomas Ravis (Dean, 1596–1605) agreed to an annual payment of £10 per annum, over and above his rent, up to a total of £170, to meet his defaults.[52]

Windfall income

Of course, rental income and manorial profits were not the only forms of revenue. There were occasional windfalls. However, while large and welcome, these could not be relied on year in, year out. For Christ Church these irregular boosts to the coffers – at least to the coffers of the dean and canons – came from two principal sources: timber and coal mining.[53]

Timber was potentially a source of considerable wealth, in demand for construction and shipbuilding.[54] But, unless strictly managed, the harvesting of timber was open to abuse.[55] In the post-Restoration years of the 1660s and 1670s, Warden Michael Woodward of New College would visit woods personally to ensure that new trees were planted to replace cut timber.[56] And in the early eighteenth century Canon Burton of Christ Church visited the college's manor of Swanton Novers in the company of the Chapter Clerk, John Brooks. The men made sure to investigate the amount of timber on the estate and its condition as well as looking at the buildings and land usage.[57] Most college leases included a clause that reserved timber – the large standing trees (rather than brushwood, scrub and coppice used commonly for fencing and fuel, including charcoal) – for the use of the college.

Christ Church's 'home' wood, from 1562, when Dean Cox conveyed it in trust to the Dean and Canons, was at Chandlings (or Chandence), on the edge of Bagley Wood, then just over the county boundary into Berkshire between Boars Hill and Abingdon.[58] The terms of the lease of the wood were stringent: the tenant, who paid £8 per annum in cash plus another £4 in corn rent, was allowed to take, and sell or use, the underwood, coppices and hedgerows on the condition that these were all left for a minimum of seven years between each cutting. For the profit he gained from these he was obliged to maintain all the wood banks and ditches, and to replace any trees that were cut down at the request of the Chapter with three new ones. The value of the trees, and the importance of the woodsman's role, was emphasised by the signing of a bond for £100.[59] The arable and woodland at Chandlings were kept in hand and managed directly by the Dean and Chapter until 1649: payments are recorded in the disbursement books to men sent for 'looking to the woods', dealing with moles and ensuring that hedging or fencing between the coppices was maintained.[60] After 1649 the fields at Chandlings were leased to Frances Bisley, a widow, and to Richard West, Christ Church's manciple, in whose management they remained until the end of the century. The lease of the woodland followed in 1669. Perhaps the Dean and Chapter did not forfeit too much control after all.[61]

Usually the profits from timber were divided between the Dean and the Canons; in 1779, for example, the proceeds from Chandlings were £70 10s. The Dean received an extra £14 2s. that year, and the canons half of that each.[62] However, on occasions, with the approval of Chapter, the profits could be diverted to college projects. In 1778, for example, £180 of timber profits from Wendling (Norfolk), £67 from Chandlings and £66 from Swanton Novers were transferred to the Canterbury Quad building fund. Timber from Deddington was sold specifically to raise money for the same project.[63]

The size of these windfalls made management of the timber in all of Christ Church's estates vital – many leases included a plan enumerating the timber trees. Additional plans were drawn when it was felt necessary, often before the issuing of a new lease, recording the number of trees of each type

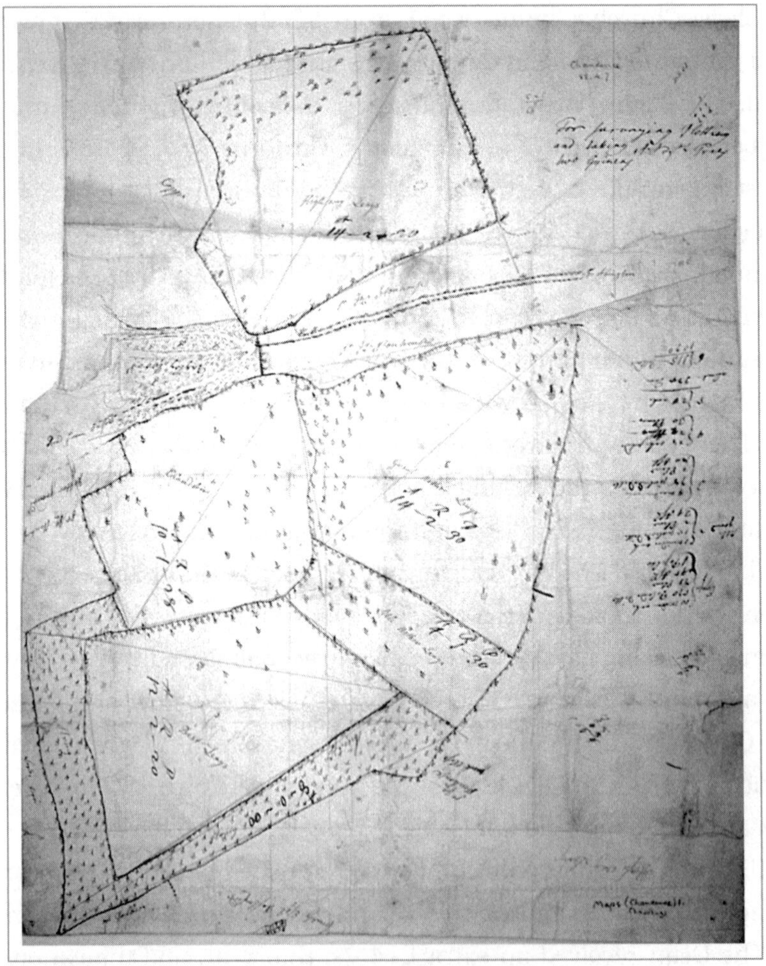

Chandlings Wood, just outside Oxford. The map, dated 1724, was drawn specifically to show the extent of the woodland, and in particular the valuable timber trees. The annotations, which are upside down, record the number of maiden oak, pollarded oak, elm and ash trees in each plot.

in each plot (maiden oaks, pollarded oaks, elm and ash at Chandlings).[64] An account was made of timber cut in South Stoke (mainly beech at this south-westerly end of the Chiltern hills) in 1636 and from whose copyhold it was taken; 190 trees, forming 128 loads, had been felled. One area, it was noted, had once been used for the production of charcoal for Christ Church.[65] But it was not just from the big timber estates such as Chandlings and South Stoke that trees were procured for college purposes: in the early years of the eighteenth century alone the parishioners of Binsey (Oxfordshire) were allowed to take a tree from the churchyard in order to rebuild a bridge destroyed by flood; two copyholders from Dorton (Buckinghamshire) were permitted to cut down eleven elm trees to repair their properties; and trees in Brize Norton were marked for Colliers Farm in Worton to repair a tenement occupied by a Mr Willesden and for the maintenance of Mr Surman's cottage in Garsington (all Oxfordshire).[66]

Property maintenance and rebuilding were a common theme in the requests to Christ Church for the felling of timber trees. Sometimes it was for the tenant's own house or for the parsonage house, and occasionally for the church itself. In 1657 William Barber of South Stoke asked for permission to fell twenty trees; he wanted to demolish the medieval hall that formed part of his property and to rebuild that end of the house. As a sweetener, he promised to improve the chancel of the local church at the same time.[67] The Dean and Chapter used timber from the local estates for its own maintenance too, and the income from the sale of trees to deal with unforeseen expenditure: trees were cut in 1689, for example, to repair the water banks by the Meadow; in 1687 it was ordered that £200 worth of trees be cut and sold to help pay off the loan made to the college by Dean Fell; in 1773 timber was sent to repair St Aldate's causeway and to build a new sawpit in the kitchen yard; and much later, in the mid-nineteenth century, timber was sold to help augment the depleted buildings funds. That timber was expensive and a valuable resource was brought home in 1838, when it was discovered that workmen doing repairs about college were taking old timbers home with them to be used as firewood. Chapter issued a decree that this was to be stopped forthwith and any future occurrence would be met with dismissal.[68] Old wood could still be sold and the profits added to the coffers.[69]

William Barber had presumably taken his twenty trees from Christ Church's coppices in South Stoke, which were named after Dean Sampson and four of the early canons.[70] While the manor and rectory were leased in the same manner as any other property, in the sixteenth and early seventeenth centuries, to the Palmer family of college auditors, Abbots Wood was managed in-house for many years.[71] In 1646 the tenant, Richard Hannars (or Hannes), requested a warrant to cut thirty loads of firewood, as part of the entitlement of his lease, but at the same time he suggested to the Dean and Chapter that the wood on the copyhold lands of the manor was being wasted and that a professional woodman should be appointed.[72] No doubt the Chapter was preoccupied at that moment, as Christ Church had been host to Charles I for the preceding four years and the Civil War had caused chaos throughout city and University.[73] But in 1649, when things had settled down, albeit under a new regime, and Christ Church needed to maximise its income to aid recovery after the royal residence, the college began to investigate. John Wheeler, of Turkdean, who held Abbots Wood in trust for the Dean and Canons, was to be investigated and, if necessary, taken to court.[74] It would seem that Dr Mills, the Treasurer, came to the conclusion that it was not necessary to go to law over the matter but a new lease was to be issued with more stringent terms. An agreement was drawn up between the Dean and Canons and Wheeler which stipulated that, for a consideration of £300, Wheeler would hold the South Stoke woods in trust for Christ Church.[75] He was obliged under the terms of the covenant to manage the woods efficiently and to leave twice as many trees per acre as were stipulated by statute. As £300 was a considerable sum it must have both focused Wheeler's mind and given the Chapter a sense of some security.[76] The statute for the Preservation of Woods, passed in 1543, required there to be a minimum of twelve timber trees per acre. After the dissolution, with so much property changing hands, the statute formalised what had been common practice for centuries and its requirements became a usual clause in woodland leases.[77]

The value of timber was graphically demonstrated, coincidentally, in Turkdean (Gloucestershire). The Dean and the Treasurer had visited the estate, of which Christ Church was rector, in 1640, and had made the prescient statement that there was likely to be trouble between the local freeholder, William Banister, and Christ Church's tenant, William Dewey, over wood on the common. According to the survey, the rectory was due the profits from a quarter of the timber on the common, but Banister claimed it all. Sure enough, in 1674 Banister went to court claiming that he had 'casually lost' a load of timber worth £50 at Cirencester market, and that the wood had come into the possession of Dewey, who refused to give it up. Dewey denied the charge, but Banister continued to argue that the wood was legally his as it had grown on the waste in Turkdean and he was lord of the manor. Christ Church claimed that the rectory was also a manor given to them by Henry VIII, and proved it by producing court rolls from the Oseney Abbey records.[78] The same archive showed that it was the Dean and Chapter who had planted the trees, and that the plaintiff's alleged manor did not exist. But Banister produced contradictory documents, apparently showing that a manor had belonged to the collegiate church of Holy Trinity at Westbury.[79] The case raised all sorts of questions: whether the Oseney manor, as well as the rectory, really belonged to Christ Church; whether there were two manors which needed to be sorted out; whether having held no manorial courts since time immemorial rendered the manor or manors lost; and if the manors were lost, were the royalties forfeit too? John Willis, the Chapter Clerk, was evidently put to work; the Book of Evidences records his research, which took him back to the Norman Conquest and the grant of the rectory by Robert d'Oilly to St George's in Oxford and thence to Oseney Abbey.[80] The manor had come to Oseney by a different course, this time from Paulinus of Theydon.[81] Willis came to the conclusion that both rectory and manor had come to Christ Church and had been leased together since the foundation.[82] The court heard evidence from both sides, with Christ Church's defence hanging on custom. The Gloucester assizes eventually decided in favour of Christ Church and Dewey. The rights to timber, turf and quarrying on the common were confirmed to the Dean and Chapter.[83]

Similarly, in Worcester in 1635, the Dean and Chapter were called before Chancery to answer a complaint from the tenants of a portion of Christ Church's estate there.[84] The Rowlands (also known as the Steyners) claimed that they had a ninety-nine-year lease on the estate, which included a coppice called Perry Wood, dating from 11 December 1566 but, because of some libel that they had not paid their rent and that they had committed waste, the Dean and Chapter had seized all the documents and were declaring the lease invalid. The Chapter responded that the rent had been unpaid

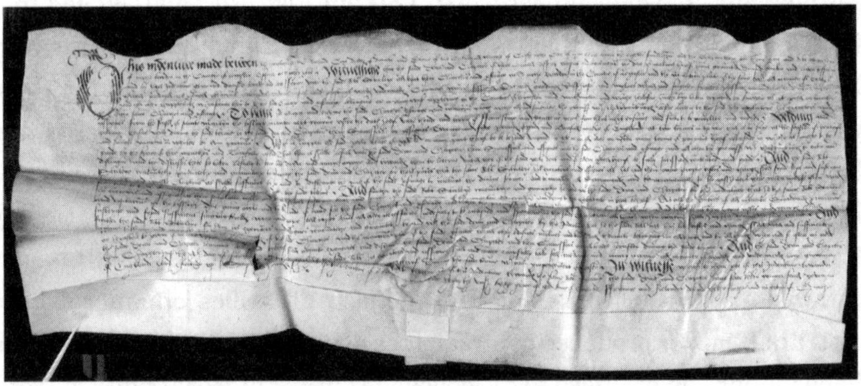

Ninety-nine-year leases, of which this is an example from Great Bowden, would cause problems for Christ Church, particularly when the Governing Body wished to run out its beneficial leases and replace them with rack rents.

for two years, that they reserved the right to re-enter the estate for non-payment and that the tenant had cut down more than 2,000 trees – mainly oak, with some elm – in Perry Wood. They had not taken the original documents but rather had used a letter of attorney to demand the rent. A lawyer had been engaged, who was taking the matter to the King's Bench and had organised the arrest of the poor sub-tenants of the estate for trespass. The lease, in their opinion, was forfeit, and they had issued a new lease to a different tenant.[85] Witness statements were drawn up, concentrating on the loss of the valuable timber. Substantial numbers of trees had been cut until, in 1635, Dean Samuel Fell had forbidden any more felling, but the order had been ignored. Neither side would budge. In May 1640 an injunction was issued ordering the Steyners to stop cutting trees, but in late June it was reported that another 660 trees of more than fifty years' growth had been felled. The Dean and Chapter insisted that they be allowed free access to the wood to be able to remove the newly cut trees, and demanded the payment of the overdue rent and a valuation of the timber already lost, which they estimated to be about £120.[86] The Rowland-Steyners were less than happy with Dean Fell and the court action: 'if you had binne pleased to have ended this suite without the rigor of the law', Robert Steyner suggested, 'your fame had flowne up to heaven.' The evidence suggests, though, that the Steyners had never been going to settle amicably, and it was another two years before articles of agreement were drawn up which finally allowed Christ Church to retrieve its timber from the wood, receive some compensation and settle with the tenant.

By 1820 the tenant of Perry Wood complained that his re-entry fine should be reduced as the products were so mean and the prices so low, particularly for the underwood,[87] and just a few years later there was a valuation, by George Davenport, surveyor, which described how a corner of the wood had been made into a pleasure ground for Burlingham's house, which had given Christ Church's tenements a beautiful situation but also indicated that the oaks were being cut too soon, depriving Christ Church of its timber. The surveyor suggested introducing a new clause into the lease, and into the lease for the nearby Nunnery Wood, which insisted on a given number of standard trees.[88] The tenants were less than happy; with these new clauses the property would be just about worthless. Much of the oak from the wood was felled for its bark, and the price had dropped. Davenport could see the tenants' point of view; there was not a lot of timber available on the Worcester estate, and he proposed that a more profitable scheme would be to permit the building of small houses, perhaps offering either timber to assist in the construction or an extension of the post-construction lease. He favoured the latter, especially if the Dean and Chapter sanctioned the construction of new roads across the estate, as the lack of wood available was not much of an incentive.

In 1834 Davenport reported that, over the previous seven years, £935 had been spent on Perry and Nunnery Woods (largely on grubbing up and labour expenses), but the return over the same period had been only £1,020. The areas of the woodland that had been converted for tillage had failed. He hoped that the new tenant, who was a decent man, would do something to improve the estate.[89]

Just a few years earlier, in South Stoke, there was a dispute with the tenant of part of Abbots Wood over the right to cut oak timber. For a while after the new management system was instigated in the mid-seventeenth century, things appear to have improved; new maps of Abbots Wood were made in 1726 and 1778 by a professional surveyor, Thomas Wood. In the intervening fifty years, only 17 of more than 200 acres of timber had been felled and the ground turned for tillage in the area known as The String. Abbots Wood, sometimes called College Woods, contained 98 acres of arable and 197 acres of beech wood.[90] However, while the management of the beech woods appears to have been in good hands, no one had been watching what had been happening to the oak trees.

In 1806 Thomas Piercy had renewed his lease of Sampson's Coppice, which had a penal fine attached of 40 shillings for every acre converted from woodland to tillage.[91] In the lease Piercy had covenanted to replace all trees that had been felled, to ensure that the coppice was properly hedged and ditched, and to cut only according to the local custom. He also promised to make a terrier of the estate – a document describing the extent, boundaries and uses of land – showing the amount of timber currently growing.[92] In 1813, when the time came for the renewal of the lease, the Dean and Chapter discovered that Piercy had chopped down £700 worth of oak since 1803, which had not been taken into account when the entry fine was being calculated. Piercy countered that the oak had been included in the sale price of the lease, and Christ Church was forced to admit that it had neglected to include the reservation of the oak in the lease. However, Christ Church's lawyer argued that, while the oak had not been specifically mentioned, the tenant was not permitted just to grub up the timber and had committed waste, and that Christ Church was entitled to the oak. Piercy did his own calculation and accounted for £209 worth of oak felled between his purchase of the lease and its renewal. Piercy's sub-tenant, Slatter, reckoned it was nearer £450.[93] Piercy's sons appealed for some leniency, and it would appear that the Dean and Chapter did not push for the refund.

The acreage of Abbots Wood has remained unchanged. In 1862 the small farm, with its unsurprisingly timber-framed buildings and arable ground suitable for stock or non-grain crops, had a gross annual value of around £170.[94] By 1883, however, in the depth of the agricultural depression, a rather despondent minute in the Governing Body papers said that it was to be let for whatever could be achieved.[95] Apart from a small quantity of land leased to the Air Ministry during the Second World War, the wood was kept in hand until its final sale in 1960.[96]

* * * * *

So, although Christ Church did not maintain complete central control over its estates, the Dean and Chapter were definitely interested in their management. After all, their stipends and the well-being of both college and cathedral depended on a reliable income derived from five main sources: the profits of directly managed land; profits from fee-paying members of the college; capital windfalls; entry fines; and rents.[97]

3

Parsons and parsonages: Christ Church's incumbencies

Along with general estate management and agricultural change, Christ Church also had to manage its advowsons – the clerical incumbencies in its gift – in nearly one hundred parishes in England and Wales.[1] The rectories, with the profits from the great tithes and sometimes including glebe land, were generally leased out like any other rural property, with the great tithe being a profitable advantage for a landowner.[2]

Glebe land, which could be in a single block or scattered throughout a parish in the open fields, was the area of land belonging to the rector and from which the incumbent's living was derived. The division of tithes – into great (grain crops, hay and wood) and small (all other produce) – was determined by the lease and by local custom. Usually the great tithes were reserved for the rector (Christ Church) and the small tithes were for the vicar (the incumbent). In Down Ampney (Gloucestershire), for example, the small tithes due to the vicar included: a cash payment of 4d. from every yardland of hay; the tithe of wool; 2d. for every cow in milk; a tithe of lambs on St Mark's Day (25 April); every tenth calf, pig and goose; the tithe of apples, wardens and other types of pears, walnuts, honey and beeswax; the tithe of eggs from hens, turkeys and ducks; and the tithes of hemp, flax and hops.[3] Not every vicar was so fortunate.

The Dean and Chapter reserved to itself the right to present the vicar or curate to the parish, although he was paid by the tenant. As such, the livings were both a source of revenue and a means of patronage.[4]

The universities of Oxford and Cambridge were, to a great extent, factories of the nation's Anglican clergy. Grammar schools, some of which were directly under the control of the bishop or a cathedral, provided a good grounding, with masters often educated at Oxford or Cambridge and already clergymen. Those men who took degrees but who were not elder or eldest sons, who would inherit the family estate or take their seats in Parliament, would in all likelihood take holy orders. Even as late as the middle of the nineteenth century, three-quarters of all ordinands were educated at Oxford and Cambridge.[5]

Students at Christ Church who wished to continue studying beyond their BA and to retain their stipendiary status were required to be ordained at least to the diaconate.[6] However, the course towards a BA was not designed to be specifically theological or vocational. Undergraduates were expected to arrive at college with their catechism by heart, and were indeed required to read their way through the Scriptures, in Hebrew and Greek, to study the Thirty-Nine Articles and, from the middle of the seventeenth century, Bishop Pearson's *Exposition on the Apostle's Creed*.[7] Divinity lectures were also compulsory. These studies, though, were intermingled with readings of classical texts in both Greek and Latin, designed to teach not just the languages but also the skills and knowledge contained within, as well as classes in rhetoric, dialectic, algebra (particularly Euclidean) and trigonometry, and logic. Outside tutorials, men could hear courses of lectures on law, all aspects of natural science, and music.[8]

Ordination was, of course, a diocesan matter rather than one for the Dean and Chapter. At Christ Church the relationship between the bishop and the diocese and the cathedral was at best distant and at worst hostile until late into the nineteenth century. On a number of occasions the bishop was refused permission to prepare candidates for ordination in the cathedral.[9] But men were ordained, occasionally in the cathedral, sometimes in other Oxford churches or in other dioceses.

Students of Christ Church were first in line for incumbencies in the gift of the Dean and Chapter after ordination and passing their Bachelor's examinations; when there was a vacancy, these positions formed their first step on the clerical ladder.[10] The best livings were often given as almost retirement presents or rewards, rather than because the Student particularly wanted a cure of souls. In 1766, for example, Edward Smallwell was permitted to hold the rich living of Batsford (Gloucestershire) in conjunction with his Studentship and his additional role of librarian 'by special favour in consideration of his incommon Trouble and great Diligence in placing and making Catalogues of the Books in Peckwater Library'.[11] If they requested it, Students were usually granted a year of grace, which meant that, on presentation to a living, a man had a 'cooling-off' period during which he retained his Studentship. The first record of a year of grace is in 1650, when Mr (probably Thomas) Hancock's Studentship was declared void.[12] There is no indication that this was the start of something new, so it seems likely that the practice was perfectly normal but just undocumented in the earlier Chapter Books.

In most cases, when the year of grace terminated, the new vicar continued in his incumbency and resigned his Studentship.[13] But there was the odd case when a man elected to come back to the familiarity of Christ Church. That this was rare is evident from the response to Robert Bourne's request to return. Bourne had come up to Christ Church as a commoner in 1678, and received a Canoneer Studentship in 1679.[14] He held a Morris exhibition, and was appointed a tutor and catechist before being presented to the comfortable living of Chalgrove (Oxfordshire).[15] No reason is given in the Chapter Book, but in December 1701, just six months after his appointment to the living, Bourne asked to return. The Dean and Chapter, although evidently surprised, allowed him to do so, not just as a Student but also as catechist. He was, however, prevented from taking another college living in the future. Only one other incident of a Student requesting to return is recorded in the Chapter Books: in 1773 William Maximilian Freind resigned his preferment in Ireland, as a prebend of Armagh, on account of his ill-health, and requested to continue his Studentship. This was granted and his year of grace revoked.[16] A further case does appear in a volume of correspondence: Matthew Skinner, who was appointed to the living of Wood Norton

(Norfolk) in 1803, was, according to his father, 'depressed in spirits'. Skinner's request to return to his Studentship was granted, with the warning that he would not receive another opportunity. Skinner did not follow up the offer and remained in Wood Norton until 1825.[17]

* * * * *

Oxford men were largely destined for the church until the later nineteenth century, and college livings were often valuable, eagerly sought-after gifts.[18] At the end of the eighteenth century the living of Staverton (Northamptonshire), the richest of the Dean and Chapter's incumbencies, generated an income of over £400 per annum, and several others were worth over £200.[19] After the Restoration particularly, there was an increasing expectation that clergymen should be university-educated and thus generally from either Oxford or Cambridge. As a result, the nation's clergy gradually became more gentrified. Under deans such as John Fell, who worked hard to ensure that the intake to Christ Church was increasingly from the gentry and aristocratic classes, this was even more evident. Benefices were nowhere near plentiful enough, however. There were twelve perpetual curacies (in 1778) that could be held alongside Studentships, most of which were within relatively easy riding distance of Oxford, but men who took on benefices that produced sufficient revenue for a decent quality of life were obliged to resign their Studentships.[20] But even livings that looked good on paper were subject to the vagaries of the economy and farming fashions. During the period 1688–91, for example, the severely depressed price of corn had a knock-on effect on the value of tithes made worse by high levels of taxation. In the late eighteenth century the Revd George Periam in Lathbury (Buckinghamshire) explained that the annual income of the parish varied 'according to the manner in which the tenants occupy their land'. The tithes were much reduced when the tenants kept cattle for fattening, but after a few years he had persuaded the tenants to switch to grain and dairy, which were much more profitable – from Periam's perspective, at least.[21]

Insufficient income to meet all demands was a problem frequently raised by parsons. In 1613 the bishop of Lincoln decreed that the stipend

The church and comfortable parsonage house in Staverton, photographed in 1868. The parsonage was built in 1778 and enlarged in 1833 to include four reception rooms, eight bedrooms and three dressing rooms, along with service rooms and servants' quarters.

of the curates of St Mary in Arden (a chapelry of Market Harborough, in Leicestershire) was so small that 'no sufficient scholar will take the living'.[22] A century later there were pots of money that incumbents could draw on to help: the Clergy Residences Repair Act of 1776 allowed incumbents to draw money from Queen Anne's Bounty for repairs and, from 1811, for new buildings, but the Bounty had been in existence since 1704, when Queen Anne, a passionate supporter of the Church of England, redirected Henry VIII's 'First Fruits and Tenths' ecclesiastical tax into a new fund, operated by Trustees, to augment the incomes of poorer clergy through the purchase of land.[23]

Christ Church had its own funds to assist its poorer clergy too, the biggest of which was the South Trust, set up almost contemporaneously with Queen Anne's Bounty in the early eighteenth century. Robert South (1634–1716) had been an undergraduate at Christ Church during the 1650s, somehow surviving in spite of his staunch and outspoken High Anglicanism to become a canon in 1670. He held estates in Caversham (Oxfordshire) and Kentish Town (Middlesex), which he left, on his death, in reversion to Christ Church. South had by all accounts been very careful to ensure that the curates who attended the parishes of which he was vicar or rector were well paid, and in his will he stipulated that three-fifths of the proceeds from the estate should be used to augment a list of specific small livings in Christ Church's patronage to the tune of £10 per annum, on the condition that the vicars or curates were not accused or suspected of grossly immoral behaviour, including fornication, drunkenness, common swearing and any conduct against the Act of Uniformity. Any surplus was to be directed to the maintenance of six poor scholars from his old school of Westminster.[24] In the nineteenth century the Trust was redrawn and the portion dedicated to the augmentation of small livings was fixed at three-fifths and extended to all livings of which the Dean and Chapter were patrons.[25] Dr Stratford's Trust, founded in 1726, performed a similar function, although grants from the canon's fund were subject to further augmentation by Queen Anne's Bounty (later the Ecclesiastical Commissioners).[26] The bequest made by Canon Stratford allowed the purchase of a farm in Cutteslowe, the income from which went towards increasing the value of various livings, which were, under the terms of the will, in Oxfordshire, Berkshire, Yorkshire, Cheshire or Lancashire.[27]

In spite of augmentations, it was still common for the Students not to reside in their parishes, or even to do much of the pastoral work expected. Drayton St Leonard (Oxfordshire) was often held by Students who made no bones at all about employing a curate to undertake the actual work of the parish, and Samuel Long was granted permission to continue to hold the curacy of Benson (Oxfordshire) in 1767 on the condition that he found a resident curate and maintained the house in good repair.[28] His successor, William Judgson, was allowed the same dispensation.[29] In the late seventeenth century the churchwarden at Stratton Audley (Oxfordshire) appealed to the Dean and Chapter for an increase in the curate's stipend, not least to help him find somewhere decent to live; the lease for the rectory stipulated that the curate was to live in a two-roomed flat in the parsonage house. Unsurprisingly, Stratton Audley was neglected as the incumbent chose to live and work in another parish.[30] Sometimes there seemed to be some deviousness in the augmentation of livings: in 1774 the Revd Judd Collins surrendered his nomination to Tring, Long Marston and Wigginton (Hertfordshire) so that he could have two distinct nominations – one for Tring and Long Marston and one for Wigginton. A couple of Chapter meetings later it was decided to grant the curacy of Wigginton with £200 from Stratford's benefaction so that it could receive further augmentation from Queen Anne's Bounty.[31]

The huge parishes in the north of the country, particularly, which could incorporate a number of hamlets as well as the principal township where the parish church was situated were potentially a drain on the resources of an incumbent. The Lancashire parish of Kirkham, for example, halfway between Preston and Blackpool, included the townships of Kirkham itself with Barton, Copp, Goosnargh, Hambleton, Lund, Ribby with Wrea, Treales, Warton with Freckleton, Weeton and Whitechapel. Similarly, the Yorkshire parishes of Northallerton and Osmotherly (Christ Church's most northerly until modern times) included North Kilvington, North Otterington, Romanby, Thornton-le-Beans, Thornton-le-Moor, Thornton-le-Street, Ellerbeck, Nunhouse and Thimbleby.

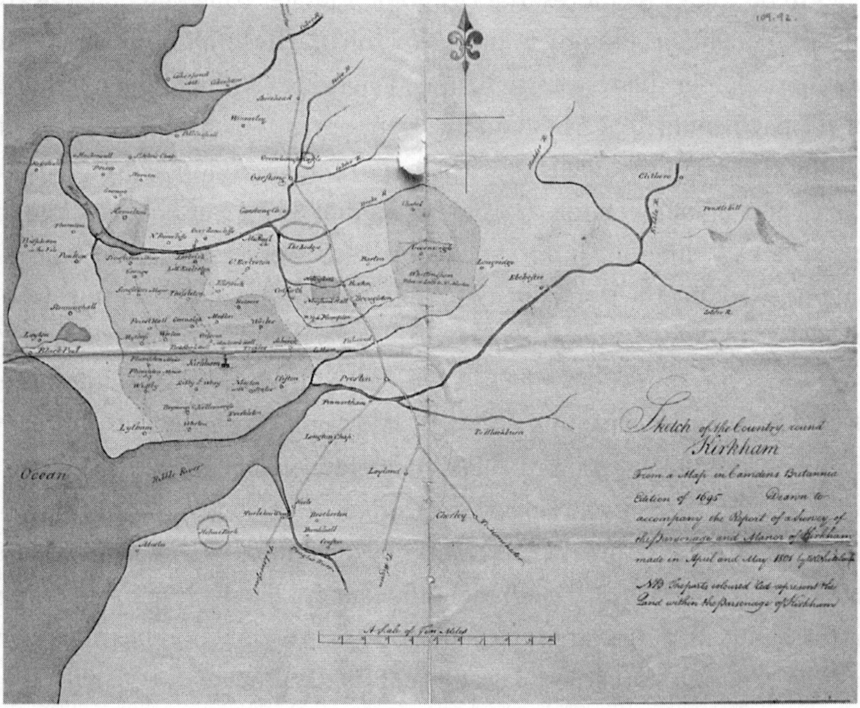

A map showing the extent of the huge parish of Kirkham in 1801, which was managed by one vicar and a curate out in the detached township of Goosnargh. It was immense parishes such as this that were broken up during the nineteenth century into smaller units that were easier for pastoral care but which required the funding of new churches and new parsonages.

A vicar could attempt to serve the entire parish or pay a curate to assist. In Rostherne, for example, the vicar in 1561, Robert Swan (who had probably been appointed to the living in the late 1550s), complained to the Dean and Chapter that he received a stipend of only £23 6s. 8d., out of which he had to pay £8 to the curate of Knutsford and £7 10s. to the curate of Peover. He paid 20s. in subsidy to the queen and 18s. for Tenths, with a further 20s. to Robert Mainwaring (the manorial lord). In the last two years he had repaired his still dilapidated parsonage house and now found himself in great debt. Swan asked the Chapter for some relief and a quarter of his year's salary so that he could take some ground on which to graze his cow. Never ones to do things by halves, the Dean and Chapter called up many of the historic documents relating to the advowson and its funding, including the appropriation of the rectory to Launde Priory in 1507 and the regulation of the payment of £23 6s. 8d. to the vicar, out of which he was to provide for the curates in the townships. The priory had been duty-bound to build the vicar a suitable house.[32] It would seem that Swan was not successful in his plea, as William Shenton, one of his successors, complained in 1632 that he was still only receiving the £23 in spite of the rectorial estate being valued at £700 per annum and the Chapter's promise to raise the vicar's stipend to 100 marks (about £66).[33] Christ Church quibbled; at first they denied that the schedule that Shenton cited as making such a commitment ever existed, but they soon modified their stance and stated instead that it had never been approved. However, the Book of Evidences records that the allowance had been raised to 100 marks by the time of its compilation in the 1660s, the extra paid by the tenant of the estate.[34] There are many instances of the Chapter giving grants, particularly to help repair churches or parsonage houses, from the earliest days through to the present.[35]

* * * * *

A large number of the decisions made in Chapter about land and property were associated with the incumbents of college livings and the management of the property attached to the parish. Students were constantly being instituted to livings all around the country, and the properties attached to the vicarages and curacies were often in need of attention. The state of parsonage houses was one particular problem, and letters of complaint from the Chapter, expecting the tenant to undertake repairs, and from the tenants, requesting assistance, were travelling backwards and forwards almost from the foundation in 1546.

In Great Bowden (Leicestershire), a sixteenth-century account of the parsonage recounts that the malthouse, slaughterhouse, kitchen and backhouse, as well as two bays of the residence itself, were on the verge of collapse and should be repaired by the farmer.[36] How much was done then is not recorded, but in 1846, when discussions were under way about the provision of a house for the new curate, it was decided that the rectory was not only too large but too dilapidated.[37]

John Stone, the vicar of Ardington (Berkshire), complained that his house was too large, very old and ruinous, and that the income from the parish was insufficient for him to build afresh. On 10 August 1691 the Dean and Chapter gave permission for Stone to take down the old medieval hall which formed part of the vicarage and to use the materials to make good the remainder.[38] It would seem that Stone adopted a make-do-and-mend approach; not much more than a century later, in 1807, William Wiseman Clarke, a local man who had been Christ Church's tenant for a short time in the 1790s, wrote to the Treasurer to inform him that the living was impoverished and the house so wretched that it had prevented residence for fifty years.[39] He anticipated that, with the present state of affairs, no more could be expected than that a clergyman from another, better preferment would turn up once a week to do what was necessary. Clarke proposed that the Dean and Chapter sell him the reversion on the rectory and then he would enclose the parish farmland, improve it and build a new parsonage house. He commented that the 'secession from our regular Church to Meeting Houses is so frequent that nothing short of a resident Minister will remedy the increasing evil'. The onward march of nonconformity would, as we will see, cause considerable distress to Anglican clergymen across the country.[40]

In 1767 John Chawner was permitted to retain £20 from the sale of timber on the Hawkhurst estate in Kent in order to repair a house on parish land but actually lived in rented rooms. The parsonage house, which was occupied by farm labourers, was described as 'mean', with an earth floor in the kitchen. By 1820 the incumbents had had enough: there had been five curates in seven years, all dissatisfied with the living arrangements and the meanness of the salary. A petition was sent by forty-six locals to the Dean and Chapter insisting that the minister should be able 'to live in such manner that he ensures the respect and esteem of the parishioners' and to 'maintain that appearance and to exercise that Liberality towards them which tend in great measure to produce confidence and good will on their part, without which much of the salutary effect of the Ministry must be lost'. Edward

Salter, the new vicar, evidently liked Hawkhurst but found that he was struggling to make ends meet; he had to give up his pony and chaise, and the small house that he had taken was expensive. He asked for financial aid. The Dean and Chapter refused to build a parsonage but did allocate funds towards the improvement of the estate.[41] It was not until 1826, when Henry Cleaver took on the curacy, that something was done about decent lodgings for the parson; the farm labourers were given notice to quit the old glebe house, and plans were put in place to rebuild something substantial and fitting.[42]

In 1770 Edmund Goodenough was given £15 to repair the curate's house in South Littleton.[43] During the 1780s new vicarages were built in Marcham (Berkshire) and in Badby (Northamptonshire), the latter coinciding with the enclosure of the parish, and a new house for the curate was erected at Daventry.[44]

It was not uncommon for the vicars to take on the improvement of their houses themselves. In 1778 Revd Edward Whitmell, Matthew Skinner's predecessor in the fairly rich parish of Wood Norton, described the parsonage house as being in good condition, two-thirds of it having been built by himself and the remainder by his immediate predecessor. The ancillary buildings included a backhouse (perhaps a wash-house or scullery), dairy, coal house, wagon and cart shed 'with convenience for Pidgeons over it', a chaise house, a new barn, stables from which the thatch had been removed and replaced with tiles, new cattle sheds, straw barns, pens and yards. Inside he had replaced the beams in the lower rooms, created a cellar and built a new staircase and a handsome study 'wainscotted with convenience for books'. Over the study there was a chamber with a garret. The kitchen had been rebuilt and was supplied from new gardens, in which he could grow nectarines and peaches. All this had cost about £150, nearly one year's income from the glebe estate, which suggests a comfortable lifestyle.[45] Similarly, in Sheering (Essex), while one half of the parsonage house was old and its lath and plaster walls, Dr Richard Hind advised, would soon require attention, the other half had been built by him in the mid-eighteenth century and included a new kitchen and pantries, and a wine cellar. He had also rebuilt all the outhouses.[46]

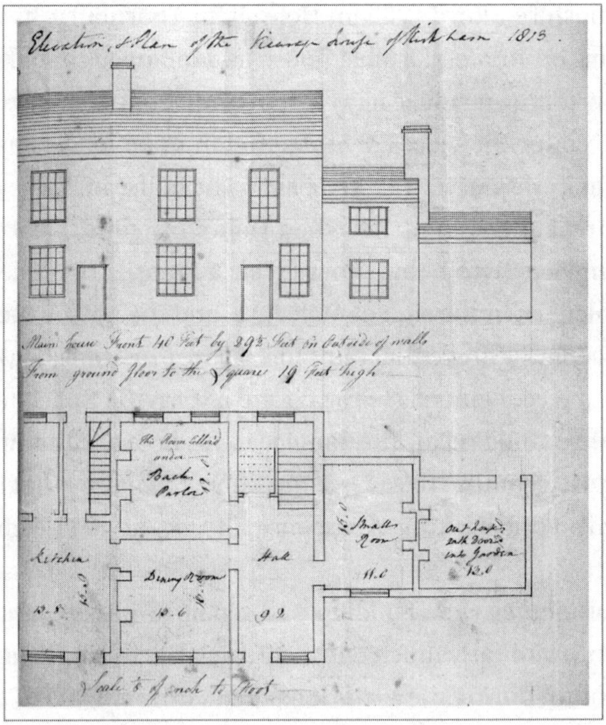

Sketch plans of 1813 for an extension to the parsonage house in Kirkham. The Dean and Chapter gave a loan of £300 to help with the improvements.

The condition of parsonages was often brought to the attention of the Chapter by newly arrived vicars: in 1658 Guy Lawrence, the vicar of Thornbury (Gloucestershire), was permitted to pull down the parsonage and to start from scratch, and in 1661 the same thing happened in Market Lavington (Wiltshire).[47] By the late eighteenth century, and right through the nineteenth, repairs, maintenance and new-builds filled the records of the Chapter. These were probably encouraged by the passing of the Clergy Residences Repair Act, passed in 1776, which allowed incumbents to borrow against the income from their parishes specifically for the maintenance and rebuilding of parsonage houses.[48] An increasing intolerance of pluralism – holding more than one incumbency – and of non-residence also required the construction of new parsonage houses.[49] In 1780, £200 was borrowed to build a new parsonage for Hamlyn Harris, the new incumbent at Badby

(Northamptonshire). Revd William Holwell, in Thornbury, had spent considerable sums on his comfortable house and intended to make use of the Act to borrow more and make it even better.[50] In contrast, a few years later, leave was given for the vicarage at Ardington to be made smaller, on the condition that it was put into good repair.[51] The house in Semley (Wiltshire) came under real attack in 1778, when Holwell, a cousin of Peter Foulkes who was then vicar, wrote that 'I never saw a more dirty unpleasing situation [...] Semley [is] in the sink of Wiltshire, and the parsonage house is in the sink of Semley.'[52] Torrential rains just before Christmas 1800 prompted the Chapter to give 5 guineas to the curate at Drayton St Leonard (Oxfordshire) so that he could repair the damage to his house, although they were quick to make it clear that this was a one-off payment and that it was not to be considered an undertaking of responsibility for the general maintenance of the property.[53]

There was much new building and repair of parsonages during the later eighteenth and early nineteenth centuries, but this work acquired even more momentum during the Victorian period, driven by three factors: new legislation against plurality and non-residence in the 1830s; massive urban growth as a result of the Industrial Revolution, which saw 50 per cent of the population living in towns and cities by 1870; and the adoption of neo-Gothic as the predominant style of ecclesiastical architecture.[54]

* * * * *

Of course, it was not just the parsonage houses that could be dilapidated; the churches themselves often required attention. Traditionally, maintenance of the chancels fell to the rectors of the parish, and Christ Church was rector of many. The rectory – with its valuable great tithes and land for exploitation – was almost invariably leased out as any other piece of property, so the liability was passed on to the principal tenant. The rest of the church building was the responsibility of the parish. In both cases the Dean and Chapter often made donations, either financial or with materials. The first mention of church repairs in the Chapter minutes comes in 1657, when William Barber, the tenant at South Stoke, asked permission to demolish the old hall that formed part of his house. He was granted twenty trees on the condition that he repaired the chancel too.[55]

In 1721 the college's tenant in Cowley (Oxfordshire), Sarah Wastie, and the Chapter agreed to put a new pew in the church for the use of Dr Bernard Gardiner, the Warden of All Souls College. It was to be next to the curate's pew, five feet long, removable so that burials could be made underneath or around it, and subject to a rent of 6d., to be paid to Mrs Wastie.[56] There were more drastic repairs needed sometimes, and in other places remedial measures had to be taken to ensure the safety of the building. In 1775 a decision was made that no new burials could be permitted in the chancel of St Thomas's in Oxford except on 'paying a fee of 5gns before the sexton break the ground and that every grave be arched with brick and properly secured with clay from the water'.[57]

But it was later in the nineteenth century, when the Victorian obsession with church restoration kicked in, that the real work began in Christ Church parishes. There was, of course, a new fashion for Gothic architecture expounded by the Ecclesiologists (the Cambridge Camden Society), which went hand in hand with a revival of sacramental and liturgical theology taking the Church back to its supposed medieval piety. Prime movers included John Henry Newman, A. W. N. Pugin and John Ruskin. But, more practically, many vicars were arriving in their churches to find that they had been sorely neglected throughout the previous century.

Ralph Barnes, the vicar of Ardington, approached the Treasurer in 1845 for a contribution towards the restoration of the church there. Work began well until the archdeacon visited and demanded that the tower be taken down and rebuilt, the roof be stripped and replaced, the pulpit and the reading desk – which were in a 'deplorable state' – be repaired, a new communion table purchased and the seats, coping and paving repaired. As if this weren't enough, even the church Bible and the bell had to be replaced. The Dean and Chapter ordered their lessee to do the work on the chancel, which was by far the smallest part of the costs, but he refused to contribute anything until the rest of the work was completed. The parish was hard hit; the repairs that they had expected to pay for had suddenly doubled with the archdeacon's demands. Christ Church said that they were under no obligation to make a donation, and offered just £20 towards the chancel work. The estimated total was over £600, of which much was to be met by mortgage and a levy on the rates. The arguments ran backwards and forwards. After a year of negotiation the Dean and Chapter offered £70, on the condition that the lessee gave £35. By this time, of course, the costs had risen still further and were creeping above £800. Once the work did restart, even more difficulties arose when it was discovered that the chancel roof timbers were in a terrible state, and that a new roof would be needed. The Dean and Chapter refused to budge, and insisted that all the work be done and within the original budget. The parish somehow did as it was told, perhaps assisted by the Vernon family at Ardington Hall, who funded the rebuilding of the north chapel, and the chancel was ready for Easter 1847.[58]

Revd Marah's appeal for assistance to repair the chancel of St Denys's in Little Compton (Gloucestershire) was accompanied by a desperate account of parish life.[59] In some ways the Dean and Chapter must have been relieved to have an incumbent who took an interest in the parish; his predecessor, Thomas Hillier, had been a thorn in Christ Church's side for several years, refusing to live in the parish partly because he wanted to live in the town where his children went to school and partly because the parsonage house needed rebuilding and the parish was poor. When Marah took over the parish in May 1857, almost the first thing he did was to submit plans for a new house to the Chapter for approval. He wasted no time, and by November the roof was on and he was off to Birmingham to buy stoves for his new residence. Then there was time for a holiday in the Caribbean.[60] A year or so later the Gothic Revival architect Edward Bruton noticed that the east wall of the chancel was out of alignment and its window in a sorry state.[61] The roof of the church, too, needed repair. It was decided that, rather than just mend and refurbish, the whole church would benefit from almost total rebuilding, which would allow additional seating. Some of the funds to pay for all the work would be met from local charities, including that of the Warneford Ecclesiastical Charity, established in 1855 by the will of Samuel Warneford, a benefactor to both local churches and hospitals. The Charity contributed to this project, in spite of having turned down several applications from other colleges, because it considered Christ Church to be an ecclesiastical body rather than an academic one. The Dean and Chapter refused to subscribe, the responsibility for the chancel belonging to the rectorial tenant. But the tenant, Richard Davis, from nearby Evenlode, had recently died, and it would seem that it took a few years for the estate to be sorted out and a new head lease issued.[62]

Marah battled on regardless. He tried another tack and appealed to the Chapter through an account of the behaviour of his parishioners rather than the buildings. No doubt he hoped that the dean and canons would be horrified and immediately offer their assistance to improve the church facilities. The first thing Marah noticed when he arrived in the parish, he recalled, 'was a band of musicians in the gallery: clarinet, fife, bassoon, etc. The band sang when and what they liked, and gave out their own psalms, hymns, and anthems. The young men in the belfry, which is open to the nave, laughed, talked, and drew on the walls.' [63] The throwing of stones at the walnut trees in the churchyard led to the treading down of gravestones and the breaking of church windows. Many went to the 'Antinomian chapel', as there had been no regular morning service in the parish church, but most people stayed at home.[64] 'Offices of nature' were performed 'openly and unblushingly', and the local women apparently dried their underwear on the hedges. Poor Revd Marah was 'terrified at the approach of Lady Visitors'. Marah neglected to remind the Dean and Chapter that no sooner had he been instituted at Little Compton than he had disappeared to the West Indies for his health, but he assured them that changes for the better would definitely be seen. His appeal worked; the Dean and Chapter relented and contributed over £400 to the restoration of the church.[65]

Also driving the erection of new churches was the spread of nonconformity, particularly Methodism and particularly in the northern counties. In Shropshire, in 1827, the tenant of one of the Careswell farms caused George Haslewood, the vicar of Quatford, a bit of a headache. The Careswell Trust, argued Haslewood, had been set up to support the established church but, he said, the tenant at Hillhouse in Quatford, with his brothers, had built

The parsonage at Little Compton built by the Revd Marah in 1857 to replace the run-down house his predecessor had refused to occupy.

a meeting house right next door to the church and expected all their labourers and servants to 'desert the church for their chapel'. Mr Haslewood had just established a group of Psalm singers at some considerable expense, and now one member of the chapel was trying to poach them. The appropriately named Mrs Sing, the wife of Christ Church's tenant, had entered into an agreement with the parents of one local lass that she could be employed on the condition that she only went to chapel. The young servant was evidently upset by the restriction, especially as all her friends were members of the Psalm-singing group. Haslewood approached Mrs Sing with a compromise: perhaps the young lady could go to chapel in the morning and then church in the evening? Mrs Sing was inflexible: 'My conscience', she said, 'will not permit me to allow any servant of mine to go to church.' Haslewood implored the Careswell trustees to give Mrs Sing notice to quit.[66]

But this was a relatively minor and local problem. Far bigger was the problem of large rural townships, where many of the population lived at some distance from the parish church. The Church of England was prompted to provide chapels in the outlying hamlets and villages to encourage attendance and to draw parishioners back to the fold from chapel and meeting house. In the Cheshire parish of Frodsham, residents of the townships of Norley and Kingsley met together in 1830 and unanimously agreed that they needed a new church: Frodsham was just too far away. The parish was five miles long, and many of the residents either did not go to church at all or went to Dissenter meetings.[67] A committee was set up and subscriptions opened. The Dean and Chapter turned to a previous vicar of Frodsham, John Fanshawe, for his advice.[68] Fanshawe was in full approval, and offered to contribute £10 per annum to the stipend of a new minister – provided, of course, that he could make the appointment. Christ Church said that they would help, but not with very much as there were many calls on their money. True as this no doubt was, the farmers of Kingsley and Norley were less than impressed, and their views were made clear to the Chapter via the local Whig MP, George Wilbraham:

> Many remarks not very propitious to the church establishment are made by the farmers and others, tending to show their surprise that, while such large sums are annually taken from them in the shape of great tithes paid to the college and of small tithes paid to the non-resident vicar, a small stipend for the express purpose of upholding the establishment and of supporting the interests of Christianity [...] should now be apparently grudged.[69]

The Dean and Chapter offered £200 towards a permanent stipend on the condition that funds for the church building were raised locally. This was not enough, and in the end the bishop of Chester, John Bird Sumner, who was particularly keen on improving church provision for the poor of his diocese and in assisting his clergy in their work, decided to make the new church a chapel of ease dependent on Frodsham and served by a curate.[70] He asked for the £200 given by Christ Church to be diverted to building the curate a house. After a year or two a local wealthy widow, Mrs Woodhouse, came to the rescue. She wrote to the Chapter informing them that over 300 people lived more than two miles from Frodsham church, that she had purchased a building in Norley that could be converted and that she had invested £1,160 in fitting it up. Mrs Woodhouse also intended to endow the church with £1,000 and an additional fund for repairs.[71] Norley was the first of Frodsham's townships to be made a parish in its own right, and was provided with a church in 1832–4. This was replaced in 1879 by a Gothic building by the established Gothic Revival architect John Loughborough Pearson.[72] Kingsley followed in 1851, after four years of fundraising and negotiation over the new church (designed by George Gilbert Scott) and parsonage house.[73] The ancient chapel at Alvanley was rebuilt largely at the vicar's expense or through his efforts, and the village became a parish in 1861; Helsby followed suit in 1875.[74]

Many of the huge parishes of the north – in Cheshire, Lancashire and Yorkshire – were divided into smaller units at this time. The sum of £150 was given towards the endowment of a chapelry at Copp in Kirkham (Lancashire), and a new lease was to include a clause that 'competent provision [must be made] for the spiritual wants of that extensive parish'.[75] Another chunk of Kirkham was hived off just the following year, when a chapel was built for Weeton and Westby with Plumpton, and a £100 annuity promised for its endowment.[76] But it was not just in the large parishes with their multiple townships that new chapels were erected: Ticehurst hamlet in Hawkhurst was given a new district church in 1840, to which Christ Church contributed £50.[77]

The growth and spread of towns and cities also meant that new parishes needed to be created, and little village churches that had once been the centre of small communities suddenly found themselves swamped by large industrial towns. The first Church Building Act was passed in 1818 in the wake of alarming statistics: according to the returns, there was an excess of population over church spaces in England and Wales of 2,528,505.[78] In Oxford, St Thomas's parish church could no longer cope with the hugely increased population of the parish, and St Frideswide's church was built on Osney Island to cater for the developing suburb, and in 1859 a temporary iron church was erected at the St Clement's end of Cowley.[79] According to the vicar, writing in 1862, the population of the township of Whitwood in Featherstone parish (Yorkshire) had trebled in just eleven years and a new church was needed urgently to serve the inhabitants, who were mainly potters, glassblowers, brickmakers and colliers.[80] A few years later, in 1874, Purston township was separated off from Featherstone – with the railway line as the boundary between the two – and a new church provided along with tithes and stipends for the new incumbent.[81] The vicar of Featherstone, Revd Hinde, arranged for the sale of some land to raise funds to build a parsonage in Purston.[82]

Correspondence to and from Leeds (Yorkshire) changes rapidly from a discussion of the produce grown in each township in the parish in the first third of the nineteenth century to a despairing response to a questionnaire, dated 7 September 1842, by the vicar, Walter Farquhar Hook, about the state of those same hamlets. Hook was experienced in managing an urban parish, having been vicar of Holy Trinity in Coventry before going to Leeds, and he had developed a strong social concern as well as a desire for spiritual revival. When he arrived in Leeds, he found that Methodism was preeminent; where there were twenty-two Wesleyan Methodist chapels in the townships of the city, there were only thirteen Anglican chapels of ease, served by just eighteen clergy, many of whom were absentee. Hook had an uphill battle to win over his largely nonconformist parish, but he gradually succeeded and re-established Anglicanism, by building a new parish church, completed in 1841, and conducting formal, sacramental worship. The congregation increased ten-fold in just four years.[83]

But there were problems beyond the main parish church. For example, in Hunslet, a township to the south which by the middle of the nineteenth century was busy with flax mills, chemical and glass works and potteries, there were now 12,000 souls without a church, and another 4,000 in Wortley to the west, a 'village' by then dominated by railway tracks and gas works. Hook's letter was passed to the Treasurer at Christ Church by Canon Pusey, who gave his opinion that Christ Church could not, in all conscience, take its share of the tithes: 'I for one', he said,

> wish to have nothing to do with Leeds tithes. The holders of the tithes are responsible for the spiritual welfare of the people [...] The state of

> our great towns, their often worse-than-Heathenism, the very brutalizing of our people, whom no one cared to humanize, was not known to them as it is to us. But now that we know it, and what a pestilence it is breeding in our country and drawing down the wrath of Almighty God, I certainly (and I know you share my feelings) had rather have no share of the responsibility. Our portion of the Leeds tithes is little to give up.

While he was morally outraged at the state of the poor inhabitants of the city, Pusey was torn between the maintenance of the Christ Church endowment and the need to help. He felt that those who had 'erected the recent large population for their own selfish ends ought to have the building and endowing of the new [churches]'.[84]

In 1844 Hook wrote a letter to his parishioners explaining that Leeds was now so large he was finding it impossible to do his work. The population was already over 150,000, and there were twenty churches or chapels of ease in addition to the parish church. He described the history of the huge parish (some 21,000 acres) and how, as the villages grew, each wished for a church of its own. While curates were appointed, the vicar still had to perform the sacraments and retained the cure of souls of the whole parish. His scheme, prepared with the approval of the bishop, laid down the conversion of all the chapels of ease into parish churches in their own right and for the curates to become vicars. The division of the parish was enacted in Parliament.[85] Almost immediately letters flew backwards and forwards between the new incumbents and Christ Church as assistance was sought for the building of new churches, parsonages and schools. By 1847, £100,000 had been spent with six new churches consecrated and thirty-seven schoolrooms erected, and by the time Hook left Leeds for the deanery of Chichester, he had doubled the number of Anglican churches and increased the provision of parsonages from six to twenty-nine and of church schools from three to thirty.[86] But the population boom did not stop: in New Wortley, by 1874, the number of residents had risen from 7,000 to 14,000 in only nine years, and the district created in 1844 had been split into two. A new church was under construction in Purston in 1875, and a new building was required to replace the temporary iron church in St Hilda's to serve the population of colliers and furnace men.[87] It was all a very long way from Little Compton and the Revd Marah's concerns over laundry drying on the hedges.

The provision of schools often went hand in hand with chapels and church restoration. Keeping the education of the nation's children firmly in the hands of the Anglican Church was seen as important, and schools were set up for both boys and girls, and new pews were set up in churches especially for children.[88]

Christ Church had, historically, always had an interest in the provision of schools. In 1553 Anthony Cave established a free grammar school in Lathbury in a chapel in the churchyard, leased for ninety-four years from the Dean and Chapter. One of the stipulations in Cave's will was for his sons, with the assistance of Chapter, to select two boys to become students at the University and then clergymen. The boys were to receive a stipend of £6 a year each, paid, until they were twenty-four, to the Treasurer and then to the scholars themselves until such time as they received a living worth £10.[89] Similarly, in the eighteenth century Christ Church was granted land in the Isle of Wight to fund the foundation of a grammar school in Portsmouth.[90] Scholars from Westminster School were elected to places at Christ Church and Trinity College, Cambridge, from 1566, and boys from grammar schools in Shropshire and Staffordshire arrived from 1741.[91]

In the nineteenth century education for the poor began to be seen as something essential. As early as 1811 the Treasurer was required by the Dean and Chapter to pay £100 as the contribution of the Dean and Chapter in support of a recently formed institution, the National Society for Promoting the Education of the Poor in the Principles of the Established Church throughout England and Wales.[92] On one day in 1850 (19 December) £200 was given to augment the chapel of Boston in Bramham, £20 was donated towards the purchase of a building for a school in Turkdean, £30 towards new schools in Harrow (Middlesex) and, because cleanliness was next to godliness, £200 was contributed to the Committee for Establishing Baths and Wash-Houses.[93]

* * * * *

Most House men were exemplary and diligent incumbents, and many went on to high office in the church, including the twenty-three who have held archbishoprics in England and Wales.[94] The niggles between them and the Chapter were much as would be expected. However, once in a while there was a real difficulty.

In Marcham in 1649 sixteen parishioners wrote to the Dean and Chapter to explain that they were dissatisfied with their minister, Mr Read, and requesting that they be sent a new man.[95] It was not his doctrine that was the problem, but his voice was just too quiet and they were unable to hear him. The canons replied, suggesting that the parish give the man three or four months to settle in and then, if things were still unsatisfactory, they would try to persuade Read to give up the living.[96] Either he improved with practice or the parish learned to manage or the Chapter just ignored the issue, but Read remained at Marcham until 1669. But this was as nothing compared with the problems that the parish suffered just thirty years later.

David Jones, a Welshman from Flintshire, who had matriculated from Christ Church in 1681, was appointed vicar of Marcham in 1699. Quite why the Dean and Chapter should have taken such a risk – unless it was just to rid Christ Church of the man – is difficult to guess. In July 1688, as a Student working his way towards his MA, Jones had to apologise for some misbehaviour towards the sub-dean, and a year later seems to have been rusticated, for his name no longer appears on the books.[97] He evidently made a name for himself as an outspoken preacher, and certainly did not mince his words with his congregation in his first parish of St Mary Woolnoth, in London.[98] Perhaps unwisely, if bravely, for the minister of a church in Lombard Street, he made a point of attacking usury and wealth. He was dismissed, and returned to Christ Church long enough to receive his MA in 1693, when he was presented to the living of Great Budworth (Cheshire).[99] Only three years later he was back in Oxford, attracting crowds with the 'impetuousness of his voice, the fantasticalness of his actions, and the ridiculous meanness of his images and expressions'. After Jones berated the University for allowing one of its employees to mow the grass in the parks on the Sabbath, the Vice-Chancellor had Jones thrown into the prison at Oxford Castle for six months.

Jones appealed on a writ of habeas corpus, and won. In 1700 he was free to take up his new post in Marcham.[100] The conclusion of Jones's year of grace was marked in the Chapter Book with unusual relish: on 31 October 1700 the Clerk recorded that the 'year of grace granted to Mr David Jones wilbe expired on Saturday next And it was therefore ordered that then his name be struck out of the Butlers Book'.[101] Immediately after appointment, Jones asked for three trees from the college woods at Chandlings to build himself a new study in the vicarage.[102] This was duly granted, but within a year the parish was drawing up a list of complaints, ranging from his unsoundness in religion and his refusal to carry out many of his most basic duties to his unreliability with female servants. The presentments were taken to the diocesan courts in Salisbury, and Christ Church sent a syndic at least once to appear for the Dean and Chapter.[103]

But it almost seems as though Christ Church turned its back on the poor parishioners of Marcham, as nothing appears to have been done to ease their problems. In fact, the Chapter protested that the parishioners were trying to extend Jones's responsibilities by insisting that he took services, or paid a curate to do so, in the nearby chapel of Garford. This, along with another hamlet, Frilford, was indeed part of the college's estate which paid tithes both to the rectorial tenant and the vicar of Marcham, but, argued the Dean and Chapter, there had never been any charge on them to repair or service the chapel.[104] For much of Jones's incumbency the churchwardens paid for a curate, and the parish was administered by the diocese. Marcham coped valiantly with Jones, as complaints and legal disputes continued to build, until his death in 1724. Many of his flock had given up, and just upped sticks and walked to neighbouring Besselsleigh, four miles away, for their baptisms, marriages and burials.[105]

Non-resident priests were a recurring problem. In 1665 the parishioners of North Otterington (Yorkshire) petitioned the dean, John Fell, concerning their curate.[106] They considered that the residency of a curate was desirable, and until that time there had been no difficulties at all. The present incumbent, however, had decided to withdraw his presence, leaving the people on weekdays like 'sheep haueing no sheepheard'. In emergencies, children could not be baptised or the dead buried, and there was no one to go to for 'spiritual imergences and parochial distempers'. It was reasonably well paid and there was a decent house; tithes were paid on time and the congregation obedient to the Church of England. It was important, they insisted, that services be conducted in the chapel of ease in the village as infirm, elderly and young parishioners were unable to walk as far as the church in Northallerton, nearly three miles away. The final request was that the Dean and Chapter should not send 'yonglings to teach us'. The guilty party appears to have been a man called Thomas Smelt, a Cambridge graduate who had been headmaster of Northallerton School during the Commonwealth years but was then appointed to the vicarage of North Otterington in 1661. However, Smelt was hardly a 'yongling'; he had matriculated from Trinity College in 1629. It seems a distinct possibility that Smelt senior had sent his son or his nephew, both Thomas, to officiate as curate in his stead. If this was the case, then the good men and women of North Otterington would have been more than justified in their complaint; neither Thomas Smelt junior was even ordained until 1668. The Dean and Chapter evidently did not heed the request of the parish, as Smelt senior remained vicar until his death in 1686.[107]

Around the same time that Marcham was coping with David Jones, Bledington (Gloucestershire) was also suffering from absentee priests. In 1708 Christ Church had appointed John Hawkins to be curate in the parish.[108] But Hawkins lived in London and so had delegated his duties to a man of his own choosing, Benjamin Hart. Hart was accused by the churchwardens of neglecting his duties, both clerical and pastoral, and so, having failed to answer the presentment and for his contumacy, he was suspended by the chancellor of the diocese, Sir Henry Penrice. The living was sequestered. Hawkins, perhaps wisely, resigned. Appointment of a new curate was left in the hands of the churchwardens, who promptly chose a man called Arundel. The Dean and Chapter, in whose opinion the living was theirs to fill, appointed Henry Proctor, a local man and a Christ Church graduate. Arundel and Proctor found themselves in a tug of war between the Dean and Chapter and Penrice.[109] All sorts of questions were raised. Could the profits be sequestered from Hart, as they really belonged to Hawkins? Could the sequestration be lifted so that Proctor could receive his dues? And how could the Chapter remove Arundel?[110] The archive does not record how long it took to resolve the dispute, but it would appear that confusion reigned for some time, with another vicar, Henry Lamb, who is not mentioned in the Christ Church records at all, also being accused of being equally neglectful of his duties. However, it does appear that Christ Church's man, Proctor, remained curate throughout the muddle in Bledington until 1730.[111]

The recording of these cases is unusual and probably reflects just how rare serious complaints about Christ Church's incumbents were. Most estates correspondence from the eighteenth century deals with the financial management of estates, particularly surrounding the setting of the periodic entry fines. The case of David Jones and Marcham is indicative of the general neglect of patronal duties by the Dean and Chapter – in parallel with the eighteenth-century neglect of the diocesan function of the cathedral – and, apart from the announcements of appointments to curacies and vicarages in the Chapter books, barely any mention is made of incumbencies until the nineteenth century, when estates correspondence is completely refocused on the problems of Christ Church's clergymen and their churches.[112]

Christ Church incumbents could also be caught up in the wider affairs of the church. The college's few estates in Wales – Guilsfield, Meifod, Buttington and Welshpool – were hit, like many others, by the Welsh tithe war.[113] The predominantly nonconformist, chapel-going communities were increasingly angry that they were obliged to pay a tithe to the Anglican Church.[114] Denbighshire particularly was affected by rioting, but the disaffection spread across the whole of the country, resulting in the Anti-Tithe League. A report on Christ Church's tithes from Wales showed that they were worth about £2,000 in 1886.[115] Dinner was provided once a year for all those who paid the tithe rent charge, which was cheaper than employing a door-to-door collector. However, said Christ Church's agents, Castle, Field & Castle, it seemed unlikely that, in the light of increased dissatisfaction, dinner would be sufficient in future. Two-thirds of those who paid were Dissenters and objected to the tithe charge on principle.

Many of the farmers in Wales assumed that every Student at Christ

Livings and curacies belonging to Christ Church in 1778

Bedfordshire: Flitton, Cople

Berkshire: Easthampstead, Marcham, Ardington, East Garston

Buckinghamshire: Slapton, Lathbury, Dorton and Ashendon, Willen, Hillesden

Cheshire: Frodsham, Runcorn, Great Budworth, Daresbury

Cornwall: St Tudy

Devon: Great Torrington

Dorset: Tolpuddle

Essex: Sheering

Gloucestershire: Batsford, Iron Acton, Thornbury, Wotton-under-Edge, Twyning, Turkdean, Lower Swell, Bledington, Temple Guiting, Little Compton, Aldsworth, Down Ampney, North Nibley

Herefordshire: Staunton-on-Wye

Hertfordshire: Tring and Long Marston

Kent: Hawkhurst

Lancashire: Kirkham, Great Bowden

Leicestershire: Market Harborough with St Mary in Arden

Norfolk: Wood Norton and Swanton Novers

Northamptonshire: Staverton, Badby and Newnham, Daventry, Flore, Ravensthorpe, Easton Maudit, Harringworth

Oxfordshire: Wendlebury, Westwell, Pyrton, Chalgrove, Spelsbury, Black Bourton, Brize Norton, South Stoke, Stratton Audley, Cassington, St Mary Magdalen (Oxford), St Thomas (Oxford), Binsey, Cowley, Benson, Caversham, Drayton

Shropshire: Wentnor

Somerset: Odcombe, Midsomer Norton, Batheaston

Wiltshire: Semley, Market Lavington, Chippenham, Charlton, Maiden Bradley

Worcestershire: North and South Littleton, Offenham, Badsey and Wickhamford, Hampton

Yorkshire: Featherstone, Wath, North Otterington, Bramham, Skipton, Preston, Kildwick, Broughton, Carleton, Adwick

CCA D&C i.b.6, 297-302; xiv.b.2, 4–9

Church was an aristocrat and Anglican. The general feeling that no poor man, or nonconformist, could study there only increased the reluctance to pay tithe rent charge. The rent charge collector in Wales, George Peterson, suggested that the money be used for educational purposes. A letter was sent to Peterson stating that many members of the Governing Body were laymen, and that there were several non-Anglicans, including one Hindu (probably Manmohan Ghose, who won an open scholarship and came up in 1887), receiving assistance from the college to study. It seems unlikely that such reassurances would have made a huge difference to the animosity felt in Wales.

Like all farmers at this time, the Welshmen had been affected by the depression, and they pleaded for some alleviation. Things turned ugly; the local archdeacon tried to help by agreeing a reduction in the tithe rent charge, but he had not consulted the Governing Body, and Dean Liddell was evidently angry, both with Archdeacon Thomas and with the principal tenants for not taking the burden of tithes on themselves, rather than distributing it among their sub-tenants. Selling the land seemed to be a non-starter too, as the local auctioneers were afraid of reprisals if they were seen to be working with the 'enemy'. The usual process for recovery of tithes from defaulters involved a visit, at which the collectors would, if the tithe was still not forthcoming, issue a ten-day notice of intention to distrain. A second visit would set aside stock or produce to the value of the tithes, which was usually left on the farm sometimes on trust and sometimes in the care of a bailiff. The third visit was for the auction of the stock or goods, which could be farcical with the produce hidden or stock moved about the farm to prevent the bailiff from catching the selected animals.[116]

When auctions for distraint were necessary, they were evidently highly charged events and occasions for militant speeches. At one auction in August 1888 when six farms came up for sale, serious disturbance was only narrowly avoided: 'The noise and yelling were extraordinary and it was only through the strenuous exertions of some magistrates and other leaders of the anti-tithe movement that we were able to obtain hearings.'

Christ Church hinted that it was willing to help in cases of real distress but still insisted on payment. The incumbent at Meifod, Archdeacon Thomas, suggested a 10 per cent rebate. This did not go down well in the parish, as other landlords were offering 15 per cent, or at Christ Church, where the Governing Body required full payment from any farmer who would make any sort of profit. Thomas gave the rebate regardless in order to get at least some payment, but neither side was impressed by this. In April 1887 Christ Church pushed for distraints, which met with considerable local intimidation; auctioneers gave up the struggle, and the local chief constable seemed to be on the side of the non-payers, if only to avoid riots. Christ Church's agent, David Owen, wisely stayed away from the auctions. Throughout 1888 Christ Church stuck to its guns, insisting on its lawful dues and even expressing a desire that military assistance be given. The Montgomeryshire authorities tried to find compromises and, slowly but surely, charges were paid, often with assistance from landlords. Most of the money was in by the end of 1889, which to a certain extent vindicated the Governing Body's rigorous insistence on payment in full, especially with the support of the Ecclesiastical Commissioners, who were even more reliant on tithe income. However, it was relatively easy for the tithe-owners in faraway Oxford to be demanding, far less so for the tithe recipients in the locality, who would rather make a rebate and receive something than be victim to at least loss of income and at worst physical danger.[117] In 1891 the responsibility for tithe rent charge was laid squarely at the feet of the landholder, rather than of his tenants, and much of the impetus for rioting was removed.[118] However, the unrest led eventually to the Welsh Church Bill, which sought to disestablish the Anglican Church in Wales. Under Clause 21, Christ Church would have had to hand over its Welsh rent charges to the Ecclesiastical Commission. As so often before, the Governing Body pleaded the uniqueness of Christ Church and obtained agreement that it would be excluded from Clause 21. In the event, the Act fell flat on the defeat of the Liberals at the 1895 general election.

The Welsh Church Act of 1914 came into force in 1920 and effectively severed any connection between the Welsh 'Anglican' churches and the English state. Although there was no legal requirement to do so, Christ Church continued to assist the churches in Montgomeryshire which were given in 1546.

After 1867, with the changes in the college's constitution, the right to present to college livings was retained by the Governing Body. Only if they failed to fill a vacant benefice within three months would the right of presentation pass to the Dean and Canons. Now the situation is much the same, although vacancies are managed by a committee consisting of the Dean and Canons with two elected members of the Governing Body.[119] The Three-Fifths South Trust still assists Christ Church incumbents with all manner of things and still makes donations towards the repair and maintenance of churches and parsonage houses. The increase in the number of parish churches in the nineteenth century has now been reversed, and parishes are being amalgamated into group ministries, with patronage often in the hands of several bodies or individuals. In some cases the right to present is taken on by one patron for the whole group, but in others the responsibility is shared. In all, Christ Church still has links with around eighty incumbencies spread as widely as they were in 1546.

4

Managing the agricultural estate II: expansion and improvement

Restoration and recovery

After the Restoration, Christ Church and many of the other colleges set about re-establishing their title to their land. The confusion caused by the Civil War, not just from sequestrations but also simply from the damage of battles and troop movements, meant that uncertainty about land ownership was common. Finances were often in a complete mess: Balliol, for example, was in dire straits, made worse when the Great Fire of 1666 erased one fifth of rental income, and both Jesus and University colleges were in financial distress. Matters were not helped by the loss of records; in 1647 the Parliamentary Visitors had required all the colleges to hand over any documents relating to their affairs. Royalist heads of houses and fellows smuggled out not just money and valuables but also account books and registers, some of which were never returned.[1] With the Restoration, across Oxford college leases and grants that had been made since the start of the Civil War were legally confirmed, but concerns about money prompted new efforts towards better financial management.[2] Christ Church appealed to its alumni and raised £6,400 in a few years after the Restoration to re-establish itself. Much was put towards the completion of the Great Quadrangle.[3]

At Christ Church the Chapter Clerk, John Willis, was charged with producing an exhaustive list of all the estates, recording title, rental income and the history of tenancies as far back as he could. He was assisted by Anthony Wood of Merton College, the antiquarian and historian of all things Oxford. Wood evidently thought himself indispensable to the project and implied in his account that Willis had chosen the time to do his research purely to take advantage of Wood's presence:

> John Willis, yonger brother of Dr Thomas Willis the famous physitian, was then chapter-clerk of Ch Church; and he designing to make a repertorie of records belonging to the said church made choice of that time to do it [i.e., from July 1667], to the end that he might have the assistance of A.W.; which he freely imparted, and demonstrated to him several evidences what encroachments that church had suffered in many places in Oxfordshire on their lands and tenements, which formerly belonged to St. Frideswyde and Osney.[4]

The pair put their heads together through July, August and part of September, working at a phenomenal speed to plough through every deed, many of which dated back to the high middle ages – the lease registers, which recorded every deed sealed by the Dean and Chapter from 1546, manorial court records and the medieval cartularies of Oseney, Eynsham and St Frideswide's – to produce the definitive catalogue. The result was the Book of Evidences – Christ Church's Domesday Book – which still serves as one of the most crucial documents in the archive.[5] A massive tome, the Book, written in Willis's clear hand, arranges all the foundation properties by county and, after a statement of the college title, leases of each property are particularised from 1547 to *c.*1682, and references are given to the copies in the estates ledgers.[6] The position of urban properties is described by reference to the properties and streets on each side. Many medieval title deeds are described in detail, and accounts are occasionally given of litigation involving the college, making reference to papers still to be found in the estates records. Court rolls are noted and frequently abstracted.[7]

Even this great work, however, did not define the college's land 'on the ground' or really resolve any of the issues concerning boundaries. The theory was all very well, but tenants needed to know just what they were entitled to farm, and the Chapter needed to know on what they were entitled

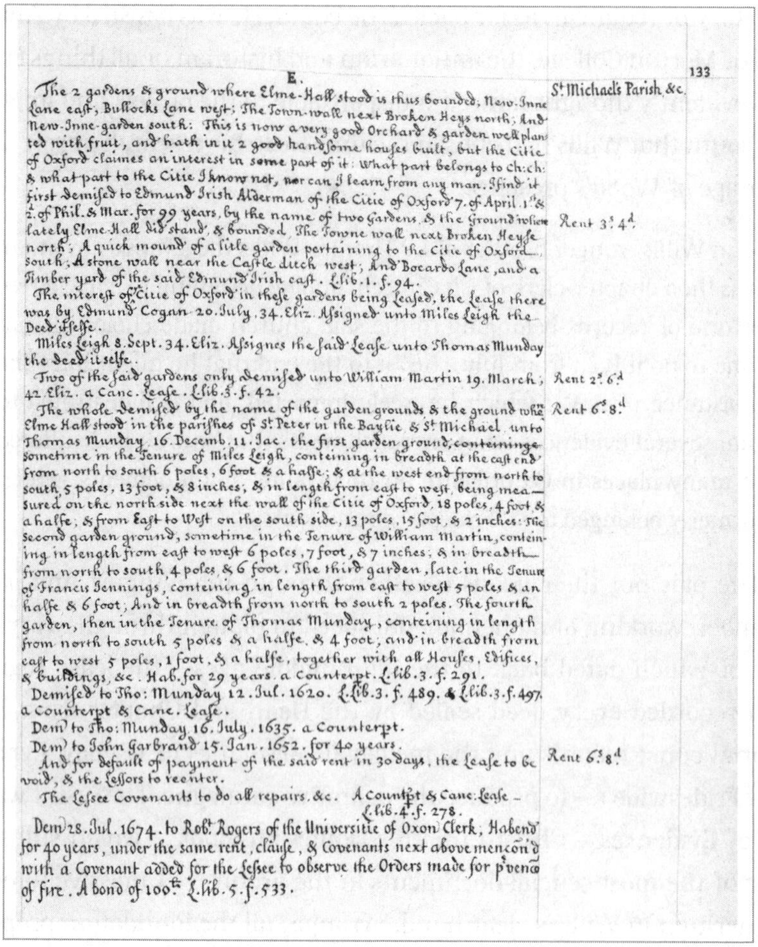

E. 133

St Michael's Parish, &c.

The 2 gardens & ground where Elme-Hall stood is thus bounded; New-Inne Lane east; Bullocks Lane west; The Town-wall next Broken Heys north; And New-Inne-garden south: This is now a very good Orchard & garden well planted with fruit, and hath in it 2 good handsome houses built, but the Citie of Oxford claimes an interest in some part of it: What part belongs to Ch:Ch: & what part to the Citie I know not, nor can I learn from any man. I find it first demised to Edmund Irish Alderman of the Citie of Oxford 7. of April. 1st & 2d. of Phil. & Mar. for 99 years, by the name of two Gardens, & the Ground where lately Elme-Hall did stand, & bounded, The Towne wall next Broken Heyse north; A quick mound of a litle garden pertaining to the Citie of Oxford south; A stone wall near the Castle ditch west; And Bocardo Lane, and a Timber yard of the said Edmund Irish east. L.lib. 1. f. 94. — Rent 3s. 4d.

The interest of ye Citie of Oxford in these gardens being Leased, the Lease there was by Edmund Cogan 20. July. 34. Eliz. Assigned unto Miles Leigh the Deed itselfe.

Miles Leigh 8. Sept. 34. Eliz. Assignes the said Lease unto Thomas Munday the deed it selfe.

Two of the said gardens only demised unto William Martin 19. March; 42. Eliz. a Canc. Lease. L.lib. 3. f. 42. — Rent 2s. 6d.

The whole demised by the name of the garden grounds & the ground where Elme Hall stood in the parishes of St. Peter in the Baylie & St. Michael unto Thomas Munday 16. Decemb. 11. Iac. the first garden ground, conteininge sometime in the Tenure of Miles Leigh, conteining in breadth at the east end from north to south 6 poles, 6 foot & a halfe; & at the west end from north to south, 5 poles, 13 foot, & 8 inches; & in length from east to west, being measured on the north side next the wall of the Citie of Oxford, 18 poles, 4 foot, & a halfe; & from East to West on the south side, 13 poles, 15 foot, & 2 inches: The second garden ground, sometime in the Tenure of William Martin, conteining in length from east to west 6 poles, 7 foot, & 7 inches; & in breadth from north to south, 4 poles, & 6 foot. The third garden, late in the Tenure of Francis Jennings, conteining in length from east to west 5 poles & an halfe & 6 foot; And in breadth from north to south 2 poles. The fourth garden, then in the Tenure of Thomas Munday, conteining in length from north to south 5 poles & a halfe, & 4 foot; and in breadth from east to west 5 poles, 1 foot, & a halfe, together with all Houses, Edifices, & buildings, &c. Hab. for 29 years. a Counterpt. L.lib. 3. f. 291. — Rent 6s. 8d.

Demised to Tho: Munday 12. Jul. 1620. L.Lib. 3. f. 489. & L.lib. 3. f. 497. a Counterpt & Canc. Lease.

Dem' to Tho: Munday 16. July. 1635. a Counterpt.

Dem' to John Garbrand 15. Jan. 1652. for 40 years.

And for default of payment of the said rent in 30 days, the Lease to be void, & the Lessors to reenter. — Rent 6s. 8d.

The Lessee Covenants to do all repairs. &c. A Countpt & Canc: Lease — L.lib. 4. f. 278.

Dem 28. Jul. 1674. to Robt. Rogers of the Universitie of Oxon Clerk, Habend' for 40 years, under the same rent, clause, & Covenants next above mencon'd with a Covenant added for the Lessee to observe the Orders made for pvencon of fire. A bond of 100li. L.lib. 5. f. 533.

An example of an urban property from the Book of Evidences. St Michael's parish in Oxford is on the north side of the city, within the city wall. Elm Hall was at the junction of what are now George Street and New Inn Hall Street.

to charge rent, make valuations for fines and collect tithes. The idea of using a map to show ownership was only just beginning to take hold among landowners. On the evidence of surviving maps, only 25 per cent of those produced before 1545 were estate maps. During the seventeenth century, though, this figure rose to around 68 per cent.[8]

Christ Church was a bit slow to see the advantage of maps; Merton, Corpus Christi and All Souls colleges, for example, were commissioning

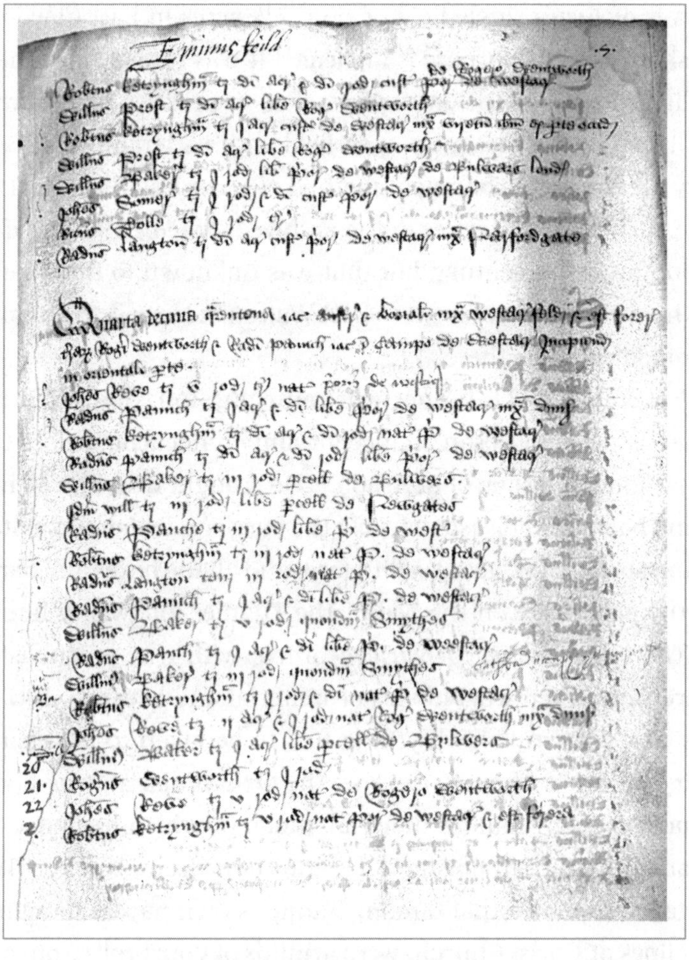

A page from the 1494 terrier of the manor of Howard and Stranges in East Walton. Before maps became commonplace, written accounts of the open fields, strip by strip, were the norm.

detailed estate maps in the late sixteenth century, and some private landowners earlier still.[9] The Dean and Chapter did commission a 'map' or plan in 1612, but it was produced to help Christ Church fight its corner in a dispute that concerned not an agricultural estate but land right on the doorstep near Oxford Castle.[10]

Apart from this one example, Christ Church does not seem to have produced an estate map until 1697. Even this, though drawn by a professional surveyor, is of just a single field of only 2½ acres in East Claydon (Buckinghamshire), and its purpose is unclear.[11] It was rare at this time, too, for Christ Church to use written surveys of its properties. There were a few terriers listing each strip in an open field with its tenant and its size, but generally there was no consistent method of recording the actual extent of an estate.[12] The earliest terrier in the archive is dated 1494, pre-dating the foundation by half a century, but that was unknown to the Chapter until Canon Thomas Tanner was sent to East Walton in Norfolk to attempt to sort out the muddled estate there.[13]

In November 1731 Tanner was returning to Oxford from Norwich, where he had been diocesan chancellor and archdeacon, before taking up his new position as bishop of St Asaph.[14] He brought with him all his manuscripts and books, but disaster struck: the barge on which the material was being transported sank near Wallingford, and all the boxes and barrels containing the papers lay on the bed of the Thames for twenty hours before rescue. The *Northampton Mercury* recorded, with true journalistic relish, that there were seven wagonloads of material and between 200 and 300 volumes of manuscripts. Everything had to be taken to pieces and hung out to dry on lines. Thomas Hearne, the Oxford diarist, was horrified by the damage to such valuable material, much of which had once belonged to William Sancroft, archbishop of Canterbury from 1674 to 1690, but Hearne failed to notice that, among Tanner's own papers hanging on the washing lines of Christ Church, were armfuls of court rolls from one of the manors of East Walton.[15]

Tanner visited Norfolk often, not just on clerical business but on behalf of the Dean and Chapter as well.[16] Christ Church's estate – the manor of Howard and Stranges – in East Walton was in a most confused state; quite apart from the conflicting claims of the three manors in the parish, none of the landowners or tenants seemed entirely sure what land belonged to whom.[17] A single family, the Barkhams and their descendants, leased two of the manors and owned the third freehold. Over time the medieval copyholds had been bought up and all the manorial functions of renewing had been abandoned. In 1497 the Howard and Stranges manor had consisted of 774 acres. When Tanner started digging, he realised that between two and three hundred acres of copyhold land had been 'lost'.

In 1716 the Barkham property passed to a creditor called Naish. Naish died while abroad in 1726, and Christ Church took its chance. Canon Tanner determined that the tangle would be straightened; in March 1726 he stormed the offices of the Swaffham attorney who acted as steward to Christ Church's tenant demanding 'in the name of the Chapter' that he be given the ill-fated court rolls, and then called a special manorial court, softening up the tenants beforehand with 'a little beer and thick ale'.[18] It was at this point that the previously unknown late fifteenth-century terrier was produced; Tanner was aware that it would have been difficult to apply its descriptions to the present situation but nevertheless had a translation made from Latin to English, and attempted to make sense of the intermixed estates and manors.[19] In 1731 Tanner returned to his canonry in Christ Church, with all the documents he felt that the Dean and Chapter needed to finally iron out the discrepancies. But the arguments rumbled on for decades, becoming even more confused when Christ Church's agent mistakenly added the land of Abbots Manor to Christ Church's property. The Dean and Chapter were advised to take the matter to Chancery but decided against yet more legal expense and entered into a compromise with Spelman, the Barkham heir, that he would pay a lump sum of £461 for arrears of rent and then be admitted to the copyholds. But no attempt was made to define the actual land for which the rent was due. Tanner had died in 1735; he must have been spinning in his grave. Needless to say, the failure to pin everything down securely was a disaster. By the middle of the nineteenth century Spelman's estate had been sold to the Hamond family, who had taken advantage of the chaos and gradually held the whole village in various forms of tenure. The copyhold land of Howard and Stranges was recorded as only 492 acres; over a century of discussion had resolved nothing. The Governing Body lost patience and decided not to renew the manorial lease. It was a decision made in frustration; for decades the lease had only brought in tiny sums. In 1897 Hamond asked to purchase the manor, but again Christ Church ignored professional advice to accept the offer and attempted again to reclaim what it had lost and to reserve from enfranchisement woodland, mineral and sporting rights.[20] It was a hopeless cause; had Christ Church attempted it some years earlier they might have stood a chance, but the Copyhold Act of 1894 required that copyholds be turned into conventional freehold or leasehold tenures (enfranchisement), and besides, the problem that had caused Tanner's gallop to East Walton in 1726 still stood: Hamond's copyholds and freehold were so intermixed that no one knew which was which. It was 1900 before the disputes over East Walton were finally ironed out when Christ Church received £1,038 for the enfranchisement.[21]

East Walton was not, unfortunately, the only property in a state of confusion. The major changes in agricultural practices across England during the eighteenth and nineteenth centuries particularly caused many such cases to be uncovered as landowners struggled to determine the extent of their holdings in order to reap the full benefits of new methods and of enclosure, by then administered by professional commissioners and completed by Acts of Parliament.

A volume of terriers covering many of the college's estates was produced in the late seventeenth century, perhaps as a complement to the Book of Evidences, but is minimal in its coverage and comes nowhere near to balancing the detailed documentation of estate history recorded in the Book of Evidences with an account of real land.[22] It would seem that the first efforts of the Dean and Chapter to clarify where their lands lay were not terribly successful. In many cases they were still unaware that there *were* problems to be unravelled.

However, by the early eighteenth century the Dean and Chapter, in common with the governing bodies of other colleges, were anxious to capitalise on the increases in agricultural productivity which they, as 'hands-off' landlords, had done little or nothing to promote. Higher profits meant larger entry fines and bigger windfalls, which, as we have seen, came to the Dean and Canons as bonuses. Increasingly, Christ Church employed professional surveyors to visit estates rather than relying on the intermittent visitations by the Dean or one of the canons. A Chapter order, given in September 1698, had decreed that no fine was to be set until a 'sufficient terrier

The church of St Laurence, which was the centre of the priory at Blackmore, in Essex. It was dissolved on 10 February 1525, when it had just a prior and three canons in residence. Just a year later it was given to Cardinal College.

The chapel at Bradwell Priory, in Buckinghamshire. The priory seems not to have recovered from the Black Death and was very small and poor from the middle of the fourteenth century through to its dissolution in 1524. Its poverty, however, ensured its strict observance of the Benedictine rule.

Queen Elizabeth I, concerned for the incomes of Oxford and Cambridge colleges during periods of inflation, introduced legislation which tied a portion of rental income to the local price of corn.

The archive room stipulated in the statutes for Cardinal College was never constructed, but the intention would have been to create a secure store similar to that in the Muniment Tower, seen here, at Wolsey's alma mater, Magdalen College.

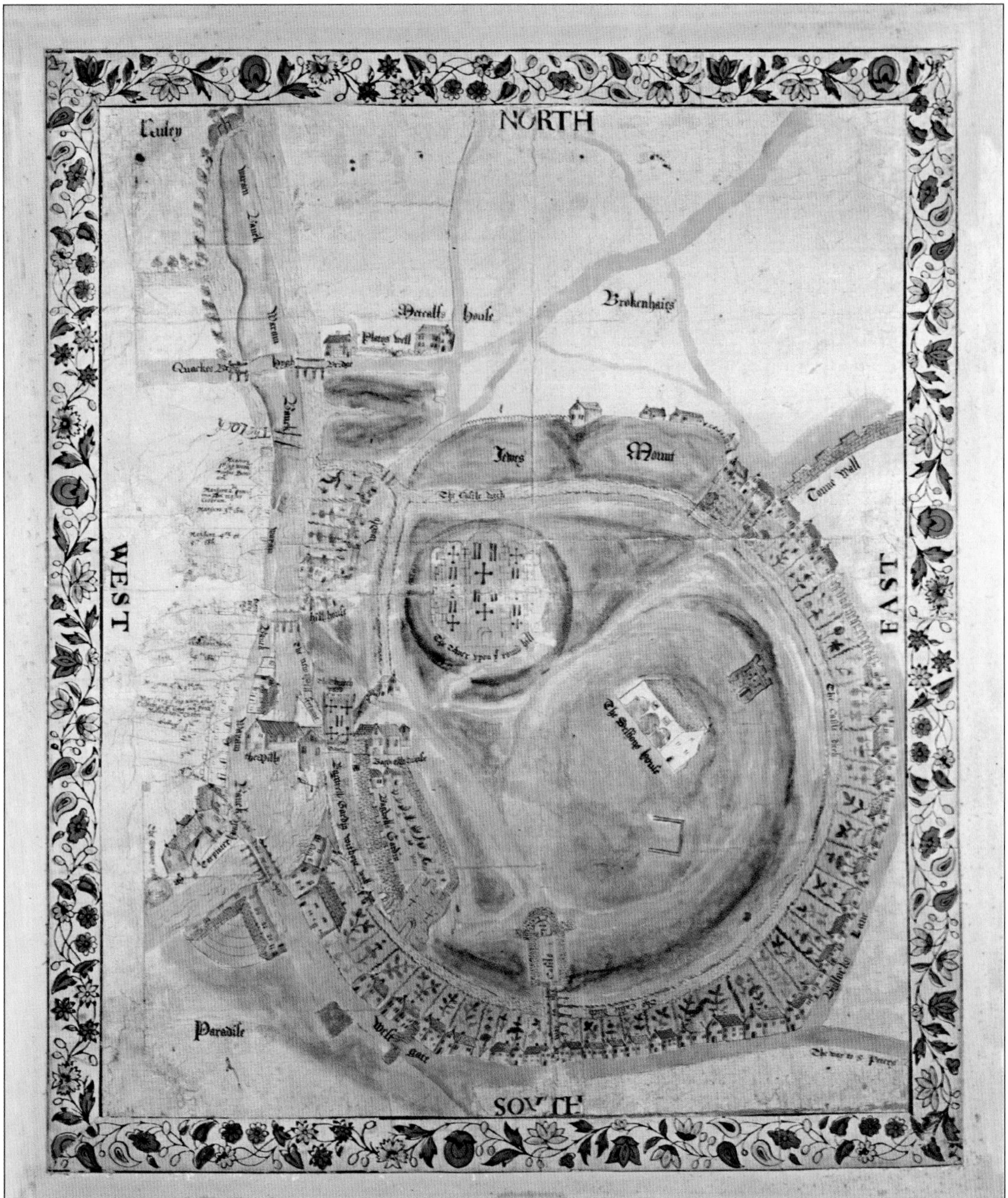

The earliest plan, or map, in the Christ Church archive is this illustration of Oxford Castle, drawn around 1617 to use as a visual aid in the Chancery case between the college and the City council over ownership of the houses below the castle walls.

Canon Thomas Tanner (1674–1735), who spent many years trying to sort out the complicated landholdings of Christ Church's Norfolk estates.

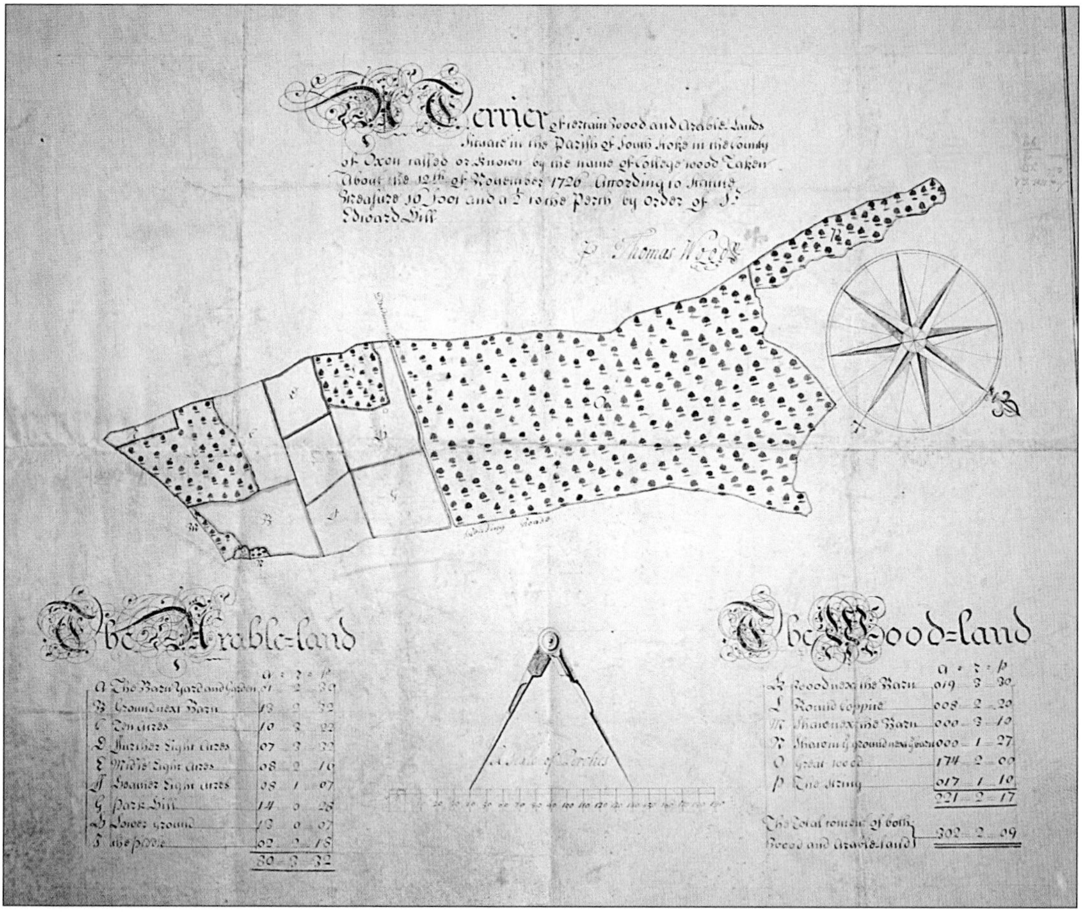

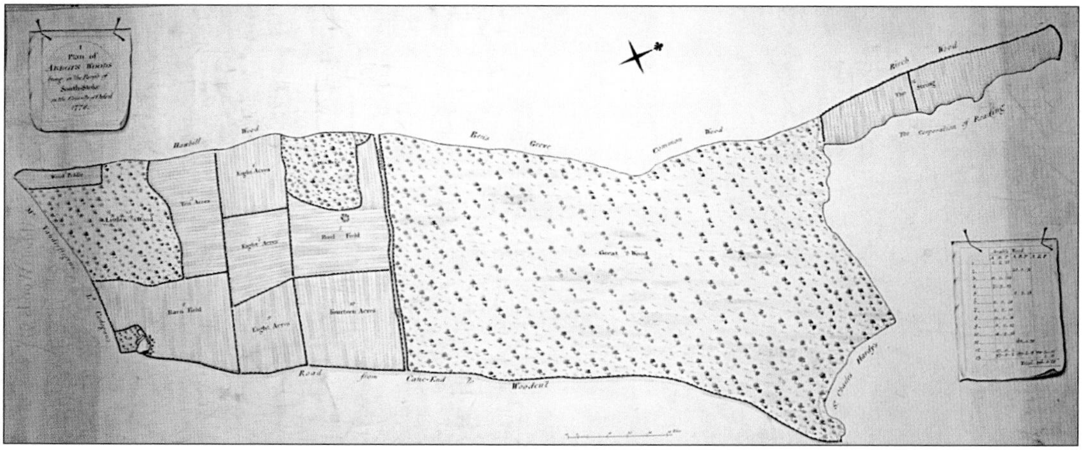

Two maps showing Abbots (or College) Wood in South Stoke in 1726 (at top) and 1778 (above). In the fifty years between the two surveys, only a very small portion was taken out of timber production for arable use. The woods were held by Christ Church until 1960.

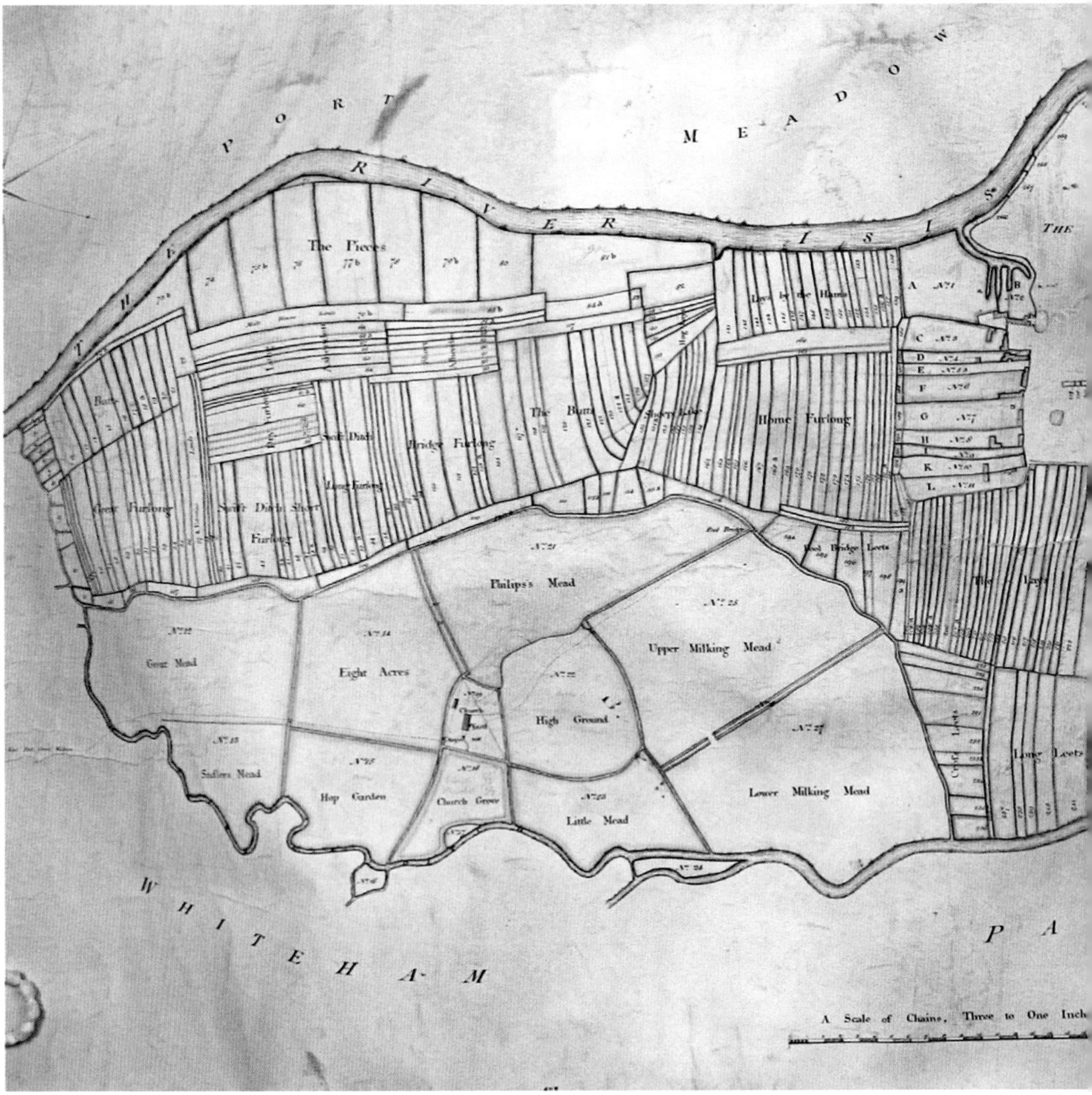

This map of Binsey, made by Richard Davis of Lewknor in 1792, shows clearly, by colour, the distribution of strips in the arable fields among the various copyholders. The low-lying, and frequently flooded, land is evident from the names of the meadows. Well-watered meadow could be profitable – hay was an expensive commodity – but Binsey was exceptionally prone to inundation, and better drainage was one of the drivers of the enclosure which took place in 1820.

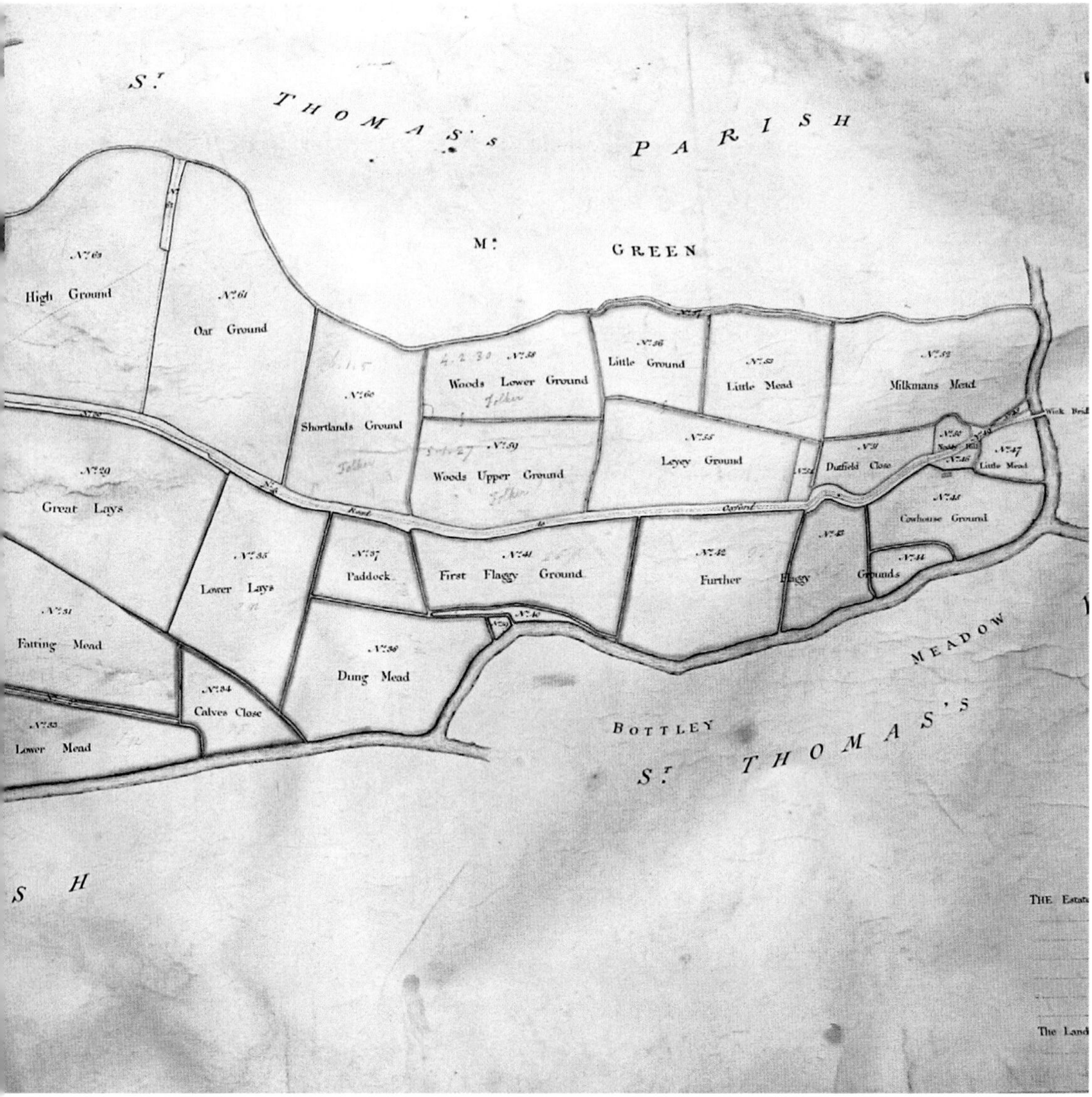

ST THOMAS's PARISH
Mr GREEN
High Ground
Oar Ground
Shortlands Ground
Woods Lower Ground
Woods Upper Ground
Little Ground
Little Mead
Milkmans Mead
Leyey Ground
Dutfield Close
Little Mead
Cowhouse Ground
Great Lays
Lower Lays
Paddock
First Flaggy Ground
Further Flaggy Grounds
Fatting Mead
Dung Mead
Calves Close
Lower Mead
Road to Oxford
BOTTLEY MEADOW
ST THOMAS's
S H
THE Estate
The Land

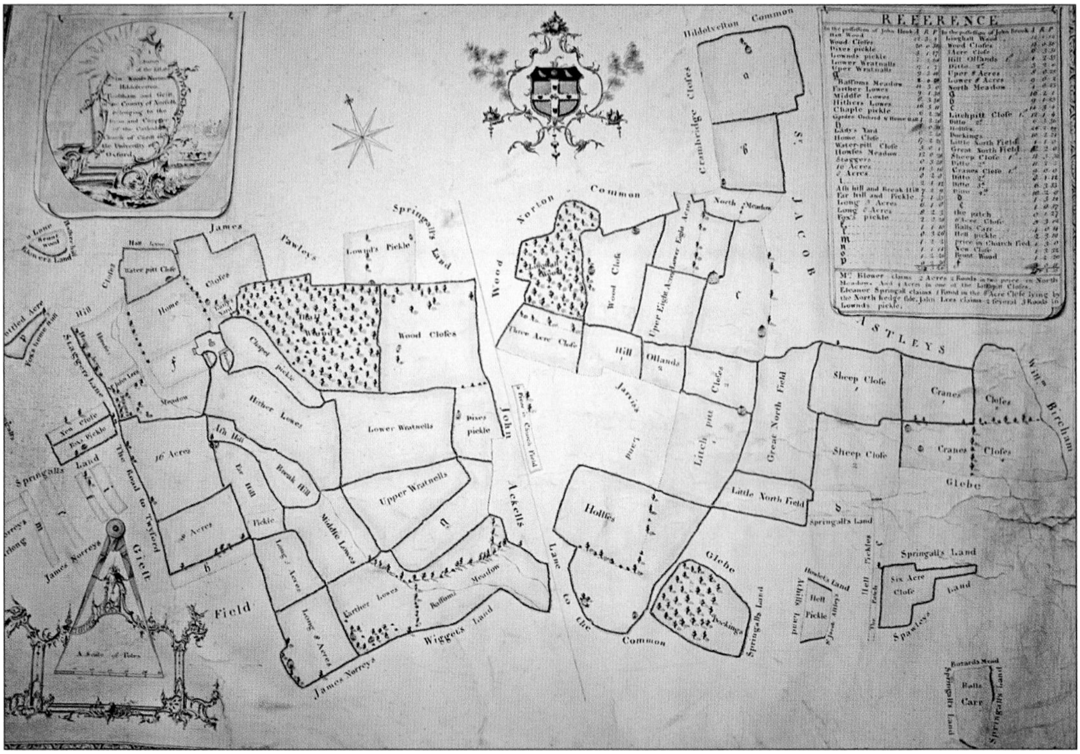

A map of Wood Norton, dated 1757. Ownership of land in the parish was confused, and the map was drawn at the suggestion of Canon Thomas Tanner and of James Jones, a surveyor, who had been appointed specifically to clarify the situation for the Dean and Chapter.

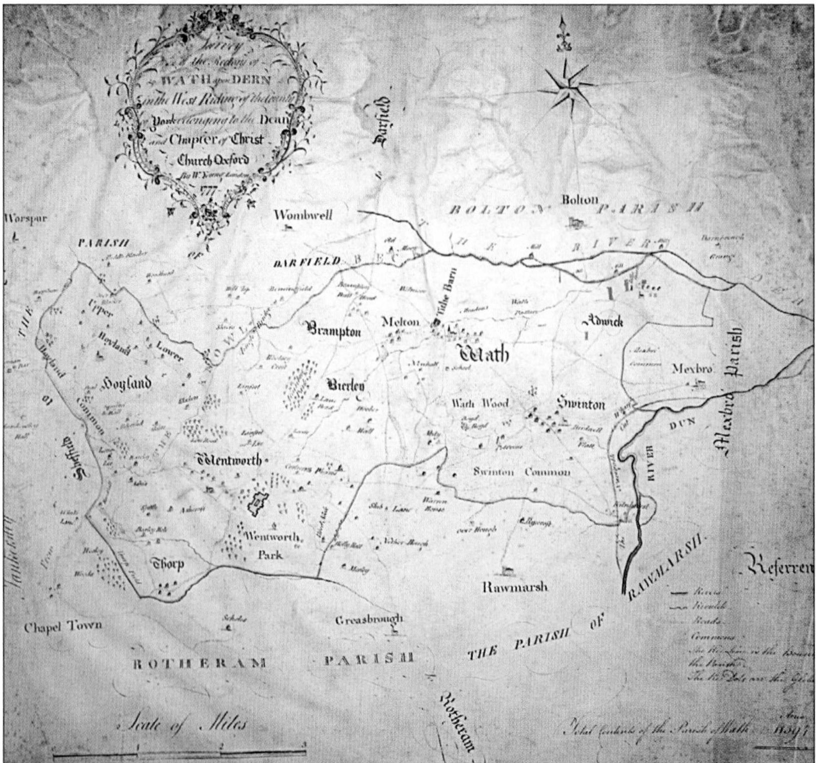

Wath upon Dearne in 1777, as surveyed by William Young to assist with the valuation of that estate. Wentworth Woodhouse, home of Christ Church's tenant, the Marquess of Rockingham, is clearly shown.

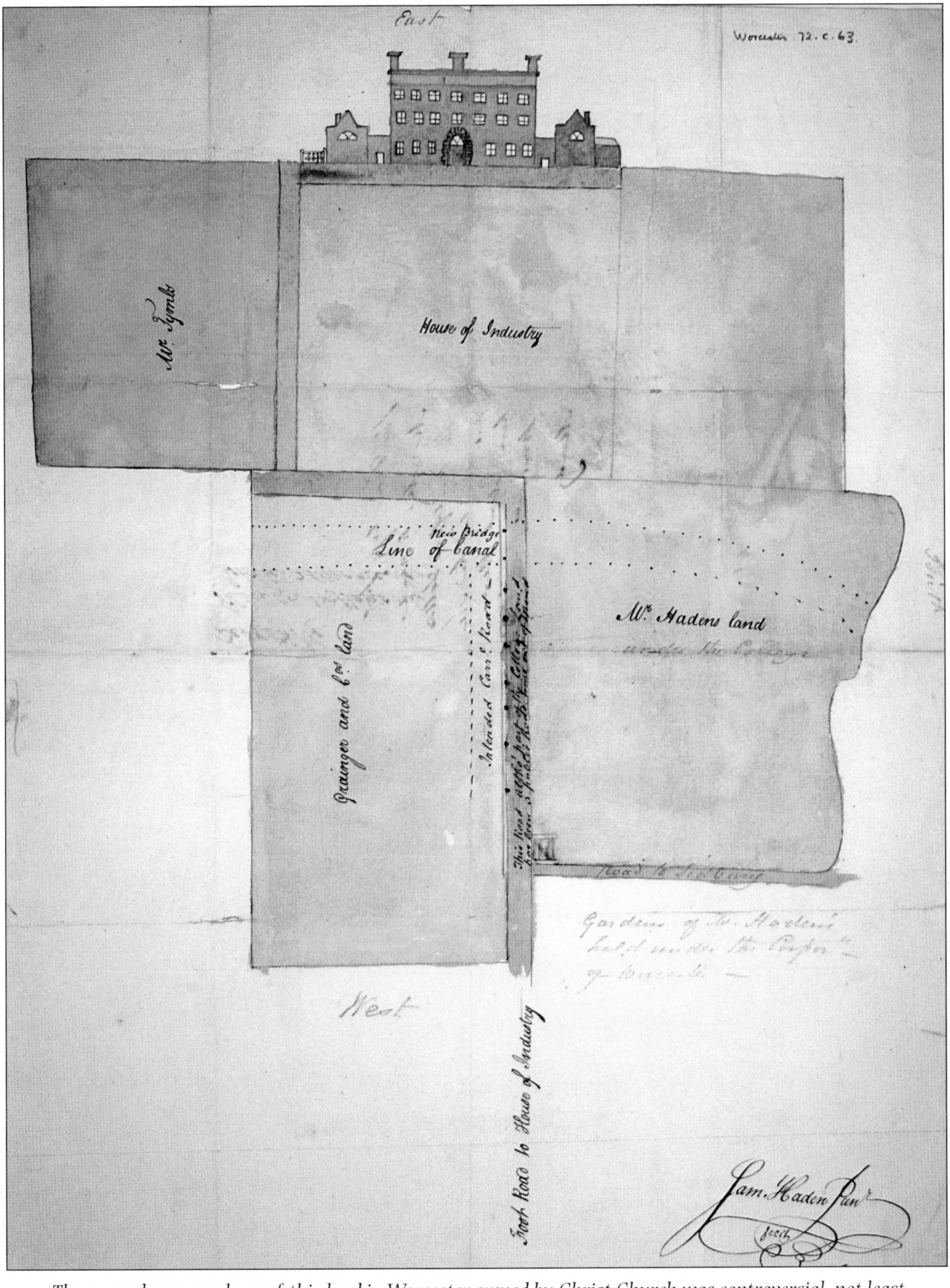

The compulsory purchase of this land in Worcester owned by Christ Church was controversial, not least because the intention to build a canal close by (its proposed course is faintly marked across the centre of this 1814 plan) meant that the value of the property was considerably higher than the college was offered.

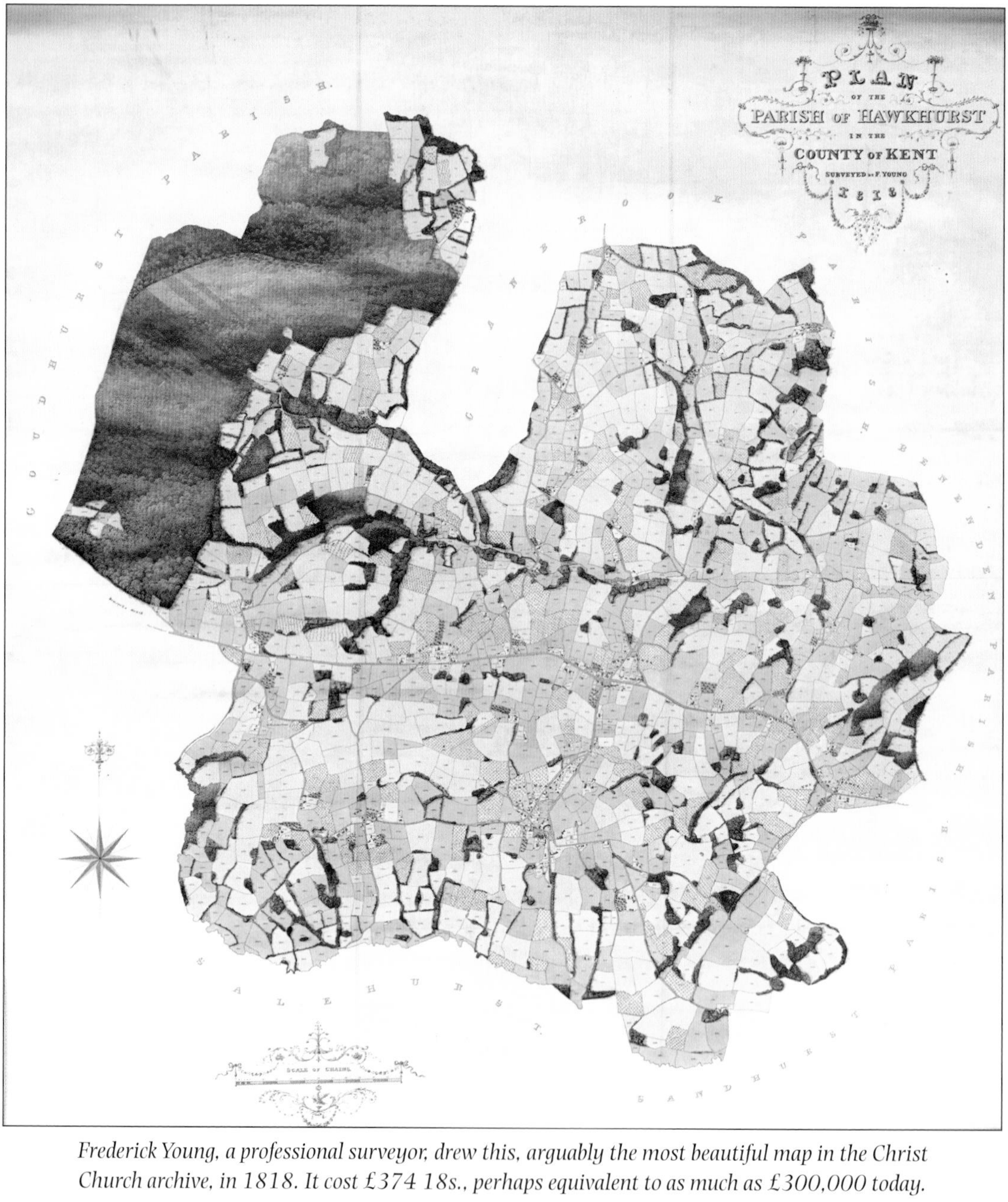

Frederick Young, a professional surveyor, drew this, arguably the most beautiful map in the Christ Church archive, in 1818. It cost £374 18s., perhaps equivalent to as much as £300,000 today.

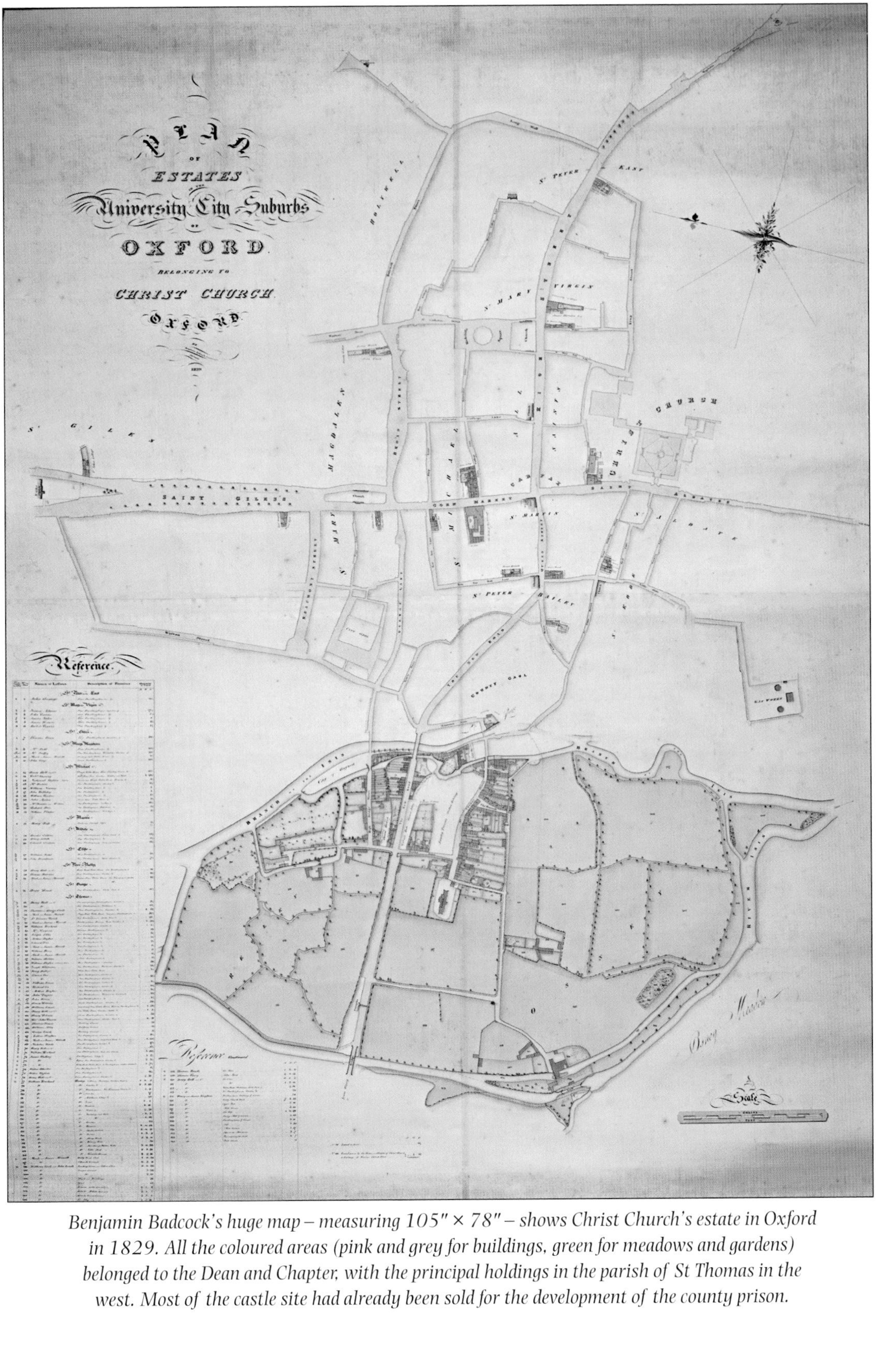

Benjamin Badcock's huge map – measuring 105″ × 78″ – shows Christ Church's estate in Oxford in 1829. All the coloured areas (pink and grey for buildings, green for meadows and gardens) belonged to the Dean and Chapter, with the principal holdings in the parish of St Thomas in the west. Most of the castle site had already been sold for the development of the county prison.

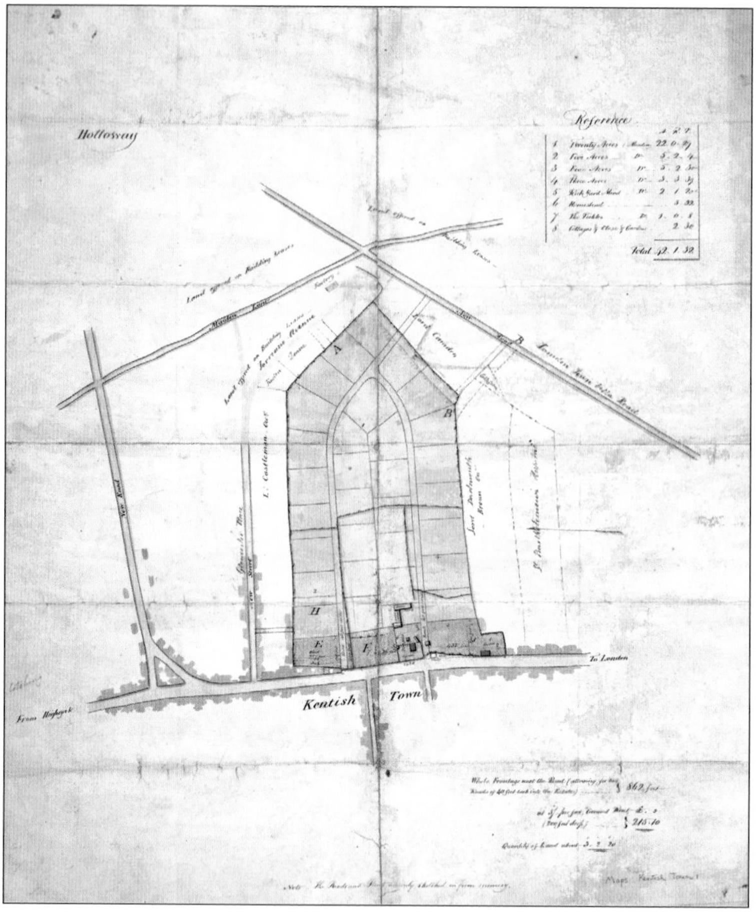

Canon Robert South (1634–1716) left the reversion in his properties in Kentish Town and Caversham to Christ Church. This plan of 1832 shows the extent of the small farm in Kentish Town and the beginnings of the development of the suburb around it. The shape of the farmland is still evident in the street layout today.

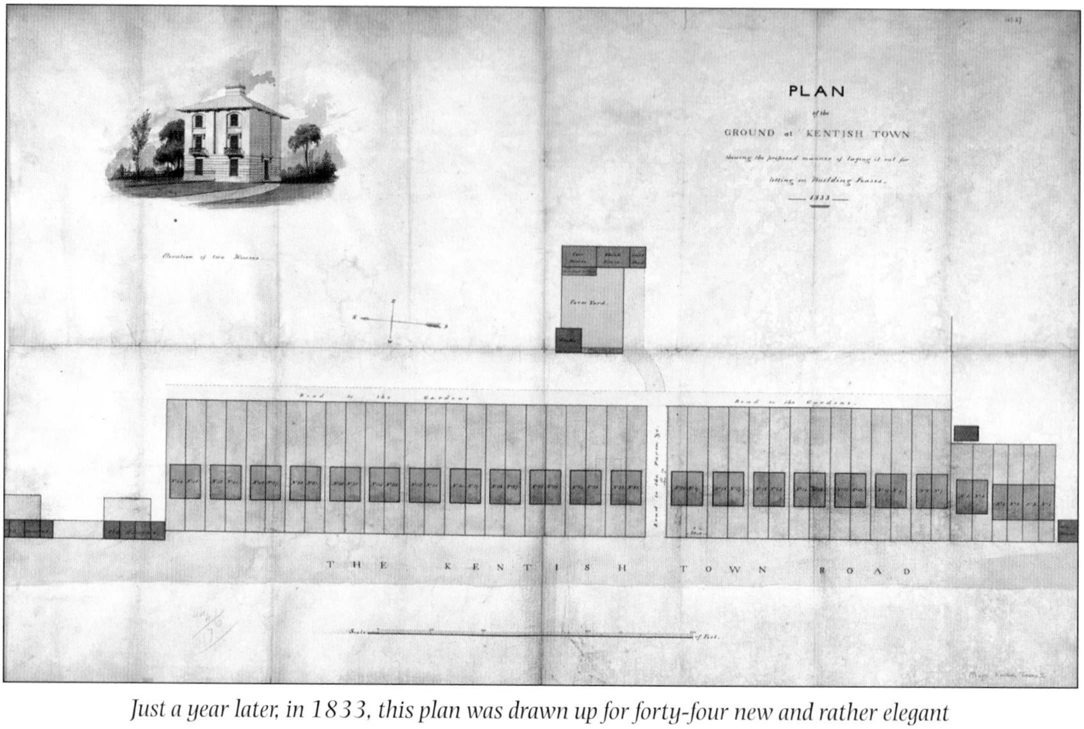

Just a year later, in 1833, this plan was drawn up for forty-four new and rather elegant villas along the Kentish Town Road. The farm was still functioning behind them.

Hillesden, mapped in 1847. The large open fields were fenced and hedged in 1652 to make smaller units suitable for the local breed of sheep and for cattle to graze.

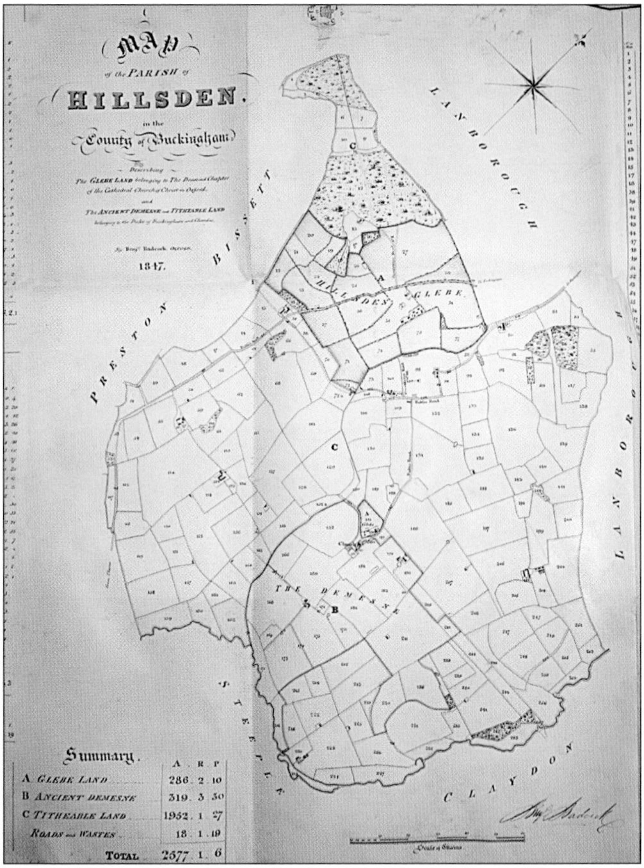

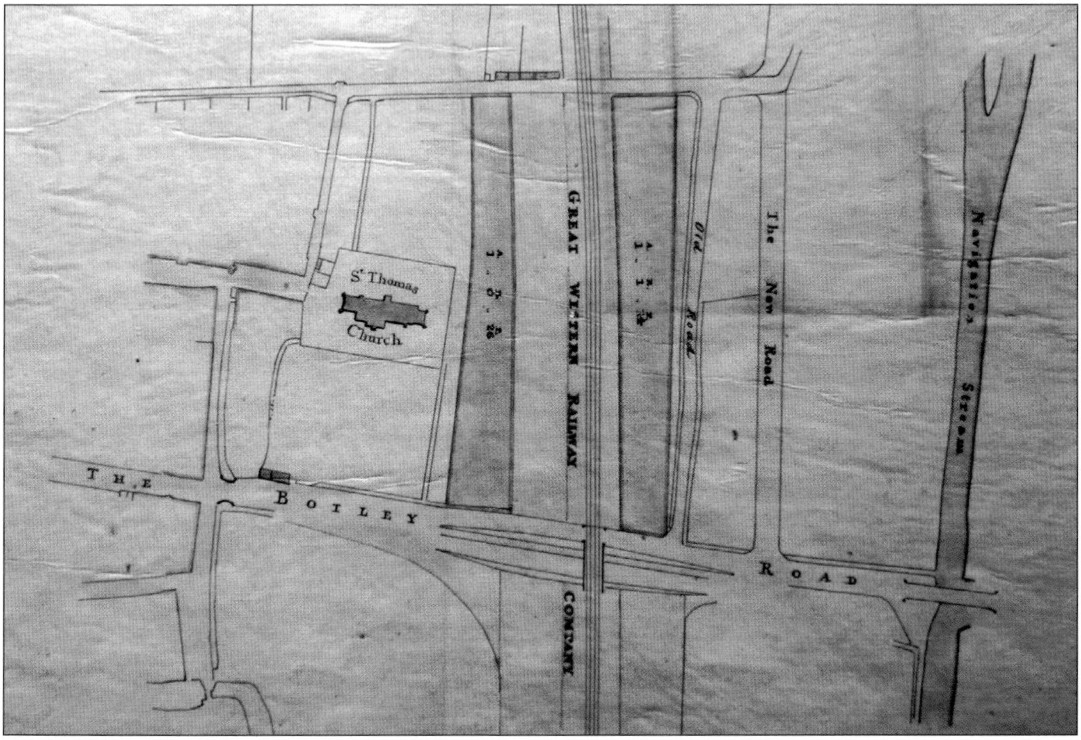

Land sales (of the areas marked in blue to either side of the railway line) in Oxford to the Great Western Railway in 1852.

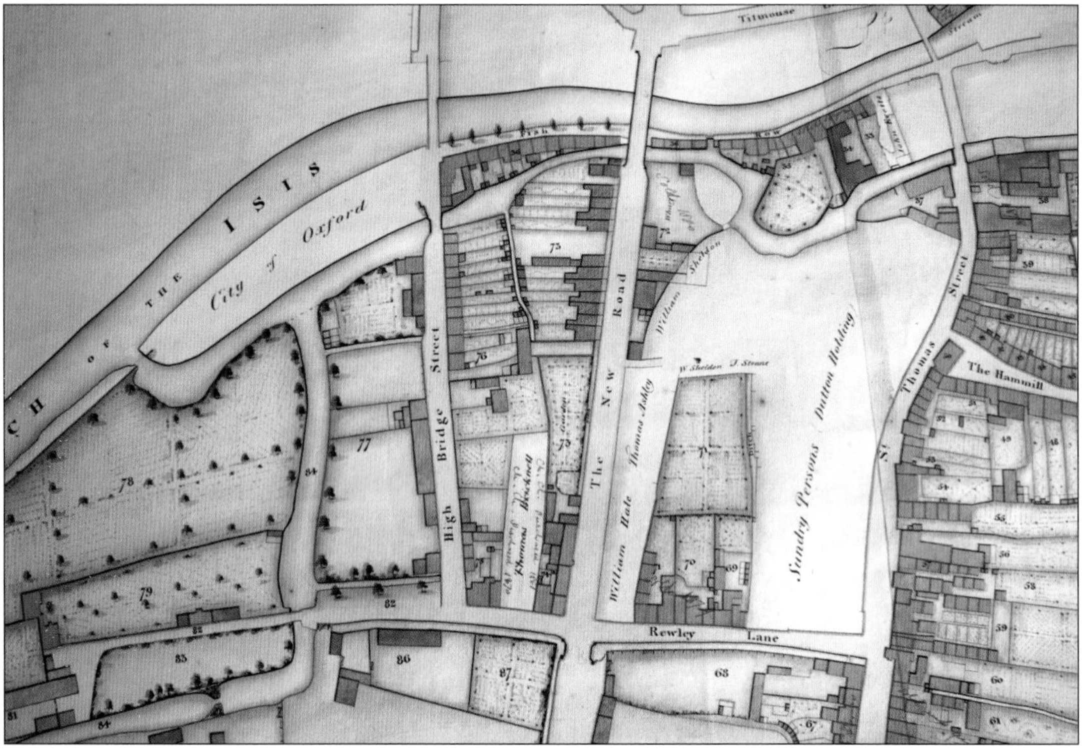

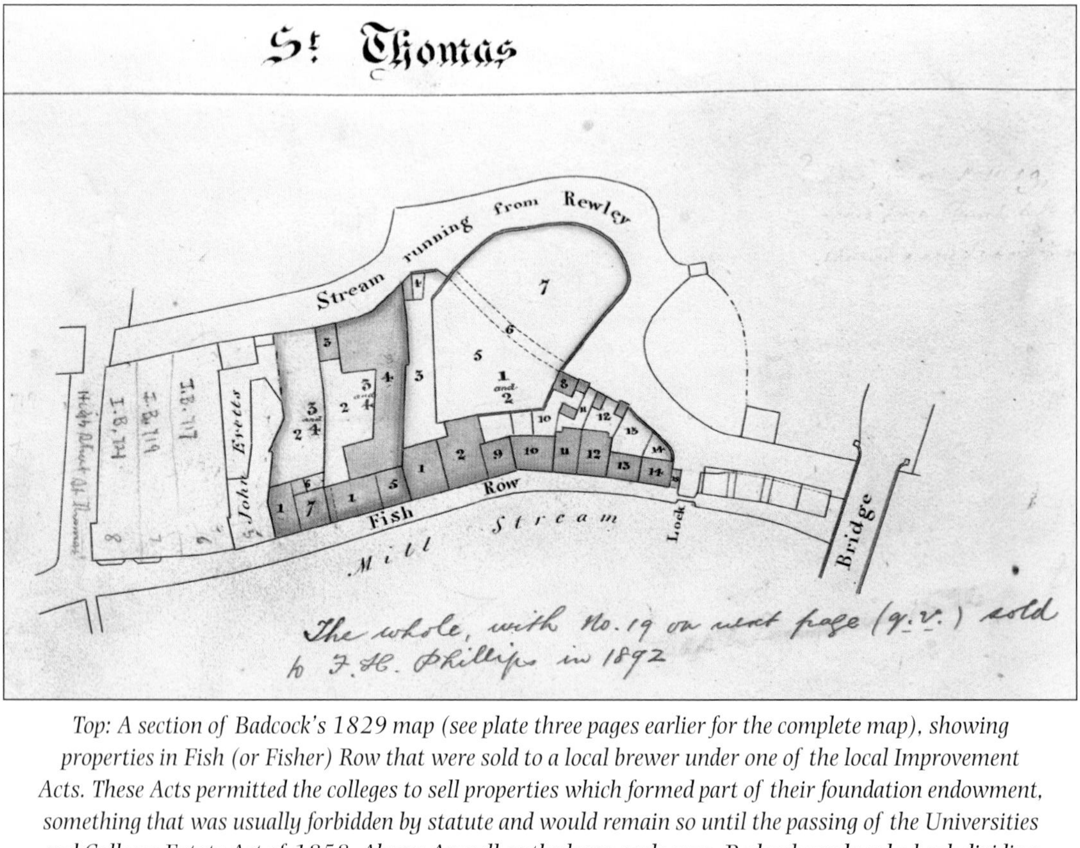

Top: A section of Badcock's 1829 map (see plate three pages earlier for the complete map), showing properties in Fish (or Fisher) Row that were sold to a local brewer under one of the local Improvement Acts. These Acts permitted the colleges to sell properties which formed part of their foundation endowment, something that was usually forbidden by statute and would remain so until the passing of the Universities and Colleges Estate Act of 1858. Above: As well as the large-scale map, Badcock produced a book dividing the map into small sections for ease of use. This page, again showing Fish Row, records a later sale.

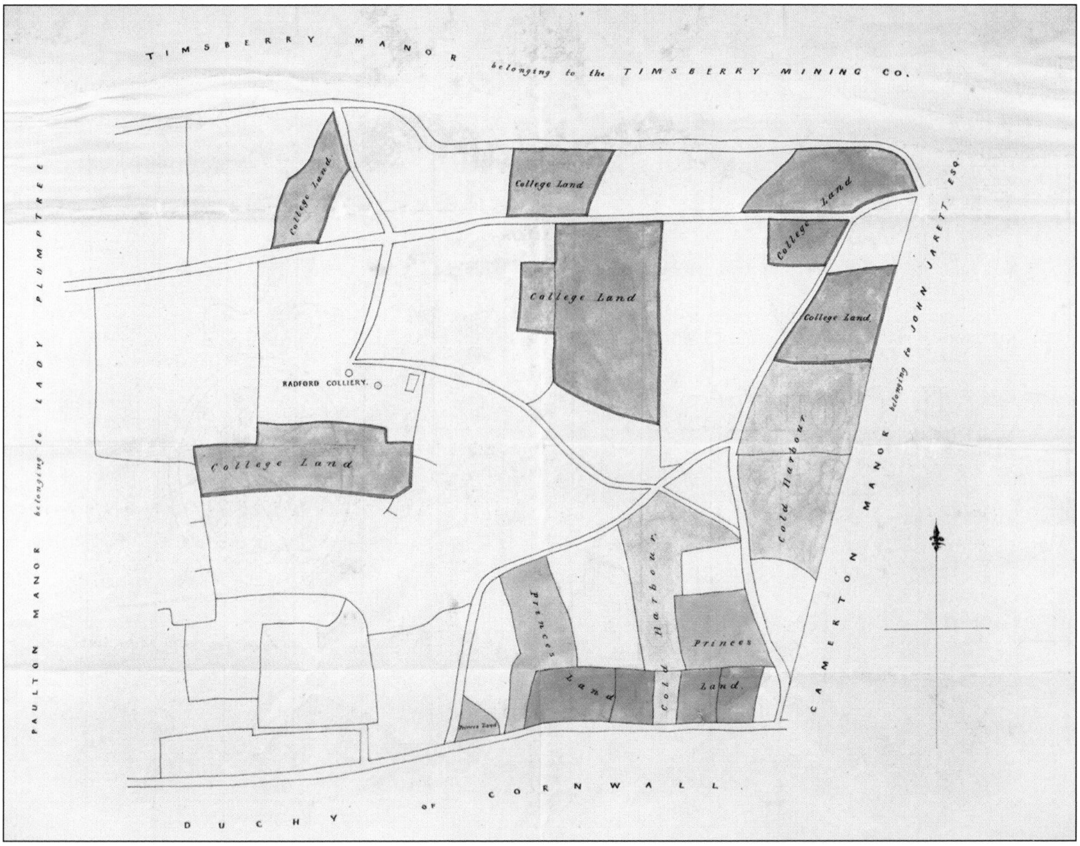

Radford colliery, in the Somerset coalfields. These two plans of 1840 show (above) Christ Church's landholdings above ground and (below) the workings beneath. The proximity of land held by other people, not least the Prince of Wales, made management difficult.

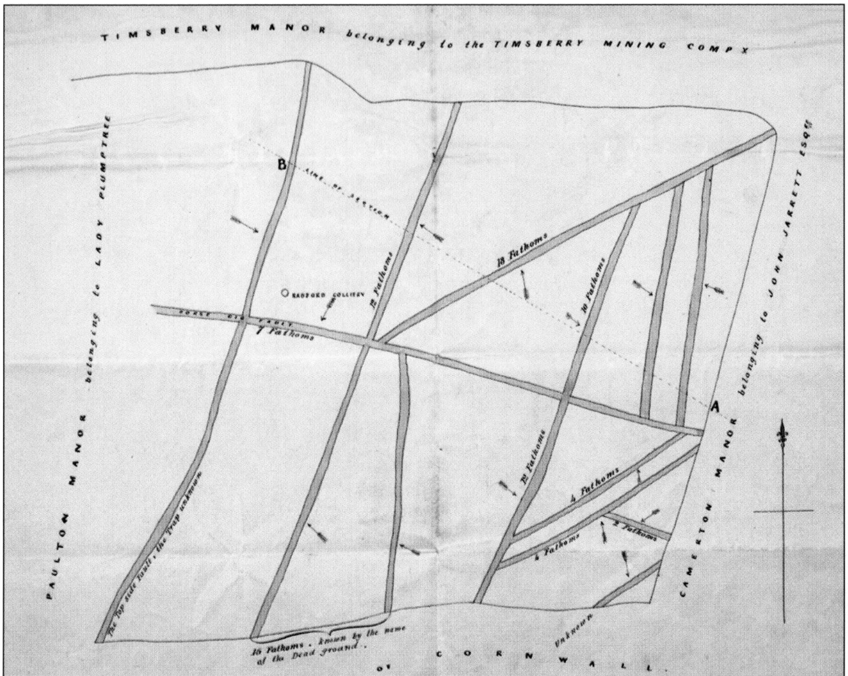

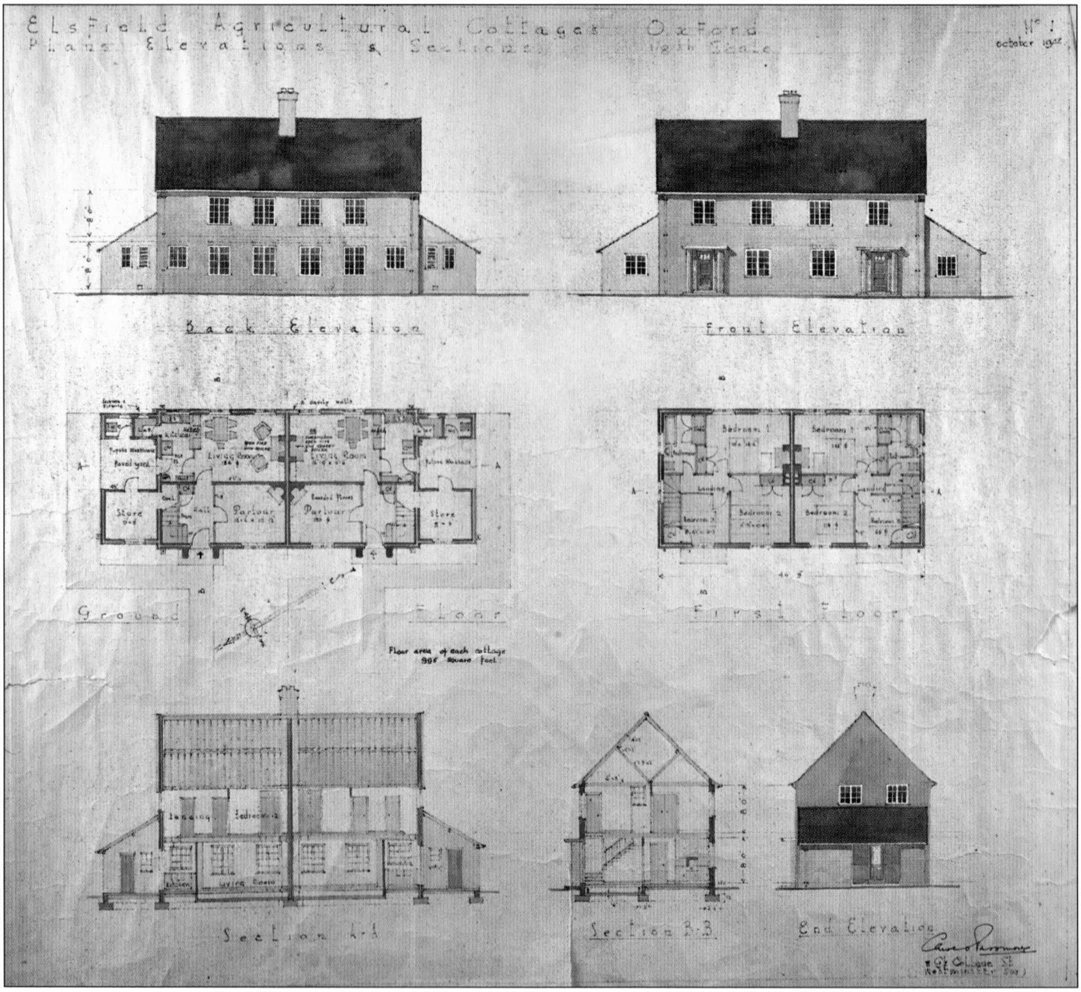

New agricultural labourers' cottages designed in 1946 by London architects Caröe and Passmore for Elsfield. Christ Church purchased the Elsfield estate in 1919, along with the nearby woodland at Shotover, partly to protect the green belt around the city from excessive development.

In the following year Smith-Woolley, Christ Church's land agents, designed these cottages for Wragg Marsh Farm, near Spalding.

be first made and brought in of the estate to be renewed', and then in 1704 the Chapter restated the decree, noting that 'many suits and controversies are like to arise [...] several of them touching the contents and boundaries of their lands and tenements. So that in time great part of the College Lands are like to be lost Unles Speedy care be taken to prevent the same.' [23] Never was a truer word spoken, but, as a result, more accurate valuations began to be determined. Tenants often offered considerable resistance to the surveyors, anticipating rising entry fines.

The Marquess of Rockingham, for example, Christ Church's tenant in Wath upon Dearne (Yorkshire), complained vociferously in 1778 about the surveyor, William Young, who, according to the peer, had valued the estate ridiculously high – about £235 more than his own estimate – and had made 'flippant' suggestions about his use of the land for stud horses – racing was one of Rockingham's favourite leisure pursuits – rather than for arable.[24] Rockingham was certain that the land was worth more as grazing. He had purchased the lease in 1769 from Samuel Tooker, in whose family the property had been for over a century. In 1773 the vicar of Wath, John Rowley, wrote to Christ Church's solicitor, James Morrell, suggesting that Rockingham had been taking tithes to which he was not entitled and had been enclosing common land in ever-increasing quantities. When this land was added to the common that had already been enclosed to provide incomes for the new chapelries of Swinton and Wentworth, the losses to the vicar's income were substantial.[25] So, when the lease came up for its seven-year renewal, Christ Church commissioned a survey and valuation, to be accompanied by maps of the glebe lands. Young earned his £89 4s., and was very thorough.[26] There is a large-scale map included in the survey which is simple, delineating only the fields and properties that formed the glebe, but renders them all identifiable even on a modern Ordnance Survey map. Young's other map, at a smaller scale, shows the whole parish with the glebe plots in context. The written survey, in contrast to the simplicity and clarity of the maps, is detailed, listing the occupiers of each plot of land in the townships of Wath and what is grown in each, whether that be barley, wheat, oats and beans or clover.[27] He enumerated each field that was lying fallow, or was pasture or meadow, giving its acreage and its value. Young included descriptions of the tithes that were due to the vicar, and explained the customs, or moduses, for the area, which included the right to every eleventh stook of corn. Rowley may have had some reason to be miffed; the distribution of tithes was evidently very confused. Even the tithe of potatoes was divided: if they were grown in gardens, then the tithe went to the vicar; if in the fields, then it went to the rector, presumably a differentiation between domestic and commercial cultivation. Perhaps unsurprisingly, Young noted that 'there are not many grown in this Parish'. But it did appear that the vicar was pushing his luck a bit; he had filed a Bill in Exchequer to demand the payment of the tithes on turnips, flax and rape. Young reckoned that tithes had never been paid on turnips.[28] The eighteenth century saw the beginnings of serious debate about the abolition of tithes, and the constant resort to law over the tiniest of things pushed matters on.

Dean Bagot, strongly conservative and renowned as rather a snob, made sure that he was directly involved in negotiations with Rockingham and offered a concessionary rate, down from the £693 that Young had suggested to £600.[29] There was more blustering from the indignant nobleman, but Bagot won and on 1 July 1778 Christ Church received £600, which was duly distributed between the dean and canons, the dean receiving, as usual, twice the amount allocated to his colleagues. John Rowley, the vicar, was still not happy; he requested that his name be entered into the memorandum book 'in large characters (that I may not be overlook'd)' for the first vacant benefice.[30]

Similar stories can be found throughout the archive, but it was not only the principal tenants who could be difficult. Sub-tenants, too, were often reluctant to help the landlord's stooges; to them, Christ Church's primary tenant appeared more of a landlord than the Dean and Chapter ever did, and they were unwilling to appear to be siding with the wrong party. The devil one knew was a far safer bet. Canon Tanner in East Walton resorted to a mild form of bribery with his beef and beer, but Christ Church often relied on its only man on the ground, the local vicar, to supply relevant information to the surveyor. Some of these men, too, were unhappy about alienating either their flocks or the resident of the big house near by.

The crux of the problem with the Marquess of Rockingham was the size of his re-entry fine. After the Restoration, entry fines had stood at around one year's income (so, if the estate was valued at £100 per annum, the entry fine was set at £100); by the 1750s, this had risen to fifteen months' income. Rockingham had neglected, no doubt deliberately, to add the extra quarter year to his calculation. Even so, he was still better off than he would have been as a tenant of another college as rates in most had been increased to fifteen months some time before the end of the eighteenth century. Christ Church was slow to follow suit – it was 1811 before the Dean and Chapter increased the entry fines to this level.[31] In spite of the difficulties of obtaining accurate and mutually acceptable valuations in order to set entry fines, the colleges still seemed reluctant to let go of the old beneficial leases and to move over to a more commercial system of rack-renting.[32]

From the middle of the eighteenth century, innovations in farming techniques and changes in land management forced Christ Church to a new level of, if not estate management, estate awareness. At this period there were clues that land management was becoming more and more professional as trust estates required purchases and sales, proceeds from sales were invested in stocks and shares, colleges were acquiring London bank accounts and leases were amended to ensure that land was measured and valued correctly.[33] In 1781 the Chapter decided that no new lease should be issued for a rural estate without the requirement for a terrier or for an urban one without a clause allowing the Chapter to inspect the property. If necessary repairs were not done, then the lease would be void.[34] And new regulations were drawn up about twenty-one-year agricultural leases. Some tenants had evidently been neglecting to renew their leases after fourteen years had passed, and the Dean and Chapter tried to use this to begin the running out of beneficial leases. Should three months pass with no attempt to have the estate revalued and to pay a fresh entry fine, the tenant would forfeit the right to renew.

The enclosure movements: enclosure by agreement

While the setting of fines was a major issue that kept the Dean and Chapter busy, particularly in the eighteenth and nineteenth centuries, changes to the physical landscape – and the consequent potential changes to income – of the estates were often going unnoticed.

Christ Church's tenants were sitting pretty with low rents, infrequent fines and probably undervalued land. A widely dispersed estate meant that valuations were often dependent on local agents, whose interests may have lain more with the tenant than with the landlord. And, of course, much of the agricultural land from which Christ Church derived its income was still farmed in two, three or even four large open fields, in which all the residents of a village or manor had strips scattered throughout.

The origins of the open-field system in England are obscure, but in the Midlands, where the multi-field arrangements were most developed and long-lived, it appears to date from the late Saxon or early Norman period.[35] Its original purpose was to divide the good and bad land of a manor or parish fairly, and to allow efficient management of crop rotation and fallow fields by the local courts. Alongside the fields, tenants had rights of common, access to underwood and other allowances on payment of labour dues and rents. Following the Black Death in 1348–9, when much land was left empty and uncultivated, and agricultural labourers were suddenly in short supply, men began to realise their worth and that they were free to seek waged work.[36] The feudal system, which had been the rural norm for many, now began to break down. Land was taken out of common use, plots were joined together and vast tracts converted for pasture as the price of wool began to increase. A growing number of farmers with their own small estates wanted to ensure that their land reaped maximum profits, although there were still huge acreages managed in the medieval manner, which made it hard to determine the precise location, and therefore the value, of every portion that contributed to the coffers. In 1598, for example, it was stated that the common fields of the hamlets of Shippon and Dry Sandford (Berkshire) were so intermingled that it was impossible to distinguish one from the other.[37]

The enclosure of the open fields was probably the greatest change that affected nearly all of Christ Church's estates, particularly those in the Midlands. It has been said that Oxford University and its constituent colleges were particularly slow in embracing the change and the benefits that it offered. Christ Church certainly was. The Dean and Chapter never initiated the enclosure process, but neither did it make any objections when tenants wished to go ahead, unless smaller landholders would be damaged or, more prosaically, profits came under threat.[38]

The first wave of enclosures in the Midlands was well under way even as Christ Church was founded. In the late fifteenth century Northamptonshire had seen great swathes of countryside converted from arable to pastureland to accommodate profitable sheep. The breed of sheep, the Midland longwool, was chosen specifically by enclosing farmers as they fared better in smaller fields than those more used to wandering widely. Buckinghamshire and Oxfordshire followed Northamptonshire's example. These three counties – areas in which Christ Church had numerous estates – saw more early enclosure than any other. The 1517 Enclosure Commission showed that over 80 per cent of enclosures in Buckinghamshire had been for pasture to take advantage of the rising price of wool.[39] Although these enclosures frequently met with opposition – because of the fear of depopulation and then over the enclosure of common land, which deprived the peasantry of their common rights of grazing and wood, for example – the distance of the region that included south-west Northamptonshire, north Buckinghamshire and north-east Oxfordshire from major rivers made pastoral farming more economically viable than grain husbandry.[40] Cattle and sheep, and even geese, could walk to market.[41] Smaller farmers began to participate and, by the time of the 1607 Enclosure Commission, which had been created after the Midland Revolt of that year against enclosure (with its loss of commons and, in the earlier days particularly, of depopulation) in neighbouring counties, opposition had died right down, and a new round of enclosures began, frequently with the agreement of all involved.[42] The Christ Church picture is interesting: the pattern of enclosures on the college's estates mirrors the general pattern in the Midlands, particularly in Buckinghamshire, where the division of enclosure in the north (undertaken early) and enclosure in the southern Chiltern area (late) is very striking.

In a number of cases, Christ Church's more business-minded tenants had effected changes in their style of farming without the knowledge of the Dean and Chapter. In Hillesden (Buckinghamshire) the Denton family, who leased the rectory with its great tithes and glebe land from Christ Church for an annual rent of £13 17s. 4d., and who owned much of the rest of the parish, set to work soon after the Civil War. A terrier written in 1652, on the eve of enclosure, confirms that the parish was still farmed principally in common fields, but also reveals that enclosure had been gradually creeping across the parish from the early sixteenth century.[43] In 1086 about 1,800 acres (out of 2,500) was under plough, and much of the rest was woodland. Just before the enclosure in 1652, this acreage had been substantially reduced for pasture and for arable farming in small closes, but there were still 600 acres under plough in open fields in the hands of the Dentons and a few other small landholders. The Dentons initiated the enclosure of the parish, as did their neighbours and relations the Verneys, in the adjoining parish of Middle Claydon.[44] One lease dated 1629, which obliged Nicholas Butterton, a tenant farmer of the family, to allow his landlord to enclose at will, suggests that the taking in of arable land was already at the forefront of the Dentons' minds, and the demesne lands (those held by the lord) had already been consolidated into a single area, rather than being scattered throughout the remaining open fields, before 1652. One of Christ Church's tenants, Mr Phillips, assisted the surveyor, John Kersey, with the practical laying out of the enclosure, which may indicate that the changes were not widely opposed. By this time smaller farmers were beginning to see that enclosure brought advantages, and many schemes were carried out amicably and with an element of compromise. Other examples close to Hillesden were at Astwood, where the lord of the manor called the inhabitants together in 1613 to agree the terms of the enclosure, and at Great Linford, where a more formal agreement was drawn up in 1658.[45]

After enclosure, however, the arable land in Hillesden was reduced to about 100 acres – all the rest was converted to pasture, and the farms, anticipating the later practice of enclosure by Act of Parliament, were moved out from the village to become isolated in the fields.[46] North Buckinghamshire, like the west of Northamptonshire, was not ideal for arable farming – even into the 1970s the land at Hillesden was largely used for grazing – so the parish was slowly converted to pasture by a long process that was begun in medieval times and largely completed with the enclosure in 1652 and the transfer of all the land into the Dentons' hands.

The Hillesden enclosure, like many in the early modern period, was done purely for profit; Edmund Denton inherited the estate from his father, who had died in prison during the Civil War. Much of central England – particularly Buckinghamshire, which had formed a front line between the opposing sides – was devastated by the effects of the fighting and billeting of soldiers. In order to pay debts and to rebuild the family mansion, which had been destroyed by parliamentary forces, Edmund invested heavily in the improvement of the estate. It was not, however, until 1714, when a dispute arose over the payment of tithes, that Christ Church had even the slightest hint that agricultural practice in Hillesden had changed.[47] The parsonage land, which was leased to Denton by the Dean and Chapter, was now entirely indistinguishable from anyone else's as it had been included in the enclosure of the entire parish. If such dramatic changes went unnoticed so close to home, it is not surprising that more difficulties arose on estates further afield.

Occasionally the Dean and Chapter were made aware of changes happening on an estate as they happened. In 1634 Christ Church was sent a copy of the formal agreement between the lord of the manor and Christ Church's rectorial tenant, Richard Grenville of Wotton Underwood, and the freeholders, to enclose a piece of land in Ashendon (Buckinghamshire). Thomas Ridgel and his fellow freeholders agreed that Grenville could enclose and hold an area of the common fields, significantly called the Sheepwalk ('Shipwalke'), for a trial period of six years in spite of the fact that the tenants of the estate had been accustomed to the first crops from the fields there. In recompense, the lord of the manor was restricted in the number of sheep he was permitted to keep in the open fields. If everything worked out, and no one was inconvenienced by the new arrangement, the agreement would become perpetual. Otherwise, intercommoning would be restored.[48]

Christ Church also became involved if a dispute over the terms of the enclosure was brought to the attention of the Chapter. In 1633 complaints were made against Sir Christopher Yelverton about his past and intended enclosures in Easton Maudit (Northamptonshire). The locals had told the Chapter that the enclosures were prejudicial to the interests of the college, and Yelverton wrote to the Treasurer to defend his cause.[49] He had, he said, with the consent of the townships of both Easton Maudit and the neighbouring Bosiat (Bozeat), and at his own cost, severed and divided the bounds of the two parishes. He denied that he had injured Christ Church land, insisted that he had done nothing unlawful and had, in fact, turned a blind eye to the encroachments of the college's tenants onto his own land. He was reluctant to go to court over it, he wrote, but 'in a Justifiable way, I may take for the future such courses as may improve my estate, if I find not a reciprocall correspondence from you'. Christ Church hurried to reply, apologising to their influential neighbour for being 'jealous' over enclosure but describing it as 'ye ruine of their Inheritance'. Just five years later both parties found themselves in the Chancery court, with the Chapter raising a complaint against Yelverton for 'defacing' the bounds of the college's land. Yelverton recited a recent lease by Christ Church which at least showed what Christ Church *should* have: 30 acres, of which 24 were in Easton Maudit and 6 in Bozeat. According to the ancient common rights, Christ Church's tenant should have common for six cattle and thirty sheep. He acknowledged that the lands were intermixed and confused and so offered to stake out 27 acres as a single plot in the open field known as Yardley and 6 acres in Bozeat. The court evidently felt this was fair and advised the Chapter to accept, which it would appear that they did. In 1639, following the court case, Yelverton actually became Christ Church's tenant in Easton Maudit and a series of questions was sent to him by the Chapter to make sure that he had fulfilled the terms of the court decision. It would appear that he had become an ideal tenant; where he found problems in determining whose land was whose, he made compensation by granting other parcels and fencing them off at his own expense. Physically enclosing the new fields was no small undertaking. In the Midlands most would have been done with quickset hedges, which of course resulted in the establishment of specialist nurseries to grow the huge numbers of shrubs that would have been required, and to provide the grass seed for new pasture. Hedges for the earlier enclosures tended to include timber trees, whereas later hedges were more uniformly quickset species.[50] The Verneys, when enclosing their land in East Claydon in 1741, purchased their hedge plants from a nursery in Syresham (Northamptonshire), mixing crab, aspen and elm with the occasional oak, choosing the species that would work best on wet or dry soils. Some of the grass seed was purchased, at some expense, but some came also from their own meadows left to grow specifically for the seed.[51] Timber from estates would have been felled to make the fences that delineated the fields while the hedges filled out.[52] On upland estates stone walls would have been constructed, and in fen- or marshland drainage ditches would have served as boundaries.[53]

Twenty years later Sir Christopher's son Henry made Christ Church an offer of 72 acres of enclosed land in exchange for the rectory and parsonage, including all tithes. He would repair the chancel of Easton Maudit church and build a house for the tenant of Christ Church's new land. The Chapter took a 'causeless dislike' to the proposal, and once again the two sides found themselves in court. It is hard to see why Christ Church was so opposed to the suggestion unless it was the loss of tithe income that concerned them. However, Yelverton continued to lease the land at the same rent as before, and Christ Church retained the advowson and the rights to timber.[54]

At Tetbury (Gloucestershire), the Commissioners for Depopulation were called in when the major landholders of the parish were accused of enclosing land for pasture 'to the great prejudice of the tenants of the Dean and Chapter'.[55] In February 1638 the Commissioners demanded that much of the newly created pasture be restored to arable, and that the offenders pay a £50 fine to the king.[56] How much of this was done is not clear, but it is evident that the value of Christ Church's rectories could be much reduced by enclosures; profits from tithes on grain produce inevitably fell with conversion to pasture. The tenant at Tetbury, for example, paid an annual rent of

£10 plus a fat wether of 13s. 4d. at the audit. The value of the estate in 1638 is not easy to determine – the receipt books record only the £10 rent paid in two instalments, in May and November, and there are no fine books from this period – but the value of the tithes was said to have fallen by £30 subsequent to the enclosure, and was likely to fall further as more land was laid to grass.[57] In theory, this didn't matter too much to Christ Church as the Dean and Chapter were still receiving the stipulated rent; it was only the vicar who was losing out. However, if the value of the tithes was dropping, the value of the land certainly was not – no farmer undertook the expensive process of enclosure lightly. Profitability was the key motive. Under the system of beneficial leasing common to most landowners at this period, it was to the tenant's advantage to hide the actual value of his land; if he could conceal the value, the entry fine could be kept down, and his income could therefore be increased. In contrast, particularly at times of inflation, the land*owner* needed to constantly review his estates and their value, otherwise relative income declined. Valuation became increasingly important.

Outside the Midland area, in Northallerton (Yorkshire) the Dean and Chapter took a case to Chancery in 1635 to sort out the confused ownership of their property. The estate had originally been the property of the monastic hospital of St James and included tithes, houses, farms and land not just in Northallerton itself but also in the neighbouring townships of Romanby, North Otterington, Thornton-le-Beans, Thornton-le-Street, Thornton-le-Moor and North Kilvington.[58] Christ Church claimed that it was being deprived of rents as local freeholders and copyholders insisted that they had an interest in the properties from before Christ Church was founded. To confuse matters still further, much land had been enclosed for pasture, including waste, and it was proposed to take in the whole of the villages. It was impossible to tell whose land was whose, and as a consequence the tithes were of no value.[59] The tenant, Francis Lassells, denied all of this, saying that his lease had been granted by Richard Morison, master of the Hospital of St James, in 1545 for ninety-nine years and that neither he nor any of the earlier tenants had once defaulted on the rent and none of the land had been enclosed. In fact, he countered, Christ Church had taken the tithes which were his by right.[60] The records fail to record the outcome of the dispute – although Lassells's lease was renewed in 1638 – but the affair was yet another indication that there was considerable confusion over land ownership and rights.

It is noticeable that the records of early enclosure, whether by grand tenants and landlords, or by agreement across an estate with freeholders and tenants alike, are mainly from the Midland counties, where so much took place. In another Buckinghamshire parish, Lathbury, where Christ Church held the rectory, a dispute over common rights – specifically grazing for the vicar's cow – took a ridiculous turn in 1630, when the vicar, Walter Evans, and some local farmers – Alin, Pinkard and Garner – came to blows. Evans had apparently sent the cow out to the common ground for pasturing, but the farmers drove her away, insisting that Evans did not have the right to do this. The poor cow was pushed backwards and forwards day after day. One morning, Evans sent his daughter to stand guard over the cow, but the farmers defeated her and dragged the cow back; on another, the farmers had locked the gate, so Miss Evans and one of her father's men found a plank to place across the ditch to the common so that they could let the cow graze. Another local, Frances Clerke, accused the Evanses of stealing the plank. This evidently continued for some time until the morning when Revd Evans left his house early to get the cow to the common before anyone else was up and about. But his effort was in vain, and he found himself face to face with Pinkard. The vicar stood in the gateway with his walking stick confronted by Pinkard, waving a pitchfork, and Pinkard's mother, who was 'railing at me with very uncivile wordes'. Pinkard forced the cow out of the field, past Evans, who was pushed into the muddy ditch. The dispute escalated; the next day the men acquired a warrant and had Evans – with his wife, daughter and manservant – up before the justices. The farmers all swore that they were only doing what Richard Hampden, the lord of the manor, had ordered. The magistrate, Tyringham, was a bit dubious, finding it hard to believe that such action against a minister of the church could ever have been done with Hampden's consent.[61] Over the course of the hearings it came out that there was a disagreement about the amount of common land belonging to the vicarage and how many animals the vicar could graze there. The judgement allowed Evans to keep two beasts in the fields and meadow when other herds were there and required him to pay 2 shillings each year for each cow.

The matter seems to have been resolved and appears to have been just one of those village disagreements which go from molehill to mountain and back again in the shortest of times. However, the argument about the vicar's holdings and common rights was just a precursor to later issues over the behaviour of the lord of the manor. In 1656 it would appear that the minister, Isaiah Davis, corresponded with the Dean and Chapter about the tithes that were due from his glebe land and problems with enclosure. It was one of those occasions when a personal visit from a senior man was required, and Ralph Button (canon and sub-dean throughout the Commonwealth period) set off to Lathbury to

> view Sqr Hampden's great ground (newly enclosed); to inquire what the Corn tithes arising there when it was used to bee sowne with corn might in likelihood bee worth per annum; what the land (now inclosed) is worth by the aker (& glebe of it) & to take notice whither the land bee in all places the feild of equally goodness. Beside to inquire what other grounds of Sqr Hampden (beside that great feild) our Tenant Sqr Andrewes hath now tith of.[62]

Button's enquiries revealed that the vicar's few acres of arable and pasture fell within the manor's single 240-acre open field, which had recently been enclosed. Hampden had divided the field, laid it to pasture and leased the closes. Hedges had been run across the vicar's land, dividing it into four or five pieces; his rights were thoroughly undermined, and the lease of the rectory had been damaged.[63] The Chapter negotiated a deal between its tenant and its curate: the glebe land would be thrown in with the rectory and the tenant would pay 25 shillings per annum directly to the minister and his successors; Christ Church's rectorial tenant (and lord of the manor), Henry Andrewes, surrendered his lease of the tithes and would pay a fixed sum of £32 to the Dean and Chapter instead.[64] In the unlikely event of any tithes being recovered from Hampden, they would be returned to Andrewes. But the solution turned out to be ill conceived; legally, the curacy – supported by land that had never been let before – could not be let separately. Hampden offered to set out land to compensate Christ Church and actually met with the Auditor in London. Everything went round in circles for a while, with all the interested parties, and others, wanting to buy bits of the land or to lease the parsonage. In November 1660 the case went before Sir Richard Newdigate, a serjeant-at-law and newly created lord chief justice, who decided that, in his opinion, the owner of a freehold within an enclosure with rights of common could throw down the enclosure and make gaps for his cattle. He decreed that some measure should be taken to overthrow the enclosure.[65] Exactly what happened in Lathbury is not recorded, but it is perhaps interesting to note that in 1662 Isaiah Davis took over the tenancy of the rectory estate.[66]

By the middle of the seventeenth century wool prices had ceased to be the driver behind enclosure, and there was a lull in activity for perhaps a century. But it was during this period that Christ Church saw its estate begin to expand with benefactions. Some bequests were made specifically to fund buildings; between 1660 and 1792 more than £54,000 was donated. Others were designed to pay for places for scholarships and exhibitions. In 1772 the annual rental receipts from Christ Church's trust estates for exhibitions was £2,760 per annum.[67]

Benefactions and trusts

Throughout Christ Church's history benefactors have given land, or funds to purchase land. The first gift from Mary Tudor, that of the manor of Tring (Hertfordshire), brought the endowment to its expected level. But apart from this, the earliest benefactions were made in the middle years of the seventeenth century, beginning in 1633, when Joan Bostock gave three houses in Peascod Street in Windsor to help four Students in need and 'of the towardliest hope for learning and conversation'.[68] Mrs Bostock was very precise in her instructions; at least five members of Chapter had to sit down in the Audit House between the hours of 1 p.m. and 3 p.m. on 18 December every year to select the fortunate Students. It is not understood why Mrs Bostock chose to give these properties to Christ Church, although it is possible that the undergraduate Charles Bostock, who received his BA in 1627, was a relation. This was soon followed by the gift of the manor of Wyld Court in Hampstead Norreys (Berkshire) by John Morris, the regius professor of Hebrew.[69] The income was to fund seven exhibitions to encourage the study of Hebrew. It took a long time for the bequest to be useful; Morris's wife did not die until 1681, and even then the terms of the will were confusing. The first exhibitions were not awarded until 1693, and it would seem that the income was never sufficient to meet Morris's terms; in 1833 Chapter received Chancery approval to reduce the number of recipients from seven to just one.[70]

There was a lull in benefactions, unsurprisingly, during the period of the Civil War and Commonwealth, but new ones began to be made soon after the Restoration.[71] Other seventeenth-century benefactions included that from Mrs Rachel Paul, the widow of the bishop of Oxford, of 38 acres – the Broad Closes – in Eynsham (Oxfordshire) to fund places for the sons of poor clergymen;[72] Canon Richard Gardiner, who had paid for the creation of Mercury, the pond in the centre of Tom Quad, left a small estate in Bourton-on-the-Water (Gloucestershire);[73] Edward Cotton, a canon of Exeter Cathedral, bequeathed his lease of the tithes of Thornmow in the parish of Ottery St Mary (Devon) to assist with the maintenance of two graduate Exhibitioners from Devon, Cornwall or Oxford;[74] and John Fell, dean of Christ Church after the Restoration, left considerable money in his will, finally settled by Chancery in 1699, with which the Chapter purchased the advowsons of Sheering (Essex), Batsford and St Tudy (Cornwall) for the benefit of Christ Church Students.[75] Fell also left property in Northmoor, Standlake, Shifford and Bampton (all Oxfordshire).[76] Holwood Farm in Chatteris (Cambridgeshire), along with a tithe rent charge, was purchased with the £7,000 left to the college in 1692 by the bishop of Lichfield, Thomas Wood, to benefit the senior holders of Masters of Arts degrees on the foundation, and Thomas Thynne, first Viscount Weymouth, gave the advowson of Wentnor (Shropshire) in 1675.[77]

There was one seventeenth-century gift that was forgotten for many years. Robert Chaloner, a Student of Christ Church from 1564 to 1577, left an estate in Garsington in his will, dated 20 June 1620, to fund a lectureship in divinity.[78] For over a century it appears that the rents had come in regularly but had been added to the corporate pot, rather than being used for the desired purpose. The Chapter did not really have much excuse; there were definitely documents on file about the bequest dating from the 1639. Perhaps they could have claimed the confusion of the Civil War if that had been the only mention of the estate, but it had come up again in discussion in the 1660s, when one of the other landholders in Garsington asked Christ Church to sort out its boundaries. Apparently the Chaloner lands were so intermixed with other properties that it was hard to tell whose was whose.[79] It was not until 1750 that the Dean and Chapter resolved to appoint a lecturer whose task was to read two lectures in English on the Thirty-Nine Articles in the Latin Chapel in the cathedral.[80]

Bequests continued into the eighteenth century, and it was during this period that Christ Church received some of the large estates that were to bring considerable benefit to the House and its members.[81] Perhaps the most substantial was that from Canon Robert South in 1714, of property in Kentish Town and Caversham.[82] The purpose of the trust was, in the first instance, to augment the livings of South Stoke, Brize Norton, East Garston, Netherswell, Ardington, Charlton, Little Compton, Drayton, South Littleton, Offenham, Stratton Audley and Dorchester by £10 per annum each.[83] Once this requirement was met, the antique sum of 'twenty nobles' – a figure that amounted to £6 13s. 4d., the noble being worth 6s. 8d. – could be given each year to six poor scholars from Westminster School, with any surplus being put towards new building work. The Kentish Town estate was a single farm when the reversion came to Christ Church, but during the nineteenth century the property was gradually built up, becoming just a part of the metropolis; Caversham consisted of four or five houses with land.[84] Later in the century, in the 1750s, Matthew Lee, physician to the Prince of Wales, bequeathed his property in London, Bath, Worcestershire and Essex, specifically stating in his will that these were to be sold and a new estate purchased specifically to fund the teaching and study of anatomy at Christ Church.[85] The chosen estates were farms in Butlers Marston (Warwickshire) and Helsthorpe (Buckinghamshire). Each was worth about £500 a year.[86]

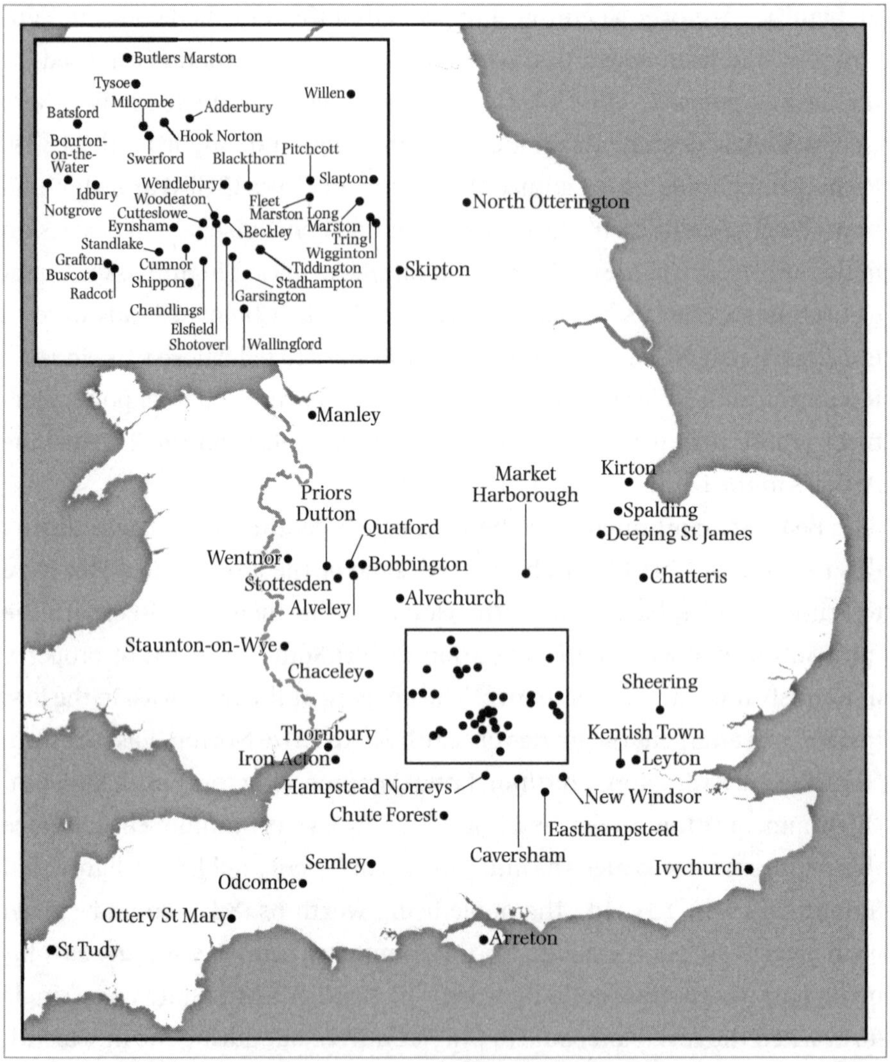

The location of properties acquired after the foundation through purchase or benefaction from the seventeenth to the twentieth centuries.

The archbishop of Armagh, Hugh Boulter, who had been dean of Christ Church from 1719 to 1724, bequeathed the sum of £1,000 in 1742 to endow exhibitions for the poorest commoners.[87] For many years this bequest was managed just as a cash fund, but in 1873 it was combined with moneys from the Fell and Bostock trusts to purchase the 227-acre Essex Farm at

Blackthorn (Oxfordshire) for £11,000.[88] Similarly Elizabeth Holford, the daughter of a coachman from Stanton St John, near Oxford, evidently a shrewd woman, left a generous but ambitious benefaction.[89] A rich merchant, Henry Harbin, had rather taken a fancy to her – she was recorded by the diarist Thomas Hearne as a 'handsome, plump, jolly Wench' – and married her, but he died leaving her with a son. Elizabeth married again, this time an impoverished baronet, giving her a title alongside the wealth from her first husband. Henry junior came up to Christ Church in 1696 but died young, and Lady Holford founded, in his memory, exhibitions for scholars from Charterhouse to Christ Church. If there were no boys at the school suitable to take up the positions, then the exhibitions could be offered to Charterhouse men in other colleges, as long as they migrated to Christ Church. The terms of the exhibitions were, though, that they could be held for up to eight years, right up to the point of receiving an MA. Lady Holford died in 1720, and it was soon discovered that by that time the bequest – more than adequate when the will was made – was only sufficient to fund three-quarters of her legacies.[90] The Dean and Chapter accepted a sum of £1,500 in 1728 and allowed it to accumulate until they were able to use the funds to purchase a farm in Cutteslowe, on the outskirts of Oxford.[91] For a short while all was well, but the tenant of the estate found himself in considerable difficulties in 1749 after losing much of his stock to the Europe-wide cattle distemper pandemic.[92] This had entered the country in Essex and over the following two or three years spread almost nationwide. Only the far west of the country was untouched. Even with government compensation, Isaac Silverside was unable to pay his rent for six years. Christ Church stuck with him as a tenant, understanding his difficulties and appreciating his honesty, but at the end of the six years Silverside owed over £540, of which he had managed to pay only £50. He sold up, raising a further £93 towards his debt.

Education was at the heart of Christ Church, and many of its benefactors, as we have seen, were keen to make it easier for young men from poorer or less privileged backgrounds to come up to Oxford. However, unlike other colleges, Christ Church did not, at its foundation, have strict ties to particular schools or to regions of the country. Thomas Wolsey, when he founded

Cardinal College in 1525, intended that there be a string of feeder schools in every diocese of the country, but only Ipswich School was founded, and its connection with Oxford was severed when Wolsey fell out of favour in 1529.[93] In 1561 Elizabeth I founded the Westminster Studentships, by which just three or four boys from Westminster School would be chosen each year, by interview and examination, but this was all. However, in the late seventeenth and mid-eighteenth century two bequests would establish new links between Christ Church and schools.

In 1732 Dr William Smith bequeathed to the dean and canons East Standen Farm in Arreton, on the Isle of Wight.[94] His intention was that Christ Church would use the income to support a new grammar school in his home town of Portsmouth. Portsmouth had grown into a large town as the Navy expanded from the reign of Charles I, through the transfer of the shipbuilding industry to the town from the Thames, and into the eighteenth century, but facilities had not kept pace. At the time when grammar schools were being founded throughout the country, Portsmouth had been too small to sustain one. By the early eighteenth century those who could afford to pay for education sent their sons away to schools outside the town. Smith, a long-standing and influential resident, evidently resolved to do his part in widening the access to schools. His will, however, left Christ Church with two properties to run: the income-generating farm and – once the properties had been purchased and equipped for purpose, not least with a schoolmaster and an usher – the income-spending school.[95] It was difficult to generate enough income from the farm, which was on uneven, hilly and stony land, and it was decided to wait until the accumulated rents produced a healthier pot before attempting to find a site and to establish the school. It was eight years before a search began, and it was not until 1751 that a suitable house, in Penny Street, was found for conversion and extension.[96]

Some years earlier, in 1690, Christ Church was left, in reversion, several farms in Shropshire and Staffordshire to fund exhibitions for eighteen boys from local schools, or the parishes in which the farms were located, to come to Oxford.[97] Each boy was to have £18 per year as undergraduates, £21 for the next three years as Bachelors, and then another £27 per year for their first three years as Masters. It was some years before the estate came into Christ Church's hands as the benefactor, Edward Careswell, left the farms first to his sister, then to Andrew Charlton, who was housekeeper to the king at Newmarket, and then to Thomas Lloyd of Whittington. It was 1736 before all three had died, and it was not until 1741 that a scheme for administering the trust was laid before the Attorney-General at the request of the headmasters of the schools. Careswell had also stipulated that, if the estates were improved sufficiently, the number of exhibitions should be increased. It was a bequest with big demands attached, and it was only too evident that the income from the properties was insufficient to meet the primary terms of Careswell's will, let alone the extras.[98] The document revealed that the income was, in that year, £321 14s. 6d., which was £3 5s. 6d. short of the required amount. Having decided to reduce, hopefully temporarily, the number of scholars to ten, drawn from only four of the proposed feeder schools, Christ Church set to improving the farms and so increase the revenue. In 1769 the Chapter commissioned John Probert to survey and value the estate.[99] Probert produced an extraordinary document, designed to be practical, with a map, a description of each farm, its current value, and observations and recommendations for improvement. But it was more than a working document; Probert's 'atlas' was beautifully drawn, on parchment, and bound in tooled red morocco.[100]

Sydnall Farm, in the parish of Ditton Priors (Shropshire), for example, is represented on a fold-out map with its title cartouche bizarrely taking the form of a rather grumpy-looking elephant.[101] The farm buildings are carefully drawn, and each field around the homestead is numbered and named. A key on the front page of the atlas shows what the shading means – whether arable, meadow and pasture or orchards. In the arable fields, even the direction of the plough strips is shown. On the opposite page a table gives the acreage of each plot, its quality and use, its value per acre and finally its overall value. Following the survey and valuation, Probert wrote his observations and opinions. He describes Sydnall Farm thus:

> This farm lies 6 miles from Bridgenorth near the Road from thence to Priors Dutton. It is in general a poor weak thin Soil on a Clay which holds the Water so that the Tillage Lands are very Hazardous and the

The title page of the survey of the Careswell Trust estates in Shropshire and Staffordshire, drawn by John Probert in 1769.

Pasture produces a hard pink Grass and some of it throws up Heath and Furze. The Fields for the most part being too large should be Divided into Closes of 6 to 8 Acres well ditched round, which ditches would serve as Receivers of the Water that flows over and Starves all the Lands in the Winter. The two Meadows 11 and 13 should be well drained after which great part of them may be Improv'd by Water the former from the Proposed Reservoir a. at the North West corner thereof and the latter from the Barn and Lane North of the House. The lower Gorst, after it is properly divided, should be Cultivated by Fallowing etc. and then layed down for a Pasture as should great part of the Rough No. 9.

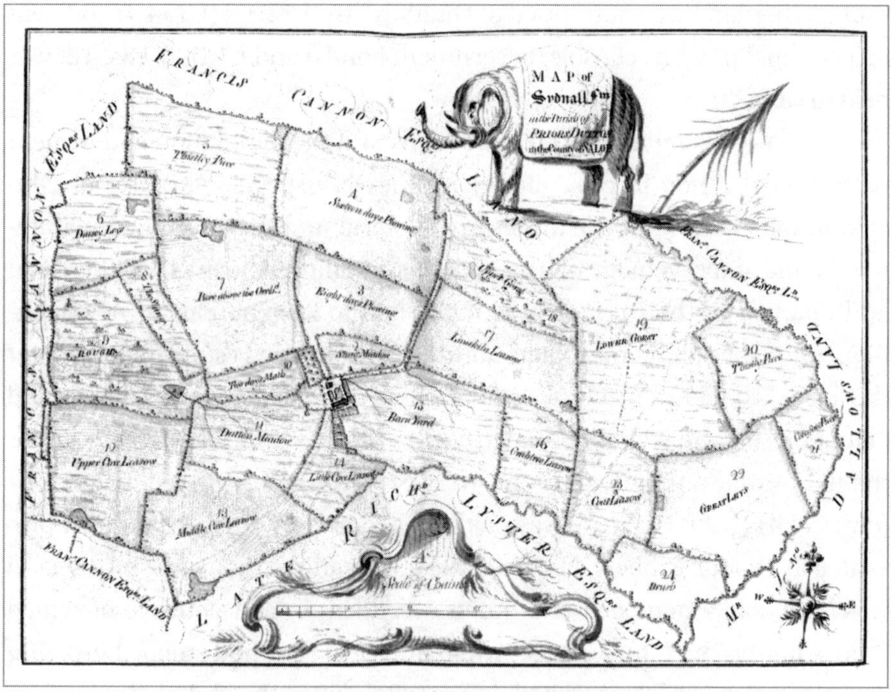

Map of Sydnall Farm in Shropshire, drawn by John Probert for his survey of the Careswell Trust estates.

> This Farm has a right of Common on the Brown Cleehill which is 3 Miles from the Farm, the road to it to the Coal and Lime is from the Gate in the North West corner of the rough N0.9 through three Farms of Mr Cannons, in Tenure of Geo. Harries, Wm Hyde and ...[102]

Probert does the same for each of the farms: Walkerslow Farm in Stottesdon, Hillhouse Farm in Quatford, Barrets Farm in Alveley and Bobbington Farm in Bobbington. His estimates of the increased value of the necessary work – mainly better drainage, which was a fashionable and successful improvement of the period generally – suggested that each farm could produce about 50 per cent more revenue.[103] Just two years later, Probert's valuation of £312 per annum and his estimated improved value of £476 was on its way to being realised. In 1772 Mr Ashby, the receiver, collected £426 13s. 6d.[104] By 1813 the trust was in surplus, and two years after that further land was purchased at Quatford. By 1820, £9,394 7s. 6d. was invested in 3 per cent consols (government bonds) and £1,093 18s. 1d. was held in cash.[105]

The management of both trust funds and the foundation endowment with the obligation to raise money for the very specific purposes of education, the running of the diocesan cathedral and the continued maintenance and improvement of the college's buildings meant that the Dean and Chapter, or their principal tenants, had to keep abreast of new techniques and developments in agriculture. Without good estate management the farms would not meet the requirements of benefactors, so surveys and valuations of land were essential to ensure that revenue was maximised. Of the trust estates, the property in Ottery St Mary was reviewed in 1816 by John Coldridge.[106] His work was neither as thorough nor as beautifully presented as that of Probert, but he made observations that some of the land was 'very badly managed and much overtilled, in consequence of which it does not produce half crops', while another farm had stopped growing crops completely.[107] This period, immediately after the end of the Napoleonic Wars, was one of agricultural depression and unemployment as men were demobilised from the army and navy. The price of wheat plummeted from a wartime high of 100 shillings per quarter to three-quarters or even half of that after 1816. Other farm produce followed suit.[108] Coldridge's valuation must be seen against this background. Gentlemen farmers across Devon had reduced their tenants' rents by up to 25 per cent, and Coldridge hoped that the Chapter would understand why he had done the same to one of the Ottery farmers, Mr Chapple at Cadhay Farm. Chapple fell deeper into debt, and the Chapter were feeling the pinch when the lease of the tithes came up for renewal and the College of Windsor demanded its entry fine. In 1841 the tithes were commuted to a money rent; two years later Chapple was declared bankrupt and Christ Church found a new tenant for Cadhay Farm. Within a decade, however, John Wheaton was also asking for an abatement on his rent. In 1869 the Chapter gave up on an estate that had proved particularly complicated to administer and sold the tithes of Thornmow to the Ecclesiastical Commissioners.[109] Administering estates that were failing, especially if their revenue was supposed to support a specific purpose, was not easy.

However, the new professionalism meant that the Dean and Chapter became increasingly aware of potential improvements that could be made to their properties. Richard Davis, speaking of Aldsworth in 1782, said that the simple, two-course husbandry in the open fields would be greatly improved after enclosure. Although the farmers were already leaving half the land fallow to recover, Davis suggested that the introduction of turnips and grass into the sequence would improve soil nutrition and provide winter fodder. He was right: in 1771 Christ Church's estate in the parish was worth £116; the enclosure took place in 1793, and by 1821 the value had risen to £584.[110]

The enclosure movements: enclosure by Act of Parliament

From the middle of the eighteenth century agricultural innovations begun during the sixteenth and seventeenth centuries – crop rotation, new and varied forms of fertilisation, new crops – built up a new head of steam. As the population grew, and with the impact of the Napoleonic Wars, a new form of enclosure emerged which would be implemented by private Acts of Parliament.[111] It was this new enclosure movement that would suddenly bring the management of estates, rather than just the renewal of leases, much more to the fore in Chapter meetings, where the decision to enclose was, unsurprisingly, dependent on the prices of farm produce and the potential revenue gains.[112]

Open fields were increasingly seen as inefficient. While they were managed and crop rotation, including fallow periods, was normal from the earliest days, the open fields allowed no autonomy to individual farmers. The arable land, commons, waste, pasture all had to be regulated communally. Increased productivity was considered a given once enclosure had taken place. Fields that had been enclosed for pasture were re-ploughed for arable and drained using new methods.[113] Christ Church's records are riddled with surveyor's estimates of improved land values and evidence that they were correct. If productivity on the land was higher, then rents or entry fines could be raised. Of course, enclosure was an expensive exercise, and this was a major consideration. Costs included not only the expenses of the legal and parliamentary process, with payments due to commissioners, surveyors and clerks, but also the practical costs of fencing, roads, drains, grass seed and agricultural losses during the actual process. Even new buildings might be necessary, as enclosure was often accompanied by a move of farms from the centre of a settlement out into the fields so that it sat central to the new allotment of land. So the enclosures of the late eighteenth and early nineteenth centuries saw changes to the landscape and to the shapes of villages. In 1780, in Stratton Audley, Christ Church's tenant, Charles Arnold, wrote to explain that he had built new farmhouses as a consequence of the enclosure and wished to pull down those he no longer needed. The same happened in South Stoke, but this had to some extent been visible earlier. In Hillesden, for example, the settlement, which had been a single, if long and straggly, village, had been divided into four small hamlets with farms scattered throughout the fields.

Parliamentary enclosure was not entirely new; some seventeenth-century enclosures were enacted, the first being that of Radipole (Dorset) in 1604, but from about 1730 right through to the end of the nineteenth century this became the conventional and commonplace means to enclose.[114] The peaks were between 1760 and 1779 and then from 1790 to 1819, with 85 per cent of all parliamentary enclosure on the statute book by 1830 and nearly half of that taking place during the years of the Napoleonic Wars. Only Oxfordshire and Cambridgeshire saw a significant amount after that date, largely owing to the slowness of the colleges to respond to the changes that had pushed improvement elsewhere.[115] The two periods of parliamentary enclosure were not the same, however. The earlier enacted enclosures were in a similar band of counties that had been most affected in the sixteenth and seventeenth centuries – across the Midlands and into Lincolnshire and lower-lying Yorkshire – while the later activity tended to deal with more marginal land. It was never quite that simple, but, in essence, the lighter soils and wastelands were brought into cultivation during the war years much as they had been, and would continue to be, in times of need.[116]

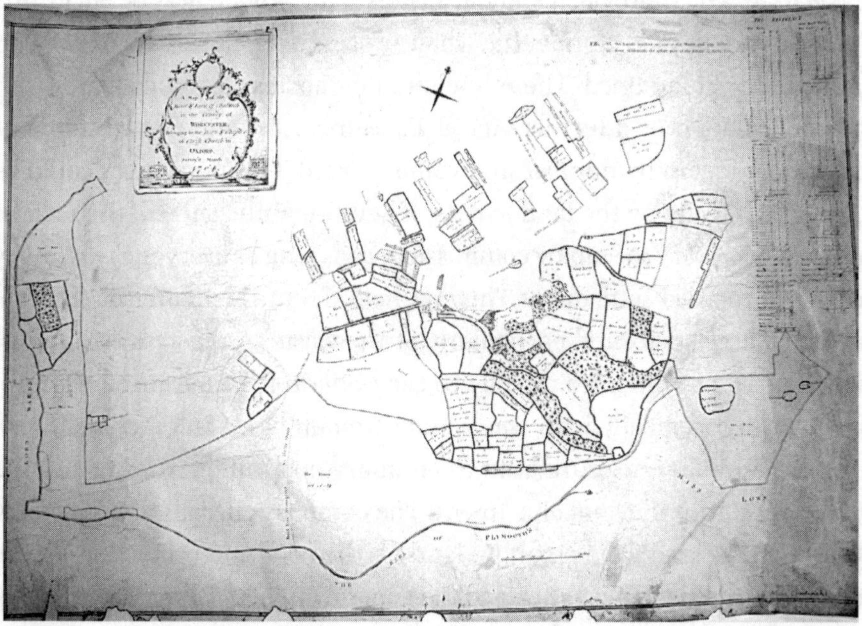

A map of Chadwick in 1764, showing the changes brought about by enclosure in the parish.

The Inclosure Act of 1773 attempted to bypass the expense of enclosure and still improve cultivation by enacting that 'where there are open or common field lands, all the Tillage or Arable lands lying in the said open or common fields shall be ordered, fenced, cultivated, or improved in such manner as three-fourths in number and value of the occupiers shall agree, with consent of the owner and tithe owner'. The Act was not particularly successful in its aims, but at least it laid down in statute the need for majority approval of the scheme, something that had easily been overridden in the past by those who owned the most. The Board of Agriculture, founded in 1793 with the express aim of encouraging improvements in farming, continued mulling over the issues, being particularly concerned about the improvement of waste land and the provision of assistance for the poorer members of a community in the form of larger gardens, access to common land and exemption from the costs of enclosing.[117] In 1801 a further Act was passed which provided standard clauses for private acts of enclosure, but it was not until 1836 that the whole process of enclosure by Act of Parliament was streamlined. The Act allowed for enclosure to take place with the confirmation of a further Act of Parliament as long as two-thirds of proprietors (again by number and value) agreed. Commissioners could be appointed directly by the landowners. If seven-eighths agreed, then it was not even necessary to employ commissioners as long as everyone was happy with the proposed settlement. This Act helped, but the matter of cost still hindered large enclosure, particularly of the waste. A report was commissioned in 1844 which led directly to the General Enclosure Act of 1845, which dealt specifically with waste and common land. This Act laid down the procedure for enclosure from the primary application, through all the local meetings to the final enactment. The commissioner also had say over issues such as land for recreation, land for the poor and protection for the rights of the lord of the manor and the general public.[118]

Christ Church's administrative records are riddled with notices of enclosure during the eighteenth and nineteenth centuries. Once commissioners were involved, and permission from all landowners became a requirement, it was no longer possible for such major changes to take place without consultation. At Christ Church there appear to have been only a small number of enclosures that affected their land in the first phase. Just three are mentioned in the Chapter Books: that of Bledington, Butlers Marston and East Garston.[119] The Bill for 'Dividing and Inclosing certain Open and Common Fields, Common Meadows, and other Commonable Lands and Waste Grounds, in the Parish of Bleddington, in the County of Gloucestershire' was presented in 1768. The glebe land – Christ Church's property as rector – was surveyed and found to include the parsonage house with its appurtenant buildings and the tithes from 48½ yardlands, the value of which amounted to £161 3s. 6d. In addition, there were moduses (local variations on the usual tithes) which included an additional 2d. on every milked cow and 5 farthings on every dry cow. Christ Church's surveyor thought that the common land, of about 200 acres, should remain intact if enclosure took place. The enclosure award (the final settlement) was made in December

1769, with Christ Church being allotted just over 340 acres with a new valuation of £245 10s. 5¼d.[120]

In 1768 Lord Cadogan applied for permission to extinguish common rights in his tenanted woods in Caversham, and in a very short period of time seals were attached to the enclosure bills for East Garston, Butlers Marston, Stratton Audley and Little Compton. Trees were purchased from the University to fence the new enclosure in Bledington.[121] Although Christ Church rarely initiated enclosure, as we have seen, there were still matters to be dealt with. In Badby the bishop of Peterborough objected to the Chapter's agreement that the vicar could grant leases for the new allotments created by the enclosure. The issue was really over the increase in income to the vicar, which was to treble. There were disputes between all the parties over the allotment of land in lieu of tithes, but just nine days after the complaint the Dean poured oil on troubled waters and on 18 March 1779 the bishop acquiesced.[122] In Tetsworth (Gloucestershire) the vicar was thanked for his support to the Chapter in a dispute with Lord Ducie, one of the neighbouring landlords.[123] Not least, estates had to be valued so that the Chapter could be certain of receiving their fair share in the re-allotment of land in a parish planning enclosure.

Not all enclosure was quick and painless, even by Act. In 1829 the proprietors of the open fields in Benson, Berrick and Ewelme (Oxfordshire), where Christ Church was rector, protested that Thomas Newton, Christ Church's tenant and the owner of considerable property in the area, had been trying to force through the enclosure for thirty years.[124] Certainly, all through the last years of the eighteenth century there were numerous valuations and surveys, including one by the king's surveyor, Richard Davis, in 1789.[125] Davis's estimate for the survey, which included making a map and compiling reference books and a terrier, came to £207 18s.[126] Joseph Glaspole, Christ Church's tenant, made an offer for the rectory on behalf of a Miss Boote, apparently another freeholder in Benson, of 5,000 guineas. The Dean and Chapter refused the offer.[127] Enclosure, though, was already being whispered about, and the tithe-holders were concerned about their potential loss of income if the land were laid to pasture. The contribution would only be small tithes, due to the incumbent, rather than great tithes, due to the rector. In the early years of the nineteenth century it would seem that some of the locals began to push for enclosure, and to offer the Dean and Chapter commutation, but around 1820 Newton took on the Christ Church lease in addition to his own freehold property. Almost immediately he defaulted on his entry fine. He said that his own tenants were grumbling about the size of the tithe, that some were already two or three years in arrears and that agricultural produce was falling in value. Chapter were less than impressed as promise after promise to pay the fine was broken.

Newton began to push harder for enclosure against the wishes of the local small farmers. The only person who had enough land to benefit was Newton, they argued, and the costs – not least of working out the bounds of the land, which were intermixed with those of neighbouring Ewelme and Berrick – would be enormous. The small proprietors would be ruined, and the plans were being driven solely by Newton's 'notorious avarice'. The vicar and the local gentry, including the lady of the manor, Lady Stapleton, were all opposed. Newton continued to agitate further, offering a commutation and to leave the land subject to tithes for those who objected. Christ Church refused to consent, so Newton tried another tack: would the Chapter remain neutral to an enclosure without commutation? The value of the tithes, he said, would rise as a result. It seemed that nothing would stop Newton in his quest; he determined to bring an enclosure Bill before the Commons advising them that he had purchased an estate that gave the appearance of a much larger interest in the parish than he actually had. His deception was uncovered, but a Bill still somehow made its way to parliament. The bishop of Oxford, also rector of Ewelme, dissented because the farmers did, not because of any conviction of his own. Next, Newton tried a bit of bribery; if an enclosure took place, and he was granted possession of the wharf on the Thames, he would increase the salary of the curate to £200. Christ Church still refused to budge, the Dean and Chapter refusing to allow the name of the college to be used to promote the enclosure. Besides, the man was still defaulting on his rent and fines.

In November 1830 a notice appeared in *Jackson's Oxford Journal* announcing that Newton would be making a third application for a Bill.

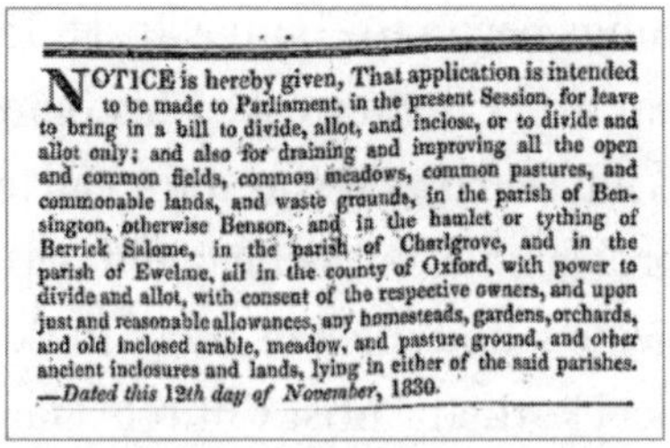

NOTICE is hereby given, That application is intended to be made to Parliament, in the present Session, for leave to bring in a bill to divide, allot, and inclose, or to divide and allot only; and also for draining and improving all the open and common fields, common meadows, common pastures, and commonable lands, and waste grounds, in the parish of Bensington, otherwise Benson, and in the hamlet or tything of Berrick Salome, in the parish of Chalgrove, and in the parish of Ewelme, all in the county of Oxford, with power to divide and allot, with consent of the respective owners, and upon just and reasonable allowances, any homesteads, gardens, orchards, and old inclosed arable, meadow, and pasture ground, and other ancient inclosures and lands, lying in either of the said parishes. —*Dated this 12th day of November*, 1830.

Advertisement in Jackson's Oxford Journal, *13 November 1830, announcing the intention to apply for a Bill to enclose the parish of Benson.*

On Sunday 21 November a crowd gathered at the church in Benson to see Newton pin up the required paper on the door. He failed to turn up, and the crowd, raised to fury, took sledgehammers to his house at Crowmarsh Battle Farm to force a guarantee that enclosure would not take place. The violence resulted that day in the breaking of Newton's barn doors and the destruction of his threshing machines. There was more the next day, when farm equipment at Ewelme was broken. The opposition to enclosure was not confined to Benson; the Swing Riots had begun in Kent earlier in 1830 in protest against enclosure and agricultural mechanisation, which were threatening pay and jobs, and tithes, which were increasingly seen as a tax on hard work. There had been protests against enclosure, both peaceful and more aggressive, for many years.[128] The men who attacked Newton's machines were soon in court, and some, apparently outsiders, were punished severely, with nine being transported and another five imprisoned; but their concerns were real. The agricultural 'improvements' of the second enclosure period were responsible for the unemployment of many farm labourers.[129]

In the meantime Newton was still not endearing himself to Christ Church. The sickness card followed the bribery; Newton announced that he had been very ill and was unable to meet with Christ Church's representative who wished to speak to him about non-payment of rent. The following year, 1833, the villagers of Benson, Ewelme and Berrick, unbowed by the punishments meted out after the riots, met together at the Crown Inn in Benson to resolve proper measures to oppose Newton's application for an enclosure Bill. Everyone there was convinced that only Newton and his son would sign.

Slowly, however, things began to change. In 1835 a new vicar arrived in Benson, and the Dean and Chapter asked his opinion of the proposed enclosure. Revd Parsons advised that it was the small proprietors in Ewelme that were causing the problem; as far as he could tell, there were only two men in Benson who objected, and most of those in Berrick were in favour. By 1838 Benjamin Badcock, then Christ Church's favoured surveyor, was attending meetings to sort out the commutation of the tithes, and deaths in the area altered the balance between the dissenters and those who were neutral. Even so, it took until 1852 for a Bill to be promoted and another eleven years for the Act to be passed and the Enclosure Award made.[130]

* * * * *

Right through from the last quarter of the eighteenth century into the later years of the nineteenth, documents for enclosure were regularly laid before Chapter for sealing.[131] But it was not just for enclosure that professional surveyors were now far more regularly employed. Mr Gregg was paid £105 for surveying Christ Church's coal-mining estate of Midsomer Norton. The task had evidently been a difficult one; he had few authentic documents, and had met with opposition particularly from the agent of the Prince of Wales, who had also commissioned a survey of his own land in the area.[132] Richard Davis, as we have seen, was sent to Benson, where he conducted a survey of the whole parish producing a plan and two books, containing a terrier and a valuation. The books were beautifully produced with titles highlighted in gold, and technically unusual, using decimal fractions for both acreages and shillings.[133] Davis also went to Helsthorpe (Buckinghamshire), Ravensthorpe (Northamptonshire), Brize Norton and Binsey (Oxfordshire), and Offenham (Worcestershire). John Dugmore was sent to Norfolk to assess all the college estates there, and a local man from Bideford – Lawrence Pridham – was commissioned to survey Great Torrington.[134] The experience of the two men could not have been more different: Dugmore surveyed Upton (Norfolk) in March 1798, enclosure was suggested in August and the Bill was read for the first time in February 1799. Pridham, on the other hand, had a terrible time, squashed between the rock of the Dean and Chapter and the hard place of the college's principal tenant, Lord Rolle. The farmers were unwilling to let him near their land, fearing increased rents, and Rolle, in spite of pestering for a renewal of his lease, did not want the goodwill between him and his leaseholders disturbed.[135]

In 1772 an extensive examination of the estate at Stratton Audley was conducted by William Chapman. It recorded not just the glebe land, in which Christ Church was most interested, but the whole parish, revealing that a tiny portion had been enclosed in the sixteenth century but otherwise nearly all cultivation was still in open fields.[136] The survey gives a rare insight into the crops grown on an estate (wheat, beans and barley) and in what quantities, how much common there was and how much meadow.[137] The common (open) fields, called The Clays and Stone Fields, extended over 1,039 acres, and references to fallow and stubble suggest that a system of rotation was commonly practised. Chapman examined the draft articles of agreement too and confirmed that the portion allocated to the Dean and Chapter's tenant – three-twentieths – was fair, provided that the land was of a decent quality.[138] This may have been a preliminary to enclosure, which took place in 1780. Here, though, only four tenants were involved – only one of whom was actually resident in the village – so a private agreement was reached.[139] Sir John Borlase Warren, Richard Arnold (Christ Church's tenant) and another landowner, Joseph Bullock of Caversfield (there in his own right and as a representative of the vicar of Caversfield), thrashed out a draft agreement.[140] It is evident that some enclosure had already taken place, at least of the area called Mawmore and other meadow and grazing land. The arable land was still, by all accounts, in open fields.[141] Of the 2,000 acres in the parish, 919 were in arable strips, 740 acres were common pasture, 50 common meadow and 300 acres enclosed meadow. Chapman reported that the proposed allotment to Christ Church – 217 acres in place of its land in the parish and 251 acres in lieu of tithes – seemed fair as long as the quality of the land was good.[142] Dairy farming became the principal activity after the enclosure was carried through, and remained so even with an increase in arable farming during the World Wars.[143]

Arnold immediately set to making the new farm functional and convenient. He had already built two farmhouses with all the associated structures by the time he wrote to the Dean and Chapter in 1794 requesting permission to take down the White Hart public house, the old tithe barn and most of the malthouse so that he could build a cowhouse and stables. He also wanted to make improvements to the parsonage house, which he said was the only property on the estate fit for a family residence. Chapter agreed to the changes.[144]

* * * * *

Maps, too, became far more commonplace, produced by professional surveyors and cartographers. The map of Butlers Marston (Warwickshire) was made specifically for the enclosure of the parish; that for Chadwick (Worcestershire) records the effects of the enclosure showing change and rationalisation of land ownership, defining which pieces of land paid tithes and which were tithe-free, and placed all glebe land in identifiable parcels.

5

From tillage to towns: Christ Church's urban estates

Although most of Christ Church's endowment was rural, there were a number of properties that were already urban or suburban at the time of the foundation and others that would become urban with the massive expansion of towns in the nineteenth century. In some cases the Dean and Chapter, and later the Governing Body, were active in this development; in others their involvement was more passive as towns and cities grew.

In Oxford, of course, there were houses and halls throughout the city in every parish. Some were residential houses and some commercial, including inns and shops, but most were a combination of the two. Many were leased to University men, such as Gerard Langbaine, dramatic cataloguer and son of the provost of Queen's College, who leased a house and shop in All Saints parish on the High Street.[1] Other properties were leased directly to colleges and were often later sold to those colleges so that holdings within the city could be consolidated, such as the string of shops with residential accommodation behind in Market Street (then Cheyney Lane) to Jesus College.[2] Benjamin Badcock's map – drawn before the Estates Act, which permitted sale of foundation property, was passed – marks Chapter property as it was in 1829; but already, with legislation such as the Oxford Mileways Act of 1771, which allowed the improvement of roads in the city, particularly Broad Street and the High, some property had been sold.[3] On the other side of town, in 1881, a strip of land was sold to allow the widening of Magdalen Bridge to make room for tram lines.

The earliest map or plan in Christ Church's archive shows Oxford Castle with the Norman motte and bailey. The site, with the chapel of St George in the castle, had been granted to Christ Church at the foundation, with all the properties that had been built around the outside of the walls. The 'Great Suite' between the Dean and Chapter and the City of Oxford was over the ownership of houses and a mill built by the City in Warham Bank (now Fisher Row). The Chapter, concerned at potential loss of revenue, appealed to the Lord Chancellor, but the City countered with the argument that Warham Bank was not as long as Christ Church claimed, and that the new houses were on City land.

The formal enquiry before Chancery commissioners began on 8 April 1617 at the Star Inn on Cornmarket in Oxford.[4] Commissioners John Dormer and George Carleton called numerous witnesses, beginning with those who gave evidence for the Dean and Chapter. Christ Church's problem was to produce witnesses who could testify to encroachments on its property which had taken place as much as forty years earlier. The first two had no local knowledge at all but were 'expert witnesses', retired soldiers who had served on the continent: Timothy Chamberlaine and John Swayne. Both these men described castles that they had seen on their travels; if Oxford Castle was the same as these then there was, they asserted, no question that the land in dispute belonged to Christ Church. Next, the Dean and Chapter relied on the evidence of two venerable Oxford residents. John Woodson, eighty-two years old, recalled the tenancies of the various properties on Warham Bank; all, he said, belonged to the Dean and Chapter, but he recounted, not very helpfully to Christ Church, that it was the mayor and alderman who had rebuilt and repaired the properties when they had fallen down. Margaret Moore, who was allegedly 109, said that she thought the properties once belonged to Oseney Abbey (and thus to Christ Church), but she too told of the mayor's rebuilding. Although the Dean and Chapter produced younger and more active witnesses, much of Christ Church's case depended on the words of two soldiers from out of town and two very elderly tenants who were trying to remember events from decades before.

It was not until July that the City had a chance to put its case before the Chancery Commissioners. Benjamin Gamon (labourer), William Farr and John Cook (fishermen), Roger Moore (painter), William Cakebread (tailor) and William Inglesby (glover) all gave very precise information about the properties in question. The Attorney-General's summing up seemed to confirm the adage that 'possession is nine-tenths of the law'; Sir Henry Yelverton ruled, on 26 October, that the new mill stream had been cut through Christ Church land but required the Dean and Chapter to grant a lease to the City, with no further argument, and that the ownership of the land on which the houses had been built must be tried at law. The final settlement was not reached until 1622, when, according to the Chapter Clerk, John Willis:

> All the advantage the College had by this tedious and Chargeable Suite was onely that of 20s per annum paid for the New Cut [...] The whole Castle Mills with the tithes are by the City now enjoyed, the three houses on Wareham Bank, and all the houses on the Castle ditch.[5]

* * * * *

Christ Church's principal estate in Oxford was in the parish of St Thomas, to the west. Until the mid-nineteenth century it was divided into two distinct areas: a small and densely populated area close to the walls of the city and the castle, and a large area of open meadow and pasture interlaced with the various streams of the River Thames. During the medieval period the area was dominated by the two monasteries of Oseney and Rewley. Most of the land belonging to those two abbeys in St Thomas's was given to Christ Church at its foundation in 1546.[6] Although Hythe Bridge Street was, from at least the thirteenth century until the eighteenth, the principal road leading west out of the city, the most developed area of the parish was a T-shape consisting of the High Street, which led from the city's west gate towards the small parish church, and a row of cottages below the castle known as Fisher Row, populated largely by bargees, brewers and fishermen, along the branch of the Thames and the castle mill stream. The area was defined by the river and then, as the Industrial Revolution took hold and more efficient means of transporting goods across country were necessary, by the canal. Oxford and the Thames were finally connected with the Midlands (at Coventry and Rugby, with connections to the Grand Union Canal), and a new wharf was opened at Hythe Bridge, in January 1790. A new bridge, a substantial stone warehouse and a canal office all serviced the wharf.

The advent of the canal, however, was to have less effect on the development of St Thomas's than the new turnpike road between Witney and Oxford, which received royal assent in two Acts of Parliament in 1767. The original plan was for the new road to follow the ancient route of Hythe Bridge Street, but a petition proposed, and its suggestion approved, that it would be far better if the new road formed an extension of one of the main streets (Queen Street, or Butcher Row) leading out from the centre of the city rather than Hythe Bridge Street, which led to the north gate. The New Road, or Park End Street as it cut through St Thomas's parish, was opened in about 1770. For a while the two streets out of town developed together, but there were significant differences. Hythe Bridge Street was poorer and more industrial, occupied by builders' yards and small businesses focused on the river trade. By the time of the 1851 census the street was full of labourers, some working locally, others still employed on the canal or by the canal owners. By the middle of the nineteenth century Hythe Bridge Street was in a poor state, and the local board put it to the Dean and Chapter that something ought to be done to improve this entrance into the city by widening and properly paving the road. By 1869 building leases had been granted for the construction of new properties and an hotel at the west end.

Park End Street, on the other hand, dominated by the Hollybush coaching inn at the western end and the Park End Wharf at the city end alongside the canal terminus receiving, storing and trading in a huge variety of goods, began its rise as the 'street of wheels'. Throughout the nineteenth century the south side of Park End Street filled with large breweries using all the new technologies, and an immense and modern furniture repository constructed using the latest steel-frame methods. The other, north side of the street started differently. New residential properties were built in the

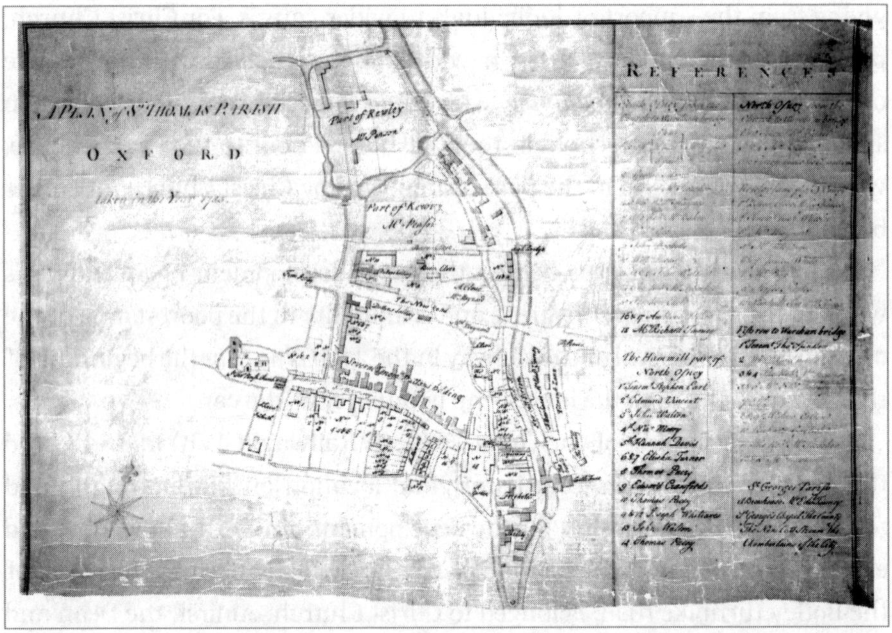

St Thomas's parish in Oxford in 1785, soon after the New Road was built but before redevelopment of this west end of the city began.

late eighteenth century which, by the beginning of the nineteenth, were developed and altered into small businesses, including a confectioner, a hairdresser, a tailor, a bootmaker, a fishmonger, a fruiterer, a saddler, a bicycle maker, a chemist and, for all the new residents and workers, refreshment rooms.

At the same time Christ Church was fulfilling its responsibilities in other parts of the parish. Concerns over health and sanitation had persuaded the Dean and Chapter to demolish six properties in Fisher Row, for example, in the late 1830s and rebuild them at the level of the road to make them drier. Later in the century, the Model Dwellings in the Hamel, a small area off St Thomas's High Street, were commissioned. The property was a three-storey block of thirty tenements, built in polychrome brick with slate roofs, with open staircases for better ventilation and with an enclosed drying yard-cum-playground, and indoor sanitation. The construction of the Model Dwellings demonstrates a very Victorian change in the emphasis of charitable giving from the support of individuals to wider causes. For Christ Church, particularly, the building of the new dwellings coincided with the closure of the Christ Church almshouse, which had housed twenty-four poor men since 1525.[7] The new school in the parish, next door to the vicar's house, was just one of several in the parish supported by Christ Church and other benefactors.

However, the impetus behind the rapid development of St Thomas's was not just concern over hygiene and criminality in the poorest area of the city, but also the arrival of the railway in the 1840s and, at the beginning of the twentieth century, the increasing popularity of the car.

With the coming of the Great Western Railway (GWR) in 1843, and the move of the station from its original location on Marlborough Road to Rewley, the stage was set for the development of the rural meadowland either side of the new track. Much of this land, particularly to the south of the Botley turnpike road, belonged to Christ Church. At first, the Dean and Chapter benefited from the sale of land to the two railway companies: 11½ acres to the GWR in the 1840s followed by another 9 some years later, and 12 acres, valued at £12,355, to the London and North Western Railway (LNWR). Christ Church was, however, slow to respond to the sudden urgent need for housing. G. P. Hester, the town clerk, presumably with a little insider information, was quicker off the mark, purchasing Osney Island (just outside Christ Church's land) in 1851, just as the LNWR station opened. Within a decade, 795 people were living on the Island in 141 houses.[8]

Among the principal reasons for Christ Church's reluctance to build was that the area's historic shabbiness and poverty, its semi-industrial working-class nature and its proximity to all forms of transport would inform its development. The last thing the Dean and Chapter wanted was to be held responsible for creating a slum. Unlike St John's College, with its fashionable expansion north of the city, Christ Church was concerned that a low-class estate would not hold its reversionary value.[9] But, having seen Hester's success, by the mid-1860s the Chapter had succumbed and had allocated land to the west of the railway for artisan housing and light industrial development. Mill Street and its side-roads were the first to be constructed, followed in the next decade by Cripley and Abbey roads. New buildings were also constructed along Hythe Bridge Street.

Another difficulty faced by the colleges was the permitted length of leases. They were still bound by the Ecclesiastical Leases Act of 1572, which permitted nothing longer than forty years. Builders were reluctant to take on building leases of a such a short length as there was little hope of recouping the costs of construction. Those that did sign such a document often built cheaply. One solution was to apply for a private Act of Parliament to permit leases of ninety-nine years. Christ Church had done this in 1851 when it wished to build on its valuable estate in Kentish Town, and St John's College followed suit in 1855. For a poorer estate, though, the costs of an Act were not worthwhile. However, in 1858, the Universities and Colleges Estates Act was passed, which released these bodies from the Elizabethan restrictions, permitting longer leases and the sale of endowment property.[10] Christ Church opted for a standard term of eighty years. Other than outright sale, building leases were an obvious and relatively easy way for a landowner to develop property. By taking a low ground rent for a given period, the landowner passed on the risk of development while hoping for a good return on rack-rented houses – with the quality of the houses stipulated clearly – at the reversion of the lease.

One other obvious effect of the railway was a sudden proliferation of hotels, inns and lodging houses. The Chapter (after 1867, the Governing Body) were reluctant to sanction the building of many new pubs (and most leases made it a condition that none of the new-build properties should be such), but they did promote hotels, both existing and new.

By the beginning of the twentieth century the age of the river and canal was past. Road traffic was increasing, and the bridge over the river had been lowered and widened, effectively stopping all vessels from proceeding down-river. The use of the canal had almost ceased too, and in 1954 the basin was filled in and the site set aside for the construction of Nuffield College. The medieval cottages that had lined the banks – sold by Christ Church to Morrell's brewery in 1898 – were pulled down. Cars and buses became the dominant forms of transport, with Christ Church approving the

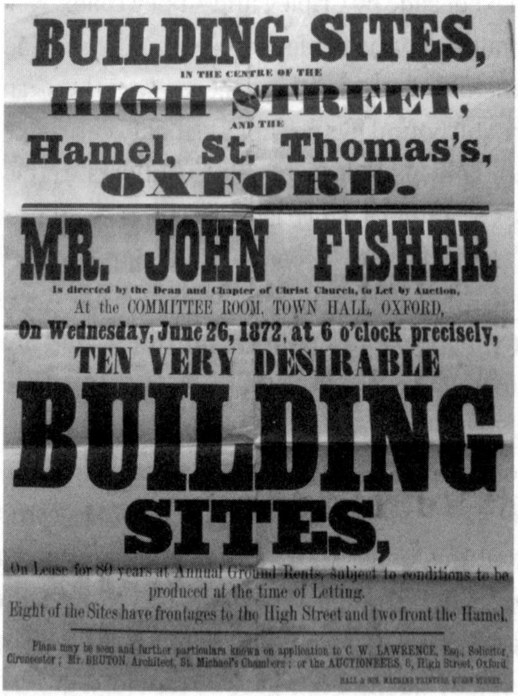

A poster advertising the sale of building plots in St Thomas's parish in Oxford in 1872. There had been cottages in this area for centuries, but the arrival of the railway had opened the city authority's eyes to the slum nature of the area. Redevelopment became an important issue.

construction of new motor showrooms and workshops on a newly widened Park End Street, alongside shops, hotels and apartments, all in the elegant Art Deco style.[11]

The leases of properties in Mill Street, Abbey Road and Cripley Road houses began to revert to Christ Church in the 1950s and 1960s, and there was some controversy in the newspapers about the sudden 'windfall' that was landing in Christ Church's hands. Within the Governing Body there was much discussion about how to manage the properties, many of which required considerable modernisation, if not serious repair. Some of the properties were sold almost immediately, others retained, with many of the residential houses in St Thomas's rented to college staff on short leases. Over the years, particularly in the 1980s and 1990s, much (but not all) of the St Thomas's estate – developed in the later nineteenth century – has been sold.

* * * * *

Another major urban development was in Kentish Town. Christ Church was bequeathed part of the manor of St Pancras by Canon Robert South in 1714. In 1795 Thomas Gregg – who seems to have been travelling backwards and forwards between Somerset and Middlesex with some regularity – described the Kentish Town estate as an old farmhouse, a large barn with stables, a smaller barn, sheds and an old slaughterhouse which had been converted into five small dwellings of two rooms apiece. It was a dairy farm, but the tenant, William Morgan – whose family had been farming in the area possibly from the seventeenth century – was anxious to get permission to increase his income from the hay produced in his meadows, which he would take to London, returning with dung to spread on his fields. He was too far from London, he said, to make any profit from milk, and he frequently requested abatement of his rent. Gregg was cautious; he advised the Chapter that building was already on the increase in the area and felt that a renewed lease longer than seven years would be a mistake. Presumably he saw that land prices in the area might begin to rise in spite of the difficulties with water supply. He wanted time to see whether development would continue apace or whether the speculators were pushing their luck just a bit too far. A short, seven-year lease would allow him to assess the situation.[12] It seems that Gregg was correct: seven years later Morgan returned to Christ Church for another renewal, offering a small increase in rent but requesting some advice in a boundary dispute with a neighbour who was marking out his property for building.[13] New roads appeared around the farm, and as early as 1804 the estate was beginning to look like a rural island in the burgeoning townscape, with just a few houses built in one corner fronting Old Chapel Row.[14] The building boom continued, and the Christ Church estate was soon targeted as an abundant source of gravel, which was coveted by the trustees of the Archway and Turnpike Road, who were working on improving road links out of London to the north.[15] Morgan was less than happy;

he depended on the hay production and sale to pay his rent, but more and more of his land was being taken by the gravel diggers. The farmer appealed, repeatedly and unsuccessfully, for a reduction in his rent.[16] In 1821 he tried yet again; the rates had gone up and the price of hay had dropped. Christ Church's agent and surveyor, now Richard Crabtree, maintained that the rent was still manageable at £260 per annum; he valued the estate at £276 18s., suggesting that the land could be let out as market gardens.[17] By this time Christ Church was letting the estate on an annual basis and Morgan felt no obligation to undertake repairs; consequently the buildings were becoming increasingly dilapidated. By 1831 Morgan was defaulting on the rent and, although Crabtree suggested a small reduction, the farmer decided not to renew after holding the estate for fifty-eight years.[18] The 42 acres were to be advertised in *The Times* in November, but Crabtree found a tenant, a London butcher by the thoroughly appropriate name of Giles Silverside, who would pay the £260 that Crabtree had thought was fair. But Silverside was no fool; he offered to take the property on a full repairing lease (fire and tempest excluded) as long as the Dean and Chapter brought the premises up to scratch during 1832 and put a fence around the whole property. Christ Church reserved the right to take in hand the road-side frontage to allow for building leases in future, and either party could determine the lease after seven or fourteen years.[19]

The correspondence of 1831 suggested that the prospect of building on Christ Church's Kentish Town estate was some years off, but there were some plans in place by November 1833; even before then, while discussions were taking place concerning the restoration of the farm, there are hints that some buildings were not considered worth much expenditure. One structure on the road frontage was to be demolished after the college's builder decided, conveniently, that it did not warrant repair. The plans for this part of the farm included elegant houses on plots 120 feet long and 20 feet wide, set back 30 feet from the road. The total projected annual income from the building leases was £354, with the houses themselves worth between £700 and £800 each year.[20]

It would appear that nothing came of these plans, but from 1842 there was renewed competition for building leases, in conjunction with an appeal for a new church in the area to accommodate the rising population.[21] A new church would also encourage the 'best' tenants. The Dean and Chapter were conscious that the Kentish Town property was a trust estate, and, as such, they could only use the profits from the estate for the purposes laid down in the trust; but, as trustees, it was their duty to maximise the income. If a church would allow higher rents, then they would contribute.[22]

By 1849 the principal farmhouse was still in place, but three-quarters of the land was occupied by new streets – Gaisford Street, Islip Street, Hammond Street, Caversham Road, Aldrich Street and Wolsey Mews – arranged within the old farm boundary.[23] Access to the new development was a bone of contention between the Christ Church developers and the surrounding landowners, but offers of co-operation over the site of a new school and the construction of a new church eased the way, particularly with the Marquess of Camden, who was evidently uncomfortable with the idea of a link between his development and that of Christ Church.[24] Through the 1850s discussions were in place for further development, and in the summer of 1859 a memorandum was issued to the Governing Body explaining how the building would progress, including the construction of a new church at the apex of the estate.

The idea that Christ Church was participating in the gentrification of the area was short-lived (the other side of the Kentish Town Road, developed by the Earls of Southampton, was already thought rather downmarket), although the archive is quiet on this.[25] Much of the building appears to have been speculative and poor. In 1859 one terrace of houses in Gaisford Street apparently collapsed before it was even completed.[26]

The plans were then thrown into disarray when the railway arrived. On 28 February 1863 C. W. Lawrence, Christ Church's solicitor, wrote to the Treasurer that he had managed to obtain satisfactory terms from the Midland Railway Company, whose new line from Bedford into London was to run straight through Kentish Town and chop the Christ Church property neatly in half.[27] Did the Dean and Chapter know in advance that this was to happen, and allow building to continue, anticipating higher compensation for houses than for undeveloped land? Again, there is no evidence either way.

A rival railway company, the Metropolitan, had also proposed bringing a line across the development, and to take land for a coal depot. Christ Church vehemently opposed this second line, which had the potential to completely annihilate the estate.[28] In the end the Metropolitan extension came to nothing, and the estate was completed around the path of the Midland. Peckwater Street was constructed parallel to Islip Street, and Oseney Crescent – with the new church of St Luke's, funded by the compensation from the railway company – was linked to the neighbouring development by Busby Place.[29]

In a matter of thirty years Christ Church had gone from being landlord of one small farm on the outskirts of London to owner of more than 500 individual properties, albeit on long building leases.[30] Although the Midland Railway was carefully constructed to have a minimal effect on the residential estate, it had an immediate effect on the quality of tenant in the area. For a short while the properties had been considered to be quite upmarket, but by 1871 more than half of the houses were shared with extended families or took in lodgers.[31] A letter of 1865 describes the tenants: Wolsey Terrace and Kentish Town Road properties were let to 'respectable tradesmen' at rents of around £65; houses on Frideswide Place, at rents of £30, were occupied by city clerks; Islip Street and Gaisford Street, a little more expensive, had respectable inhabitants; but Peckwater and Hammond streets, at rents of only £25 to £33, were for poorer people who often took in lodgers.[32] Residents there included 'better-class mechanics' and some city clerks, but all had sufficient means 'in proportion to their lot in life'. A second letter, just a month later, suggested that this might have been wishful thinking; some properties in Peckwater Street were occupied by three or four families.[33] Caversham Road was the best street, with houses let for as much as £75 per year to solicitors, gentlemen and large tradesmen.

The use of some properties changed. On Wolsey Mews, for example, the stables and coach houses for the shops on Kentish Town Road were no longer needed by those premises and had been leased out to cab proprietors.

Christ Church's Kentish Town estate, originally a single small farm, had become, by the middle of the nineteenth century, a bustling suburb of London, with rapidly expanding shops (such as those shown here, c.1900) and a variety of residences.

In 1893 it was noted that the stone arches at either end of the road, presumably now a hindrance to the new tenants and damaged by the traffic, were on the verge of demolition. An appeal to the Dean and Chapter was made to save at least part of the stonework, as the responsibility for the arches fell to none of the lessees.[34] As shopping habits and fashions changed, so permission was sought to alter premises, particularly those on the main street. Norris & Son, who ran a drapery business at 250–252 Kentish Town Road, asked to make openings in the party walls so that they could make the two properties into one establishment, and to change the mews at the back of their premises to extend their workshops and storerooms. The Treasurer was advised that 'It is quite the order of the day now, to unite in one general establishment several trades, and these larger establishments, by giving greater choice and convenience to their customers, and reducing staff and establishment charges, seem to succeed better than the smaller and ordinary shops confined more strictly to one trade'.[35] Three years later the same company, now Norris & Beal, requested permission to make the same alterations in the neighbouring shops (at numbers 246 and 248). A few months later, another company, Speight & Co., boot- and shoemakers, followed suit. Christ Church's agent, Mr Bedells, recommended approval. Although there would be no immediate benefit to the college, the value of the reversions would improve.[36] Around the same time, the Midland Railway purchased property in Oseney Crescent to allow for an extension to the line.[37]

Managing a large urban development was, in some ways, exactly the same as administering the agricultural estate; the Governing Body in Oxford oversaw the signing of leases, gave permission for alterations and donated to churches and schools. In other ways it was completely different. The removal of forecourts along Kentish Town Road, so that the London County Council could widen the street, caused considerable debate in 1900. The private forecourts were used by many of the tradesmen to display their wares, and many included ventilators, which improved conditions in the properties. Clement Upperton, Christ Church's solicitor, proposed a clause in the Council's Bill to leave the ventilators undisturbed.[38] The Governing Body immediately submitted a claim for the reversionary value of the right to use the forecourts for display, and £1140 was put forward as a reasonable figure. The Council countered with an offer of £384, which must have been met with derision in Oxford. A revised figure of £700 was accepted (the solicitor admitting that the reversionary value forty years later could only be speculative), and so conveyances of forecourts along a considerable stretch of the road were sealed in 1903.[39]

A bigger problem was the digging of the Hampstead Tube by the Charing Cross, Euston and Hampstead Railway Company. The underground line had been on the cards since the passing of the enabling Act in 1893, but it was not until 1903 that finances were in place and work could begin seriously. The railway caused a general hue and cry over fears of the damage it might cause to Hampstead Heath, but Christ Church was concerned more about the potential risk to forty-one of its houses. The Governing Body, on the advice of Clement Upperton, commissioned a set of photographs 'so that we may have evidence if necessary hereafter of the state the premises were in before the Tube was made'.[40] In 1904 the lawyer counselled Christ Church to accept the £662 offer by the railway company (substantially less than the £1,033 demanded) as he was of the opinion that any arbitrator would come down on the side of the railway. In 1905 an easement and conveyance was granted by the Governing Body for the subsoil.[41]

One application that seemed completely to throw Grafton Bedells, Christ Church's agent in London, was for the adaptation of two properties to create a 'biograph theatre'. He asked Upperton for guidance; retail business in Kentish Town Road was not in a good state at the time (1909), and he evidently wondered whether the cinema could kick-start trade again. In any case, a considerable amount of money would be spent on the premises by the lessee, which could only be a good thing.[42] The Gaisford Street Cinema was opened in 1910.[43]

After the First World War, a number of houses on Peckwater and Islip streets were purchased by St Pancras Borough Council, but otherwise (apart from the small number of properties purchased for the construction of the Midland Railway) the estate remained as it had been since its development. The Governing Body had expended some sums in repairing war damage and making more general repairs. They also commissioned new building on cleared sites, including two blocks of flats (called Wolsey House and Peckwater House, on Oseney Crescent) described as 'architect-designed and of superior construction with brick walls, tiled roofs, fire-resisting floors and metal window frames, with balconies and a pleasing front elevation'. They had perambulator lock-ups and Marley tiles throughout the interior.[44] However, in 1955, soon after the reversions had fallen in, the Governing Body decided to sell the entire estate. An auction catalogue was drawn up by the company of Jones, Lang, Wootton & Sons, consisting of thirty-eight lots, beginning with three public houses, two banks, eighteen main road shops and over 300 residential properties. The gross rent roll was £62,375 per annum.[45] The auction never took place, but the residential estate was sold to St Pancras Borough Council for just over £260,000. The commercial estate – including the shops, pubs, banks and cinema, mainly on Kentish Town Road and in Wolsey Mews (now largely back stores and lock-ups for the premises on the main road) – was retained until 1973.

There were other estates that began rural but which became urban over the years, including 21 acres in Hillingdon, allotted in lieu of tithes at enclosure in 1825, and tithe land in Harrow (both Middlesex).

Harrow, with its proximity to London, had always been a prosperous farming area, concentrating in the seventeenth and eighteenth centuries on wheat production. Christ Church's right to tithes extended across the whole parish, including the hamlets of Harrow itself, Greenhill, Preston, Kenton, Sudbury, Roxeth, Alperton, Wembley and Pinner. The tithe barns of Wembley, Alperton and Pinner were also included in the estate. The rent in 1546 was over £74, but the tenant could potentially reap ten times that, as the tithes were valued, at least by the mid-eighteenth century, at over £700.[46] From that date, there was a gradual swing from arable farming to meadow as London grew and the need for hay and meat rocketed. In 1797 over 3,500 acres of land in the Harrow district was meadow, twice the area laid down to other crops. There were discussions between all the principal landholders, as well as the Dean and Chapter as tithe-holders and rectors, concerning enclosure of the parish, with Richard Davis approved as Enclosure Commissioner.[47] In Harrow the process was reasonably quick. The preliminary discussions took place in January 1802, and the draft Bill was ready by April. It did not pass first time, partly as local variations in the payment of tithes – moduses – established for cows, sows, orchards and gardens, particularly land in front of their cottages, had not been taken into account. Amendments were proposed in February 1803 suggesting that the college be offered a corn rent in lieu of an allocation of previously 'waste' land. After three months small changes were made to the Bill, and it was soon passed. All tithes were extinguished, and Christ Church was granted 912 acres and so became one of the largest landowners in the parish. It was also awarded £1,005 in corn rents.

The transportation of hay to the metropolis was made quicker and easier once the Paddington branch of the Grand Junction Canal opened in

1801, crossing the corner of the parish. The canal also carried Londoners out of the city on pleasure trips. The turnpike road, described as 'dangerously narrow for considerable distances, confined by high banks with plantations and often houses on them, [with] many dangerous turnings almost at right angles, and [...] often impassable by the overflowing of the River Brent', was improved in 1826.[48] But, as at Kentish Town and in St Thomas's, Oxford, it was the arrival of the railway – particularly the new LNWR stations at Pinner, Harrow and Sudbury – that caused an explosion of suburban development, beginning with substantial villas but soon expanding to include smaller houses, factories and, of course, Wembley Park with its stadium and arena. Christ Church sold most of its estates in Preston, Kenton, the Weald and Roxeth between 1921 and 1933.[49]

* * * * *

Canals and railways, which had had significant effects on Christ Church's estates in Oxford and Middlesex, were to have an impact in all areas of the country. The dean and canons were not old-fashioned men and embraced new ideas rapidly, especially if there was a chance of profit. Oxford benefited economically from the arrival in 1790 of the Oxford Canal, which connected the Midlands to London via the River Thames, but the city was soon to be bypassed as the Grand Junction Canal opened in 1800 from Braunston (Northamptonshire) directly to London. However, the spread of the canal system across the country caused considerable interest, and before long Christ Church sold land in Oxford and Northamptonshire to both the Oxford and the Grand Junction canal companies, and moneys derived were often invested in government stocks. The Grand Junction Canal Company requested land for a new reservoir at Daventry, for example, offering £80 per acre for 54 acres in 1803. Christ Church's tenant, Revd William Rose, thought this was a bit stingy. He wanted £100 but would settle, he said, for £95. The agent for the canal company, a Mr Barker, was evidently persuasive for, after just a week or so of discussion, Rose settled for the original offer of £80 per acre and compensation of £800 for the mill that would be destroyed in the work.[50]

In addition to the income derived from sales, the Chapter purchased

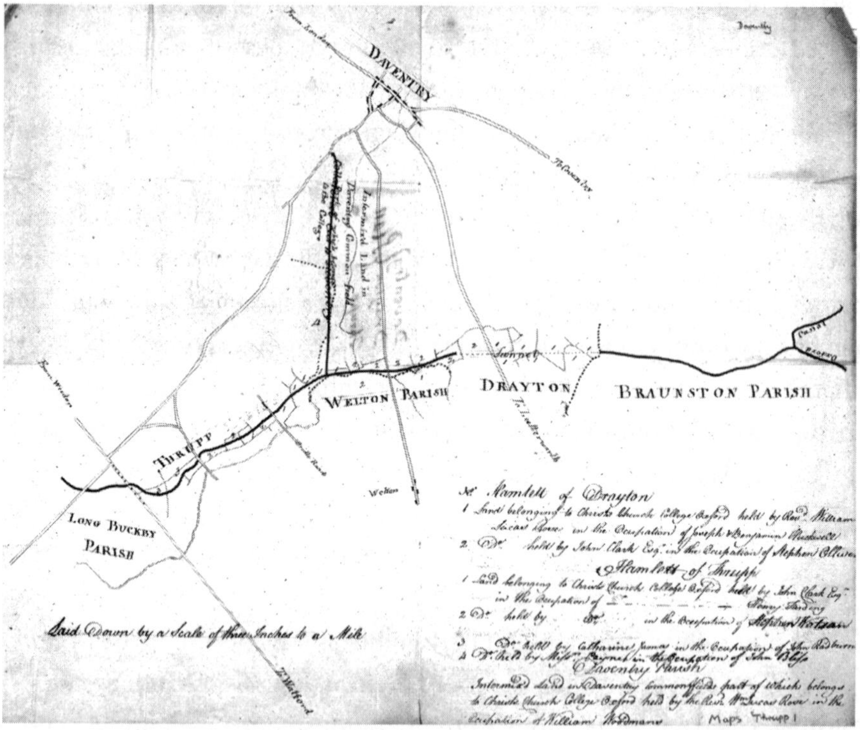

Sketch plan showing the line of the Grand Junction Canal across Christ Church land near Daventry.

shares in the canal companies, doubling the college's chance of making money in the new ventures.[51] Tenants who were ousted from lands sold were compensated accordingly; Mrs James in Thrupp was given half of the proceeds. Similar arrangements were made for tenants on land needed for the new railways that spread rapidly across the country from the 1840s. In Oxford the railway was resisted by the University for some time, largely for fear that the sudden proximity of London would have a detrimental effect on student morality, but there was also fear that estates would be damaged. In 1846 the proposed branch between Oxford and Cowley from South Hinksey would be 'injurious to Cowley, separating Church Cowley from Temple Cowley', but it would also, said the petitioners writing to the House of Commons, obstruct the flood waters in wet seasons and cause problems for the neighbourhoods. Even the proposal to connect Oxford and Cambridge by rail, something that could perhaps have been seen as a good thing, was resisted 'on the grounds that estates would be materially damaged, that there was insufficient intercourse between the two places to support a railway, and that the welfare of neither university would be improved by increased access'.[52] The Dean and Chapter declared that they were not duty-bound to renew leases for land that was likely to be acquired for railway construction, but they insisted that any moneys received for such land should be placed in the account of the Accountant General of the Court of Chancery and invested in public funds in the name of the Dean and Chapter. Any dividends were to be paid to tenants until the end of their term.[53]

* * * * *

A single house in St Sepulchre's parish, near the Old Bailey, was Christ Church's only foundation property in the City of London. Forming a small part of the original endowment, it would seem that the tenement had belonged to the Charterhouse, a Carthusian monastery from the late fourteenth century until the dissolution, just a short distance to the north. In 1525 Prior William Tymbigh leased the house to Sir John Mordaunt, courtier and royal counsellor, which suggests that it was a substantial and decent house.[54] At the time of the Great Fire in 1666, the property was leased to Richard Collins, a lawyer at the Inner Temple. The house was destroyed on the third or fourth day of the conflagration, and the following year, after the establishment of the Fire Court charged with handling issues between landlords and tenants, John Willis, the Chapter Clerk, was sent to London on behalf of the Chapter.[55] The court permitted lease extension beyond the usual forty years for an urban tenancy. Collins, who lived in York but had come down south specifically to attend to the extraordinary affairs, advised the court that he had taken on the tenancy in 1653 and he asked for an extra forty years. The court granted him thirty-five years at the same rent on the condition that he rebuild the property. The record suggests that Collins had already begun the work of reconstruction but, rather than restore the house as it was – one residential property with shops on the street frontages

– he had built nine or ten smaller houses. By 1806 a survey of the estate indicated that these had been divided up into still more smaller properties: six properties in Dean's Court, nine in Fleet Lane and four in Seacoal Lane. In 1806 they were all in good shape, but fifty years on, while in the tenancy of the Blacket family, woollen drapers of West Smithfield, the property was in a sorry state, with those houses on Fleet Lane and Dean's Court ready to be condemned. The surveyor recommended a claim for dilapidations; the proposed railway from London Bridge to Farringdon would cut through the estate, but, he advised, even if it took place, the value of the land would not be increased. Christ Church, in the throes of major constitutional reform at home and no doubt preoccupied, decided to cut their losses and sold in 1860.[56]

There were other small urban properties, including houses in Banbury (Oxfordshire) and the rents from two water mills there, which were given in compensation for deficiencies in the original endowment.[57] Three properties in Peascod Street in Windsor were given in trust in 1633, which seem to have been perpetually in a bad state of repair. In 1763 the first house, occupied by a surgeon called Heyes, was evidently on the verge of collapse, and the tenant in the next property, Dame Freeman, only made ends meet by renting out rooms to the 'lower kind of people'. The third house, leased to a carpenter called John Brown, was described as 'old and indifferent'.[58] For a short while things did improve, with new tenants who took their repairing leases seriously, but by 1843 Christ Church's agent, William Ingalton, had to ask for leniency for Mrs Ward, the tenant of one house; she lived with a schoolmaster son in Brighton whose private establishment was failing with the growth in the number of National schools. Another son was a clerk at the Bank of England but suffering with cancer of the tongue, and the third boy worked for the Post Office and was unable to provide much assistance at all.[59] It was all very sad, and a month after the appeal for consideration for Mrs Ward, one of the occupiers offered to take over the properties. He was anxious to avoid his neighbour turning the backyard into a shooting gallery! At least one of the properties was infested by rats, and the Windsor Board of Health was demanding attention to the drains.[60] Considering that the street

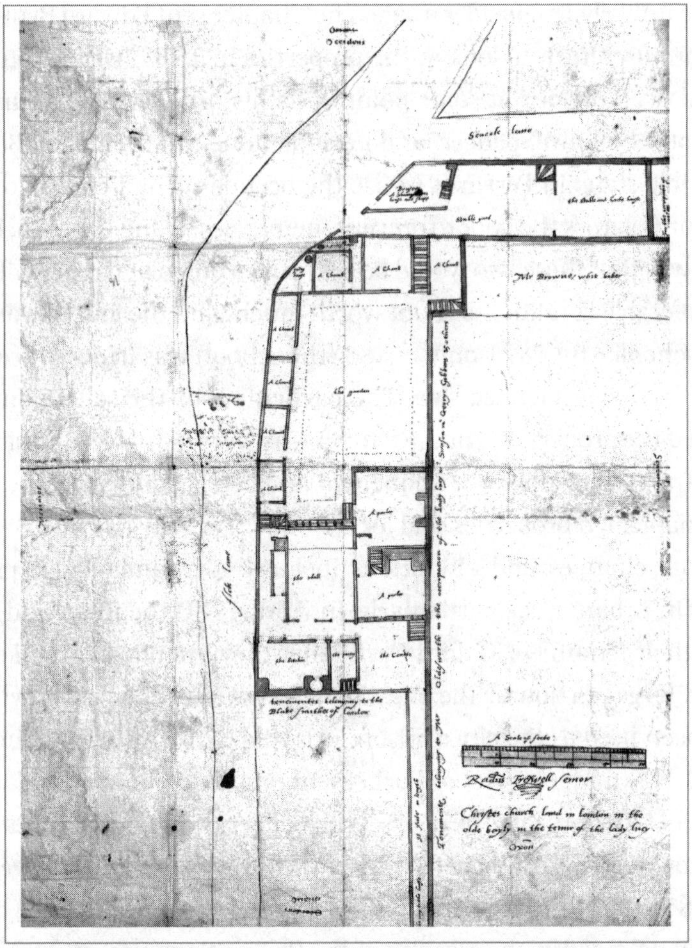

Christ Church's only foundation property in London was a single house in the parish of St Sepulchre, near the Old Bailey. This plan of the house is dated 1610, but the property was destroyed during the Great Fire of 1666 and later rebuilt as a speculative venture, not as a single residence as it had been before but as nine or ten smaller and poorer houses, probably with shops on the ground floors.

was an ancient and direct thoroughfare up to the gates of the castle, this was a sorry state of affairs.[61]

Mr Spencer, he who wished to stop the shooting gallery, asked whether the Chapter would consider selling his house, but the Treasurer replied that Christ Church was aware of the 'improvable value' of the houses and would be unlikely to consider a sale. The Chapter sent Edward Bruton, their consultant architect, to look at the properties in 1857. Of the four houses (one had been divided at some point in its history), two were leased from the Chapter by John Spencer, and he sublet one to Mr Perrins. Both were in a terrible state; in Perrins's house the occupants had even had to place loose boards across the floor to prevent themselves falling through. Bruton's opinion was that these two would be best pulled down and rebuilt. The third was in tolerable condition but not worth much, and the fourth was used as a small school.[62] By 1871 only no. 83 (the school) was in decent condition, and Bruton recommended sale. The particulars of the sale optimistically advertised the properties – nos. 80 to 83 – as 'very valuable' and situated in the 'central part of the most frequented and best Business Street'. The four rather dilapidated properties sold for £4,020.[63]

Social changes and alterations in local government also prompted changes in urban areas particularly. In April 1780 the Dean and Chapter notified their tenants of Oxford Castle that they intended to retake possession of a large portion of the site. A few years later the castle, which had always been used as the city's prison, was sold to the justices of the county for £333 10s. under an Act of Parliament passed to allow the enlargement of the gaol.[64] Technically, of course, the colleges were not permitted to sell foundation property until the passing of the Universities and Colleges Estates Act in 1858, but improvements to the city allowed the rules to be bypassed on occasions, aided by the creation of the Paving Commission established by the Oxford Mileways Act of 1771. The Commission was a joint body of city and University men and had tremendous powers to raise income through the rates to improve roads and bridges, to construct the Covered Market and deal with paving, cleansing, lighting and general city improvements.[65]

In 1786 one of the houses in St Martin's parish was sold to its tenant as part of the property was needed for road-widening.[66] The property may well have been one that Christ Church was pleased to part with: the college had few houses right in the centre, and the odd one or two, surrounded by those owned by other colleges and the city, were potentially a nuisance rather than an asset. The case of Elm Hall was an example. In 1792 a dispute arose

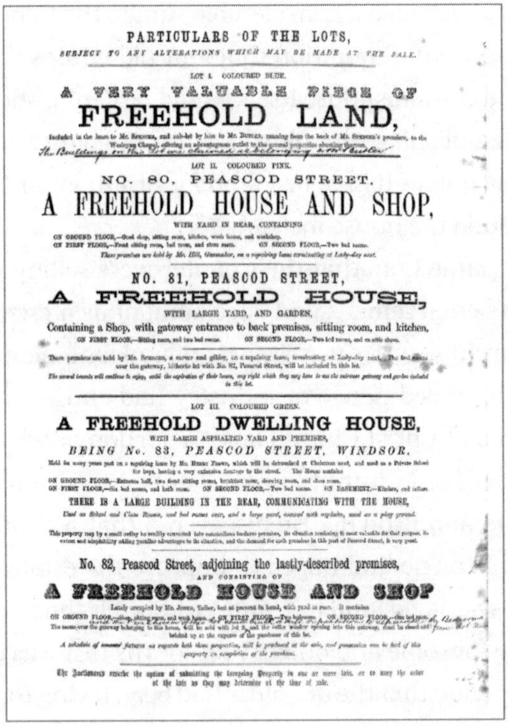

PARTICULARS OF THE LOTS,

SUBJECT TO ANY ALTERATIONS WHICH MAY BE MADE AT THE SALE.

LOT I. COLOURED BLUE.

A VERY VALUABLE PIECE OF

FREEHOLD LAND,

Included in the lease to Mr. Seymour, and sub-let by him to Mr. Butler, running from the back of Mr. Seymour's premises, to the Wesleyan Chapel, offering an advantageous outlet to the several properties abutting thereon.

LOT II. COLOURED PINK.

NO. 80, PEASCOD STREET,

A FREEHOLD HOUSE AND SHOP,

WITH YARD IN REAR, CONTAINING

ON GROUND FLOOR,—Good shop, sitting room, kitchen, wash house, and workshop.
ON FIRST FLOOR,—Front sitting room, bed room, and store room. ON SECOND FLOOR,—Two bed rooms.

These premises are held by Mr. Hill, Gunmaker, on a repairing lease terminating at Lady-day next.

NO. 81, PEASCOD STREET,

A FREEHOLD HOUSE,

WITH LARGE YARD, AND GARDEN,

Containing a Shop, with gateway entrance to back premises, sitting room, and kitchen,

ON FIRST FLOOR,—Sitting room, and two bed rooms. ON SECOND FLOOR,—Two bed rooms, and an attic above.

These premises are held by Mr. Seymour, a carver and gilder, on a repairing lease, terminating at Lady-day next. The bed rooms over the gateway, hitherto let with No. 82, Peascod Street, will be included in this lot.

The several tenants will continue to enjoy, until the expiration of their leases, any right which they may have to use the entrance gateway and garden included in this lot.

LOT III. COLOURED GREEN.

A FREEHOLD DWELLING HOUSE,

WITH LARGE ASPHALTED YARD AND PREMISES,

BEING No. 83, PEASCOD STREET, WINDSOR.

Held for many years past on a repairing lease by Mr. [illegible], which will be determined at Christmas next, and used as a Private School for boys, having a very extensive frontage to the street. The House contains

ON GROUND FLOOR,—Entrance hall, two front sitting rooms, breakfast room, drawing room, and close room.
ON FIRST FLOOR,—Six bed rooms, and bath room. ON SECOND FLOOR,—Two bed rooms. ON BASEMENT,—Kitchen, and cellars.

THERE IS A LARGE BUILDING IN THE REAR, COMMUNICATING WITH THE HOUSE,

Used as School and Class Rooms, and bed rooms over, and a large yard, covered with asphalte, used as a play ground.

This property may by a small outlay be readily converted into commodious business premises, its situation rendering it most valuable for that purpose. Its extent and adaptability adding peculiar advantages to its situation, and the demand for such premises in this part of Peascod Street, is very great.

No. 82, Peascod Street, adjoining the lastly-described premises,

AND CONSISTING OF

A FREEHOLD HOUSE AND SHOP

Lately occupied by Mr. Jones, Tailor, but at present in hand, with yard in rear. It contains

ON GROUND FLOOR,—Shop, sitting room, and wash house. ON FIRST FLOOR,—Two bedrooms. ON SECOND FLOOR,—One bed room.

The rooms over the gateway belonging to this house, will be sold with lot 2, and the cellar window opening into this gateway, must be closed and bricked up at the expense of the purchaser of this lot.

A schedule of tenants' fixtures as regards both these properties, will be produced at the sale, and possession can be had of this property on completion of the purchase.

The Auctioneers reserve the option of submitting the foregoing Property in one or more lots, or to vary the order of the lots as they may determine at the time of sale.

Sales particulars for the Dean and Chapter's houses in Windsor.

over the ownership of property: the city owned part of it and Christ Church the remainder, but which bit was whose, and how they were divided, had become confused over the years. The first recorded internal committee was set up, consisting of just three men – the sub-dean, Benjamin Blayney and Arthur Onslow – to negotiate with the city council.[67] It took just six weeks for the joint committee to come to the conclusion that there was no way to determine the division of the tenement so it made sense for Elm Hall to be sold, and for the profits to be split equally between college and city. The proceeds, £84, were invested in the 3 per cents, and the interest was added to the SIGA account,[68] along with the income from the sale of land to the Oxford Canal Company in both Fenny Compton (Warwickshire) and Oxford. It was the Paving Commission which had pointed out to Christ Church, in 1834, the poor state of its almshouse just to the south of St Aldate's church.

The Chapter had subscribed a considerable sum to the Commission's appeal to widen the street on the condition that four old houses that stood in front of the church and the almshouse itself would be demolished. It turned out, however, that demolishing the almshouse was going to be difficult, not least because new homes had to be found for its inhabitants. Christ Church undertook to rebuild the house instead.[69]

Around the same time that the Chapter were selling the castle site to Oxford City for its enlargement and development as a prison, in Worcester a compulsory purchase order was issued on land for a new workhouse. The directors of the intended house of industry had chosen, and already surveyed, a small area of Christ Church land, a portion of which was occupied by a Mr Browne.[70] Christ Church's agent, Val Vickers, went into negotiation with the directors and Browne. He discovered that a canal was to be dug on the land, and Browne had hoped to improve the estate by constructing a wharf there. It was good land too, and Vickers felt that the directors' offer of £4 4s. per acre for some and only £3 8s. for the rest was rather paltry. He was also of the opinion that the directors had been trying to play the Chapter off against their tenant by dealing with each separately. He suggested thirty-five years' purchase at £4 10s. per acre. The negotiations continued for some months over the winter of 1792–3, and the deal was eventually settled in February, when the directors paid the requested £4 10s., but only for thirty-one years' purchase. The piece of land under discussion was less than 2 acres.

* * * * *

Over the years, while Christ Church's estates remain largely agricultural, properties in towns such as Bedford, Tonbridge and Wembley have been bought and sold, and new developments on college land have expanded towns and villages such as Brize Norton (Oxfordshire) and Daventry.

6

Managing the agricultural estate III: reform

The process of enclosure began the gradual change of the sources of much of Christ Church's endowment income from the profits from rectories, tithes and manorial courts to the rental proceeds from physical land and buildings. Parliamentary enclosure often, but not always, included the exoneration of tithes by making allotments of land in lieu.

Christ Church received many tithes with the rectories given in its original endowment. Historically, these would have been 'in kind': crops, poultry, sheep, pigs and other more local produce, shared, as we have seen, between the rectorial tenant and the vicar or curate. Over time, and by the middle of the eighteenth century at the latest, most were commuted to cash, partly for convenience and partly to deal with practical difficulties: if the tithe was, for example, one lamb in ten, what happened if there were only nine lambs?

Tithe commutation

By the late eighteenth century, if not before, tithes began to be seen as anachronistic, a tax on yield that discouraged endeavour and improvement, a hindrance that damaged relationships between a community and its vicar and, as men grew rich in commerce and industry, as a tax that penalised agriculturalists. Some also saw them, particularly the great tithes, as an easy income for the tithe-owners, who grew rich at the expense of others' labour. To some extent this was justified: some livings were rich, and the owner of the rectory (or its lessee) could be very comfortably off. Others, often the curates who did the work in the parishes, were very poorly paid indeed, and many had to do more than one job, sometimes a second clerical position or, for example, teaching, in order to keep body and soul together.[1] At one meeting in 1831 of the Ashton under Lyne Reform Society, a speaker called tithes 'unjust' and 'tyrannic':

> unjust as they take from the useful and industrious part of society a tenth of the products and improvements of the land to support luxury and idleness. They are tyrannic as they are taken as a substitute for a public robbery committed by a tyrant King, who seized the land and revenues appropriated for the support of the church and distributed them among an overgrown aristocracy.[2]

The abolition of tithes was part of the discussion surrounding the Reform Act of 1832. There were arguments for keeping them, as well as the vociferous clamour against, not least over fears that this would be a step towards the disestablishment of the Church of England. Concerns over revolution were also to the fore for some years after the end of the Napoleonic Wars.[3] The same points had been raised when the University proposed lifting the requirement to subscribe to the Thirty-Nine Articles before a student could matriculate.[4] But after 1832 the case for abolition appears to have been accepted, and it was the practicalities that formed the basis for the debates over the next few years. Tithe Commutation Bills were introduced into each session of Parliament between 1833 and 1836. In the end, it was the Bill laid before the House by Lord Russell that made it through to royal assent on 13 August 1836. A new office was established, with Tithe Commissioners and an army of local assistants whose task would be to assess the average value of tithes over the previous seven years (based in equal parts on the price of wheat, barley and oats over the period). This would be converted to a money payment to be known as the tithe rent charge. While the payment was still attached to the land in some ways, it was no longer a tax on yield, so increased productivity was no longer penalised.

The Act resulted in a series of standard maps and surveys covering the whole country in order to determine how much land was titheable.[5] At Christ Church, immediately after the passing of the Act, the Dean and Chapter arranged for trusted attorneys to be sent nationwide to manage the changes and ensure that Christ Church received its dues; men such as Benjamin Badcock, a local map-maker and surveyor, who was given charge of estates across Oxfordshire and Gloucestershire.[6] The Act was probably also responsible for stimulating the employment of professional land agents more generally; Badcock was certainly used for more than just commutation business and later, from around 1878, it was the firm of Field and Castle whose expertise was utilised.[7] From January 1838 tithe commutation agreements were being laid before Chapter in a rush to get voluntary agreements – which worked much like enclosures had done – in place. After October that year the Tithe Commissioners had powers to impose compulsory commutation. It became quite a costly exercise; expenses were paid by the land- and tithe-owners.[8] In 1840 the Dean and Chapter agreed to borrow £5,000 to cover commutation expenses but no more. They were evidently optimistic, as another £2,000 was added to the pot in 1842.[9] Although a rent charge was more acceptable to landowners and tenants alike, no one had quite heard the end of tithes. There would be more trouble to come.

Beneficial leases and rack rents

If Christ Church was beginning to adopt modern methods of land management, or to accept that both tenants and the government wished it, it was in the continued use of the beneficial lease that the colleges, and Christ Church in particular, remained old-fashioned. Most landowners had been running out their beneficial leases and switching to rack-renting (that is, leases on a commercial rent) since the 1630s. By the time of the Napoleonic Wars only the Crown, the church and the universities were lagging behind. William Pitt the Younger reformed the management of the Crown estates in 1794; the church had reform forced upon it in the 1830s, but most colleges continued with the old system into the 1850s and beyond.[10]

Some changes had taken place with local Improvement Acts allowing some sales of property to allow for better roads and drainage. The Oxford

Paving Act allowed the Dean and Chapter to dispose of several houses in the city of Oxford – some to private individuals, others to colleges – in the 1770s. Using the excuse of tidying up the city, property was consolidated. Jesus College bought a house next door on Cheyney Lane (now Market Street), and Pembroke College purchased a garden that abutted their site on the west side of St Aldate's. In St Thomas's parish, houses in Fisher Row were conveyed to Edward Tawney, one of the local brewers.[11] Other property was sold under the Act for Lighting and Cleansing the Streets, various Canal Acts and the Worcester House of Industry Act. From 1802 land could be conveyed away for the redemption of land tax on other property. The sale of a few enhanced the value of others.[12]

Land Tax had been introduced in 1692 to raise funds for William III's war effort against Louis XIV and for the first five years was assessed on the actual rental values of land. In 1698 this was altered, and each county was given a fixed quota. Land Tax Commissioners and local assessors were appointed. In the 1690s the Land Tax brought in around 35 per cent of national revenue, but as the rate never varied (becoming fixed at 4 shillings in the pound in 1776), it slowly became of far less significance, dropping to 17 per cent in the 1790s, and became more inconvenient to collect than it was to pay. A Land Tax Redemption Office was established in 1798, which allowed landowners to redeem the tax and be exonerated from future taxation by paying a lump sum (the equivalent of fifteen years' tax), which would be invested in 3 per cent consols in government stock yielding an annuity exceeding the tax by 20 per cent. Not all landowners rushed to do this, but some opted to buy themselves out straight away, such as Charles Arnold, Christ Church's tenant in Stratton Audley. Other landowners sold a small piece of their estate to cover the cost of redemption, but Arnold decided that he would not reduce the farm but just pay the purchase price of the redemption outright.[13]

Christ Church sold the rectories of Caversham and Claines (Worcestershire), and the income from the money raised was to be split between the SIGA account and the fund for augmenting small livings.[14] The sums raised were, in some cases, quite substantial; the rectory of Temple Guiting

(Gloucestershire) went for nearly £9,000, and a farm in Daventry for more than £3,000.[15] But more general sales were not permitted: endowment property had been given for a specific purpose – to fund the primary function of education and, in Christ Church's case, the administration of the cathedral. Alienation of any of the original gift was forbidden in statutes in other colleges and in those of Cardinal College by which Christ Church, informally, operated.

The 1830s saw Parliament tackling not just political reform and tithe commutation but also seeking to reform church administration. Part of Earl Grey and Robert Peel's proposal was to do the same in the church as they had done with rotten boroughs: to root out all unnecessary clergy (particularly non-residentiary canons and others without a cure of souls) and to reinvest the wealth released to augment poor livings and establish new parishes in growing urban areas. Church estates, it was argued, were not being managed to their full potential. The cathedral estate of St Paul's, for example, had a potential revenue of £39,000 per annum but was actually bringing in only £14,000, and the prebendal estate was in an even worse financial position.[16] St Paul's was held up by the bishop of London, Charles Blomfield, as an example of the iniquities of mismanaged cathedral wealth, when there were slums only a short distance away which had only one church and one clergyman for every eight or ten thousand people. The reports of the Ecclesiastical Duties and Revenues Commission resulted, in 1840, in the Cathedrals Act, by which estates, and the profits from the abolished prebendaries and canonries, were handed over for administration to the Ecclesiastical Commissioners (the successor body to Queen Anne's Bounty). As usual, though, Christ Church was exempted.[17]

Another Act, in 1850, established within the Ecclesiastical Commission an Estates Committee which gave authority to manage all church estates vested with the Commission, including dealing with beneficial leases.[18] During the 1850s both Oxford and Cambridge universities appealed for similar legislation to help their positions.[19] In 1858 the Universities and Colleges Estates Act was passed, permitting the colleges to sell land, followed by another Act in 1860 which allowed the colleges to raise loans to compensate their members for the loss of fine income.[20] The Fellows of some colleges were, if not content, then ready to suffer a drop in income to allow the beneficial leases to be run out, but Christ Church was particularly reluctant and the loans were to cause considerable financial stress in the years to come. The Dean and Chapter were wary of running out the old leases, afraid that they might lose control over the income from their land, although they were conscious that rack rents would give far more stability than low rents and periodic entry fines.[21] Even so, the Act gave colleges that had been reluctant to start running out the beneficial leases another stimulus to begin. But reform was a slow process, and many colleges were only half-way through when the agricultural depression hit.[22]

At the same time as the government was working on the reform of cathedrals, a similar effort was being directed at the universities and their colleges in ways other than the administration of estates. The arguments were, in some ways, similar to those used against cathedrals: huge endowments were being used to fund large fellowships, many of which were little more than sinecures. At Christ Church, as long as a man took his Bachelor and Master degrees at the correct times, was ordained to the diaconate and remained unmarried, he could remain on the Student body, with a stipend from the endowment, for life with no duties to perform at all, at a time when the University Commissioners felt the universities and colleges should be reaching out to a wider community and poorer students.[23] Internally, at Christ Church, reform was also sought in the administration of the estates or, to be exact, in the distribution of the income from the estates. For more than a decade, between 1855 and 1867, arguments raged and reforms were discussed in Chapter meetings, in the Common Room and no doubt in corners all over college and in the cathedral. The Students' main aim was to achieve the same position in the governance of the college that their colleagues in other colleges enjoyed. Eventually, after the Christ Church Ordinance of 1858 failed to meet the demands of the Students, the Christ Church Oxford Act was passed in 1867, creating the sometimes parallel and sometimes divergent Governing Body and Dean and Chapter. The Governing Body would be led by the Dean, with members of Chapter and all the

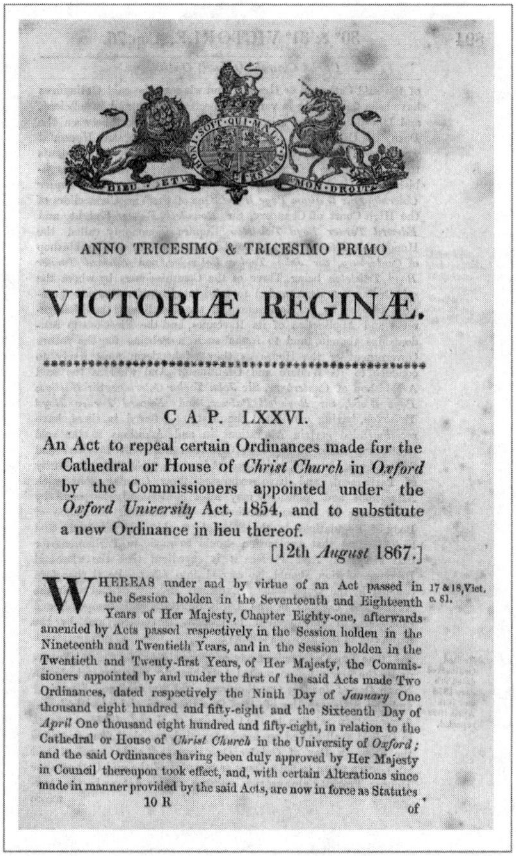

ANNO TRICESIMO & TRICESIMO PRIMO

VICTORIÆ REGINÆ.

CAP. LXXVI.

An Act to repeal certain Ordinances made for the Cathedral or House of *Christ Church* in *Oxford* by the Commissioners appointed under the *Oxford University* Act, 1854, and to substitute a new Ordinance in lieu thereof.

[12th *August* 1867.]

WHEREAS under and by virtue of an Act passed in the Session holden in the Seventeenth and Eighteenth Years of Her Majesty, Chapter Eighty-one, afterwards amended by Acts passed respectively in the Session holden in the Nineteenth and Twentieth Years, and in the Session holden in the Twentieth and Twenty-first Years, of Her Majesty, the Commissioners appointed by and under the first of the said Acts made Two Ordinances, dated respectively the Ninth Day of *January* One thousand eight hundred and fifty-eight and the Sixteenth Day of *April* One thousand eight hundred and fifty-eight, in relation to the Cathedral or House of *Christ Church* in the University of *Oxford*; and the said Ordinances having been duly approved by Her Majesty in Council thereupon took effect, and, with certain Alterations since made in manner provided by the said Acts, are now in force as Statutes of 17 & 18, Vict. c. 81.

10 R

The first page of the printed version of the Christ Church Oxford Act of 1867, which altered the constitution of Christ Church and caused the introduction of new committees and, in years to come, the employment of professional financiers to manage the endowment

Students (now fellows, as in other colleges), and would have power over the disposal and management of all the foundation's revenues.[24] The Dean and Canons would continue to manage the cathedral with funds set aside specifically for the purpose.

The uses of revenue began to change with the new constitution. Before 1858, and certainly before 1867, most men leaving their colleges were going into the church with a ready stipend. Once their year of grace was over, Christ Church brought someone else into the fold, and outgoings remained

Canon Robert Payne Smith (1818–1895) was the regius professor of divinity and the first Treasurer under the new constitution.

reasonably static.[25] However, the University reforms, and the changes to Christ Church's constitution, meant that men were likely to stay longer and to hold down scholarly careers until retirement. As the almost inevitable career move into the church (with their positions for life) became less ubiquitous, so pensions became an issue, and funds derived from the endowment were put aside for this purpose.[26]

With a much larger Governing Body, committees became the normal means to conduct business. One of the first to be established, at the very first meeting of the Governing Body on 16 October 1867, was the Treasury (soon Finance) Committee with responsibility for the management of funds.[27] (A dedicated committee was the only way to manage the new affairs, although it was some years before an experienced professional financier or estates manager was appointed as Treasurer or bursar.[28]) After the position ceased to be held by a clergyman, the Treasurers were, for the best part of a century, primarily 'estates' men, often farmers in their own right, rather than financiers.[29] Governing Bodies began to establish committees with specific responsibility for the administration of estates from 1870. Once the business of college landholding had gone beyond the sealing of leases, the setting of entry fines and the presentation to livings, a new means of administration became necessary. The running out of beneficial leases meant that local matters which had usually been dealt with by the principal tenant of an estate – subscriptions to schools, church restoration appeals, parsonage improvements etc. – suddenly fell to the Students to deal with at Governing Body meetings. The first Treasurer under the new constitution was still a canon, Robert Payne Smith, the regius professor of divinity. He resigned his canonry in 1871 to take up the deanery of Canterbury, and into his place came Robert Godfrey Faussett, a Student since his matriculation in 1845, who was immediately thrust into dealing with the agricultural depression and Christ Church's near-bankruptcy.[30]

Agricultural depression

The middle years of the nineteenth century were years of prosperity in agriculture, with high productivity caused more by the widespread adoption of machinery and better drainage and the consequent need for far fewer labourers than by the application of new science and technology (although this did continue the advances of the previous century), and the growth of urban markets with the transport system to feed them.[31] Most colleges had seen a rise in income between 1850 and 1871, although the increases were widely different, with Merton, which had run out its beneficial leases early and successfully, seeing more than a doubling of its revenue but Balliol a rise of only 3 per cent.[32]

But the beginnings of the depression were already forming, with an increase in the importation of agricultural produce since the Corn Laws had been lifted in 1846 and the consequent collapse of grain prices in the following decades, and new diseases – such as foot and mouth, rinderpest and pleuro-pneumonia – brought in as the transport of live animals increased.

In the early 1870s the importation of grain rose by 90 per cent and the figures were higher still for meat, butter and cheese. And then, from 1874, a run of bad harvests and twenty years of bad weather (floods, droughts and extreme winter conditions) just made matters worse: cheap American imports meant that farmers were no longer compensated for low harvests by the high prices that could be commanded in times of dearth.[33]

The diary of John Simpson Calvertt, who took on two Crown farms near Leafield (Oxfordshire) in the Wychwood Forest area of the Cotswolds, on the same cornbrash soil as Christ Church's estates in Enstone and Bledington, covers the period of the depression.[34] While much of the diary is taken up with socialising, gossip and hunting, it records the misery of the bad weather and consequent failed harvests. On 30 April 1879, for example, he writes: 'April has been cold, frosty, foggy, snow, rained & been most irregular throughout – everything is backward and the present farming prospects very disheartening.' The next day there were snowstorms and Calvertt still had 45 acres of barley and 85 acres of oats to drill. Later that year 21 June was 'drizly, cold, and windy, like March', and on 20 July the farmer entered into his diary that there had been 'heavy rain in the early morning – and terrible showers during the day – the most awful season – for frosts, cold, & rain, during April, May, June, & till present date – ever experienced by the present generation'. On 22 August 'continues the most cursed, ruinous weather on record – cannot thrash oats – plough fallows – skerry turnips, nor even carry manure on the clover land for wheat!!! – and this state of things been going on *all over* the *country* since last *April*!!!' Harvest was a disaster; already the bringing in of the fodder crops, sainfoin and clover, had taken an extraordinary forty days, and in September harvest was only possible on odd days and it was the worst he had ever gathered with neither quality nor yield – 'worthless'. Calvertt wrote that there were sales of farms all over the district. On 31 December his diary entry reads: 'Wind and rain most of the day – no work done!!! So ends the most *ruinously* ugly *seasoned* year, of *this century*'.[35]

The effect of the depression on Christ Church's tenants is visible throughout the mass of estates correspondence, particularly in the papers about farms in the Cotswolds, which appear to have been hit especially hard. Many tenants found themselves unable to pay rents, let alone entry fines, but it was generally accepted that it was better to have a tenant on a farm, particularly an experienced man, than to evict one who was unable to pay and then be unable to re-let.[36]

Calvertt certainly survived because he was able to negotiate his rent down by 25 per cent.[37] In Netherswell in 1888, the land agent, Hayward Field, recommended that Mr Clifford, the tenant, be kept on in spite of his inability to pay either current rent or his arrears. To evict Clifford would have meant that the college would have had to take the farm in hand, as no new tenants could be found.[38] Mrs Badger's crops failed on her farm in Brize Norton, and, according to Field, she would be unable to continue farming if the Governing Body were not lenient.[39]

In 1887 a Mr Lane, the occupier of a farm in Aldsworth, was suffering so much from the effects of the crisis he wanted to give up his lease.[40] But Christ Church's agent, Hayward Field, held out no hope for a new tenant; he recommended allowing the lessee to stay on at a nominal rent, just to keep the farm going.[41] A year later, however, Field had changed his mind and decided that Lane was so far behind with the rent that it would be better if he gave up the farm. Opinions at Christ Church differed on whether to allow Lane to stay and receive no rent or to attempt to find a new tenant in such difficult circumstances. The overriding principle in all the debates was not to be stuck with managing any farm directly; the Governing Body were told how Magdalen College had tried and lost out to the tune of nearly £2,000 by attempting to manage four farms in-house.[42] As a consequence, the college was prepared to be very lenient. Aldsworth farm was let to a new tenant at a very low rent – Lane had been paying, or trying to pay, £351 per year; Walker, the new man, paid only £100.[43] Christ Church was fortunate to find a man prepared to pay any rent; so anxious were some landlords to keep the farms operating, rather than fall into disrepair, that there was land in the Cotswolds that could be taken for no rent at all. In some places it was decided to lay the fields to grass to weather the Depression.[44] Grazing for sheep and cattle was less likely to fail than root crops and grain. It did not always work, however; Lane had been instructed to sow seed, just in case he was unable to keep up the farm – it was easier to have an empty farm laid to grass than full of unharvestable arable crops – but even this failed. Field struggled at many of Christ Church's farms to persuade the tenants to stay on: a farmer at Offenham (Worcestershire) had been persuaded to keep going, while in nearby Littleton the farmer wanted to leave but no new tenant could be found. Field recommended nearly halving the rent.[45]

Some areas of the country not only made it through the years of the Depression but actually increased farm output, with Sussex, Lancashire and Cheshire all making percentage increases in gross farm output of more than 10 per cent. But most of the counties that did well were pastoral or grew specialist and local crops, such as hops and fruit in Kent and Sussex. One positive result of the depression was the tendency of farmers to diversify. Alternative husbandry sprang up everywhere.[46]

The counties that suffered most were all in Christ Church's farming heartland, from Worcestershire (with a decline between 1873 and 1894 of 4 per cent) to Oxfordshire and Berkshire (20 and 21 per cent respectively). Worcestershire may, however, have mitigated the worst effects of the poor grain harvests by diversifying into horticultural and vegetable crops, which were not taken into account in the official figures.[47] Acres of glasshouses were erected in the decades after the tax on window glass was lifted in 1845, and between 1875 and 1895 the recorded area of market gardens and orchards across the country rocketed. With the growth of the railway system, and innovations in food preservation and refrigeration, specialist local crops could be transported much more easily, and quickly, into the major urban areas of the country. The vicar in Badsey (Worcestershire) wrote to the Governing Body in 1902 asking for a contribution towards a new clock for the church tower as nearly all the locals were market gardeners and needed a clock to get their produce off by train.[48]

In the Vale of Evesham, where Christ Church had considerable estates, horticulture (which included fruit and vegetables as well as flowers) was long established, since the Middle Ages, but it expanded in the nineteenth century, with improved roads in the early part of the century and then with

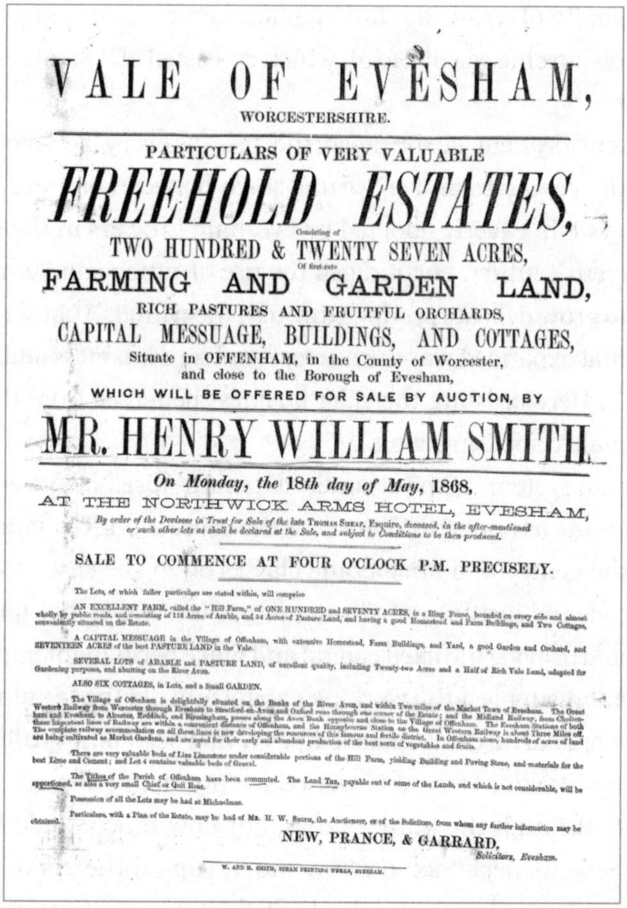

VALE OF EVESHAM,
WORCESTERSHIRE.

PARTICULARS OF VERY VALUABLE
FREEHOLD ESTATES,
Consisting of
TWO HUNDRED & TWENTY SEVEN ACRES,
Of first-rate
FARMING AND GARDEN LAND,
RICH PASTURES AND FRUITFUL ORCHARDS,
CAPITAL MESSUAGE, BUILDINGS, AND COTTAGES,
Situate in OFFENHAM, in the County of Worcester,
and close to the Borough of Evesham,
WHICH WILL BE OFFERED FOR SALE BY AUCTION, BY

MR. HENRY WILLIAM SMITH

On Monday, the 18th day of May, 1868,
AT THE NORTHWICK ARMS HOTEL, EVESHAM,
By order of the Devisees in Trust for Sale of the late THOMAS SHEAF, Esquire, *deceased, in the after-mentioned or such other lots as shall be declared at the Sale, and subject to Conditions to be then produced.*

SALE TO COMMENCE AT FOUR O'CLOCK P.M. PRECISELY.

The Lots, of which fuller particulars are stated within, will comprise

AN EXCELLENT FARM, called the "Hill Farm," of ONE HUNDRED and SEVENTY ACRES, in a Ring Fence, bounded on every side and almost wholly by public roads, and consisting of 116 Acres of Arable, and 54 Acres of Pasture Land, and having a good Homestead and Farm Buildings, and Two Cottages, conveniently situated on the Estate.

A CAPITAL MESSUAGE in the Village of Offenham, with extensive Homestead, Farm Buildings, and Yard, a good Garden and Orchard, and SEVENTEEN ACRES of the best PASTURE LAND in the Vale.

SEVERAL LOTS of ARABLE and PASTURE LAND, of excellent quality, including Twenty-two Acres and a Half of Rich Vale Land, adapted for Gardening purposes, and abutting on the River Avon.

ALSO SIX COTTAGES, in Lots, and a Small GARDEN.

The Village of Offenham is delightfully situated on the Banks of the River Avon, and within Two miles of the Market Town of Evesham. The Great Western Railway from Worcester through Evesham to Stratford-on-Avon and Oxford runs through one corner of the Estate; and the Midland Railway, from Cheltenham and Evesham, to Alcester, Redditch, and Birmingham, passes along the Avon Bank opposite and close to the Village of Offenham. The Evesham Stations of both these important lines of Railway are within a convenient distance of Offenham, and the Honeybourne Station on the Great Western Railway is about Three Miles off. The complete railway accommodation on all these lines is now developing the resources of this famous and fertile district. In Offenham alone, hundreds of acres of land are being cultivated as Market Gardens, and are noted for their early and abundant production of the best sorts of vegetables and fruits.

There are very valuable beds of Lias Limestone under considerable portions of the Hill Farm, yielding Building and Paving Stone, and materials for the best Lime and Cement; and Lot 4 contains valuable beds of Gravel.

The Tithes of the Parish of Offenham have been commuted. The Land Tax, payable out of some of the Lands, and which is not considerable, will be apportioned, as also a very small Chief or Quit Rent.

Possession of all the Lots may be had at Michaelmas.

Particulars, with a Plan of the Estate, may be had of MR. H. W. SMITH, the Auctioneer, or of the Solicitors, from whom any further information may be obtained.

NEW, PRANCE, & GARRARD,
Solicitors, Evesham.

W. AND H. SMITH, STEAM PRINTING WORKS, EVESHAM.

The auction particulars for Hill Farm in Offenham. Francis Field, Christ Church's land agent, recommended its purchase as the conversion of pasture to 'garden grounds' dramatically increased land values in the area.

the rail network.[49] Along with other crops, apple and pear orchards began to flourish.[50] In 1859 there were 60 acres of market gardens in Offenham, successfully cultivated by fifty or sixty men. Christ Church's agent, Francis Field, reported back on the college estate in Great and Little Hampton in 1864.[51] It was, he wrote, let to numerous occupiers as garden ground at a high price, and Field recommended that the purchase of more market garden land – already in use as such – in the vicinity would produce a large rental. The conversion of pasture to garden grounds had doubled the value of the land,

and the proximity of a railway station made it even more valuable. In 1868 Christ Church purchased Hill Farm, which consisted of 188 acres of market garden land.[52]

The 'Kent' system encouraged the use of every available piece of ground, with vegetables and soft fruits sown between orchard fruits, and the French system, eagerly adopted by Evesham growers in the early years of the twentieth century, encouraged the use of much smaller frames and bell glasses to grow delicate produce through the winter. Another specialism of the area that expanded was the nursery and seed business and, of course, asparagus. In Herefordshire the cider business benefited from the renewed interest in quality apple growing.[53]

The estate system, with its landlord–tenant–hired labourer structure, was seen by some as one of the causes of the depression. The land was there to support the gentry and aristocratic classes or, in the case of Oxford colleges, an academic institution whose main interest was not farming. The landlord would provide the fixed capital and make permanent improvements while the tenant supplied the working capital and did the farming. In times of prosperity or dearth, the responsibilities would become more fluid. During the depression landlords were criticised for not doing enough to support their tenants through the harder times, but how much could be invested into improvements depended on how much capital there was to spare.[54] Rental income from Christ Church's landed estate was its principal source of revenue. If that was reduced, for whatever reason, then there was far less in the kitty to play with.

By 1886 Christ Church had taken out loans of £200,000 (more than three times its income on the revenue account) to see it through the difficult time without entry fines, and although net income from lands now at rack rent instead of on beneficial leases had risen, the difference was lower than anticipated and insufficient to meet the repayment of fine loans.[55] Between the mid-1870s and 1897 the gross value of Christ Church's agricultural estate may have fallen by as much as 39 per cent.[56] The rents themselves were diverted to 'do up' any neglected estates, as rack-rented estates needed to be attractive to prospective tenants. In the past, under the beneficial lease system, tenants had treated their farms almost as their own property and generally looked after them in order to maximise their profits, or minimise expensive repairs and maintenance at lease renewal. However, once the landlord had refused a lease renewal and decided to run out the lease, any incentive to take care of the property evaporated.

The redemption date for the loan coincided with the fall in rental income caused by the depression. Christ Church, to add to its difficulties, had recently invested in the construction of its new residential wing, Meadow Buildings, a major overhaul of the cathedral, the building of the Wolsey and Fell Towers, and twice in a reordering of the Great Quadrangle. Whether or not it had been profligate – spending close to £100,000 over twenty years – debts were far in excess of income.[57] The college came as close as it has ever done to bankruptcy – only the hugely increased rents from urban property kept the place afloat.[58]

The appalling state of Christ Church's finances was not entirely unexpected. In 1874, even before the onset of the agricultural depression, the Governing Body had informed the Vice-Chancellor that Christ Church's income would be stationary for the next ten years, and in 1877, the Copyhold Commissioners were warned of the same: 'the finances of Christ Church will be seriously affected during the next seven years by the operation of running out leases and raising loans in lieu of fines.' The Governing Body advised the Copyhold Commission that they anticipated that things would begin to improve after 1885.[59] However, on 2 March 1886 the Finance Committee reported to the Governing Body that 'the indebtedness of the House is very greatly in excess of that of any other College, in proportion to its available external income.' Further borrowing had to cease immediately, except for emergencies, and the sum that was to be paid into the pension fund should be held back.[60] Seven recommendations were made:

- separate bank accounts should be kept for corporate and trust funds;
- the Steward should keep a separate account for the Tuition Fund, into which fees and the Governing Body's capitation grant should be paid;
- the capitation grant should be restricted to £1 per head, and for 1885

the sum of £50 should be paid into the existing pension fund, which then stood at £581 16s. 9d.;

- 5 per cent of the quarter's dividend should be kept back from all Studentships;
- an application should be made for permission not to elect to empty Studentships for one year;
- the dinner allowance and Governing Body lunches should be suspended until further notice;
- there should be no gaudy.[61]

The Treasurer, Robert Godfrey Faussett, warned that these solutions were probably only the tip of the iceberg.[62] If income continued to fall, then salaries would have to drop. He discussed which estates were likely to bring in increased rents or were ripe for development. Income would be steady, but expenditure was excessive. Much of this was 'one-off' capital expenditure, which would eventually be offset by income. In the short term Faussett proposed two ways in which the excess of expenditure over income could be met: £4,000 could be borrowed, and the regular vote of moneys to the Pension Fund – this time £1,300 – could be rescinded. He also suggested that the Land Commissioners be approached for an extension to the period of loan repayment from twenty-eight to thirty years.[63]

The committee report was taken to the Governing Body meeting on 17 March, when all that was agreed was to defer discussions until the October meeting, although a number of Students, along with the Dean, Canons and Censors, signed a resolution agreeing to the proposed reduction in salaries. Although not recorded in the Governing Body minutes, Thomas Vere Bayne – Secretary to the Governing Body and Liddell's Man Friday – motioned, at Faussett's request, that the Treasurer be relieved of his position, on the grounds of ill-health, from Michaelmas. The debate about finance in the Governing Body was a thinly veiled attack on Faussett and his Treasurership, which had already been battered by the Cleveland Commission fourteen years earlier. Appointed in 1872 to investigate college finances, the Commission slated Christ Church particularly for the alleged misapplication of its

Robert Godfrey Faussett (1827–1908) had been a Student at Christ Church since his matriculation in 1845. When Payne Smith resigned his canonry to take up the deanery of Canterbury, Faussett was elected Treasurer (he was also Steward, or domestic bursar) and was thrust into coping with the agricultural depression and the near-bankruptcy of Christ Church.

income. The figures, at least in the synopsis, revealed that Christ Church had the same number of undergraduates as Balliol College but an income over six times greater (£49,000 compared with £8,000), and yet still managed to be in dire financial straits. Many college bursars responded angrily to the summary report of the Cleveland Commission, and Faussett protested most vehemently that Christ Church had responsibilities that were unique.[64] Charles Dodgson defended Faussett, preparing a paper, in consultation with his close friend Vere Bayne, which challenged the statements made by the Finance Committee, and proposing that the Pension Fund be used as a temporary source of revenue, to meet the £6,000 annual interest repayments.[65]

Thomas Vere Bayne (1829–1908) was one of the leading lights in the reform of Christ Church in the mid-nineteenth century. He was Dean Liddell's right-hand man, and largely responsible for the administration of Christ Church for several decades.

How far the condition of Christ Church's finances really was Faussett's fault, and how far it was just circumstance and the buck having to stop somewhere is difficult to judge, but the stress was evidently great within college at the time. Bayne stated in his diary that 'I never wish for such another ten days'.[66] At the start of Michaelmas term Bartholomew Price was appointed to draw up a report on the financial state of Christ Church.[67] Price presented his paper to the Governing Body at the meeting on 11 December, laying out the state of finances. In November 1886 there were loans outstanding of £18,000 for buildings, £2,000 for drainage and £2,000 on estate improvements, which were all being paid back on thirty-year terms. Additionally, Christ Church was paying back Fine Loans, which were made to carry the

Bartholomew Price (1818–1898) was a mathematician and Fellow of Pembroke College. His financial skills were demonstrated in his successful role as Secretary to the Delegates of Oxford University Press. In 1886 he was asked by the Governing Body of Christ Church to investigate and report on the state of the college's finances.

House over while beneficial leases were being run out, and which amounted to the phenomenal sum of £203,556 10s. 6d. The loans had been agreed on the conditions that interest was paid annually out of income, and that a sinking fund be created with an amount equivalent to one seventh of the whole loan deposited in the fund annually from the twenty-second year of the loan to the twenty-eighth. Some £63,000 of these grants had been borrowed from the Land Commissioners on twenty-eight year terms.

Projections, according to Price, showed that income would steadily rise over the next few years. In the short term, this would be insufficient to deal with the debt, so Price proposed approaching the Land Commission for a two-year extension to the loan period, from twenty-eight to thirty years, as Faussett himself had already suggested, and to take out further, smaller, Fine Loans. He did not think, though, that it was necessary to suspend appointments to Studentships (although new ones should not be added without great caution), or to reduce the dividends: 'economy is necessary, but we see no reason why the immediate interests of the House should be sacrificed, or the existing members put to personal inconvenience.'

The meeting evidently went off without a hitch; Price's recommendations were accepted, including a proposal, mooted in Dodgson's paper, concerning the Pension and Tuition Funds, and the contributions to and from both.[68] However, by 1897 not much seems to have changed. William Skene, then Treasurer (and the dean's son-in-law), wrote a memorandum for the Governing Body insisting that a policy be decided for the discharge of loans.[69] In 1889, he said, loans had amounted to nearly £217,000, and although, sinking funds had been established and then held a total of £55,000, fresh loans had been taken out and the total debt was still around £180,000, excluding the £40,000 owed to the Board of Agriculture. The cause of most of the debt, said Skene, was the agricultural depression, which had wiped between 30 and 35 per cent off the rental value of estates. Christ Church was worse hit than other colleges, as it had to use half its income to maintain the Chapter.[70] Skene reckoned that using the Pension Fund, and possibly the Carey Trust, could be used to cover the deficit until 1901.[71] The remainder, which had to be paid off by 1908, could be met by yet another loan.[72] Clause 4 of the new Universities and College Estates Bill caused some consternation not just at Christ Church but to the other colleges as well. It had intended to provide some relief by extending the time for repayment in certain cases from thirty to fifty years, but the Board of Agriculture wanted to restrict extended loan periods to estates from which the income was less than the required loan repayments. The Governing Body wanted no restrictions, but the Board of Agriculture did not accept Christ Church's arguments. Negotiations continued even beyond the second reading of the Bill, and eventually it was agreed that some relief could be given although the method was still up for discussion.[73] Skene sent up estimates of receipts and expenditure for 1898 and 1899, and proposed an annual repayment of £7,000. This was not enough apparently, and a counter-proposal was made suggesting that the Chapter and Students reduce their income from college revenues in proportion to the losses caused by the agricultural depression. In the end, a fresh amendment to Clause 4 was proposed to grant full extension in every case in which the sum required for the repayment of a loan exceeded one half of the net annual value of the land after deducting the rent reserved by the old beneficial lease. If this were accepted, said Skene, then the relief that the Governing Body needed would be met.[74]

It was the debt burden that was causing Christ Church's problems; in actuality, right at the end of the nineteenth century, its gross income was beginning to rise again, and the revenue from Trust estates was healthy.[75] Selling more property to reduce the debt was not an option; the proceeds from sales permitted by the 1858 Estates Act had to be invested with the Copyhold Commission until it could be reinvested. But what did help with the rebalancing of the books was housing.[76] Christ Church was already running out leases at the time of the 1872 Cleveland Commission, and the Estates Act had permitted new building on ninety-nine-year leases. The need to do something about the slums of west Oxford and then the arrival of the railway prompted a string of new development projects in St Thomas's parish at almost no expense.

7

The right of 'coleing': Christ Church's mining estates

Christ Church was given the manor and parsonage of Midsomer Norton at its foundation. The property had formerly belonged to Merton Priory in Surrey and had been leased by the priory to Nicholas Prideaux in 1533.[1] At some point in the five years before Merton was dissolved in 1538, Prideaux's lease was surrendered and a new one issued, for a term of sixty years, to John Wychell. There seems to have been some dispute over the payment of rents and the re-leasing of the property, possibly surrounding Queen Elizabeth's Act of 1571 laying down the maximum terms for agricultural and urban tenancies. It was a lucrative property, with an annual beneficial rent of £19, and the Dean and Chapter would have been anxious to sort it out. Once sorted, William Ridge and then his son Hugh settled down to enjoy the profits of the parsonage and the manor, including all the buildings, gardens, agricultural land, tithes and court profits, but with a covenant to pay pensions and additional charges should they fall behind with the rent. Christ Church retained for itself the timber trees, as was usual, the profits from wards and marriages, and an annuity from the church at Martock.[2] What was not mentioned at all in the earliest leases of the manor and parsonage was the presence of coal under college property, or the rights to mine it.

The coalfields of Somerset were in a small area around Midsomer Norton, Radstock and Paulton, about ten miles south-west of Bath. The earliest mining was at Paulton, where the coal was exposed and could be easily extracted. Around Radstock mining was more complicated, as the seams could be faulted and dipped sharply.[3]

Christ Church evidently had retained the right to 'coleing' in Midsomer Norton and Radstock from the foundation, but the first mention in the archive is in 1708, when a consortium of local clothworkers and miners were granted a lease for twenty-one years to mine on any land belonging to the manor of Midsomer Norton at a rent of 2s. 6d. per pound's worth of coal raised.[4] Before this date, correspondence was concerned largely with the administration of the manor's agricultural land and the income from tithes and courts, but by the early years of the eighteenth century an increasing number of property owners and tenants were beginning to understand the potential for profits to be realised from mining. Even so, production was limited in the early years, partly owing to the terrible state of the roads in the area; coal had to be carried out on horseback. Turnpike roads, run by the Bath and Bristol Trusts, came nowhere near the mines.

The early diggings were either adits, where the coal seams broke the surface, or relatively shallow bell pits (an ancient form of mining which involved sinking a shallow shaft and then hollowing out a chamber beneath to extract minerals along the seams closest to the surface).[5] As one pit was emptied, another would be dug close by, and the first used to take the spoil from the second. Work could be hindered by the complicated intermixing of land owned by different landlords. The proximity of estates belonging to the Duchy of Cornwall was a particular problem until the first half of the eighteenth century, when local landowners and entrepreneurs began to acquire leases specifically to allow them to mine across larger areas.[6] The local vicar, Thomas Coxeter, wrote in October 1727 to Canon William Stratford in Oxford to describe the setbacks that the Christ Church lessees had suffered, including water ingress into the mines, but he explained that the miners had now obtained leases on contiguous areas and had constructed an underground gutter to improve drainage. Extraction could begin in earnest, or so they thought.[7]

In February 1728 Henry Swymmer, one of the aldermen of Bristol, applied for the tenancy of the manorial land in Paulton. He had purchased an adjoining estate specifically to search for coal, and wanted to expand

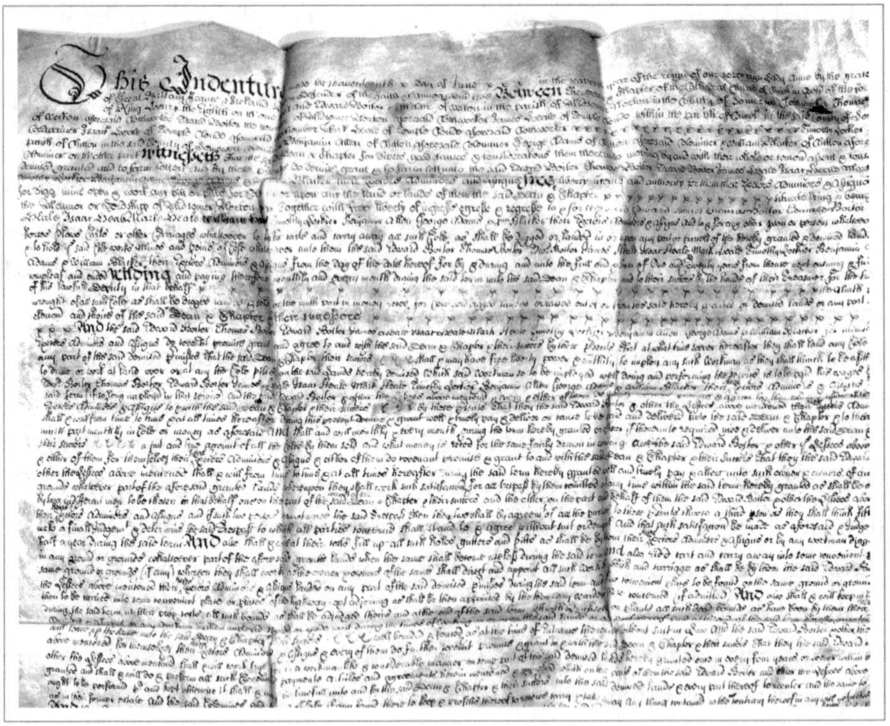

The lease for the right to mine coal on Christ Church land in Midsomer Norton, dated 17 June 1708.

his investigations. Swymmer offered the going rate of 2s. 6d. in the pound, and to make good any damage from digging to the sub-tenant of the fields in question. Just a week later, presumably in response to a letter from the Chapter, Sir Abraham Elton, the local MP and mayor of Bristol, and Christ Church's principal tenant in Midsomer Norton, wrote to Dean Bradshaw advising that it would be wise to jump on to the 'coleing' bandwagon, and to let the experts do the work properly, rather than leave the coal unquarried. Elton knew who would be best for the job, and recommended Swymmer.

Within two weeks, a draft agreement was drawn up offering Swymmer a twenty-one-year lease for the royalty of 1.25 per cent on the coal extracted and an additional royalty of 10 per cent for any stone sold. Royalties were to be paid on 1 March and 1 September. Christ Church's tenant was to receive compensation for damage to the land; any failure to work the mine for more than six months would render the lease void; a professional accountant was to be taken on (paid by Swymmer), and employment given to at least ten local men. Pits were to be filled once the coal had been extracted and the land returned to its original state, including field hedges and fences.[8]

Swymmer's arrangement – confirmed in a lease of 7 March – was met with bewilderment by the men who thought that they had the lease to work on Christ Church's land.[9] The lease of 1708 had been surrendered in 1719 and reissued, for a further twenty-one years, to three miners: John Emery, Thomas Tyler and Benjamin Allen, who had been a signatory to the 1708 lease.[10] Technically, the right to mine was theirs until 1740 at least. The local vicar, Thomas Coxeter, penned another appeal to Canon Stratford explaining that the miners had invested considerable sums of their own money in their search for coal and were well placed and well qualified to continue the work successfully.[11]

Henry Swymmer was a cool customer; he wrote to Christ Church's Auditor and Chapter Clerk, John Brooks, suggesting that, as no coal had been extracted for six years, he assumed that Emery, Tyler and Allen's lease was forfeit, and besides, Coxeter was both ancient (he was seventy) and had a personal interest, as his son was working in the coal business at nearby Welton and was in partnership with Emery at Midsomer Norton. Swymmer advised Brooks that he already had four or five men at work, and his pit was looking promising.[12] But the other men were not going to take this lying down; no, they admitted, they had not extracted any coal, but they had done all the preparatory work – sinking pits and setting up works. And then, just as they were about to succeed in their efforts, Swymmer had swanned in and claimed their rights. The men were certain that the covenants in the lease had not been broken.[13] Coxeter had warned Chapter that the men were prepared to go to law, if necessary, and it would appear that this is exactly what they did. However, there is no further correspondence in the archive until 1734, when the men petitioned Christ Church reiterating that they had been searching for and later extracting coal on Duchy land, and were working their way over to Christ Church property. Swymmer had begun his investigations on Chapter land but was still unsuccessful. Christ Church had offered them a bond, which they had refused, but not a renewal of their lease, which they now requested, with Coxeter junior as one of the partners. Christ Church's lawyer, Joseph Taswell, advised against this course of action; if the lease were to be renewed, then it must only be to men who also worked the Duchy land which was intermixed with Christ Church's. To try to have leases with two separate parties was potentially disastrous; when quarrels broke out – as they inevitably did – it was not unknown for one party deliberately to flood the mines of the others.[14]

Eighteen months later Tyler and Allen tried another tack, and asked Chapter to grant a lease to work coal at Midsomer Norton to Mrs Elizabeth Mogg. Mrs Mogg already had a lease with the Duchy, and Tyler and Allen had several leases on adjoining property where coal had already been found. Tyler and Allen were prepared to surrender their 1719 lease to the college if a new one was granted to Mogg; they would then invest their money into working college coal. That Christ Church and the Duchy should lease to the same people seemed sensible and vital to the success of the enterprise. Swymmer's interest in Christ Church's coal seemed under threat.[15] However, the lease register confirms that the lease of Christ Church's mining business was passed from Henry Swymmer to his three unmarried children: William, Anthony and Bridget. Perhaps this is nothing surprising: the Swymmers were merchants in Bristol and the West Indies, as was Abraham Elton, the tenant of the parsonage and manor of Midsomer Norton (excluding the mining activities). John Day, to whom Elton's lease was granted after Elton's death, was his grandson. Henry Swymmer's brother Anthony was a signatory to the marriage settlement between Peter Day and Elizabeth Elton.[16] It was all wheels within wheels.

For a short while, correspondence between the Dean and Chapter and the estate at Midsomer Norton related to agricultural matters but did include digging for marl, which had recently been discovered in the area. Drawn up from 'wells' of about seven fathoms depth, the marl was used as a soil improver and increased the value of the arable land without the need for further fertilisers. For the local vicar, good cider years increased his income from tithes by around 12 per cent.[17]

The Somerset coalfields were never highly productive, partly because of the difficulties of transportation out of the area and partly because Bristol, the largest nearby town and potential consumer, had its own supply on the doorstep. In 1791 the surveyor, Thomas Gregg, was asked by the Dean and Chapter to survey the lands of the manor 'as they had but faint knowledge of it'. His report did not make happy reading. Long disputes with the Duchy of Cornwall over ownership of parcels of land had caused considerable dissatisfaction; Christ Church's land was scattered among freehold land, and even the copyholders themselves were uncertain of the boundaries of their tenancies. Gregg persuaded them that this needed to be corrected. Christ Church's tenants needed to be treated carefully, and documentation was hard to find. Gregg put together as much information as he could gather, including a survey that had been made of the manor in 1777, which had emphasised the complicated land ownership, and then commissioned a map, which he laid before the manorial court for approval.[18] In his report to the Chapter, Gregg first summarised the tithe income from the rectory and then went on to advise that the Dean and Chapter needed to inspect the coal workings annually. Prospects, he said, were gloomy; after considerable expenditure on the college coal lease, work had stopped, and everyone was anticipating that the mines would be abandoned with the arrival of cheap and plentiful supplies from Pontypool. However, the Pontypool coal was, in all probability, swallowed up by local ironworking, and the future of the Somerset coalfields looked more promising when plans for a new canal were approved in 1794.[19]

In 1796 a new lease of 45½ acres was issued to a second consortium of local men (including one of the Mogg family at last). Compared with earlier leases, the document suggests a much more industrial environment than those of the early eighteenth century. Not only could the miners dig and remove coal, but the lease permitted the erection of engines, the digging of drains, the creation of roads and the quarrying of stone. The rent was a tenth of the profits from all coal except 'bag coal' (for local use) and coal needed to operate the engines.[20] Profits began to come in, slowly at first, as 'it is the invariable custom of the adventurers to get the deep coal first in

William 'Strata' Smith (1769–1839) was a civil engineer and geologist whose career began in the Somerset coalmines, surveying the geology and planning the route of the Somerset Coal Canal.

case water should afterwards prevent it'.[21] Seven years later Gregg wrote to Dean Jackson, in some surprise, that he had just paid £100 into the college's account, and anticipated more in two or three years when the Somerset Coal Canal was fully operational.[22]

By 1812 steam engines were beginning to take over from horse-power to raise the coal from the pits, which were 'astonishingly deep'.[23] As well as royalties due from mines dug on Christ Church land, the Dean and Chapter also received a share from any coal mined under its land, with an 'underground bailiff' ensuring that the free share went to the right person or institution. Four pits in the area provided these 'freeshares'. In the year ending 17 August 1816 the 10 per cent share to the Chapter from the Radford pit amounted to £75, but the following year it was only £29.[24] Gregg advised Christ Church to encourage work under its land; it was an expense-free enterprise.[25]

Portrait of William Buckland (1784–1856) by Thomas Phillips. Buckland was a canon of Christ Church and later Dean of Westminster, but is better known as a geologist, naturalist and pioneering palaeontologist.

Following the work on the mining area of Somerset by the 'father of geology', William 'Strata' Smith, in the 1790s ahead of the building of the Coal Canal, it is intriguing to note that, in 1824, two Christ Church men, William Buckland and William D. Conybeare, published a geological account of the Somerset coalfields. In it they expressed the opinion that, although the seams were very thin and would be disregarded by miners in the principal coalfields of the nation, with modern equipment and techniques they could produce a decent profit. Old and abandoned shafts could now be drained and reopened and new pits dug.[26]

The pits provided an income for Christ Church, both in direct leases and royalties or freeshares almost until the mines were taken over by the new National Coal Board in 1947.[27] Old pits closed and new ones were sunk, so the location of the pits that supplemented Christ Church's coffers changed, but the profits dropped off considerably by the end of the nineteenth century, when the pits that had contributed most to the Chapter's coffers were exhausted and closed.[28] In the late nineteenth century and the early years of the twentieth, Christ Church sold many of the individual copyholds in Midsomer Norton – sometimes to the tenants but often to mining companies, other landowners, such as the Duchy of Cornwall, or to the railway companies – without reserving the mineral rights.[29] Only a few interests were retained but, in the spring quarter of 1910, the Old Mills colliery paid a royalty of only £3, with nothing in the following three months.[30] Nationalisation was not to have much effect on revenue.

There were other estates that provided possibilities for income from mining or other extraction enterprises. In Featherstone in Yorkshire, the Governing Body were even less directly involved with coal mining than they had been in Somerset, but local agents and the local vicar were evidently aware of the rich pickings available. In 1859 the land surveyor William Paver recommended the purchase of a house, farm buildings and a croft in Purston Jaglin for £270. Paver reckoned that the property was worth £242 5s. 4d., but it was adjacent to land already held by Christ Church, and it was understood that there was coal beneath. Acceptance of the owner's price seemed a wise move.[31] A little later, in 1874, the vicar, Revd Hinde, wrote to Christ Church explaining that land had been selling at £240 per acre and up to £500 for an acre for land with a right of passage to coal. He asked permission to sell the field adjacent to the vicarage to one of the pit owners, who had promised to build decent houses for the miners.[32] It was a time of considerable expansion of the industry in the area; although mining had, as in Somerset, begun in the Middle Ages, it was only with the opening of new railways that it really took off. The Featherstone Main Colliery was opened in 1866, followed by Ackton Hall Colliery in 1873. The population was rising rapidly, with nearly three-quarters employed in the mines. Hinde certainly had his finger on the pulse.

The Dean and Chapter took Hinde's words seriously and commissioned a valuation of its lands and minerals in Featherstone from Mr White, a land

and mineral surveyor from Wakefield. He suggested a figure of £5,742 10s., perhaps equivalent to £4 million today.[33] Within twenty years the new vicar, Revd Stebbing, suggested that this value had increased to £9,000 while the value of tithes, or the tithe rent charge, had dropped as agricultural land was swallowed up by new housing and industrial activity. Stebbing proposed exchanging some of the land and coal for tithe rent charge; if this did not happen, he said, he would not be able to stay in the parish. A small quantity of land was sold, but most was retained, and in the last years of the nineteenth century and the early ones of the twentieth Christ Church leased property to the coal and cloth magnate Samuel Lister, Lord Masham, an inventor of textile machinery, and Henry Briggs, whose family company produced jute. Masham purchased the Ackton Hall estate and collieries in 1890 and immediately set about sinking and improving the Silkstone and Haigh Moor seams.[34] The mines, as they passed under Christ Church land, produced a steady income; from 1898 to 1909 the revenue amounted to £3,194 15s.[35] The leasing of coal rights in Yorkshire continued until the Second World War.

8

Managing the agricultural estate IV: the modern period

During the early years of the twentieth century Christ Church began to pull itself out of its financial difficulties. A new Treasurer, George Hutchinson, arrived in 1910 and immediately made a progress around the college estate making notes on the size and type of each farm, the condition of the buildings – both the houses and farm buildings, the water supply and drainage, and the tenants themselves.[1] Many of the farms were family concerns: College Farm in Astrop (Northamptonshire) had been tenanted by the Gregorys for over a century. Some were tiny, only 20 or so acres; others, such as Manor Farm in Brize Norton (Oxfordshire), were over 800.[2] Generally, Hutchinson seems to have been pleased with what he found, and by 1913, although income was not quite up to the level it had been in 1871 before the agricultural depression, prosperity was returning to agriculture, and rents and tithe rent charges began to increase and were supplemented by rents and ground rents from houses and building schemes. Nearly all of this was by now at rack rents or on long leases, the old beneficial leases having been almost entirely replaced. In 1871 Oxford college income from beneficial leases was nearly £11,000; by 1913 this had dropped to £800.[3] A few copyholds survived in Christ Church's portfolio in Church Cowley, Deddington, Sibford Gower, South Stoke and Westwell (all in Oxfordshire), and in Midsomer Norton. Only £121 19s. 6d. came in from the surviving beneficial leases of Manor Farm in Wood Norton.[4]

The Governing Body also began to buy land again: between 1904 and 1908 it invested in several farms in the Romney Marsh area of Kent, at least some of the money for which came from the South Trust.[5] And in 1907 Christ Church purchased Adderbury Grounds Farm (Oxfordshire) with the mineral rights. The land had been leased, at least since 1895, to the Hook Norton Ironstone Partnership at a ground rent of £50 per annum, a royalty of 2d. for every 2,520 lb. of limestone or ironstone raised, and an additional fee of £5 per acre of land utilised. Hook Norton Ironstone was taken over in 1904 by Cochrane & Co., of Woodside Ironworks, near Dudley, to whom Christ Church also leased White Gate Field.[6] In spite of the difficulties caused by the depression, agricultural land was still important and accounted for two-thirds of the income of the colleges in 1913.[7]

The First World War appears to have had very little impact on Christ Church's management of its farms and other estates: the Estates Committee's papers are full of the usual material on farm improvements, drainage schemes, repairs and refurbishment of properties, leases and renewals. New agreements were made with industrial tenants, including a new lease with Featherstone Colliery of seams under Christ Church property in Yorkshire, and a quarrying lease to Brymbo Steel for ironstone in Wroxton (Oxfordshire).[8] On the ground things were very different, with able-bodied men called up to fight and farm horses (along with crops to feed them) requisitioned. Food prices rose rapidly.[9] In November 1914 Henry and William Potter, drapers, applied for the reassignment of the lease of 28 Pembroke Street, Oxford, to their wives. At first glance it would appear that the two men had joined up and were leaving their wives, Fanny and Mary, in charge. But no, this was nothing to do with the war at all – the men were, apparently, totally incompetent at running a business and had decided (or perhaps been encouraged) to grant the women control.[10]

But other businesses *were* suffering as a result of hostilities, at least by the end of 1915, particularly shops selling non-essential goods and those who took in boarders. Approximately 15 per cent of men working in agriculture had joined up by July 1915, and many undergraduates and young tutors had also responded to the call-up. Mrs Henrietta Armstrong, at

1 Brewer Street, Oxford, appealed for a reduction in her rent as her income from lodgers had dropped by 25 per cent since the outbreak of war, and the tenant at 90 St Aldate's who provided accommodation for undergraduates asked the same.[11] Mr Eastman, proprietor of a butcher's shop at 18 Market Street, advised the Treasurer that he would have to give notice to quit at Michaelmas 1917, in spite of already having been granted a reduction in his rent. The Estates Committee pondered the case and decided that, as Eastman was a reliable and prompt payer and as it would be difficult to let the shop if the butcher were to go, then a further reduction would be wise.[12] Miss Louisa Bossom and Mrs Sarah Rodnight, who ran a sweet and confectionery shop in Park End Street, and must have been suffering terribly with the impact of taxes on imported sugar, which was arriving in much-reduced quantities anyway, and excise duties on the home-produced product, requested and were granted a 25 per cent reduction in rent from midsummer 1916.[13]

It was not just tenants in Oxford who were struggling: Mr Collett, who leased a shop in Daventry, was called up in October 1917. If the Governing Body would grant him a reduction in rent for the duration, he would keep the shop going. Much as landlords had tried to keep farms occupied, even with low or no rents, during the agricultural depression, they were anxious not to be stuck with empty urban properties. Collett was a good tenant, and was granted a 50 per cent reduction until the end of the emergency period.[14] There were appeals, too, for the suspension of building leases and contracts. Shortage of men and supplies would have made continuation difficult. Mr Burnham in Harrow (Middlesex) applied, in November 1915, for a formal deferment of his building lease until after the war, while Frank Cooper requested that he not be required to commence building on his £2,000 extension to the jam factory on Botley Road.[15]

But farming life, at least as far as the Estates Committee was concerned, continued much as before. The 1914 harvest was early, so most was gathered in before men were mobilised, and the expectation that the war would be over by Christmas meant that no one felt the need to do anything differently.[16] The government thought that rising prices would encourage increased production as farmers grasped the opportunity for increased profits.[17] The Treasurer reported at the end of 1915 on the financial situation created by the war: 'external revenues for 1916 will not be seriously affected by the War, though internal receipts will be greatly reduced.' He made a few proposals to deal with deficits in the Tuition Fund and on the Steward's account, and on managing the college's contribution to the University. His report concluded with the statement that the debit balance on the Corporate Fund at the end of 1910 had been £6,882, already a substantial reduction in the huge debt in 1900. By the end of 1914 this had been brought down still further to £3,270, which he had anticipated would be cleared, in normal circumstances, during 1915. 'Unless cash is immediately and urgently required by the University', he advised dealing with the remainder of the debt as soon as possible.[18]

It was not until 1917 that the difficulties of food production hit home, when the City of Oxford Special Committee (convened under the Cultivation of Lands Order, 1916) applied for a field in Binsey Lane and a piece of Oxpens (meadow land in the parish of St Thomas) to grow crops. As we have seen, the quantity of arable land had fallen as land was laid to grass during the agricultural depression, and this trend continued up until the outbreak of the First World War.[19] From early 1917 government policy to deal with shortages encouraged the re-ploughing of 3 million acres of grassland, with a target of returning to the quantity of land in cultivation in the 1870s. Covenants to restrict ploughing in thousands of leases had to be formally overturned.[20] The Corn Production Act was passed, guaranteeing minimum prices for grain. Later that year a portion of Merton Field was granted for allotments.[21] Timber from Christ Church's estates was purchased by the government and paid for in short-term 5 per cent war bonds, and other stocks – around £70,000 worth – were transferred into government issues during 1917 alone.[22]

Immediately after the war, applications were received from estates across the country for grants to assist with the erection of memorials. A lump sum of £150 was set aside from which the Treasurer could make individual grants, evidently very much at his own discretion as few appear in the minutes. There was, however, a donation towards the Oxford memorial at the junction of the Banbury and Woodstock roads, and permission was given to the vicar in Runcorn (Cheshire) to sell a small portion of glebe land for a garden and cross.[23] More prosaically, Christ Church expended £468 on materials from military hutments to be used for estate repairs.[24]

Agricultural productivity increased during the First World War, but colleges, like many other landlords, were reluctant to increase rents at a time of crisis, preferring instead to sell land at the high prices that could be demanded. Rents on buildings, rather than agricultural land, were limited anyway by the Rent Restriction Act of 1915, to prevent profiteering. This had come about after landlords in Glasgow had hiked rents to take advantage of the thousands who had come into the city to work in munitions factories; rent strikes by shipyard workers in support of a small group who had been taken to court for defaulting worked to push the Act through Parliament with some speed. Agricultural rents did see rises towards the end of the war.

The Universities and Colleges Estates Act of 1858 had permitted for the first time the mortgage and sale of foundation land, and it is evident that much was sold in the years following the Act, but it is the period immediately following the war that saw huge tracts of land exchanging hands.[25] In fact, colleges were actively encouraged by the Asquith Commission to sell, and fears that they might be expected to sell all their land caused the various Governing Bodies to draw back a little and argue that some land was beneficial, if not crucial, to the survival of collegiate life.[26] However, investment of the proceeds of these post-war land sales is said to have at least doubled the net receipts of the colleges.[27]

Christ Church and five other colleges that sold land in 1919 and 1920 reaped an income of £331,800. Usually sales and purchases were to consolidate holdings, and some areas of the country were almost abandoned, particularly south-west Wales but also Dorset and Sussex.[28] Most of Christ Church's sales were small and relatively local to Oxford, realising only tens or low hundreds of pounds. Large landowners were keen to sell while the prices were high and tenants, aided by mortgages, wanted to buy. Bigger sales included 9 acres on the Cowley Road to the local council for £4,250, and land, cottages and the Greyhound public house in South Stoke for a similar price; 15 acres in Harrow were sold to Debenhams for £3,900. The Great Western Railway paid over £3,600 for land, timber and iron fencing in Worcester, and the whole of the Westwell estate was sold for £11,100. The college also divested itself of its two public houses in Daventry, the Bear and the Plume of Feathers, for a total of nearly £3,000.[29] Land sales were well timed, when farm prices were high and the price of wheat and oats were fixed under the emergency measures of the Agriculture Act of 1920. But as the price of grain dropped in the early 1920s the Act was repealed and farm values began to fall, losing a third of their price between 1929 and 1932 alone. The quantity of land under cultivation dropped again – by a quarter from its height in 1918 to 1926. The new small farmers who had started the post-war years with optimism were now struggling.

Interestingly, though, while many of the colleges, including Christ Church, were busy selling property, the Governing Body was also choosing to invest in new estates. Additional farms were bought in Hillesden, and in 1919 Christ Church purchased almost the whole village of Elsfield (Oxfordshire). The manor house was immediately sold on to John Buchan, but the farms (Sescut, Forest, Church, Hill and Home farms) and several cottages were all let at rack rents. Only the woods of Elsfield and Woodeaton were kept in hand.[30] The rectory, or glebe, farm at Cassington (Oxfordshire) was also bought that year and kept in hand, alongside the properties already held in the parish which were leased. Both Elsfield and Cassington became, in effect, 'home' farms.[31]

Between the wars, colleges benefited from a building boom. By the outbreak of the Second World War college income from houses had doubled in money terms, and trebled in real terms, compared with the revenue in 1920.[32]

Copyhold enfranchisement

During the second half of the nineteenth century legislation had been passed to deal with the last remaining manorial dues and customs, and the conversion of copyhold tenure to conventional leasehold tenure – enfranchisement. Between 1841, when the first Copyhold Act was passed, and 1894, when an Act that consolidated fifty years' worth of laws was given the

Hill Farm, Elsfield, c.1950.

royal assent, it became increasingly simple for copyhold to be enfranchised by either the lord or the tenant, or both. Whoever requested the change paid the fees, and a rent charge was determined to compensate the lord of the manor for the loss of his manorial dues. Many of Christ Church's copyholds were extinguished with the passage of the 1894 Act.

Copyholds were finally abolished by the Law of Property Act in 1925. None of the Acts, however, ended the concept of manors and manorial lordships, and manorial dues could still be claimed; in 1910 a heriot was claimed in Binsey on the reversion of the last copyhold there, and as late as 1914 a heriot was still due on the death of the last copyhold tenant in Westwell. Originally set at the best live or dead chattel, by 1914 it had been settled at a money charge of one-third the annual value of the property. The widow of the copyholder would be entitled to the property for her widowhood.[33] Manorial rights still survived too. However, in some cases, the rights that had been due to the lord were extinguished with enfranchisement or when Christ Church sold the manorial lordship as part of a conventional conveyance. In 2007 Christ Church sold the mineral rights associated with Manor Farm in Black Bourton (Oxfordshire), for example. But in a few cases they continued to be of potential significance and value, and could include the rights to mines and minerals, sporting rights and rights to hold fairs or markets. In 2002, however, the Land Registration Act sought to make the existence and the ownership of these rights clearer by requiring them to be registered or, if they no longer had significance, lost. A deadline was set of October 2013; if rights had not been registered by then, they would be forfeit. The imposition of a *terminus post quem* prompted a flurry of work for all those who held manorial lordships. In most cases, at Christ Church, it was found that rights had indeed either been extinguished formally at enfranchisement of the copyhold tenancies (as at Ellerbeck in Yorkshire) or allowed to fall into desuetude (as at Maids Moreton) or conveyed with the estate and the manorial lordship (as at Deddington in 1954, Kirkham in 1870 and Swanton Novers in 1886). The decision was made not to register any manorial rights, but Christ Church does remain the lord of the manor in a number of places.

Final tithe commutation

The major change in Christ Church's relationship with the land in the twentieth century was the final commutation of tithes in 1936.[34] During the First World War the income from tithe rent charge (that is, the monetary payment that replaced actual tithes in 1836) had rocketed. Because of the index-linking of tithe rent charge to the value of grain, the charge had risen from a low of £77 in 1915 to over £109 in 1918. That year the government placed a short-term cap at the 1918 level for seven years but this did not help the tithe-payers, who therefore did not benefit from reduced charges when the price of grain fell in the immediate post-war years. The tithe-payers could, when the charge exceeded parity, redeem their liability, and many who could afford it did just that.

In 1925 the government advocated that a permanent level of £105

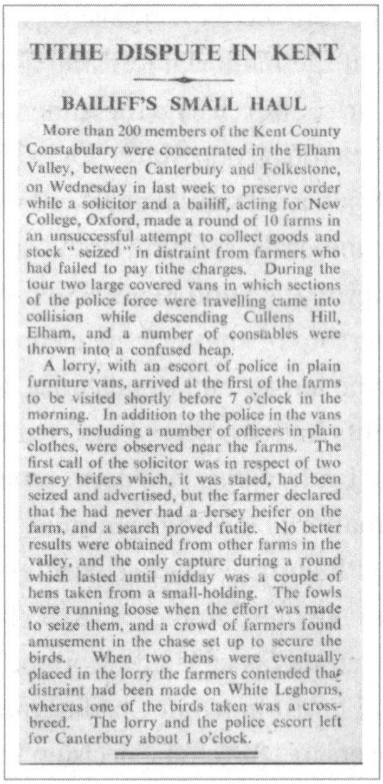

TITHE DISPUTE IN KENT

BAILIFF'S SMALL HAUL

More than 200 members of the Kent County Constabulary were concentrated in the Elham Valley, between Canterbury and Folkestone, on Wednesday in last week to preserve order while a solicitor and a bailiff, acting for New College, Oxford, made a round of 10 farms in an unsuccessful attempt to collect goods and stock " seized " in distraint from farmers who had failed to pay tithe charges. During the tour two large covered vans in which sections of the police force were travelling came into collision while descending Cullens Hill, Elham, and a number of constables were thrown into a confused heap.

A lorry, with an escort of police in plain furniture vans, arrived at the first of the farms to be visited shortly before 7 o'clock in the morning. In addition to the police in the vans others, including a number of officers in plain clothes, were observed near the farms. The first call of the solicitor was in respect of two Jersey heifers which, it was stated, had been seized and advertised, but the farmer declared that he had never had a Jersey heifer on the farm, and a search proved futile. No better results were obtained from other farms in the valley, and the only capture during a round which lasted until midday was a couple of hens taken from a small-holding. The fowls were running loose when the effort was made to seize them, and a crowd of farmers found amusement in the chase set up to secure the birds. When two hens were eventually placed in the lorry the farmers contended that distraint had been made on White Leghorns, whereas one of the birds taken was a cross-breed. The lorry and the police escort left for Canterbury about 1 o'clock.

A cutting from an unidentified Kent newspaper describing the fiasco of the distraint order at Elham in 1932. The college involved was Merton, not New College.

per £100 of nominal value be set, abandoning the index-linking to grain prices. A further payment of £4 10s. would be made to ecclesiastical persons or corporations to create a sinking fund against the eventual redemption of tithe after the distant year of 2009. Naturally, the colleges affected by this proposed reduction in income lobbied furiously, demanding either a return to the pre-war system or a scheme of commutation. Christ Church was potentially the greatest loser, having much of its income tied up in tithe rent charge; in 1915 this had stood at £23,000, but by 1920 it had risen to £34,000.

But the general depression of 1929–32, which saw the prices of farm produce plummet, prompted protests by farmers, who in stark contrast to the experience of the tithe-owners had seen their incomes more than halve while tithe rent charge stayed the same. Farmers refused to pay, and there were violent incidents when bailiffs and police attempted to distrain on farm goods in exactly the same manner as had happened in Wales in the 1880s.[35] Auctioneers at distraint sales were often under fire from angry farmers, and some refused to alienate the men for whom they usually conducted business. On occasion efforts to distrain could be farcical: at Elham, in Kent, in 1932 more than 200 policemen were needed to preserve order while a bailiff and solicitor acting for Merton College started at 7 a.m. to visit ten farms to seize goods to cover the value of unpaid tithes. After six hours of fruitless searching, not least for two Jersey cows which the farmer said that he had never possessed, all that had been seized were two hens.[36]

Christ Church's Treasurer, George Hutchinson, wrote a long article for *The Times* in which he tried to explain what the issues were by taking a fictional country parish and tracing the effects of the agricultural depression and tithe legislation upon both the tithe-owner and the tithe-payer.[37] Hutchinson attempted to give the story from both points of view: that of the tithe-owner and the vicar, and that of the tithe-payer. He pointed out that the vicar had been the one losing out when grain prices rocketed during the war but tithe payments were capped, and that the owner of the farm lost out on tithe payments during the depression when tithe-payers were granted remission of tithes that were more than two-thirds the rental value of the land. After the war the imaginary owner of the fictitious farm, brought low by death duties and poor return on investments, decided to sell to the sitting tenant. The tenant jumped at the chance as conditions were then favourable, taking out a mortgage to complete the purchase. By 1933, however, things had changed; the Corn Production Act had been repealed, and government wages boards insisted on a minimum agricultural wage. The produce of the farm was worth only half what it had been when the tenant had bought it; he was unable to pay back the mortgage; and there was no one who would wish to buy. He was also still paying the £109 tithe charge, and the notion that it would be extinguished in 2009 was cold comfort. The farm was deteriorating as there was no spare cash to do repairs, let alone make improvements. It was no wonder that he, and his contemporaries, resented the tithe. Hutchinson, while sympathetic to his farmer, also felt that it was unfair on the local vicar, who, if tithes were abolished, would be deprived of his income.

Christ Church took the same line as it had during the agricultural depression of the 1880s and 1890s: they would assess cases of hardship individually. Farmers were struggling again, from bad harvests, cheap imports and low prices. A record 600 farmers were declared bankrupt in 1932 alone. Those who survived cut the number of labourers they employed.[38] The payment of tithe was just an added burden. Some colleges, such as Merton, had come in for some publicity in their fight for tithes, but the lack of records from the 1930s at Christ Church means that it is impossible to tell whether the Governing Body had fought any public battles.[39] However, all through the depression years Christ Church was investing in improvements to farms and farmhouses, and there are only one or two instances of tenants wishing to terminate their leases.[40] The campaign of the Universities of Oxford and Cambridge, which held the bulk of lay tithes, led by the bursar of New College, Geoffrey Radcliffe, was unsuccessful, and in 1936 the Tithe Act was passed, extinguishing tithe rent charge, as of 2 October that year.[41] Government stock was issued in compensation of an amount that would yield sufficient interest to cover the gross annual value of tithe rent charge.[42] A redemption annuity would be charged on the land for sixty years after the date of the Act.[43] Tithe annuities were paid first to the Tithe Redemption Commission, which was set up by the 1936 Act, and then to the Inland Revenue from 1960. Small annuities (under £1) were abolished in 1951, and all annuities terminated by the Finance Act 1977.

By 1937, when the Agriculture Act was passed, another war was already looming on the horizon. The Act was designed to improve exhausted grassland either for better grass or better arable, should impending hostilities require additional arable cultivation. Farmers hoped that the Act would be the stimulus for preparation for war until their hopes were dashed when, in July 1938, Neville Chamberlain announced, on the advice of his minister of agriculture, William Morrison, that there was no need to increase production of foodstuffs until, or unless, war was actually declared. Morrison was succeeded at the ministry by Reginald Dorman-Smith, who had been president of the National Farmers' Union. It was not long before plans were in place under the Agricultural Development Act of 1939 to ensure that food production and distribution were organised.[44]

Negotiations were under way with the Air Ministry concerning the sale of land in Brize Norton in 1937 for the new aerodrome, and more was requisitioned in October 1939. Marlborough Farm in Burton Dassett (Warwickshire) was requisitioned by the War Department, and the tenant applied to surrender the lease. In Worcester land was acquired compulsorily for an emergency hospital, and consent was given for the Oxford City Corporation to erect air-raid shelters for Cowley St James School. As had been done in 1914, permission was sought to abandon building schemes until the war ended. No specific policy for the wartime administration of estates was laid down by the Governing Body; in fact, the papers suggest that things carried on much as usual, with grants being requested by and awarded to tenants, particularly for improved water supplies and drainage. There is some evidence that arable was being extended again: 100 acres in Wroxton, from which ironstone had been removed since the First World War, was to be used to grow corn. War damage was inevitable too. In November 1941, £21 was spent repairing a property in Brize Norton that had been hit by a drifting barrage balloon, and £450 was reclaimed from the War Damage Commission in 1942 for repairs to Little Bridge Farm in Ellerbeck.[45]

Although the war is treated with a very light touch in the Governing Body papers, there are clues that tenants in some places did suffer. The Kentish Town estate was certainly badly bomb-damaged, and a number of buildings needed repair or complete rebuilding. St Pancras Borough Council was on the look-out for sites for temporary housing too.[46] Post-war housing schemes prompted several councils to approach Christ Church for land: Worcester Corporation were looking for a site of nearly 200 acres; Southam Rural District Council bought a plot in Fenny Compton for development; and glebe land was sold in Sheering.[47] Immediately after the war, in contrast to the sales of 1919 and 1920, the Governing Body immediately began to buy, particularly commercial property, including shops in Sevenoaks and

Tonbridge (Kent), factories in Bridgwater (Somerset) and Croydon (Surrey), a bank in Kingston upon Thames (Surrey) and an office building in the City of London.

The agricultural estate was to be revalued. In a similar move to that taken by the Chapter after the Civil War and unrest of the mid-seventeenth century, when it commissioned a report on its landholdings to be drawn up in the form of the Book of Evidences, the Governing Body responded to the disruption of the Second World War by appointing the land agents Smith-Woolley & Co. to undertake a preliminary survey, followed by a more detailed valuation, of the agricultural estate for the 'purpose of securing an increase in rents'.[48] A new Treasurer, C. I. C. Bosanquet, who had taken up office in 1945, wished to assess the state of the landholdings after the war. Bosanquet had been appointed to the Treasurership in 1939, but hostilities had intervened. He saw service as Secretary of the Works and Buildings Priority Committee and then as Principal Assistant Secretary of the Ministry of Agriculture and Fisheries. A summer of touring the estates with his predecessor, George Hutchinson, evidently gave him food for thought.[49] With Smith-Woolley's reports and valuations in hand, a considerable number of farms were purchased, primarily to augment holdings that had been given at the foundation or bequeathed to Christ Church by benefactors over the centuries. Four farms, for example, were bought around Daventry to supplement the considerable property already held from the foundation, and new estates in Lincolnshire were purchased, including Chestnut Farm in Kirton and Wragg Marsh Farm near Spalding, as investment properties. The survey advised that they were on highly productive silt, suitable for all farm crops, market gardening and bulb-growing.[50] Others were sold, including three farms in Northallerton, and properties in Norfolk at Wood Norton and Wendling on far poorer soils.[51] More locally, Manor Farm at Stratton Audley was sold. Parts of the estate there had been sold between the wars, including the Plough Inn in 1929, followed in 1939 by West Farm.

Manor Farm was surveyed in January 1952 by Christ Church's land agents, Smith-Woolley.[52] It was still largely pastoral, and those acres which had been ploughed for emergency food production during the Second World

War were gradually being relaid to grass. The tenant farmer had been in place since 1919 and, according to the agents, was a good stockman but lacking in initiative and rather work-shy. The farm buildings needed a bit of attention, and the field drains had been left largely unattended, Smith-Woolley reckoned, since the late nineteenth century. The rent in 1885 had been £300, and the agents calculated that the farm was only worth £435 per annum in 1952. It was recommended that Christ Church sold, as the expense of putting the buildings right and attending to the drainage was too expensive to justify. The Governing Body took the advice and sold Manor Farm to its tenant that year.[53]

After the lifting of investment restrictions by the Universities and Colleges (Trusts) Act of 1943, colleges began to move funds into equities, and at Christ Church a new investment policy was drawn up at the end of 1946 in parallel with the survey of estates. This proposed that moneys could be invested in any funds authorised for the investment of trust funds, public stocks, government securities, local authority stocks and securities, railway and other utility shares, and other corporate shares anywhere in the United Kingdom, colonies, dependencies, India or the USA.[54] In 1948 the Governing Body purchased £66,738 worth of industrials, and changes in investments began to make a regular appearance in the Estates Committee reports from that year.[55]

Smith-Woolley continued to act as Christ Church's land agents, not just undertaking valuations and making recommendations but also supervising repairs, maintenance and improvements. By 1950 the Governing Body felt that things were in good enough order to show off a little and participated in the Royal Agricultural Society Show held in Kidlington, near Oxford, that year with a display of 'before and after' photographs of improvements to farms across the country. Bosanquet wrote a report to accompany the photographs explaining that the aim in the post-war years was to provide better farms and better houses, with farm workers, tenant farmers and landlord all working in co-operation.[56] Good water supplies were the first priority, and over £8,000 had been spent in four years, supplemented with grants from the Ministry of Agriculture and Fisheries. Tile and mole drainage

Photographs taken for the 1950 Royal Agricultural Society Show held on Kidlington airfield, just north of Oxford. Christ Church was keen to show its investment in farm buildings and housing. Opposite top: Agricultural labourers' cottages built at Wragg Marsh in 1949 to designs by Smith-Woolley. Opposite bottom: Cottages in Brize Norton in 1947 just before re-thatching. This page top: A Ministry of Works concrete hut purchased and re-erected for agricultural use by the tenant of College Wood Farm in Woodcote, near South Stoke. Above: Very up-to-date farm buildings at Manor Farm in Pitchcott.

schemes had been created, particularly at Christ Church farms on the heavy Oxford clays; hard roads had been built on eight estates that grew potatoes and sugar beet, making it easier for tractors and lorries to be manoeuvred, and yards had been concreted at many dairy farms; and a major policy of the Governing Body was to ensure that as many farms as possible had an electricity supply.

The provision of decent housing was another priority, not least to bring property up to the standards required by the local authorities. Modernisation, including the installation of bathrooms and lavatories, was carried out on a good proportion of the farmhouses, many of which were ancient and important buildings, and thirteen new houses had been built for farm workers since 1945. Cecil David Brown, employed as Clerk of Works from 1943, designed farm cottages and buildings for the estates.[57]

Adapting the farm buildings to accommodate modern techniques was another problem: keeping and maintaining old buildings and those with architectural merit while making farms usable in the modern world was not straightforward. It was, said Bosanquet, 'a constant challenge to resourcefulness to try to realise these ideals within the limits of economic expenditure'. Dutch barns were the biggest area of expenditure, followed by the improvement of the buildings on dairy farms so that farmers could secure attested status for their herds. Depending on the farmers' preference, either new milking parlours had been built or old cow sheds adapted for clean milk production. Bull boxes were a complementary provision.

Other 'improvements' done in the late 1940s would be frowned upon today, not least the bulldozing of fields to make them level (which must have destroyed acres of medieval ridge and furrow), the filling up of ponds and the removal of hedges to make larger fields, but this was part and parcel of agricultural policy at the time.

But, apart from this one demonstration of Christ Church's activities on the farms, there has been very little shouting about the college's landed estate, even in-house. Policy remained much the same throughout the second half of the twentieth century, and agricultural property continued to be an important and large part of the endowment. Acreage decreased – from around 30,000 acres in 1946 to around 17,400 in 1993 – but quality increased. Rent per acre immediately post-war was £1.24 per acre but rose by the 1990s to £51.10 (with a constant rental yield of 5 per cent).[58] In the 1980s and 1990s there were around 700 holdings, of which forty or fifty were whole farms. Policy dictated that farms which came into vacant possession were sold, and with the proceeds new tenanted farms of perhaps twice the acreage could be acquired.[59] Consolidation of the estates was still on the agenda, as was farm improvement; the geographical spread, although not the same as it had been in 1546, was nevertheless still wide, but in more productive areas and with a diverse range of husbandry, including, in 1993, a prize herd of Jersey cows, a stud farm and a substantial carrot farm. The farms varied in size too, from over 1,000 acres to smallholdings in the Vale of Evesham of no more than 10 acres each.[60] The Treasurer, Richard Benthall, aimed to maintain an agricultural portfolio of around 18,000 to 20,000 acres of grades I and II land. Occasional development windfalls were added bonuses to the corporate pot. In 1996 about two-thirds of Christ Church's income came from property, of which half was agricultural.

The Treasury acquired its own section of the Christ Church Annual Report in 1990 but the short paragraph dealt solely with new buildings and repairs to old ones within the walls of Christ Church. It was not until the report of 1994 that the Treasurer explained to the alumni how the agricultural estate was faring.[61] In 1997, towards the end of Richard Benthall's time in post, investment matters were also brought to the notice of a wider audience, and in 1999 the Estates and Finance Committees were amalgamated so that all endowment matters could be dealt with under one umbrella.[62]

* * * * *

Different colleges have managed their landed estates in different ways, particularly during the twentieth century. Some, such as Balliol, have sold all their agricultural land, but Christ Church retains some 10,500 acres.[63] The late nineteenth and early twentieth centuries saw immense changes to the estates and to their administration. Legislation has, at times, variously tied

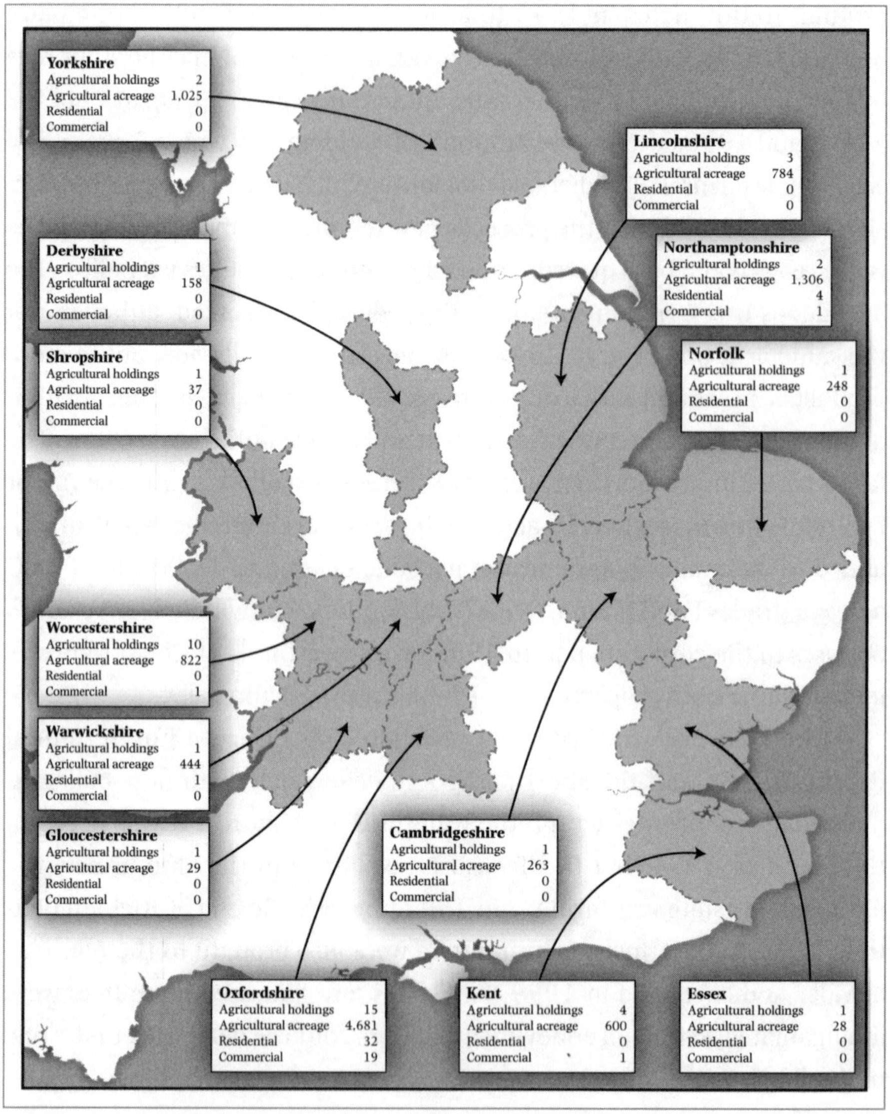

Christ Church's estate in 2020, showing the number of properties by category in thirteen English counties.

the hands of the colleges and liberated them in the management of property; world wars have caused chaos but also brought opportunities for improvement and increased income; developments in transport systems, science and technology have forced new methods; and the increased freedom of the colleges to do more with their endowments has reduced their dependency on the land.

In the late nineteenth century Christ Church, with several of the other colleges, began to build its way out of a slump. In the last two or three decades, particularly with government demands for the construction of new homes across the country, property development has once again come to the fore on farm land around towns in various part of the country, and investment in new land, often at nodes of communication, is now frequently made with the consideration of development potential. Farms are consolidated, and some houses – built over the centuries as labourers' cottages – are sold as changes in farming techniques require fewer employees. With land agents Savills (who absorbed Smith-Woolley in 2004), houses have been built on agricultural land around Brize Norton, Daventry and Evesham, and more are planned. The commercial estate – largely in Oxford but beginning to spread further afield, even overseas – still grows. Interest in land is also maintained through third-party property funds.

New opportunities have arisen with new technologies; investment in a wind farm on college land in Northumberland was considered, and rent is received from a solar farm near Brize Norton.[64] Climate change is also at the forefront of property considerations; energy efficiency – the aim to be carbon-neutral – is important in all new developments, which adds to costs, but there may be opportunities to purchase land that may have the potential to rise in value as timber plantations and rewilding become recognised as important issues by governments and environmental agencies. Corporate social responsibility and environmental social awareness need to be taken into account in the management of the main site of Christ Church and its wider estate.

Primarily, Christ Church's property is there to provide the funds for its educational and ecclesiastical functions. Its administrators were, in the early days, largely gentry clergy who understood the arcane origins of its revenues. From the end of the nineteenth century, as the old ways of beneficial leasing, manorial profits, tithes and copyholds disappeared, it became increasingly evident that the role of Treasurer had to be occupied by a professional financier assisted by a team of land agents and investment experts. In 1913 dividends and interest provided 8 per cent of colleges' gross external receipts; by 1987–8, that was up to 51 per cent. In 2018–19 assets were split almost equally between equities (and other investments) and property, although commercial and residential property is considerably more important to the portfolio now than the rural estate. And yet, for both sentimental and good financial reasons, that historic connection to the land, and to the tenant farmers, some of whom have held their properties for several generations, remains important.

Appendix 1: Monastic houses suppressed to endow Cardinal College, 1525

	Value	Manors	Rectories	Other income
Bayham, Sussex	£125	6	3	Rents and a mill
Blackmore, Essex	£85	1	4	Rents
Bradwell, Buckinghamshire	£47	1	2	Rents
Canwell, Staffordshire	£25	1	2	Rents
Daventry, Northamptonshire	£236	1	4	Rents
Dodnash, Suffolk	£44	2		Rents
Felixstowe, Suffolk	£40	1		
Horkesley, Essex	£27			Rents
Ipswich, Suffolk	£80	5	3	
Kexby and Leppington, Yorkshire	£90	2		
Lesnes, Kent	£189	2	6	Rents
Littlemore, Oxfordshire	£33	3	1	Rents
Poughley, Berkshire	£71	4	1	Rents
Pynham (Calceto), Sussex	£43	3		Rents
Ravenstone, Buckinghamshire	£66	1	1	Rents and a mill
Rumburgh, Suffolk	£30	1		
St Frideswide, Oxford	£220	5	6	Rents and tithes
St Mary de Pré, Hertfordshire	£65	3	1	

	Value	Manors	Rectories	Other income
Sandwell, Staffordshire	£38	1		Rents
Snape, Suffolk	£99	3		Rents
Stansgate, Essex	£43	1		Rents and pensions
Thoby, Essex	£75	1	1	Rents
Tickford, Buckinghamshire	£57	2	1	Rents and pensions
Tiptree, Essex	£22	1		Rents
Tonbridge, Kent	£169	3	4	Rents and pensions
Wallingford, Berkshire	£134	3	2	Rents
Wykes, Essex	£92	3		Rents and annuities
Other land and property				
Cheshunt, Hertfordshire	£30	1		
Rudby and Wetwang, Yorkshire	£190		1	Prebend

Appendix 2: Christ Church's foundation and trust endowment

Christ Church's endowment was magnificent, its income almost twice that of its nearest Oxford rival, Magdalen College. The location, type and origin of those properties are listed below. Many of the foundation and later estates were increased by purchase, altered by changes to land administration (particularly by enclosure and tithe redemption), and many have been sold, particularly after the passing of the Universities and Colleges Estates Act in 1858, and after the First World War. Those in **bold** type were the foundation properties, given by Henry VIII in the Charter of Dotation of 11 December 1546.

Bedfordshire

Cople – rectory with tithes, buildings and glebe lands, apparently from the priory at Chicksands

Flitton and Silsoe – rectory with mansion house, tithe barn and tithes, apparently in the hands of the Earl of Kent

Berkshire

Ardington – rectory with land and tithes, from Oseney Abbey

Buscot – farms, purchased in 1874

Chandlings – woods, from Abingdon Abbey, purchased by Dean Richard Cox in 1547 and transferred in trust to the Dean and Canons in 1562

Cumnor – a pasture, apparently given by Anthony Radcliffe to assist the fund for the building of Peckwater Quad, mortgage redeemed in 1692

East Garston – rectory with mansion house, glebe lands, pastures and all tithes, apparently originally from Amesbury Abbey
Easthampstead – advowson, bought by John Fell's trustees in 1701
Hampstead Norreys – manor of Wyld Court, given by John Morris in 1639
Lyford – some tithes and a close, from Notley Abbey
Marcham – rectory with houses and dovecotes, glebe lands, tithes and all other profits, from Abingdon Abbey
New Windsor – three tenements, given by Joan Bostock in 1633
Sandford – some tithes, from Abingdon Abbey
Shippon – tithes, from Abingdon Abbey, but not granted to Christ Church until 1601, after a tussle with the Duchy of Cornwall
Wallingford – land near or in the castle, purchased in 1548, formerly part of the property of the College of St Nicholas

Buckinghamshire

Ashendon – church, rectory and tithes, from Notley Abbey
Dorton – rectory with glebe land, tithes and land, from Notley Abbey
East Claydon – land, from Notley Abbey
Fleet Marston – farm, bought in 1867
Helsthorpe – estate bought in 1773
Hillesden – church, rectory, mansion house, lands and tithes, from Notley Abbey
Lathbury – rectory with tithe barn and chapel, houses and other barns, and tithes, from Lavendon Abbey
Maids Moreton – manor with lands, tenements, rents and profits, from Oseney Abbey
North Marston – house (called the Sign of the George) with houses, gardens, meadows and pastures, and cottage, from Oseney Abbey
Pitchcott – estate, bought from Baron Rothschild in 1853
Saunderton – manor, probably from Thame Abbey
Slapton – advowson, bought from the Duke of Chandos in 1730
Willen – income, given by Richard Busby in 1697

Cambridgeshire

Chatteris – farm, purchased from funds given by Thomas Wood, bishop of Lichfield, in 1697

Cheshire

Acton and Bollington – tithes, part of the rectory of Rostherne

Acton Grange and Daresbury – tithes, part of the rectory of Runcorn

Budworth – rectory with parsonage, chapels of Whitton and Peover, glebe lands and tithes, from Norton Abbey

Frodsham – rectory with parsonage and tithes, from Vale Royal Abbey

High Legh – tithes and land, part of the rectory of Rostherne; Rowley Bank Farm

Manley – fee farm rent, sold to Christ Church in 1913

Marthall – tithes, part of the rectory of Rostherne

Mere – tithes, part of the rectory of Rostherne

Newton and Hatton (with Daresbury) – tithes, part of the rectory of Runcorn

Over Tabley (with Knutsford and Peover) – tithes, part of the rectory of Rostherne

Preston – tithe barn and tithes, part of the rectory of Runcorn

Rostherne – rectory with lands and tithes, from Launde Abbey

Runcorn – rectory, from Norton Abbey

Sudley – tithes, part of the rectory of Rostherne

Tatton – tithes, part of the rectory of Rostherne

Thelwall – tithes, part of the rectory of Rostherne

Cornwall

St Tudy – rectory, bought by John Fell's trustees in 1699

Devon

Great Torrington – rectory with buildings, timber, advowson and tithes, part of the administration of Sir William Petre, possibly from Abingdon Abbey

Ottery St Mary – tithes, leased from the Dean and Canons of Windsor in 1674

South Brent – rectory with tithes, glebe lands etc., part of the administration of Sir William Petre, possibly from Abingdon Abbey

Dorset

Tincleton – house and tithes, from Abbotsbury Abbey

Tolpuddle – tithes and demesne land, from Abbotsbury Abbey

Essex

Leyton – house, given by Matthew Lee

Sheering – advowson, bought by John Fell's trustees in 1699

Gloucestershire

Aldsworth – manor and parsonage with lands and tithes, from the abbey of St Peter in Gloucester

Batsford – advowson, bought by John Fell's trustees

Bledington – rectory with glebe lands, tithes and other property, from the abbey of Winchcombe

Bourton-on-the-Water – estate bought by Richard Gardiner, and given to Christ Church in 1664

Down Ampney – rectory and parsonage with tithes and demesne land, from the hospital of St John of Jerusalem

Iron Acton – advowson, given to Christ Church in 1716 by William Jane

Little Compton – rectory, barns, glebe lands and tithes, from the abbey of Tewkesbury

Netherswell – rectory and tithes with glebe land, meadows and pasture, from Notley Abbey

North Nibley – tithes with glebe lands, meadows and pastures, from Tewkesbury Abbey

Notgrove – manor and farm bought by Christ Church in 1871

Temple Guiting – tithes and profits, from the Hospital of St John of Jerusalem

Tetbury – rectory and all tithes, from Eynsham Abbey

Thornbury – rectory with buildings and tithes, from Tewkesbury Abbey

Thornbury – house and garden purchased for the benefices of Rangeworthy in 1858

Turkdean – manor and farm, from Oseney Abbey

Twyning – rectory with tithes and glebe lands, from Winchcombe Abbey

Winson – messuage and yardland, from Oseney Abbey

Wotton-under-Edge – manor and the rectory with buildings, lands and profits, from Tewkesbury Abbey

Herefordshire

Staunton-on-Wye – advowson, given in 1621 by William Wickham

Hertfordshire

Tring – manor and rectory, with the rectories of Wigginton and Long Marston, with glebe lands, profits and tithes, given by Mary Tudor in 1555

Isle of Wight

Arreton – farm, given to Christ Church in 1732 by William Smith, founder of Portsmouth Grammar School

Kent

Hawkhurst – rectory with mansion house, buildings, gardens, lands, tithes and profits, part of the administration of Sir William Petre (possibly from Abingdon Abbey)

Ivychurch – cottages and gardens, purchased with other land on Romney Marsh, in 1906

Lancashire

Kirkham – manor, court profits and royalties, houses, and the rectory and tithes, from Vale Royal Abbey

Whittingham – tithes from the lands of the chapelry of Goosnargh, from Vale Royal

Leicestershire

Great Bowden – rectory with parsonage, mansion house, glebe lands etc., origin uncertain but possibly a property of the Earl of Southampton

Market Harborough – rectory and a benefaction of Robert Smith given in 1609

Lincolnshire

Deeping St James – land, purchased in 1949

Kirton – farm, purchased in 1953

Spalding – farms, purchased in 1947

London

St Sepulchre – house in the Old Bailey

Middlesex

Harrow – manor, rectory and tithes, reputedly from the land of Thomas Wriothesley, Lord Chancellor

Hillingdon (Colham) – tithes, from Thame Abbey

Kentish Town – part of Robert South's bequest of 1714

Montgomeryshire

Meifod, Welshpool and Guilsfield – rectories with all appurtenances, from Thomas Wriothesley

Norfolk

East Walton – manor and all profits, from the administration of Sir Richard Southwell

Saham Toney – closes, from the administration of Sir Richard Southwell

Swanton Novers – manor with all the appurtenances and profits, from the administration of Sir Richard Southwell

Upton – manor, with all the appurtenances and profits, including fishings and fowlings, from the administration of Sir Richard Southwell

Wendling – manor with all appurtenances and profits, from the administration of Sir Richard Southwell.

Wood Norton – manor, with all the appurtenances and profits, including fishings and fowlings, from the administration of Sir Richard Southwell

Northamptonshire

Astrop – farm, buildings, with all profits, from Oseney Abbey

Badby – tithes, from Evesham Abbey

Bimney – meadow, part of the administration of Sir Thomas Pope

Daventry – manor, capital messuage with all appurtenances, and property in the town, from Daventry Priory

Daventry – farms, purchased in 1947

Easton Maudit – land, from Lavendon Abbey

Flore – rectory, houses, glebe lands, tithes and profits, from Merton Priory

Guilsborough – tithes, from Bolton Priory, in Yorkshire

Harringworth – rectory with buildings, lands and profits, from Elstow nunnery in Bedfordshire

Ravensthorpe – rectory with tithes, from the Hospital of St John of Jerusalem

Thrupp – land, from Daventry Priory

Oxfordshire

Adderbury – farm, purchased for mineral rights in 1907

Banbury – tenement and land, from the administration of Sir William Petre

Beckley – tithes, part of Cardinal College, and back in Christ Church's possession in 1708

Benson – rectory and tithes, from Dorchester Abbey

Binsey – manor and profits, from St Frideswide's Priory

Black Bourton – manor and profits, from Oseney Abbey

Blackthorn – Essex Farm, purchased with monies from the Fell, Boulter and Bostock trusts in 1873

Bodicote – land, from the administration of Sir William Petre

Botley – meads, from Oseney Abbey

Brize Norton – church and rectory, with tithes and glebe lands, from Eynsham Abbey

Cassington – rectory and tithe barn with lands and profits, from Eynsham Abbey

Caversham – rectory with glebe lands and buildings, from Notley Abbey

Caversham – property from the bequest of Robert South of 1714

Chalgrove – rectory and tithes, from Thame Abbey

Clanfield – messuage, from Oseney Abbey

Clattercote – site of the priory, from the administration of Sir William Petre

Cowley – manor, with lands and pastures, from Oseney Abbey

Cutteslowe – farm, purchased through the Holford and Stratford trusts
Deddington – manors of Deddington, Clifton and Hempton, from the administration of Sir Thomas Pope
Drayton St Leonard – rectory with tithes, from Dorchester Abbey
Duns Tew – land, from Oseney Abbey
Elsfield – the 'home' farm
Enstone – rectory with glebe land and tithes, from Winchcombe Abbey
Epwell – cottage and land, from Oseney Abbey
Eynsham – closes, given by Rachel Paul in 1676, with additional land purchased with the Frampton bequest
Garsington – messuage and land, from Oseney Abbey
Garsington – farm from the Challoner Trust
Grafton – farm and manor, purchased in 1867 with funds from the South Trust
Hook Norton – land, purchased in 1874
Idbury – land, purchased in 1943
Lew – messuage and land, from Oseney Abbey
Medley – lands, purchased in 1861
Milcombe – manor, purchased in 1872
Overy – rectory and tithes, from Dorchester Abbey
Oxford:
St Aldate (with St Edward and St Michael and the South Gate) – tenements and the Meadow from Oseney Abbey and St Frideswide's Priory
All Saints – rents and tenements, from Oseney Abbey
St Ebbe – tenements, from Oseney Abbey
St George – a tenement and the church, from Oseney Abbey
St Giles – tenements, from Oseney Abbey
St Giles – house from Kidd benefaction
St John – quit rents, from Oseney Abbey
St Martin – tenements, from Oseney Abbey
St Mary Magdalen – tenements, from Oseney Abbey
St Mary the Virgin – tenements, from Oseney Abbey
St Michael – tenements and quit rents, from Oseney Abbey

St Peter-le-Bailey – tenements, from Oseney Abbey
St Peter in the East – tenement and quit rents, from Oseney Abbey
St Thomas – tenements, from Oseney Abbey
Pyrton – rectory with all appurtenances, from Norton Abbey in Cheshire
Radcot – land and cottages, purchased in 1891
Shipton-on-Cherwell – land, from Oseney Abbey
Shotover – farm, purchased in 1909
Sibford Gower – manor and copyhold land, from Oseney Abbey
South Stoke – manor and rectory with all appurtenances, from Eynsham Abbey
Spelsbury – rectory with land and tithes, from the collegiate church of St Mary in Warwick
Stadhampton – land, bought in 1747
Standlake – farms, purchased in 1638 by Samuel Fell
Stratton Audley – manor, farm, rectory house and all profits, from Bicester Abbey
Swerford – farm, purchased in 1860
Tiddington – meadow, bequeathed to Christ Church in 1726
Weald – land and farmhouse, from Oseney Abbey
Wendlebury – advowson, purchased with a bequest from Henry Smith in 1700
Westwell – manor and lands, from Edington Priory in Wiltshire
Woodeaton – farm, purchased by Christ Church in 1940
Worton – messuage and land, from the manor of Worton
Wroxton and Balscott – rectories, with timber and tithes, from the administration of Sir Thomas Pope

Shropshire

Careswell estate – five farms in Shropshire and Staffordshire given by Edward Careswell
Highley – Woolstans Woods, from St Wulstan's Hospital in Worcester, part of the administration of Sir Richard Morison
Wentnor – advowson, given by Thomas Thynne in 1675

Somerset

Batheaston – rectory, glebe lands, properties, from the monastery of St Peter and St Paul in Bath

Midsomer Norton – rectory and manor, with all appurtenances and profits, from Merton Priory in Surrey

Odcombe – advowson, given to Christ Church in 1726

Warwickshire

Butlers Marston – farms, purchased during the eighteenth and nineteenth centuries

Fenny Compton – manor site and land, from Clattercote Priory

Shotteswell – land, part of the administration of Sir William Petre

Tysoe – farm, purchased in 1861 with funds from the Lee Trust

Wiltshire

Charlton – rectory and tithes, from Ivychurch Priory

Chippenham – rectory with a tithe barn, all tithes and profits, from Farleigh Priory in Wiltshire

Chute Forest – fee farm rent, sold to Christ Church in trust for Pembroke College in 1677

Easterton – tithes, from Edington Priory

Maiden Bradley – rectory with all appurtenances, tithes and glebe lands, from Notley Abbey

Market Lavington – rectory, tithe barn, tithes and profits, from Edington Priory

Semley – advowson, purchased by Christ Church in 1717

Worcestershire

Aldington – tithes, from Evesham Abbey

Alvechurch – farms, part of the Lee Trust, and sold to buy new properties

Badsey – tithes, from Evesham Abbey
Chaceley – messuages, part of the Lee Trust
Chadwick – land, from St Wulstan's Hospital, and part of the administration of Sir Richard Morison
Claines – rectory and tithes, part of the administration of Sir Richard Morison
Clifton-on-Teme – close and house, part of the administration of Sir Richard Morison
Great and Little Hampton – tithes, from Evesham Abbey
Middle Littleton – tithes, from Evesham Abbey
North Littleton – tithes, from Evesham Abbey
South Littleton – tithes, from Evesham Abbey
Severn Stoke – messuage and land, part of the administration of Sir Richard Morison
Wickhamford – tithes, from Evesham Abbey
Worcester – closes, land and Frog Mill, part of the administration of Sir Richard Morison

Yorkshire

Bramham – tithes, from St Oswald's Priory
Ellerbeck – manor, with lands, demesne, fowlings, fishings and profits, part of the administration of Sir Richard Morison
Featherstone – rectory and tithes, from St Oswald's Priory
Kildwick – rectory and tithes, from Bolton Priory
Leeds – rectory and tithes, from Holy Trinity Priory in York
Long Preston – rectories and tithes, from Bolton Priory
Northallerton – site of the dissolved hospital of St James with land and all appurtenances, part of the administration of Sir Richard Morison
North Otterington – vicarage, sold to Christ Church in 1868
Osmotherley – messuage and lands, part of the administration of Sir Richard Morison
Skipton – glebe land, purchased in 1859

Thornton-le-Beans and Thornton-le-Moor – tithes, part of the administration of Sir Richard Morison

Thornton-le-Street – tithes, part of the administration of Sir Richard Morison

Wath – rectory glebe lands, and tithes, from St Oswald's Priory

Appendix 3: Treasurers of Christ Church

Most of this list of Treasurers was compiled from various archival sources by Dr E. G. W. Bill in the mid-1950s. There are some gaps in the early years, particularly in the middle of the seventeenth century, as sources are not always complete. It is only the first Treasurer who has been listed; in the sixteenth and seventeenth centuries it was not uncommon for there to be two or three sub- or under-Treasurers. Appointments were, historically, made in December.

1546–55	Alexander Belsyre
1556	Henry Siddall
1557	Alexander Belsyre
1558–60	Henry Siddall
1561–2	Thomas Day
1563	Thomas Siddall
1564	Thomas Bernard
1566–8	Herbert Westfaling
1569	John Kennall
1570–71	Herbert Westfaling
1572	Tobie Matthew
1573–6	Robert Dorset
1577	Herbert Westfaling
1578	Robert Dorset
1579–80	Herbert Westfaling
1581–2	Thomas Thornton
1583	Daniel Bernard
1584–5	Ralph Pickhaver
1586–8	Martin Heton
1589–90	Richard Eedes
1591–4	John Weston
1595	Arthur Wake
1596	Ralph Pickhaver
1597–8	Thomas Thornton
1599–1603	Richard Thornton
1604–5	John Howson
1606–13	Richard Thornton
1614–15	John Weston
1616–17	William Ballowe
1618–19	John Weston
1620	William Piers
1621	Leonard Hutton
1622–32	John Weston
1633	Samuel Fell
1640	John Morris
1641–4	Thomas Iles

1649	John Mills
1651–2	Henry Cornish
1653	Ambrose Upton
1656	Ralph Button
1657	Henry Wilkinson
1658–9	Henry Cornish
1660–61	John Dolben
1662–4	Richard Allestree
1665	Edward Pocock
1666–74	George Croyden
1675–81	Henry Smith
1682–9	John Hammond
1690–91	Henry Smith
1692–5	Roger Altham
1696–1704	Anthony Radcliffe
1705–10	William Stratford
1711–12	Francis Gastrell
1713	John Potter
1714	Thomas Burton
1715–26	Robert Clavering
1727–9	Thomas Tanner
1730–35	John Gilbert
1736–8	Richard Trevor
1739–46	Philip Barton
1747–51	David Gregory
1752–5	John Fanshawe
1756–9	Paul Forester
1760–62	Edward Bentham
1763–7	John Tottie
1768	William Digby
1769	John Tottie
1770–75	John Jeffreys
1776–80	Henry Bathurst
1781–2	Cyril Jackson
1783–9	Arthur Onslow
1790–95	Benjamin Blayney
1796–1801	Robert Holmes
1802–07	William Jackson
1808–12	William Howley
1813–23	Samuel Smith
1824–9	Phineas Pott
1830	Henry Woodcock
1831–56	John Bull
1857–65	William Jacobson
1866	Walter Waddington Shirley
1867	Robert Payne Smith
1868–86	Robert Godfrey Faussett
1886–1910	William Baillie Skene
1910–45	George Thomas Hutchinson
1945–52	Charles Ion Carr Bosanquet
1952–72	Francis Anthony Gray
1972–85	Keith Batey
1985–98	Richard Benthall
1998–2005	Hugh Richardson
2005–	James Lawrie

Appendix 4: Deans of Christ Church

Richard Cox	1546	George Smalridge	1713
Richard Marshall	1553	Hugh Boulter	1719
George Carew	1559	William Bradshaw	1724
Thomas Sampson	1561	John Conybeare	1733
Thomas Goodwin	1565	David Gregory	1756
Thomas Cooper	1567	William Markham	1767
John Piers	1570	Lewis Bagot	1777
Tobie Matthew	1576	Cyril Jackson	1783
William James	1584	Charles Henry Hall	1809
Thomas Ravis	1596	Samuel Smith	1824
John King	1605	Thomas Gaisford	1831
William Goodwin	1611	Henry Liddell	1855
Richard Corbett	1620	Francis Paget	1892
Brian Duppa	1629	Thomas Banks Strong	1901
Samuel Fell	1638	Henry White	1920
Edward Reynolds	1648	A. T. P. Williams	1934
John Owen	1651	John Lowe	1939
Edward Reynolds	1659	Cuthbert Simpson	1959
George Morley	1660	Henry Chadwick	1969
John Fell	1660	Eric Heaton	1979
John Massey	1686	John Drury	1991
Henry Aldrich	1689	Christopher Lewis	2003
Francis Atterbury	1711	Martyn Percy	2014

Conventions and monetary values

Conventions

In England, Wales and Ireland the Julian calendar was replaced by the Gregorian calendar in 1752. Before this date, the civil or legal year began on 25 March, rather than 1 January. In this volume, however, all years, even before 1752, are assumed to have begun on 1 January.

All archival references, unless otherwise prefixed, are to Christ Church sources.

References to the *Oxford Dictionary of National Biography* (*ODNB*) are to the name in context unless otherwise indicated.

The counties given with each place name are those in use at the time of the acquisition of a property. The majority will, therefore, be the counties before the boundary changes made in 1974.

A note on monetary values

Calculations of equivalent values have been derived from Lawrence H. Officer and Samuel H. Williamson, 'Five Ways to Compute the Relative Value of a UK Pound Amount, 1270 to Present', on www.measuringworth.com. It is not always easy to pick the correct comparator, which is why, in some cases, two values have been given.

Notes

All references to material in the Christ Church archive are prefixed 'CCA', those to material in Christ Church Library 'CCL'.

Introduction and acknowledgements

1. Curthoys (2012).
2. Fletcher (1995).

1. Foundation and endowment

1. Curthoys (2012), 4.
2. Curthoys (2012), 12–14.
3. CCA DP iv.b.1, fol. 43v. Representing, based on GDP, an annual endowment income of *c.*£40 million today.
4. *VCH Essex*, vol. ii (1907), 137–8, 162–5. All the Essex houses, except Thoby, were initially given to Cardinal College but were then transferred to Ipswich School, Wolsey's first 'feeder' grammar school.
5. William Warham (*c.*1450–1532) was educated at New College and appointed to the archbishopric in 1503. Tonbridge is not far from Warham's archiepiscopal palace at Otford.
6. *VCH Kent*, vol. ii (1926), 167–9; Wadmore, 'Tonbridge priory', *Archaeologia Cantiana*, xiv (1882), 326–43.
7. *VCH Oxon*, vol. ii (1907), 75–7.
8. *VCH Kent*, vol. ii (1926), 165–7; *VCH Suffolk* (1975), 102–3. Lesnes is in Bexley, south-east London.
9. *VCH Suffolk*, vol. ii (1975), 77–9. Rumburgh, like the Essex houses, was to be added to the property of Ipswich School. The mark was not a coin but a unit of account, valued in England at two-thirds of a pound sterling (13s. 4d.). Three hundred marks would be worth about £3 million today, using GDP per capita. A quitclaim is a formal renunciation or relinquishment of a claim on a property.
10. *VCH Sussex*, ii (1973), 86–9.
11. *VCH Berks*, ii (1907), 77–9.
12. *VCH Berks*, ii (1907), 85–6. Edward Fetyplace was treasurer to the Duke of Suffolk. The surviving part of the monastic buildings at Poughley was, until recently, the residence of the base commander for RAF Welford.

13. CCA D&C vi.c.6, 59. Wolsey's statutes stipulated that the Head of House would be called a Dean, and the scholars Canons, which suggests a collegiate or cathedral church (and so the titles make sense after the foundation of Christ Church in 1546). However, a dean could also be the head of a group of monks in a Benedictine monastery or, in a college environment, a fellow in charge of the studies and discipline of junior members. Wolsey's use of 'Dean and Canons' demonstrates that he saw his college as a natural successor to the monastery. See Curthoys (2012), 5.
14. Ward (1843), 178–9; CCA D&C vi.c.6, f01.81v ff.
15. CCA DP iv.c.1. The volume records the income for 1526/7.
16. Ward (1843), 182–183; CCA D&C vi.c.6, 60.
17. The Censor Theologiae was (and still is) the Dean's deputy on the academic side of Christ Church.
18. CCA D&C vi.c.6, 61–3. Estate papers were kept in cases with numbered drawers for many years, although it is unlikely that the Cardinal College chests were ever made. The last of these – a more modern version – was removed from the Treasury muniment room in Meadow Buildings about twenty years ago, and the incomprehensible classification system devised in the 1950s for the manorial documents may have been derived, somehow, from the arrangement of the drawers. The tower room in which the documents and moneys were to be held, the door of which was also to have three keys, was never constructed.
19. Curthoys (2017), 27.
20. Ward (1843), 188; New (2010), 79–82. Today there are three seal matrices: the 'Great Seal'; a copy of the obverse of the 'Great Seal'; and the 'Small Seal'. None is the original. The use of the 'Great Seal', for college business, must be witnessed by the Dean or one of the canons and by a member of Governing Body. The 'Small Seal' is for the exclusive use of the Dean and Chapter or Dean and Canons. See the current Statutes of Christ Church, section II.
21. Colleges were not permitted to sell foundation property until 1858.
22. CCA D&C vi.c.6, fol. 64.
23. Curthoys (2012), 15.
24. LP Henry VIII, v, 86, nos. 173, 411, 872. There is a suggestion in Wadmore's article that the property of Tonbridge Priory was assigned to King Henry VIII College in 1532, but it does not appear in the *Valor ecclesiasticus* and must have remained with the Dean and Chapter of Windsor who were granted it after Wolsey's fall, in 1530.
25. *Valor ecclesiasticus*, ii (1814), 250–53.
26. Curthoys (2012), 17–18. The prebend was worth £78 per annum in 1535, about £48,000 today using the Retail Price Index. (If using a wage index, comparing relative average income, it could be valued at near £600,000.) Relative monetary values throughout this volume have been calculated using the calculators on MeasuringWorth.com. Choosing the appropriate comparator is difficult. The canons each received £20 per annum.
27. Tresham was the only canon to serve in all three colleges: see Curthoys (2012), 17.
28. Curthoys (2012), 20–21.
29. Curthoys (2012), 40–42; Curthoys (2019), 68–75.
30. Curthoys (2012), 99.

31. It was not until the middle of the nineteenth century that the Students of Christ Church would become the equivalent of Fellows in other colleges.
32. Curthoys (2012); Curthoys (2019).
33. Perhaps an endowment income of £25 million per annum today, based on GDP per capita (see note 26 above and p. 00).
34. See Appendix 2 for a complete list of Christ Church's foundation and trust estates.
35. Neild (2008), 14, 28–29. Trinity had only two estates south of the Thames (one in Surrey and one on the Isle of Wight). Christ Church had more, scattered throughout Wiltshire, Dorset, Somerset, Devon, Cornwall, the Isle of Wight and Kent. The roughly east–west division is evident.
36. In Oxford, Magdalen, and in Cambridge, King's. Aylmer, in *HUO*, vol. iii (1986), 523. The wealth of the colleges depended on their endowment, subsequent donations and the success or otherwise of the management of that property. The scale of contributions due from the colleges drawn up for the visit of Queen Elizabeth in 1592, which remained a scale for taxation for many years thereafter, was based on rental and other external revenues.
37. The tithes were finally granted to Christ Church in 1601: CCA Leases Shippon 1b.
38. CCA MS Estates 35, fol. 1.
39. Curthoys (2012), 49ff.; Bowers (2019). Trinity College, Cambridge, did not receive statutes in 1546 either. Edwardian commissions drew up codes for both colleges, and those for Trinity were promulgated in 1549 (with amendments in 1552, 1554 and 1560). It would appear, however, that the complicated and unique institution of Christ Church defeated the statute-makers until the nineteenth century.
40. There were often two or even three men listed as Treasurer in the lists of college officers. Presumably the second and third men conducted business when the principal Treasurer was away on business or indisposed.
41. Twigg, in *HUO*, vol. iv (1997), 774. This was certainly the case at Merton and University colleges, and a bond for £5,000 does survive in the Christ Church archive from the late nineteenth century signed by William Baillie Skene: CCA xlviii.a.83.
42. CCA xii.b.1, fol. 7r; Curthoys (2012), 47. Arderne took his degrees from Merton College before coming to Christ Church. He remained at Christ Church until 1551, when he took the vicarage of South Stoke (Oxfordshire); James Curtoppe (or Courthope) was a fellow of Corpus Christi College before being appointed as a canon of Christ Church in 1547; Thomas Francis (or Frauncis) was a medic who would be appointed regius professor of physic in 1554 and Provost of the Queen's College in 1561.
43. CCA xii.b.1, fol. 12; Curthoys (2012), 53 and n.40; CCA MS Estates 5, fol. 3.
44. CCA D&C i.b.2, 103; CCA Misc deeds 85.
45. By 1620 the Auditor's fee had risen to £20 10s. per annum, perhaps £58,000 today using the wage index.
46. Curthoys (2012), 283; Curthoys (2017), 62. Around £8,000 and £20,000 respectively using the RPI.
47. Perhaps in the region of £9 million using a wage index that calculates how much would be needed to purchase the goods in and around the property.
48. CCA MS Estates 80, fols 222–266.

49. CCA D&C i.b.3, 221–222.
50. CCA MR iii.c.1/4/3.
51. The principal series of documents include the disbursement books (CCA xii), the receipt books (CCA xi), the estates registers (CCA xx) and Chapter minutes (CCA D&C i), followed, after 1867, by the Governing Body minutes (CCA GB i).
52. CCA D&C i.b.4, fols 35 and 35v, 117v, 120v and 126v; Dunbabin, in *HUO*, vol. v (1986), 285.
53. Aylmer, in *HUO*, vol. iii (1986), 521.

2. Managing the agricultural estate I: revenue

1. G. E. Aylmer, in *HUO*, vol. iii (1986), 525.
2. Aylmer, in *HUO*, vol. iii (1986), 524.
3. See, for example, the position at St Paul's Cathedral in Johnson, in Keene et al. (2004), 309.
4. The percentage varied over the years, particularly during the eighteenth and nineteenth centuries.
5. Neild (2008), 19; Challis (1989), 11.
6. Aylmer, in *HUO*, vol. iii (1986), 534.
7. Ibid.
8. Richardson (1961), 30; CCA MS Estates 56, fol. 1.
9. The leases stipulated the reserved portion in volume of grain, and specified the grain itself, depending on the staple grain of the estate. The rent of the parsonage of Great Torrington (Devon), for example, was originally £63 per annum. It was divided, after the Corn Rent Act, into £42 money rent, with 1 quarter 4 bushels of wheat and 82 quarts of malt. The corn rents always seem to have been paid in cash rather than in kind. CCA1.c.3, 884; Aylmer, in *HUO*, vol. iii (1986), 535.
10. Neild (2008), 31.
11. Aylmer, in *HUO*, vol. iii (1986), 535–41.
12. Aylmer, in *HUO*, vol. iii (1986), 543. The 1557 lease of the rectory of Batheaston (Somerset), for example, was for ninety-nine years – see CCA Leases Batheaston 8 – and that of a small property in Shotteswell (Warwickshire), in 1553, was for sixty years – CCA Leases Shotteswell 1.
13. CCA series lvi.c. and ix.b. and c.
14. E. G. W. Bill, *Catalogue of Treasury Papers* (April 1955). Typescript catalogue of the first records kept in the archive.
15. Aylmer, in *HUO*, vol. iii (1986), 525.
16. Leases North Nibley 3.
17. CCA MS Estates 3, fol. 2; CCA MS Estates 86, fol. 207v.
18. Leases Great Bowden A 1. Styrley's lease of the rectory, parsonage and mansion place with tithes, glebe, meadows, pastures, commons, fishings, orchards, gardens, mills and all fruits and profits was another of the very long leases – this time of ninety-nine years – which caused such problems for Christ Church's income. It was granted on 15 January 1547 and enrolled in Chancery in 1569.

19. CCA MS Estates 44, fols 1–3 and 5–9; *VCH Leics*, vol. v (1964), 38–49. The problem of finding a 'sufficient scholar' to take on the curacy of St Mary in Arden was still an issue in 1613. In order to make ends meet, ministers were officiating at unlawful marriages and allowing regular services to go unsaid. Proposals were made, and carried through, for St Mary's and the chapel at Market Harborough to be amalgamated.
20. CCA MS Estates 48, fol. 3. Possibly as much as £3 million today, using GDP.
21. CCA MS Estates 48, fols 5–10. The Montgomery estate soon came into the tenancy of Philip Herbert, fourth Earl of Pembroke and first Earl Montgomery, at the request of James I and appears to have remained almost a royal gift for a century. The Herberts were powerful on the Council of Wales: Williams (1958), 236. Tenants included James Palmer, who was an esquire of the King's Bedchamber, then Roger Palmer, James's son and the husband of Barbara Villiers, who was first Cup-Bearer to the king and then King's Cofferer. He was made Lord Castlemaine merely to provide his wife, the king's mistress, and her children title and status: *ODNB*.
22. CCA MS Estates 40, fols 8–25.
23. Dunbabin, in *HUO*, vol. v (1986), 285.
24. Neild (2008), 16–17.
25. OUA WPy/16/1, fol. 19; Twigg, in *HUO*, vol. iv (1997), 786. Langbaine was also keeper of the University archives: *ODNB*. Instructions were issued by Parliament in March 1644 that rents should be paid to the local County Committees which were set up as local government authorities as Parliament took over areas of the country.
26. Twigg, in *HUO*, vol. iv (1997), 777, 787.
27. Spence (1991), 19–22. Skipton Castle was the last Royalist bastion in the north of England to fall to Parliament in 1645, after a three-year siege.
28. *ODNB*; CCA MS Estates 107, fols 84–90.
29. CCA DP ii.c.1, fol. 34.
30. CCA MS Estates 16, fols 180ff. This is probably an exaggeration; just before the war the estate was valued at somewhere between £500 and £700 per annum. There had, however, been an endless court case over Rostherne rectory, which may have swallowed up much of the profit from the estate.
31. *ODNB*.
32. Aylmer, in *HUO*, vol. iii (1986), 557; Twigg, in *HUO*, vol. iv (1997), 776–9; CCA xii.b.86, 58. The actual figure given to the king by Christ Church is unknown, but it is thought that Christ Church, with Lincoln, Oriel and New colleges, contributed around £3,000 of the £10,000 total. In 1643 alone 172 lb. of plate were handed over.
33. Twigg, in *HUO*, vol. iv (1997), 785.
34. Twigg, in *HUO*, vol. iv (1997), 788. However, the dean and canons in residence after the war would have enjoyed the proceeds from the high number of new leases issued once estates management was back on an even keel.
35. Johnson, in Keene et al. (2004), 308. Using GDP, perhaps £700 million today.
36. Curthoys (2019), 114–16. Throughout its history Christ Church has benefited from being both part of the University and a diocesan cathedral. There are numerous

examples of legislation – both parliamentary and synodal – that exclude Christ Church right up to the present day.

37. CCA D&C i.b.3, fols 10 and 11. John Mills had come up to Christ Church as a Westminster Student in 1620, and was made a canon in 1648, having been a Parliamentary commissioner for the surrender of Oxford in 1646, a Visitor in 1647 and judge advocate for the Parliamentary army. He was deprived of his canonry under Dean Owen in 1651 but returned in 1659 during Reynolds's brief second stint in the Deanery, before being sent to Norwich as chancellor of the diocese.
38. CCA D&C i.b.3, fols 4, 6, 27 and 47. Christ Church manors, on the other hand, have been the easiest to begin with because, as with the court system, there was already a mechanism in place to bring together tenants, copyholders and landholders.
39. Richard Smith, clothier, had taken the lease of Great Torrington rectory in 1616. After his death in 1650 his widow, Grace, took over the estate. After her death, her heirs were chased for non-payment of rent for nearly twenty years.
40. CCA MS Estates 20, fol. 59.
41. CCA MS Estates 24, fol. 8; CCA li.c.3, 527. The manorial estates were managed through the local manor courts, the records of which, in the early modern period, generally record just admissions to copyholds with the associated costs, rather than the more detailed proceedings of the medieval period.
42. CCA MS Estates 52, fols 1–7
43. Bod MS Tanner 106, fol. 30 (with copy at CCA MR iii.c.1/7/5); CCA MS Estates 16, fols 32–49. Rostherne is about 15 miles south-west of Manchester. Christ Church also had an interest in other parishes near by, including Frodsham, Runcorn, Knutsford and Daresbury, the birthplace of Charles Dodgson (Lewis Carroll). There were properties in Lancashire (west of Preston) and in west and north Yorkshire.
44. Outside the scope of this volume, room rents and University and college fees were another significant income stream.
45. Harvey (1984), 55; Hilton (1969), 47.
46. The manors given to Christ Church at the foundation were those of: Maids Moreton and Saunderton (Buckinghamshire); Aldsworth, Turkdean and Wotton-under-Edge (Gloucestershire); Tring (Hertfordshire); Kirkham (Lancashire); Harrow (Middlesex); East Walton, Swanton Novers, Upton, Wendling and Wood Norton (Norfolk); Daventry (Northamptonshire); Binsey, Black Bourton, Cowley, Deddington (with Clifton and Hempton), Oxford St Thomas (South Oseney), Sibford Gower, South Stoke, Stratton Audley and Westwell (Oxfordshire); Midsomer Norton (Somerset); Fenny Compton (Warwickshire); and Ellerbeck (Yorkshire). A few others were acquired at later dates: see Appendix.
47. CCA1.c.2, 498–500. In this part of the country, a yardland was the equivalent of 24 acres.
48. One odd due to the manor of Maids Moreton was the suit and service due from All Souls College. There seems to have been no financial benefit to Christ Church from this, so it must have derived from a medieval due to Oseney Abbey that had since lapsed in all but the paperwork. No record appears to survive at All Souls either. A similar suit was due from Corpus Christi College out of the manor of Church Cowley.

49. Perhaps £25,000 today, using the RPI. The Book of Evidences records that a yardland in Maids Moreton was only 24 acres, which was considered large enough for thirty sheep and four 'beasts'. The area could vary from region to region between 15 and 40 acres.
50. The Cartwright family also held the Duchy manor, one of the other two (or possibly three) manors in Deddington. In addition to the manor of Deddington with Clifton and Hempton, there seems to have been another small manor called Ilbury, of which Christ Church held a portion called Ilbury Leasow. The Book of Evidences does not call it a manor.
51. CCA1.c.2, 421–422; *VCH Oxon*, xi (1983), 81–120.
52. CCA MS Estates 56, fols 18–20; CCA1.c.3, 767.
53. Mining is dealt with in Chapter 7 below.
54. There is no evidence that the shipbuilding industry decimated British woodland. If there were difficulties in the supply, Oliver Rackham suggests that this was down to poor organisation and transport or low prices offered, rather than any shortage of appropriate timber. If, he says, there had been difficulties finding timber for the tiny fleet that defeated the Armada, it would have been impossible to supply the very much larger fleet that defeated Napoleon. Shipbuilders always used British oak, except for the masts, which were always imported. See Rackham (1990), 95.
55. Thomas, in Broad and Hoyle (1997), 115.
56. Rickard [Oxford, 1949], 12.
57. CCA viii.b.1, fol. 103r.
58. The woods, previously the property of Abingdon Abbey, had been purchased by Dean Richard Cox in 1547. A licence in mortmain was granted in 1741 that allowed the Dean and Chapter to make conveyances in its corporate capacity rather than in the names of the dean and canons as individuals.
59. CCA1.c.3, fols 847–850. Perhaps an annual rent today of £30,000. The equivalent of £100 would be about £220,000.
60. See, for example, the entries under 'Reparations extrinsicall' in xii.b.23 (1580/81).
61. The manciple was, with the cook and the butler, one of the three senior college servants on the domestic side.
62. CCA xlviii.a.1. Other estates that had enough timber to generate dividends were Swanton Novers and Wendling (Norfolk), Featherstone (Yorkshire), Chadwick (Worcestershire) and Worton (Oxfordshire).
63. CCA xxxiii.b.3, 11.
64. CCA D&C i.b.5, 71; Maps CCA Chandence 1; CCA Chandence A 23. A map of the estate was commissioned in 1723, for which the surveyor was paid two guineas. The area was also used to graze most of the flocks and herds of cattle purchased by the Dean and Chapter for the table.
65. CCA MS Estates 80, fols 267–269. The felling may have been for Dean Duppa's refurbishment of the cathedral, or even in preparation for Samuel Fell's first attempt at the completion of the Great Quadrangle. Surveys of Abbots Wood had been made in 1631.
66. CCA D&C i.b.5, 72, 116, 211. Surman's property was, at least in the nineteenth century, a beer-house.

67. CCA D&C i.b.3, 87.
68. CCA D&C i.b.3, 283; CCA D&C i.b.4, fol. 4; CCA D&C i.b.10, fol. 32v; CCA MS Estates 2, fol. 239; CCA D&C i.b.10, 10; Curthoys (2017), 162–4.
69. In 1780, during the construction of Canterbury Quad, old timbers and wainscoting from the medieval Canterbury College were sold to add to the building fund: CCA xxxiii.b.3, 12.
70. Sampson's Wood (120 acres), and four coppices named after Dorset (49 acres), Weston (51 acres), Thornton (70 acres) and Howson (16 acres).
71. CCA MS Estates 80, fols 117–266. The lease of the manor was granted to William Palmer, Christ Church's Auditor, in 1569. His father, Thomas, had bequeathed £20 to Christ Church for the building of a new tower. William died in 1596, also leaving bequests to Christ Church, which his son, Barton, refused to administer. In 1608, on Barton's death, a case went to court. The Dean and Chapter took the patent of auditor away from the Palmers (it had been purchased by William for the family), which caused further ructions. The Chapter stood firm, however, and the Palmers, having embezzled Christ Church of its legacies, were not reinstated. Philip King, the brother of the Dean, held the auditorship from 1608 until at least 1630.
72. CCA MS Estates 80, fol. 274. Hannars was William Barber's father-in-law and died in 1678. William appears to have taken over the running of the South Stoke manor and estate some time before his father-in-law's death.
73. Any loss of timber during the 1640s may have been a direct consequence of the war. Certainly Hannars was concerned about a demand for timber from the governor of Wallingford Castle in March 1646: CCA MS Estates 80, fol. 765. See also Twigg, in *HUO*, vol. iv (1997), 791.
74. CCA D&C i.b.3, 4 and 9. The rectory of Turkdean (Gloucestershire) was also a Christ Church property. Wheeler would become Christ Church's tenant in Turkdean in 1662 (although only temporarily, and on payment of a lump sum to Thomas Keble of Southrop, who continued to lease the property in reversion) which suggests that any concerns over his management had been lifted.
75. CCA South Stoke B1 and 2. The woods were leased later in 1650 to Henry Bishop, a Student of Christ Church from 1642 until *c.*1650, and remained with his family until 1720.
76. Perhaps £40,000 today, using the RPI.
77. Rackham (1990), 76–7.
78. The two manorial documents are from 1501/2 (17 Henry VII) and 1479/80 (19 Edward IV): see Denholm-Young (1931), 18–19.
79. It does appear that there were two manors in Turkdean and that one did indeed belong to William Banister. He owned a copyhold of land in Lower Turkdean whereas Christ Church manor was in Upper Turkdean. The argument was clearly that the commons belonged to the upper village not the lower. See *VCH Glos*, vol. ix (2001), 217–33, and CCA MS Estates 31, fol. 527.
80. *ODNB*. Robert d'Oilly, with his brothers Gilbert and Nigel, came over to England at the Conquest. It was Robert, with his friend Roger d'Ivry, who built Oxford Castle and founded the collegiate church of St George within the castle walls.

81. Paulinus held the manor of Theydon Mount in the early thirteenth century: *VCH Essex*, vol. iv (1956), 276.
82. CCA1.c.3, 522.
83. CCA MS Estates 31, fols 517–530. In 1714 the Dean and Chapter ordered that no timber could be cut without their permission: CCA D&C i.b.5, fol. 13v.
84. CCA MS Estates 103, fols 6–150. The case was still rumbling into the 1650s. A substantial portion of Perry Wood survives today and is a nature reserve.
85. The lease, for just four years, was to Francis West, a servant of the dean, and issued so that the action could be made in his name.
86. Perhaps £500,000 today using GDP.
87. CCA MS Estates 104, fol. 209.
88. CCA MS Estates 104, fol. 274.
89. Things did not improve and it looked at one point, as the city of Worcester crossed the railway and began to converge on first Perry and then Nunnery Woods, as though all would be grubbed out. However, both woods did survive and were leased to the local council as leisure facilities.
90. CCA MS Estates 80, fol. 316v; CCA Maps South Stoke 1 and 2.
91. It would appear that the previous tenant, Richard Fisher, a London haberdasher, had been given notice to quit by Christmas 1803. The lease had come up for sale in April 1803 and included a new farmhouse and buildings, 101 acres of arable and 203 acres of beech woodland.
92. CCA MS Estates 80, fol. 355.
93. CCA MS Estates 80, fols 361–363.
94. CCA MS Estates 80, fol. 264.
95. CCA GB i.b.2, 335.
96. CCA South Stoke, B.71.
97. Aylmer, in *HUO*, vol. iii (1986), 521–4.

3. Parsons and parsonages: Christ Church's incumbencies

1. CCA xiv.b.2 records the eighty-six incumbencies in Christ Church's gift in 1778; the number was ninety in 1900, and is now (2019) seventy-eight.
2. Dunbabin, in *HUO*, vol. v (1986), 292. The rector, or the lessee, of the parish was usually responsible – until modern times – for the chancel of the parish church, and the congregation for the maintenance of the rest of the building.
3. CCA MS Estates 26, fol. 11.
4. Hill (1971), 50. The very term 'incumbent' indicates that the clergyman 'lay' upon the property, to a certain extent reducing its value. At Christ Church the gift of a living was often made to a Student and became increasingly sought after as clergymen married and had families. It was not until the middle of the nineteenth century that Students (and Fellows) in the colleges were permitted to marry.
5. Curthoys, in *HUO*, vol. vi (1997), 482.
6. Students at Christ Church, always with an upper-case 'S', were men given a stipend from the endowment, unlike fee-paying commoners. These men were elected as undergraduates (a little like an exhibitioner today) but could hold their Studentship

indefinitely as long as they did not marry, took their examinations at the appropriate times, were ordained at least as deacons and did not take an outside post that paid a living wage. Of course, most men did move on to roles outside Christ Church, whether in the Church, government, their own family estates etc. Students today (since 1867) are the equivalent of Fellows in other colleges.

7. CCA D&C i.b.1, fol. iv; Slinn (2017), 117. John Pearson, bishop of Chester, delivered a series of sermons on the Apostle's Creed which was first published in 1659. The volume remained on the reading lists of Christ Church undergraduates for more than two centuries, and was a staple text for bishops' ordination examinations.
8. Curthoys (2012), 171–5; Slinn (2017), 110–12.
9. Curthoys (2012), 88; Curthoys (2019), 104.
10. Being ordained was not only the first step on the usual career path for an Oxford graduate but was also an essential requirement of remaining a Student at Christ Church, should a man wish to stay. Every year, after the December election, men who had not taken orders within the required period were given six months to do so. Applications to be ordained had to be made to the dean a month in advance of the ceremony. If a Student had not been ordained by the end of June, his Studentship was declared void.
11. Evans (1976), 6; CCA D&C i.b.6, 158 and 163; CCA MS Estates 24. Batsford was one of the advowsons purchased with moneys left by John Fell in 1686. In 1838 the value of the living was calculated as £456. The parish, particularly the church, benefited in later years from the generosity of the Mitford family. Lord Redesdale purchased the advowson in 1860.
12. CCA D&C i.b.3, 29. Thomas Hancock came to Christ Church in 1648 as a chaplain, appointed by the Parliamentary Visitors. It is possible that he went on to be appointed vicar of Chilmark (Wiltshire) in 1661.
13. CCA D&C i.b.4, fols 51r and 118*r; D&C i.b.5, 278. A decree of 1699 seems to have been a reiteration of earlier rules concerning the year of grace. In 1709 the clause denying any man more than one year of grace was repealed. However, from this date Students were required to ask for their year of grace within thirty days of their institution to their new benefice.
14. Students were either schoolboys from Westminster School examined for and elected to their positions by a panel consisting of the Headmaster of the School, the Dean of Christ Church and the Master of Trinity College Cambridge (the Westminster Students) or were put forward for a Studentship by the Dean or one of the Canons (the Canoneer Students).
15. Bill (1988), 303; CCA MS Estates 140, fol. 147. Morris exhibitions were funded from the income from Wyld Court (Hampstead Norreys, Berkshire) through the bequest of John Morris, the regius professor of Hebrew (1626–48) to encourage the study of Hebrew.
16. Freind was appointed to another living, Chinnor, which was not in Christ Church's gift, after his Studentship was declared void on his marriage in 1778, a position he held until his death in 1804. He was also a personal chaplain to William Markham, dean of Christ Church, bishop of Chester and then archbishop of York.
17. CCA D&C i.b.4, fol. 64v; D&C i.b.6, 260; DP ii.b.1, fol. 15.

18. CCA xiv.b.2, 10. In 1778 fifty of the Christ Church advowsons were considered of sufficient wealth to be given to Students.
19. £400 in 1778 is the equivalent, using the RPI, of about £50,000. The incumbent also had use of an elegant mid-eighteenth-century house.
20. The twelve that could be held in conjunction with Studentships were: Binsey, Cowley, Oxford St Thomas, Benson, Stratton Audley, Drayton (all Oxfordshire); Ashendon and Dorton (Buckinghamshire); Aldsworth (Gloucestershire); Ardington (Berkshire); Offenham and Hampton (Worcestershire); and Hawkhurst (Kent). Perpetual curacies were, in effect, vicarages but paid by stipend from a trust or endowment fund. Many appeared when large livings were carved up into smaller ones in the nineteenth century. The term disappeared in 1868, when perpetual curates were permitted to call themselves vicars, although the legal status was not abolished until 1968.
21. G. V. Bennett, in *HUO*, vol. v (1986), 35; I. V. Doolittle, in *HUO*, vol. v (1986), 247; CCA xii.b.2, 52.
22. CCA MS Estates 44, fol. 5.
23. Jennings (2018), 31–3; Brittain-Catlin (2008), 7. 'First fruits and tenths' was an ecclesiastical tax payable by clergy in Great Britain, originally to the Pope. Henry VIII annexed it to his own revenues in 1534. The tax remained payable to the Crown until 1704, when Queen Anne diverted them for the augmentation of livings with an income of less than £80. In the reign of Anne, 3,800 livings were estimated as having an income of under £50 per annum; by the time of the 1836 Ecclesiastical Commission report, this had dropped to 297.
24. *ODNB*; Bill (1988), 104; CCA MS Estates 138, fols 252 ff; CCA xiv.b.2, 10. The livings were those of: South Stoke, Brize Norton, Drayton, Stratton Audley and Dorchester (all Oxfordshire); East Garston and Ardington (Berkshire); Nether (or Lower) Swell and Little Compton (Gloucestershire); Charlton (Wiltshire); and South Littleton and Offenham (Worcestershire). South's will demonstrates his concern for the poor more generally, with gifts towards an apprenticeship scheme in Llanrhaeadr (Denbighshire), to clergy ejected from their positions as non-jurors, to poor widows and housekeepers in Westminster, to the Greycoat Hospital for poor children in Westminster, to the verger at Christ Church who had managed South's business in Oxford, to his personal servants and to the poor of all the places where he had lived or owned property.
25. CCA MS Estates 138, fol. 269; GB i.b.2, 124. The 3/5 South Trust still (in 2020) gives grants to Christ Church clergy.
26. Queen Anne's Bounty was established in 1704 specifically to augment poorer church livings. Of the 100,000 livings in the country, half had an income of under £80 per annum, and 1,200 under £20. It was usual for augmentations from the Stratford Trust to be matched by Queen Anne's Bounty. In 1854, however, the management of Queen Anne's Bounty was altered and the co-funding was no longer guaranteed. Grants were still made by the Dean and Chapter from Stratford's fund and from other sources. At the same time, the liability to repair chancels was divided between the lessor and the lessee: see CCA D&C i.b.10, 157.

27. As with the South Trust, the Court of Chancery approved an alteration to the Stratford Trust in 1869 to permit the use of the funds for the repair and building of parsonage houses: CCA MS Estates 138, fols 269–343.
28. Long held the curacy of Benson from 1755, but was permitted to continue there after his appointment to the vicarage of Shabbington in 1768. Judgson held the curacy from 1790 until 1820 in conjunction with the rectory of Adderley.
29. CCA D&C i.b.6, 178; D&C i.b.7, 385.
30. *VCH Oxon*, vol. vi (1959), 331; CCA MS Estates 83, fols 55–56 and 166; CCA Leases Stratton Audley A 53–55; CCA D&C i.b.10, 100v. It was not until the early nineteenth century that the Dean and Chapter reserved a cottage from the lease for the use of the curate. Even this was not considered suitable by some. In 1848 a house was constructed which met with approval.
31. CCA D&C i.b.6, 251–252.
32. CCA MS Estates 16, fols 1–30.
33. CCA MS Estates 16, fols 132–326.
34. CCA1.c.3, 686.
35. CCA MS Estates, 16, fol. 132;1.c.3, 676–681. Swan's case prompted a deep and acrimonious dispute over the living of Rostherne that was to run for many years, resulting in the creation of the Vernon Studentship in 1601, and many more years of argument.
36. CCA MS Estates 44, fol. 1.
37. CCA MS Estates 44, fol. 293.
38. CCA D&C i.b.4, fol. 20.
39. The Clarke family were lords of the manor from 1606 to 1833: *VCH Berks*, vol. iv (1924), 269.
40. CCA MS Estates 2, fols 26–28.
41. Maps Kent Hawkhurst 2 is arguably the most beautiful map in the Christ Church archive (see colour plates). The total cost of the survey and the map was £374 18s., which would have gone a long way to providing a decent house for the incumbent.
42. Brittain-Catlin (2008), 30; Pevsner, *Kent* (2012), 286; CCA MS Estates 38, fols 180–185. CCA D&C i.b.6, 182; CCA MS Estates 38, fols 46 ff.
43. CCA D&C i.b.6, 202.
44. CCA D&C i.b.7, fols 419, 421 and 568.
45. CCA MS Estates 54, fols 47–50; xiv.b.2, 227.
46. CCA MS Estates 9, fol. 224; xiv.b.2; Pevsner, *Essex* (2007), 681. The advowson of Sheering was not a foundation property but purchased in 1699 with moneys left by John Fell in his will specifically for the acquisition of livings for Students.
47. CCA D&C i.b.3,109
48. The Act, the first of a series known as Gilbert's Acts, was responsible for many new parsonages in the late eighteenth and into the nineteenth centuries.
49. Brittain-Catlin (2008), 17; Jennings (2018), 31.
50. CCA xiv.b.2, 100.
51. CCA D&C i.b.7, 421. Ardington was one of the poorer parishes with a stipend supplemented by Dr South's Trust.

52. CCA MS Estates 30, fol. 144. Holwell had matriculated as Student in 174, and was presented to the living of Thornbury in 1762. His cousin Peter Foulkes had been the vicar of Semley and a prebendary at Exeter from 1759 until his death in 1778, succeeding David Gregory, who was appointed Dean of Christ Church in 1756.
53. CCA D&C i.b.8, 16.
54. Jennings (2018), 34–5; McClatchey (1960), 19–29. In a period of only fifty years nearly 3,000 new parishes had been created and 5,000 new parsonages provided.
55. CCA1.c.2, 343; CCA D&C i.b.3, 87.
56. CCA D&C i.b.5, 46v.
57. CCA D&C i.b.6, 282.
58. CCA MS Estates 2, fols 99–148; Pevsner, *Berkshire* (2010), 129. The Vernon family held the manor of Ardington from 1833 to 1860.
59. Little Compton was historically a detached parish of Gloucestershire. In 1844 it was transferred to Warwickshire.
60. CCA MS Estates 27, fols 153–167.
61. Pevsner, *Warwickshire* (2016), 435.
62. CCA MS Estates 27, fols 181–183.
63. CCA MS Estates 27, fol. 186.
64. The 'Antinomian' communities in this part of England were probably Quakers. There were a number of Quaker chapels in the area, the closest probably at Long Compton, about three miles away. Other possibilities were the Congregational or Wesleyan chapels, also in Long Compton: Royal Commission on the Historical Monuments of England (1986), 236. Antinomians in the Christian Church believe that, as salvation is through grace rather than good works, the obligation to follow Mosaic law – specifically the Ten Commandments – is null. Their faith is demonstrated through morality.
65. Almost all of Little Compton church is a Victorian rebuild, reusing some of the original features. Only the tower is medieval: *VCH Warks*, v (1949), 50–52.
66. CCA MS Estates 139, fol. 105.
67. In 1844, according to Revd John Hall, writing in 1857, there were ten Dissenting meeting houses within the parish of Frodsham: CCA MS Estates 13, fol. 314. Hall had been a Student of Christ Church from 1826 to 1845.
68. John Fanshawe had been a Student of Christ Church from 1790 until his appointment to Frodsham in 1819.
69. CCA MS Estates 13, fol. 75.
70. *ODNB*. Sumner had been consecrated as bishop of Chester in 1828. In 1848 he was elevated to the archbishopric of Canterbury.
71. CCA MS Estates 13, fols 70–94. Fanshawe matriculated as a Canoneer Student in 1790 and remained at Christ Church until his installation at Frodsham in 1818. Wilbraham chaired the committee of Kingsley and Norley residents. Martha Woodhouse was the widow of Samuel, who had been the principal landowner in Frodsham.
72. *ODNB;* Pevsner, *Cheshire* (2011), 510.
73. CCA MS Estates 13, fols 295–310; Pevsner, *Cheshire* (2011), 419.
74. Pevsner, *Cheshire* (2011), 103, 394.

75. CCA D&C i.b.10, fols 34 and 34v.
76. CCA D&C i.b.10, 42.
77. CCA D&C i.b.10, 27.
78. Port (1961), 5. The total population of England and Wales was around 13 million at the time of the 1821 census.
79. CCA D&C i.b.11; GB i.b.2, 65 and 124. In 1859 a questionnaire was sent to all of Christ Church's incumbents to assess the state of the livings, including the availability of seats in the churches for the population. Concerns were raised that, if there was insufficient space, then parishioners would be drawn to Dissenting chapels.
80. CCA MS Estates 108, fol. 219v.
81. CCA MS Estates 108, fol. 298.
82. The Parsonages Act of 1838 permitted sale of land by an incumbent. The money raised was paid to the Governors of Queen Anne's Bounty (later the Ecclesiastical Commissioners), who would then allocate it for the erection of a new house or the purchase of something suitable.
83. *ODNB*. Hook had come up to Christ Church in 1817.
84. CCA MS Estates 110, 66–69.
85. CCA MS Estates 110, 160–172; 7 Victoria, 1844.
86. CCA MS Estates 110, 278.
87. CCA MS Estates 110, 378, 399.
88. After the passing of the 1902 Education Act the Governing Body established a policy of grants to schools in parishes where Christ Church had land. Governing Body announced that it would pay the proportion of their subscription to any school to which they normally subscribed up until the date that the Act came into force. After that date the college would no longer subscribe to any school but would contribute as landlords, according to their rateable proportion, to repairs thrown on managers of non-provided schools. They would adopt the same principle for any new schools. CCA MS Estates 138, fol. 35.
89. CCA MS Estates 9, fol. 4; *VCH Bucks*, iv (1927), 379. Merton College was granted land by Cave in order to pay the schoolmaster and to find places for additional scholars. The school was ruinous by 1699 and was taken down, the materials being used to repair the vicarage.
90. See p. 98.
91. See pp. 98–102.
92. CCA D&C i.b.8, 101.
93. CCA D&C i.b.10,129v. The Committee for Promoting the Establishment of Baths and Wash-Houses for the Labouring Classes was formed in 1844. In 1846 the Public Baths and Wash-Houses Act was passed, the first legislation empowering British local authorities to fund the building of baths.
94. Christ Church carries the nickname 'The House' from its Latin tag, *Aedes Christi* ('House of Christ'). Members are often known as 'Housemen'.
95. This could have been John Read who was a chaplain at Christ Church in 1661 and 1662. The Book of Evidences (CCA1.c.3, p.838) records that Read stepped down from the vicarage of Marcham in 1669.
96. CCA D&C i.b.3, 2 and 3.

97. CCA D&C i.b.3, 287.
98. Oxfordshire History Centre, MS Oxf. Dioc. Papers d.106. Jones was ordained in Magdalen College chapel on 21 September 1690. The church of St Mary Woolnoth had survived the Great Fire and was repaired by Christopher Wren. However, it was unstable and dangerous, and so rebuilt by Hawksmoor as part of the Fifty Churches scheme in the early eighteenth century.
99. Jones's incumbency at Great Budworth is not recorded in the Christ Church archives at all, which, considering it was in the gift of the Dean and Chapter, is surprising. The only record is the certificate of institution held at the National Archives in the papers of the Office of First Fruits and Tenths: TNA E331/Chester/14.
100. CCA1.c.4, 306.
101. CCA D&C i.b.4, fol. 57v.
102. CCA D&C i.b.4, fol. 56v.
103. CCA D&C i.b.4, fol. 69v.
104. CCA MS Estates 4, fol. 169. Garford and Frilford have been part of the parish of Marcham at least since the thirteenth century. Garford has had its own chapel since that time, but Frilford has not. The parish was in Berkshire until 1974.
105. CCA D&C i.b.4, fol. 54v; Brod (2001), 12–28; *ODNB*.
106. CCA MS Estates 111, fol. 174. North Otterington was a township in the parish of Northallerton.
107. CCA1.c.3, 717; Venn (1927). It is possible that the vicar, although the position was in Christ Church's gift, may have been chosen by the lessee, Roger Fauconberg, whose family had Cambridge connections.
108. Dunbabin, in *HUO*, vol. v (1986), 292. Hawkins, if this is the same man, had come up as a servitor, one of the lowest rank of undergraduates, who performed menial duties around college in payment for tuition. He had received a Paul Exhibition, funded by a gift from Mrs Rachel Paul, the widow of William, bishop of Oxford, of 38 acres of land in Eynsham (Oxfordshire), with a preference for 'poor resident Bachelors of good life and conversation': Bill (1988), 192.
109. CCA MS Estates 25, fols 19 and 20. Possibly William Arundel who had been curate at nearby Wyck Rissington and was later appointed vicar at Twyning, a little further north in Gloucestershire and another Christ Church living.
110. CCA MS Estates 25, fols 19 and 20; Dunbabin, in *HUO*, vol. v (1986), 292.
111. Ashby (1974), 186–7.
112. Curthoys (2019), 129–139; Dunbabin, in *HUO*, vol. v (1986), 292
113. Dunbabin, in *HUO*, vol. vi (1997), 423.
114. Dunbabin (1974), 211. By this time, established by the Tithe Commutation Act of 1836, a tithe rent charge – of money – had replaced tithes in kind.
115. Dunbabin (1974), 219. Christ Church's total annual income from tithes was £24,000.
116. Dunbabin (1974), 212–13.
117. Dunbabin (1974), 218–20.
118. CCA MS Estates 50, fols 1777–1904.
119. Statutes of Christ Church, Oxford; clause VI.

4. Managing the agricultural estate II: expansion and improvement

1. Twigg, in *HUO*, vol. iv (1997), 797; Dunbabin, in *HUO*, vol. v (1986), 269. Many colleges have gaps in records from the 1640s; this is the case at Christ Church, where volumes in a number of series, particularly that of the disbursement books, are missing for the 1630s and the later 1640s. Interestingly, there are no disbursement books from the 1650s either, which does prompt the suggestion that the outgoing Parliamentarian governing bodies did the same as they left their positions in 1659 and 1660.
2. Jones (2005), 114; Darwall-Smith (2008), 182–4; Twigg, in *HUO*, vol. iv (1997), 801.
3. Dunbabin, in *HUO*, vol. v (1986), 269–70; CCA DP ix.b.1. Supplies brought in by Dean Samuel Fell for this project immediately before hostilities broke out were purloined to be used in the City's defences.
4. Clark (1891–4), vol. ii, 113.
5. The Book of Evidences was divided into two volumes in 1952 and carries the shelfmarks1.c.2 and 3. A number of the documents mentioned in the Book have since disappeared and are only recorded here. The Book was copied from a draft which also survives in the archive. It has been digitised and is available here: www.chch.ox.ac.uk/library-and-archives/western-manuscripts-0 (November 2019).
6. The estates ledgers (shelfmarks xx.c.1 onwards) form a continuous sequence from 1540 to the present day. The volumes contain copies of documents 'under seal', primarily leases but also including presentations to livings up to the mid-nineteenth century and conveyances after the passing of the 1858 Act which permitted colleges to sell foundation property. Until the late 1990s, these were beautifully bound each year in heavy red leather. Now they are kept in less appealing but perhaps more practical box files.
7. Most of the medieval papers relating to property that would become Christ Church's endowment were transferred to the Bodleian Library in 1927.
8. Bendall (1997), vol. i, 59.
9. Bendall (1997), vol. i, 24–6, and plates 1–4; Fletcher (1995), 11; McConica, in Catto et al. (1996), 96–7.
10. CCA Maps St George 1. See Chapter 5 on Christ Church's urban estates.
11. Fletcher (1995), 65 and plate 11; Bendall, (1997), vol. ii, 76; CCA Maps East Claydon 1, drawn by John Burges of Stanton St John.
12. A terrier is a register of landed property, formerly including lists of vassals and tenants, with details of their holdings, services, and rents; a rent roll; in later use: a book recording the site, boundaries, acreage, etc. of the lands belonging to a private person, or a civil or (now chiefly) an ecclesiastical corporation: *OED*.
13. CCA viii.b.54; MS Estates 51. Canon Thomas Tanner's papers, most of which are in the Bodleian, contain a large number of notes, receipts, acquittances etc. relating to Christ Church business. Tanner was particularly active in matters relating to the college's estates, particularly in Norfolk, in the early eighteenth century. Several of the letters from Tanner concerning East Walton went missing after the then archivist, Dr Bill, took notes but before the calendar was bound. Bill's summary descriptions of

the documents are therefore the only record of much of Tanner's efforts to resolve the problems in East Walton. Some terriers proved useful for other purposes: the one for Thornbury (Gloucestershire) was taken to the church there to be kept in the parish chest to clarify the method of tithings: see CCA D&C i.b.5, 277

14. *ODNB*. Tanner held the bishopric and his canonry at Christ Church *in commendam*.
15. Tanner bequeathed Sancroft's books and papers to the Bodleian Library.
16. CCA D&C i.b.5. The appointment of proxies, recorded in the Chapter Books, suggests that Tanner was away from Christ Church a minimum of three months and up to nine months of each of the years from 1726 to 1731, in spite of being Treasurer from December 1727 for three years.
17. The manors of East Walton were Howard and Stranges, belonging to Christ Church, and those of Abbots and Priors, the first held by the bishop of Norwich but in the hands of the Barkhams, and the other held directly by the Barkham family by descent since the dissolution. All three were in dispute.
18. CCA MS Estates 51.
19. CCA viii.b.55.
20. It is not surprising that Christ Church wished to rediscover its rights in East Walton. The manor was potentially rich as it included the manor house, associated buildings, mills, waters, fishing and fowling rights, meadows, warrens, customary dues, timber, woods and underwoods.
21. Dunbabin, in *HUO*, vol. v (1986), 302–4; CCA 3.f.4. All manorial rights were extinguished with the enfranchisement.
22. CCA viii.b.1.
23. CCA D&C i.b.4, fols 41v and 82v. Even urban properties, particularly those in Oxford, were subject to reviews by either the dean or one of the canons before a new lease could be issued: see CCA D&C i.b.4, fols 4v and 10.
24. CCA MS Estates 115, fols 19–21; Bendall (1997), vol. ii, 577; Fletcher (1995), 53–6. William Young was a surveyor, valuer and enclosure commissioner active across the country in the later part of the eighteenth century. Today's equivalent would be around £400,000. Charles Watson-Wentworth, Marquess of Rockingham, had been prime minister between 1764 and 1766 and would be again, briefly, in 1782. His estate at Wentworth dominated the parish of Wath: *ODNB*.
25. CCA MS Estates 115, fol. 17.
26. Rockingham had purchased the lease with two years to run, so his first renewal and entry fine was due in 1778. Young's fee was about £11,000 today using the RPI.
27. The townships were Wath itself, Brampton Bierley, Wentworth, Thorp, Hoyland, Swinton and Adwick.
28. CCA viii.b.161. Young was uncertain whether or to whom the tithes on flax and rape had been paid.
29. Bagot's reduction reduced the entry fine down from an equivalent today of *c.*£1.2 million to just under £1 million.
30. CCA MS Estates 115, fol. 33.
31. Dunbabin, in *HUO*, vol. vi (1997), 384 and 385n. By 1840 Christ Church was charging around two and a half times the net value of the estate, rather than one and

a half times the gross. In practice, it was claimed, this did not make an appreciable difference.

32. Dunbabin, in *HUO*, vol. v (1986), 281.
33. Most colleges began to invest in South Sea stock, and then began to branch out in turnpike and canal bonds, and then into consols, but land was still at the foundation. It was not until the late nineteenth century that colleges were freed to invest in securities. Even then, consent was required from the Board of Agriculture. This was not changed again until the 1960s. Dunbabin, in *HUO*, vol. v (1986), 273–4, 285; Neild (2008), 87.
34. CCA D&C i.b.6, 210 and 219.
35. Hall (2014), 209–12. Other earlier and later field arrangements were common in the north, east and west of the country.
36. See also p. 32.
37. CCA MS Estates 3, fols 256–270. The row, which was largely over receipt of tithes, rumbled until 1613 complicated by the claim that it was the queen who owned a portion of the land under dispute.
38. Wade Martins (2004), 4.
39. Leadam (1971), 153.
40. Gay (1904), 233.
41. Overton (1996), 138–9.
42. Overton (1996), 156–61; Wade Martins (2004), 6–7; *AgHistEW*, vol. iii, 89–90; *AgHistEW*, vol. iv, 232–6. Depopulation and the conversion of land from tillage to pasture, so that men could no longer grow food, was a major concern in the sixteenth and seventeenth centuries (although depopulation was probably less widespread than the rebels suggested, and many of the decayed villages may have been so since the Black Death). In an area from which grain was not readily exported, only enough for local needs would have been grown. When the land to grow that grain had been removed, shortages and rising prices caused crisis.
43. CCA MS Estates 8, fols 5–24; Curthoys (2013), 181–200.
44. Broad (2004), 48–79.
45. Reed (1984), 138.
46. The strips and furlongs of the old open fields are still visible, in their wave formations, in the pastures around Hillesden (and around many other Midland villages).
47. CCA MS Estates 8, fol. 5.
48. CCA MS Estates 6, fol. 3.
49. CCA MS Estates 55, fol. 268.
50. *AgHistEW*, vol. vi (1989), 65–6. Not all new pastures were sown; most were probably developed from the ancient system of 'leys' which left areas of arable to be temporarily returned to pasture for common usage. To create new pasture land, the leys were left larger and longer. See Lane (1980), 21, 29–30.
51. Broad (2004), 238–9.
52. CCA D&C i.b.6, 199. In 1770, for example, Christ Church purchased seventy-five young oak trees from the University for the enclosure of Bledington (Gloucestershire).
53. Turner (1984), 1.

54. CCA MS Estates 55, fols 268–284; CCA Leases Easton Maudit 6–14. Christopher Yelverton was the son and grandson of influential Northamptonshire MPs whose principal residence was in Easton Maudit.
55. Gay (1904), 195–244; *AgHistEW*, vol. iv, 232–236. A Commission of Enquiry was established after the Midland Revolt in 1607 and generally came down firmly on the side of enclosure but against depopulation.
56. CCA MS Estates 28, fol. 201. Tetbury had been, since the early fourteenth century, one of the major Cotswold sheep and cloth markets. By the seventeenth century the wool markets were beginning to decline and the reaction of the locals to much more enclosure for pasture is understandable. Hurst, *Sheep in the Cotswolds: The Medieval Wool Trade* (2005), 80, 178
57. CCA MS Estates 28, fols 205–208; xi.b.35, fol. 21. A century later, the estate was valued at £163 per annum, with an entry fine of £80 in 1733.
58. Although a northerly property, Northallerton is in the Vale of York and on fertile soil: *VCH YorksNR*, vol. i, (1914), 418. In contrast, Christ Church also had property in nearby Ellerbeck and Osmotherley a few miles to the east on the edge of the North Yorkshire Moors, where one farm, Nunhouse, was described in 1776 as 'poor land, high and cold and inconveniently situated for the market': CCA MS Estates 113, fol. 44.
59. CCA MS Estates 111, fols 8–23.
60. CCA MS Estates 111, fols 24–80. Christ Church's land in Northallerton and the surrounding townships had originally been the property of the Hospital of St James in the town. Morison was granted the property after the dissolution of the Hospital and held it until Henry VIII included it in the endowment of Christ Church. Morison was sent as ambassador to Denmark in 1546: *ODNB*; *VCH Yorks*, vol. iii (1913), 317.
61. Possibly William Tyringham who later became MP and JP for Buckinghamshire.
62. CCA MS Estates 9, fol. 17.
63. CCA MS Estates 9. fol. 18.
64. CCA MS Estates 9, fols 20–23.
65. ODNB; CCA MS Estates 9, fol. 25.
66. CCA Leases Lathbury A 4.
67. Dunbabin, in *HUO*, vol. v (1986), 295; CCA DP ix.b.1. The value of those estates in 1772 was £72,000. Bill (1988) details the bequests that were made for the funding of tuition and maintenance of scholars.
68. CCA1.c.3, 916–917; CCA MS Estates 5, 1–264; CCA DP ix.b.1, 62. See also pp.103–104
69. CCA DP ix.b.1, 46.
70. CCA Leases Hampstead Norreys 1–4 and 13; CCA MS Estates 140, fol. 147; CCA lv.c.24. The first suggestion, in 1830, was to reduce the number of exhibitions to two.
71. Twigg, in *HUO*, vol. iv (1997), 794.
72. CCA Leases Eynsham A 1–24 and B 1–8; CCA DP ix.b.1, 47 and 62; CCA lv.b.72. Christ Church bought more property in Eynsham a few years later with the bequest of £100 by Robert Frampton, bishop of Gloucester, who had been an undergraduate at Christ Church before the Civil War. In 1853 the Frampton land was exchanged for a small plot that adjoined the Paul closes before the whole was sold in 1868.

73. CCA Leases Bourton 1–22; CCA MS Estates 26, fols 340v-392; CCA DP ix.b.1, 46; CCA lv.b.62.
74. CCA Leases Ottery St Mary 1–9; CCA MS Estates 25, fols 1–502; CCA DP ix.b.1, 47; CCA lv.b.25. The tithes belonged to the Dean and Chapter of Windsor.
75. CCA MS Estates 9, fols 224–253; CCA MS Estates 139, fol. 213; CCA lv.b.30, 38–39 and 46–47; CCA Leases Sheering 1–6; CCA DP xi.b.1, 41–42; CCA D&C xxiv.b.1/5.
76. CCA MS Estates 80, fols 1–174; CCA xi.b.1, 42.
77. CCA Leases Chatteris 1–43; CCA MS Estates 11, fols 1–714; CCA Leases Wentnor 1; CCA MS Estates 84, fols 236–251. Thynne had been an undergraduate at Christ Church from 1657. He was president of the Board of Trade from 1702 to 1705: *ODNB*.
78. CCA DP ix.b.1, 40.
79. CCA MS Estates 73, fols 1–23. The property included a brick kiln – ruinous for nearly all of Christ Church's ownership – and so became known as Kiln Farm. Christ Church also had a small foundation property (just 10 acres) in Garsington, which was sold to the Queen's College in 1892: Leases Garsington A.
80. CCA MS Estates 73, fol. 116; *ODNB*. Part of Kiln Farm was sold for redevelopment in 2013, but Christ Church still holds about 41 acres in the parish. Chaloner also founded a grammar school in Amersham (Buckinghamshire) which bears his name, but spelt Challoner.
81. CCA DP ix.b.1, 44; CCA D&C xxiv.b.1/5. Smaller benefactions in the eighteenth century included that of the advowsons of Iron Acton (Gloucestershire), given by William Jane, regius professor of divinity, in 1716, Slapton (Buckinghamshire), given by Dorothy Roderick in 1730, and Odcombe (Somerset), given by William Westley in 1726.
82. CCA MS Estates 138, fols 252–268.
83. CCA D&C xxiv.b.1/5. Income from the South Trust was also used to purchase the advowson of Semley (Wiltshire) in 1717.
84. See pp. 121–8 on the development of Kentish Town. CCA MS Estates 66, fols 215–384; CCA Leases Caversham B 1–F 2. Both estates were sold, at different times, and the funds invested in a Consolidated Trust Pool but still used for its original purposes. Christ Church also had a foundation property in Caversham which included the rectory with its glebe lands and buildings. It was sold in 1799 for the redemption of land tax, but the Dean and Chapter retained the patronage of the living: CCA Leases Caversham A; CCA MS Estates 65.
85. CCA MS Estates 90, fol. 38; CCA DP ix.b.1, 65
86. CCA MS Estates 140, fol. 110.
87. CCA DP ix.b.1, 64.
88. CCA Leases Blackthorn 1–3; CCA MS Estates 64, fols 1–3. The property was sold in 1953 for £10,000.
89. CCA DP ix.b.1, 62.
90. CCA MS Estates 61, fol. 1; CCA MS Estates 140, fol. 45.
91. CCA MS Estates 61, fol. 4.
92. Broad (1983); *AgHistEW*, vol. vi (1989), 358–9. The period from 1742 to 1760 was a particularly bad one for cattle plagues in England. Another Christ Church tenant,

this time in the north Yorkshire township of Osmotherley, wrote in 1750 that there were no cattle either on the property or in much of Yorkshire at all: CCA MS Estates 113, fol. 33.

93. Curthoys (2012), 6–7.
94. Smith came from Newport on the Isle of Wight. His medical degree was from Leiden, and incorporated at Oxford in 1696. *VCH Hants*, vol. v (1912), 147.
95. CCA MS Estates 34 and 37.
96. Washington and Marsh [1976], 5; Watson (2008), 18–23. Christ Church still (in 2019) has some input into the governance of the school.
97. CCA MS Estates 39, fols 1–168; CCA DP ix.b.1, 62. The schools were Shrewsbury, Bridgnorth, Newport, Shifnal, Wem and Donnington.
98. CCA MS Estates 139, fol. 4. It is not known why Edward Careswell left his estates to Christ Church. He had no connection with the college, or even with Oxford. The exhibitioners were to come from Shrewsbury (four boys), Bridgnorth (three), Newport (four), Shifnal (three), Wem (two) and Donnington (two) schools.
99. Bendall (1997), vol. ii, 417. Probert started his career as a shoe-cleaner to Sir Watkin Williams Wynn and worked his way up to be agent to Robert Clive and his son, the Earl of Powis (all these men were educated at Christ Church), and an enclosure commissioner.
100. CCA viii.a.53.
101. CCA viii.a.53, fols 2–4. Probert names the parish as Dutton Priors.
102. There were coal measures on Brown Clee Hill, mined from the late seventeenth century into the nineteenth. The coal was used in the limeworks at the foot of the hill during the eighteenth and nineteenth centuries: *VCH Salop*, vol. x (1998), 314.
103. *AgHistEW*, vol. vi (1989), 284.
104. CCA viii.a.53, fols 16–17; CCA MS Estates 139, fol. 33; Fletcher (1995), 83–4, 131–3.
105. Turnock (1998), 57.
106. Bendall, ii (1997), 106. Coldridge was employed by the Dean and Chapter of Exeter Cathedral.
107. CCA viii.a.17; CCA MS Estates 25, fol. 426. Coldridge's survey cost 5 guineas.
108. *AgHistEW*, vol. vi (1989), 706.
109. CCA MS Estates 25, fols 426–502; Leases Ottery 9.
110. CCA MS Estates 24, fols 20 and 37.
111. Thirsk (1987), 56–61; Wade Martins (2004), 12.
112. Turner (1984), 36–52.
113. Bledington (Gloucestershire) benefited from improved drainage installed by a specialist who lived in the parish. The original drainage had relied on the ridge and furrow ploughing. This was replaced by elm pipes and covered ditches filled with thorns, and then by the laying of clay pipes. The government had set aside £4 million between 1846 and 1850 to loan to farmers for drainage improvements. Ashby (1974), 339; Langlands et al. (2008), 24.
114. Turner (1984), 16.
115. Overton (1996), 150–51; Turner (1984), 17.

116. Turner (1984), 17–23; *AgHistEW*, vol. vi (1989), 44–7; Williamson et al. (2013), 134. It must be remembered that not all areas of the country were in open fields waiting to be enclosed at any period, Kent being a case in point.
117. Curtler (1920), 178–80. The Board of Agriculture lasted only until 1822, not to be re-established until 1889.
118. Curtler (1920), 257–61.
119. CCA D&C i.b.6, 199 and 208.
120. CCA MS Estates 25, fols 21–49.
121. CCA D&C i.b.6, 192, 199 and 208.
122. CCA D&C i.b.7, 397; MS Estates 55, fols 119–122. Bishop Hinchliffe was also Master of Trinity College, Cambridge. It is likely that Dean Bagot knew him well.
123. CCA D&C i.b.7, 398; MS Estates 134, fol. 7.
124. CCA MS Estates 60, fol. 268.
125. *ODNB*.
126. CCA MS Estates 60, fol. 202. About £25,000 today using the RPI, nearly half the annual value of the estate.
127. CCA MS Estates 60, fols 210 and 218.
128. Neeson (1993), 259–93. Little, if any, evidence of violent resistance to enclosure or any other agricultural improvements can be found in the Christ Church estates papers.
129. Allen (1992), 310–11.
130. CCA MS Estates 60, fols 249–98; Tiller (2019) accessed 10 December 2019 at http://tlio.org.uk/custom-community-and-conflict-in-south-oxfordshire/
131. For example: CCA D&C i.b.8, 31v (Lyford and Wroxton); 32v (Spelsbury); 39 (Maids Moreton); 40v (Wroxton); 64 (Aldington), and 77v (Silsoe); D&C i.b.9, 54v (Bampton); D&C i.b.10, 64v (Clanfield); 115 (Pyrton); 115v (Cowley); 154v (Tring and Wigginton); 158v (Caversham).
132. CCA D&C i.b.7, 602; CCA MS Estates 87, fol. 127.
133. Richard Davis was the king's surveyor: *ODNB*. CCA MS Estates 60, fol. 202. Additional sets of the plan and books could be had at the cost of 1½d. per acre for the old enclosure and 3d. for the open fields.
134. CCA D&C i.b.7, 638, 641, 669, 670, 675; MS Estates 58, fols 27–35; MS Estates 64; fols 47–51; MS Estates 101, fols 38–48; MS Estates 52, fols 319–325; MS Estates 53, fol. 76; MS Estates 54, fols 53–61; Bendall (1997), vol. ii, 156 and 416. Dugmore also acted as Enclosure Commissioner for Upton in Norfolk, and was surveyor to the famous agriculturalist Coke of Holkham. The enclosure of the parish was completed quickly; the first suggestion was made in August 1768 and the Bill read for the first time in February 1799.
135. CCA D&C i.b.7, 668; MS Estates 20, fols 170–200. Pridham was chosen as a suitable surveyor on 11 September 1797, but it was not until the 1830s that the common was enclosed (50 acres of which was set aside for the poor).
136. Considerable exchanges of land had taken place in the mid-sixteenth century, rationalising landholding in the parish: CCA MS Estates 83, fol. 1
137. There was a good quantity of meadow, and commons for sheep, cattle and horses.
138. CCA MS Estates 83, fols 10–20.

139. CCA MS Estates 83, fols 7–8. Richard Arnold, Christ Church's tenant, resided in Stratton Audley.
140. CCA MS Estates 83, fols 10–19. Caversfield was a neighbouring manor to Stratton Audley: *VCH Oxon*, vol. vi (1959), 327.
141. CCA MS Estates 83, fol. 7; *VCH Oxon*, vol. vi (1959), 329.
142. CCA MS Estates 83, fol. 20. The commutation of tithes was a regular feature of enclosure awards.
143. *VCH Oxon*, vi (1959), 329; CCA D&C i.b.7, 420. The private Act of Parliament was passed in 1780: 20 Geo III, c.50.
144. CCA D&C i.b.7. 635; CCA MS Estates 83, fol. 27. The archive is riddled with accounts of the demolition of an astonishing number of tithe barns.

5. From tillage to towns: Christ Church's urban estates

1. *ODNB*; CCA Leases All Saints 3.
2. CCA Leases St Michael 6.
3. Dunbabin, in *HUO*, vol. v (1986), 288.
4. The Court of Chancery was where any case relating to equity, including trusts and land law, was heard. The court was abolished in 1875, and the Chancery Division now forms part of the High Court of Justice. The Star Inn was an ancient coaching inn on the west side of Cornmarket. It was renamed the Clarendon Hotel in 1863, when it was refaced. The building ceased to be a hotel in 1939 and was eventually demolished in 1954 to become a new and huge Woolworths and then a shopping centre in 1984.
5. Willis recorded the proceedings in the Book of Evidences: CCA1.c.2, 81–94 and 256. He added that he had written this down in such detail to protect Christ Church against further incursions by the city council. An annual sum is still paid.
6. Curthoys, in *Oxoniensia* (2017), 133–63.
7. Christ Church still had an eye on the corporate coffers, however. Although a second block was planned, the return of only 5 per cent gross was not deemed sufficient. See also Curthoys (1995).
8. Graham (1985); CCA MS Estates 77, fol. 347.
9. Dyos (1968); Graham (1985); Chalklin (1968).
10. Brock and Curthoys (1997), 428; CCA MS Estates 45, fol. 331.
11. CCA GB iii.b.12/2, 292. The Oxford Corporation purchased frontages in Park End Street, Rewley Road and Hythe Bridge Street in 1920, and Christ Church contributed £1,000 to the lowering of Pacey's Bridge. Most of the surviving Art Deco buildings in Oxford are along Park End Street, the majority of which, including the Royal Oxford Hotel, were built with Christ Church's approval on college land. The head lease of the 'island' site, bordered by Hythe Bridge Street, Fisher Row, the southern end of Rewley Lane and Park End Street, was recently (2015) sold by the Governing Body.
12. CCA MS Estates 45, fol. 96; Tindall (1977), 105–6.
13. CCA MS Estates 45, fols 98–100.
14. Tindall (1977), between pp. 132 and 133. Old Chapel Row is now Kentish Town Road (the A400).

15. Tindall (1977), 102–3. Northbound stage coaches passed through Kentish Town until the construction of the Archway at the beginning of the Great North Road in 1813.
16. CCA MS Estates 45, fols 104–110.
17. Bendall (1997), 118.
18. Tindall (1977), 103.
19. CCA MS Estates 45, fols 120–140.
20. CCA MS Estates 45, fol. 159.
21. CCA MS Estates 45, fols 199–209.
22. CCA MS Estates 45, fols 201–203.
23. Tindall (1977), between pp.132 and 133, and 58. All names with Christ Church or Robert South connections.
24. CCA MS Estates 45, fol. 268.
25. Tindall (1977), 166.
26. Tindall (1977), 167.
27. CCA MS Estates 45, fol. 436; Tindall (1977), 175.
28. CCA MS Estates 45, fols 440–450.
29. St Luke's was the first architectural commission for Basil Champneys, whose father was the vicar of St Pancras.
30. Universities Commission Report (1874), 673–5.
31. Tindall (1977), 166, 168.
32. CCA MS Estates 45, fol. 454.
33. CCA MS Estates 45, fol. 456.
34. CCA MS Estates 45, fols 553–556.
35. CCA MS Estates 45, fol. 552.
36. CCA MS Estates 45, fol. 596v. Speights requested permission to extend further in 1900.
37. CCA MS Estates 45, fol. 603v.
38. CCA MS Estates 45, fol. 610v.
39. CCA xx.c.46, p.39 (for example).
40. CCA MS Estates 45, fol. 633v; MS Estates 46.
41. CCA xx.c.46, p.134.
42. CCA MS Estates 45, fol. 643v.
43. http://www.londonssilentcinemas.com/ Accessed on 18 May 2019. The cinema was leased to Odeon Cinemas from 1947 until it closed in 1960, and then the property was leased to a developer: CCA xx.c.52, p.169 and xx.c.59, pp. 4 and 15.
44. The blocks, which consisted of six and eight flats respectively, still stand today.
45. Perhaps £5.2 million today, using GDP per capita.
46. Perhaps £36,000 today, using the RPI.
47. *ODNB*. Davis of Lewknor was royal topographer from 1786. He undertook many surveys for Christ Church and other Oxford colleges, often producing beautiful maps as well as his technical reports. His appointment to oversee the enclosure of Harrow reflects its financial importance to the college.
48. *VCH Middx.* iv (1971), 172; CCA MS Estates 47, fol. 278.
49. *VCH Middx.* iv (1971), 198–200.

50. CCA MS Estates 56, fols 195–221. Reading on through the papers, it becomes evident why Rose accepted the agent's offer. The mill, for which Rose was offered £800, had actually burnt down some time before and had been uninsured.
51. CCA MS Estates 136, fols 253–314.
52. CCA D&C i.b.10, fols 88 and 88v.
53. CCA D&C i.b.10, 91. The principal and interest on the sale proceeds belonged to the Dean and Chapter. It was not always from the sale of land for railways that benefited Christ Church. In 1890 Mrs Eliza Dixon, in memory of her husband, who had been an undergraduate, gave £2,000 of Great Eastern Railway and £1,500 Lancashire and Yorkshire Railway 4 per cent debenture stock to invest or to sell and reinvest: CCA MS Estates 139, fol. 195.
54. CCA Leases London St Sepulchre's 1.
55. The Fire of London Disputes Act (18 and 19 Cha. II c.7) was passed in 1666 in order to settle differences between tenants and landlords of buildings destroyed by the fire. It was repealed in 1948 under the Statute Law Revision Act. Christ Church was called before the court too, concerning the rebuilding of tenements in St Bride's parish, rents from which had been included in the will of Sir Thomas White, founder of Sion College and of the White's professorship of moral philosophy, to help poor scholars at Christ Church and Trinity College, Cambridge: CCA MS Estates 138, fol. 416; CCA DP ix.b.1, 45.
56. CCA MS Estates 45, fols 2–45.
57. CCA MS Estates 60, fol. 106.
58. CCA MS Estates 5, fol. 187.
59. CCA MS Estates 5, fol. 211.
60. CCA MS Estates 5, fols 213, 222 and 236.
61. Then, as now, Peascod Street was the main shopping street in Windsor, and three of the four houses had shops on the ground floor, including Mr Hill the gun-maker, John Spencer, a carver and gilder, and Jones the tailor.
62. CCA MS Estates 5. fol. 248.
63. CCA MS Estates 5. fols 265–269. About £3 million, using GDP, today.
64. CCA D&C i.b.7, 415 and 496.
65. *VCH Oxon*, vol. iv (1979), 232.
66. CCA D&C i.b.7, 516. St Martin's parish was right in the centre of the city. Today the Carfax tower is all that remains of the church.
67. John Randolph, the sub-dean, was, in 1792, canon and regius professor of divinity. Blayney had been made a canon of Christ Church and regius professor of Hebrew in 1787. In 1792 he was also Treasurer. Onslow was a canon of Christ Church from 1779 to 1795, before being appointed dean of Worcester.
68. CCA D&C i.b.7, 606, 607, 609 and 621. SIGA rents were small rents received from a few estates in Oxfordshire, Cheshire and Worcestershire, as well as the capon, boar and wether rents from properties, tithes from Binsey and rents from some rooms in Peckwater Quadrangle. The name 'Siga' derives from 'Sus, incrementum, gallusque, ariesque' ('Swine, rents, cocks, and rams').
69. CCA MS Estates 142, fols 210–227; Curthoys (1995).

70. CCA MS Estates 103, fols 227. The piece of land was Oldfields, leased at this period to William Russell of Worcester: CCA. Leases Worcester B.

6. Managing the agricultural estate III: reform

1. Evans (1976), ix. The curate of Goosnargh in the parish of Kirkham (Lancashire), for example, supplemented his income by teaching at the Drapers' School there: CCA MS Estates 42, fol. 50.
2. Evans (1976), ix, 16, 84.
3. Evans (1976), 86.
4. Curthoys (2012), 198.
5. Evans (1976), 88–136; Evans (1993), 13–16; Kain and Oliver (1995), 1.
6. CCA D&C i.b.10, 4 and 5v, for example.
7. Dunbabin (1997), 418; CCA MS Estates 124. One side-effect of tithe commutation appears to have been the loss of innumerable tithe barns. Although tithes had not been paid in kind for many years, the buildings must have appeared as anachronistic as the tithes themselves. For example, in Turkdean, permission was given to remove the old barn and rebuild it somewhere more useful; the vicar of Kildwick was allowed to take his down and reuse the materials for repairs to the church; the barn at Skipton was converted into a house for the schoolmaster and mistress; the building at Batheaston was sold. See CCA D&C i.b.10, 16, 124, 124v, 173.
8. Evans (1993), 15.
9. CCA D&C i.b.10, 32v and 50v.
10. Dunbabin, in *HUO*, vol. vi (1997), 377.
11. CCA MS Estates 97, fols 296–298.
12. Dunbabin, in *HUO*, vol. vi (1997), 287–8, 424.
13. Pearsall (2011); Beckett, in Turner and Mills (1986), 176; CCA MS Estates 83, fol. 29.
14. CCA D&C i.b.8, fol. 22v.
15. CCA MS Estates 97, fols 296–298.
16. Morrin, in Keene et al. (2004), 339.
17. Morrin, in Keene et al. (2004), 339–40; Curthoys (2012), 230; Curthoys (2019), 140–42; 3 and 4 Vic Cap 113.
18. 13 and 14 Vic Cap 94.
19. Dunbabin, in *HUO*, vi (1997), 385–386.
20. Dunbabin, in *HUO*, vol. vi (1997), 424–5. More general sales could not be made until 1858, and even then the proceeds could only be reinvested in land or lodged with the Copyhold Commission at 3 per cent interest. Loans approved by the Board of Agriculture under the 1858 Act also allowed improvements to drainage and sanitation, the chemistry laboratories, the library, lighting and stone repairs. They also paid for the 1911 kitchen extension and accommodation on Brewer Street in 1934.
21. CCA MS Estates 130, fols 80–94. The Chapter were concerned too that the abandonment of fines would damage their private incomes, and came up with a

complicated scheme to ensure that dividends still came their way. Counsel suggested that the scheme was, at the very least, doubtful in its legitimacy.

22. Dunbabin, in *HUO*, vol. vi (1997), 386.
23. Curthoys (2012), 227.
24. Curthoys (2012), 262. The undergraduate and graduate members on the foundation became Junior Students briefly, funded like exhibitioners, from the foundation. Eventually, the position disappeared.
25. See p. 46 for an explanation of the year of grace.
26. Dunbabin, in *HUO*, vol. vi (1997), 378.
27. Curthoys (2012), 262.
28. Dunbabin, in *HUO*, vol. vi (1997), 421–4.
29. Dunbabin, in *HUO*, vol. vi (1997), 419. New College chose a full-time professional bursar in 1862, recognising that estates business had changed beyond the capabilities or time of a Fellow.
30. Curthoys (2012), 263–5.
31. *AgHistEW*, vol. vii (2000), 125–31.
32. Dunbabin, in *HUO*, vol. vi (1997), 382.
33. Miller (1983), 8–14. The situation was not helped by the transfer of central and local power from the traditional hands of the landed gentry and aristocracy by the Reform Act of 1832, the Reform and Redistribution of Seats Acts of 1884–5 and the Local Government Act of 1888. But it was also accepted by the Conservative government and the Royal Commission on Agricultural Depression that a return to tariffs was not possible.
34. Miller (1983) 7. Calvertt came from Louth (Lincolnshire). He wanted to farm on a larger scale than was then possible in his home county, and the property he had there was inclined to flood. The farms are also close to Burford and Taynton, whence came the stone for much of the construction of Cardinal College. Christ Church sold its farm in Enstone just before the depression took hold in 1873, but still felt the impact in 1879, when asked to assist with the repairs to the church bell tower and frame. The incumbent wrote that it was difficult to raise funds locally during the Depression: CCA MS Estates 72, fol. 327. In the same year the vicar of Bledington said exactly the same thing: CCA MS Estates 25, fol. 269. In Bledington several families migrated, although there is no evidence of this in Christ Church's estates papers: see Ashby (1974), 341.
35. Miller (1983), 55–67. Emphasis in the original.
36. Dunbabin, in *HUO*, vol. vi (1997), 427.
37. Miller (1983), 12.
38. CCA MS Estates 29, fol. 149v.
39. CCA MS Estates 24, fol. 252v.
40. In contrast to the horrendously wet weather of 1879, 1887 was too dry. Calvertt recorded 'Ruination to Landlords, & Tenants!!!': Miller (1983), 143.
41. Rack-renting allowed the college to be flexible in the amount demanded of a tenant in a way that the old beneficial leases could not. Large abatements were often agreed. Field struggled at many of Christ Church's farms to persuade the tenants to stay on
42. CCA MS Estates 24, fol. 265v.

43. CCA MS Estates 24, fol. 252v and 263v–265v.
44. *AgHistEW*, vol. vii (2000), 189; Langlands et al. (2008), 58.
45. CCA MS Estates 24, fol. 252v.
46. *AgHistEW*, vol. vii (2000), 190–99.
47. *AgHistEW*, vol. vii (2000), 159–61.
48. CCA MS Estates 98, fol. 351. Badsey is close to Evesham, with its direct connections to Worcester, Birmingham, Oxford and London.
49. Martin (1985); *AgHistEW*, vol. v (1984), 167–72.
50. *AgHistEW*, vol. vii (2000), 191.
51. This Francis Field may even have been the same person as the previously mentioned Hayward Field, as his full name was Francis Hayward Field, and the Aldsworth correspondence is signed 'F. Hayward Field'.
52. CCA MS Estates 102, fols 136, 200, 234 and 325; Martin (1985).
53. *AgHistEW*, vol. vii (2000), 479–84; Thirsk (1997), 169–89.
54. *AgHistEW*, vol. vii (2000), 177–8.
55. There was no real interest any more in the prevention of over-valuation of estates for a fine loan. When the tenant was paying the entry fine, the tenant could and did negotiate.
56. Dunbabin (1975), 631–47. The valuations of the 1870s may have been optimistic, but comparison with figures from Cambridge are consistent with a decline of up to 40 per cent.
57. Dunbabin, in *HUO*, vol. vi (1997), 386. During 1874 and 1875, £12,000 had been invested in repairs alone – between £6 and 9 million today, a figure not dissimilar to the current budget for repairs and maintenance. New building and the refurbishment of the cathedral, between 1863 and the 1880s, added between £70,000 and £80,000 (£40–60 million today).
58. Curthoys (2012), 263–5.
59. CCA MS Estates 135, fol. 3; MS Estates 130, fol. 140.
60. A pension fund was incorporated into the statute revision of 1882 up to a maximum of £1,000 per annum, which could then be invested. Pensions could be granted to Students who retired owing to ill-health after fifteen years' service or, more generally, after twenty-five years' service.
61. CCA MS Estates 134, fol. 25; GB i.b.3, p.14. The capitation fee was set a maximum of £5 per undergraduate. Up to £1,000 plus 10 per cent of the tuition fund and any surplus in that fund could be added per annum to the pension fund.
62. Faussett was the son of a canon, a clergyman himself and a mathematician. He was appointed Treasurer in 1868 and, although not a professional estates man or financier, he had considerable experience representing Christ Church on external bodies such as the Land Drainage Commission.
63. CCA MS Estates 134, fols 27–38.
64. Harvie, *HUO*, vol. vii, (2000), 69–73.
65. Dodgson, *Remarks on Report of Finance Committee* [March 1886] in CCA MS Estates 134, fol. 39; Wakeling (ed.), vol. vii (2004), 26; CCL MS 536/1, fol. 15v.
66. Wakeling (ed.), vol. vii, (2004), 262–4n, and CCL MS 536/1, fol. 18; CCA GB i.b.3, p.16.

67. CCA GB i.b.3, p.29. 'Bat' Price (1818–1898), of Pembroke College, was also a delegate of the University Press, and showed tremendous skill in managing its finances and growth : *ODNB*.
68. CCA GB i.b.3, pp.34–38; CCL MS 536/1, fol. 83v; CCA MS Estates 134, fols 39–42. Price proposed that the debt due to the Tuition Fund, of £2,373, be reimbursed by the House as soon as possible, and then that excesses in the Tuition Fund thereafter be paid into the Pension Fund for investment, following the guidelines in the statutes.
69. W. B. Skene was elected Treasurer in 1886 and held the position until his death in June 1910. He appears to have been the first Treasurer to be appointed after a formal interview process that included external candidates: see CCA xlix.a.1, 74–75, 77–81.
70. CCA MS Estates 135, fol. 312.
71. CCA MS Estates 139, fol. 174.
72. CCA MS Estates 135, fol. 199.
73. CCA MS Estates 135, fols 330–341.
74. CCA MS Estates 135, fols 368–390.
75. Dunbabin, in *HUO*, vol. vi (1997), 404 and 417; Dunbabin (1975), 633.
76. Dunbabin, in *HUO*, vol. vi (1997), 428–31; Dunbabin (1975), 637.

7. The right of 'coleing': Christ Church's mining estates

1. The Prideaux family have held Prideaux Place, near Padstow in Cornwall, since the sixteenth century.
2. CCA1.c.3, 877ff.
3. Flinn (1984), 12–14.
4. CCA MS Estates 57 and 58; CCA Midsomer Norton B, 1; Fletcher (1995), 117–24.
5. Crossley (1990), 204.
6. CCA MS Estates 87, fol. 52; Flinn (1984), 14.
7. CCA MS Estates 87, fol. 41; Crossley (1990), 208.
8. CCA MS Estates 87, fols 35 and 37.
9. CCA Midsomer Norton B, 5.
10. CCA Midsomer Norton B, 2 and 3.
11. Coxeter had been appointed to Midsomer Norton in 1700; he died in 1730. He was not a Christ Church man, although the living of the parish was in the gift of the Dean and Chapter.
12. CCA MS Estates 87, fol. 43.
13. CCA MS Estates 87, fol. 45.
14. CCA MS Estates 87, fols 50–52.
15. CCA MS Estates 87, fols 53–55. The Mogg family (ancestors of the present Rees-Moggs) had a considerable interest in the Somerset coalfields from the late seventeenth century.
16. Bristol Archives 5918/46.
17. CCA MS Estates 87, fols 58–82. Marling would ultimately have a dramatic effect on tithes, as the improved land would later be turned over to pasture. Timothy Lewis, Christ Church's land surveyor, reported in 1777 that this would 'swallow up the corn tithes'.

18. CCA D&C i.b.7, 602; Fletcher (1995), 120–24 and plate 28; Bendall (1997), vol. ii, 448. Gregg was paid £105 10s. for his work on the Midsomer Norton estate, perhaps £12,000 today using the RPI. The map was drawn by William Sampson, from Bath.
19. CCA MS Estates 87, fols 127 and 146.
20. CCA MS Estates 87, fol. 129; Midsomer Norton B 9.
21. CCA MS Estates 87, fol. 135.
22. CCA MS Estates 87, fol. 138; CCA xlviii.a.1; Flinn (1984), 102; Down and Warrington [1971], 17. In 1799, the dividends from coal amounted to £40; in 1803 these had risen to £120. The Somerset Coal Canal opened in 1805, but the Radstock branch was never commercially successful (there had been all sorts of technical issues with its construction), and it was replaced by a tramway, running along the old towpath, in 1815. The Paulton arm, on the other hand, was profitable and remained in use until 1898: Flinn (1984), 183.
23. The Radstock Old Pit, on land owned by the Waldegrave family, lords of the manor of Radstock, had installed a Boulton and Watt steam engine in 1800: Flinn (1984), 102.
24. CCA MS Estates 87, fols 158 and 164. Using GDP per capita, this represents an income of around £75,000 in 1816 and £30,000 the following year. The Welton works brought an income of £75 in 1817 from 28,800 bushels of coal.
25. CCA MS Estates 87, fol. 166.
26. *ODNB*; Buckland and Conybeare (1824), 263.
27. Down and Warrington [1971], 27–31.
28. Down and Warrington [1971], 84, 102, 147, 154; CCA MS Estates 87, fol. 205. The Salisbury colliery opened in 1792 and was closed by 1873; the Paulton works appear to have been closed for geological reasons in the early nineteenth century; the Radford colliery closed around 1847. The Welton pits, sunk on Duchy of Cornwall land, were profitable: Old Welton remained productive until the 1890s; the New Welton works opened around 1822; and Welton Hill was worked from about 1815 to 1896 although it would appear that Christ Church received no income from the pit after 1840.
29. CCA GB i.b.2 throughout.
30. CCA MS Estates 88, fol. 426. Perhaps the equivalent of £300 in 2018.
31. CCA MS Estates 108, fol. 187; Bendall (1997). There appears to have been a family of Pavers working as surveyors and land agents in Yorkshire in the nineteenth century.
32. CCA MS Estates 108, fols 284–290.
33. Using GDP per capita. CCA MS Estates 108, fol. 300.
34. There is no mention in the Christ Church archives of the miners' strike of 1893, which affected collieries across the country. Briggs and Masham appear to have been relatively beneficent owners which perhaps deflected the worst of any rioting.
35. CCA MS Estates 108, fol. 442. Perhaps £2 million using GDP per capita.

8. Managing the agricultural estate IV: the modern period

1. Captain George T. Hutchinson, was a farmer himself, and had worked for the Duchy of Cornwall before coming to Christ Church in 1910. He was responsible for the

creation of the Masters Garden at Christ Church, and died in January 1948 of heart failure while out hunting soon after retirement. His notes are at CCA MS Estates 134, fols 156–270.

2. CCA MS Estates 134, fols 157 and 169.
3. Dunbabin, in *HUO*, vol. vi (1997), 429.
4. CCA xxi.b.4.
5. Perhaps a curious purchase as the land was of little use except for the pasturing of sheep, and wool prices had not been a significant portion of the endowment income for possibly centuries.
6. CCA xlviii.a.63; Leases Adderbury 1–5.
7. Dunbabin (1975), 638; Dunbabin (1994), 656.
8. CCA xlviii.a.63; CCA xx.c.47 and 48. The agreed royalty for the coal was £20 per foot thick per acre.
9. *AgHistEW*, vol. viii (1978), 70–75.
10. CCA GB iii.b.12/2, 230; CCA xlviii.a.60.
11. CCA xlviii.a.2; CCA Leases St Aldates 18.
12. CCA xlviii.a.63; CCA Leases St Thomas PES.
13. *AgHistEW*, vol. viii (1978), 75, 90 and 166.
14. CCA xlviii.a.63.
15. CCA xlviii.a.60 and 61.
16. *AgHistEW*, vol. viii (1978), 70–72.
17. Crowe, in Hoyle (2013), 268.
18. CCA xlviii.a.61. There were, of course, still huge sums tied up in Estate Improvement Loans, which cost, in 1914, about £6,500 to service: see CCA xxi.b.4, 60–64.
19. *AgHistEW*, vol. viii (1978), 2–3.
20. *AgHistEW*, vol. viii (1978), 92–4; Crowe, in Hoyle (2013), 270.
21. CCA GB iii.b.12/2, 256 and 264. The Governing Body held no gaudies between 1916 and 1918, and only served meat on Tuesdays and Thursdays once rationing was introduced in 1918: Curthoys (2012), 298–9.
22. CCA GB iii.b.12/2, 268. Considerable sums (*c.*£70,000) held in other stocks was converted into War Stocks at 4.5 per cent and 5 per cent during 1917: xlviii.a.63.
23. CCA GB iii.b.12/2, 302; GB iii.b.12/2, 280 and 290; CCA xx.c.48, 190.
24. GB iii.b.12/2, 304.
25. About a quarter of the land in England is thought to have changed hands between 1919 and 1921. See, for example, Wade Martins (2002), 194.
26. Dunbabin, in *HUO*, vol. viii (1994), 659.
27. University College, for example, sold off many unprofitable estates between 1919 and 1923, including all its Welsh property, realising over £80,000: Darwall-Smith (2008), 445.
28. Dunbabin, in *HUO*, vol. vi (1997), 426; Dunbabin, in *HUO*, vol. viii (1994), 664–5.
29. CCA1.c.14, 11–14.
30. Christ Church employees rented many of the properties in Elsfield throughout the twentieth century.
31. CCA GB iii.b.12/2, 286; CCA xx.c.48, 107.
32. Dunbabin, in *HUO*, vol. viii (1994), 663.

33. CCA xxi.b.4, 29; CCA xxi.b.10, 30. By 1920 this copyhold had been redeemed and an annuity was paid to the widow.
34. Dunbabin, in *HUO*, vol. viii (1994), 663–7; *AgHistEW*, vol. viii (1978), 162–3.
35. See pp. 69–72 for an account of Christ Church and the Welsh Tithe War.
36. Twinch (2001), 125. I am grateful to Jennifer Thorp, archivist at New College, who advised that the incident actually involved Merton College, not New College as a newspaper article reported. It seems that the names of college bursars were frequently confused in press articles at the time.
37. *Times*, 17 October 1933.
38. *AgHistEW*, vol. viii (1978), 229–40.
39. Twinch (2001), 279–85. Tithepayers' associations were formed in most counties, with the most local to Oxford representing not just Oxfordshire but Berkshire and Buckinghamshire too. The Wallingford and District branch was particularly active.
40. The tenant at Chestlion Farm in Clanfield (Oxfordshire), for example, offered to withdraw his notice to quit if his rent was reduced from £400 to £250, backdated by a year.
41. Twinch (2001), 207.
42. CCA MS Estates 133.
43. 1936 c.43. Tithe annuities were paid first to the Tithe Redemption Commission, which was set up by the 1936 Act, and then to the Inland Revenue from 1960. Small annuities (under £1) were abolished in 1951 and all annuities terminated by the Finance Act 1977.
44. *AgHistEW*, vol. viii (1978), 327–8; *ODNB*.
45. CCA iii.b.12/3 and 4.
46. CCA iii.b.12/4, 48–49, 52 and 59.
47. CCA iii.b.12/4, 50 and 54–55.
48. CCA GB i.b.7, 622.
49. *Christ Church 1944–5* and *1946–7*.
50. Kirton Seadyke Farm was sold in 1962 and Wragg Marsh Farm in 1959.
51. CCA viii.c.7.
52. CCA viii.b.102.
53. CCA xx.c.54, 61. The sale price was £10,000. Christ Church continued to be patrons of the living, appointing the vicars. In 1995 Stratton Audley was amalgamated with nine other parishes to form the benefice of Shelswell, and now the patronage is shared.
54. CCA GB iii.b.12/4, 58.
55. Dunbabin, in *HUO*, vol. viii (1994), 668. Subsequent legislation has opened investment opportunities still further.
56. CCA P.TOP.Farms; CCA MS Estates 134, fols 278–283.
57. This had begun before the war, in 1937, when grants became available under the Housing (Rural Workers) Act of 1926. Then improvements, and even reconstruction, was effected in labourers' cottages in Deddington, Spelsbury and Stratton Audley (Oxfordshire), and in Ellerbeck (Yorkshire).
58. These figures are from 1998.

59. Farmers could pass on their tenancies if there was a family member who could run the farm effectively, continuing a centuries-old practice. Between 1984 and 1993 eight farms were sold, including some in Yorkshire, and seven new ones purchased. The farms were even more widely spread than they had been in 1546, with one in the Scottish borders and two in Humberside. The quality and rental value of the land increased.
60. Benthall (1994).
61. *Christ Church 1994.*
62. *Christ Church 1997*; *Christ Church 1999*; CCA GB i.b.31, 5225 and 5246.
63. Dunbabin, in *HUO*, vol. viii (1994), 663; Jones (2005), 276. Balliol completed the sales of its agricultural property outside Oxford between the 1920s and the 1960s.
64. Christ Church is also the landlord of a crocodile farm in Oxfordshire.

Bibliography

Archival sources

The primary sources in the Christ Church Archives (CCA) have been the volumes of estates correspondence (MS Estates 1–150), calendared by Dr E. G. W. Bill, and the minutes of, first, the Dean and Chapter (D&C i.b.1–10) and then of the Governing Body (GB i.b.1 ff.). Other in-house sources include Deanery papers (DP), maps and drawings, manorial records, terriers and valuations, estates registers, disbursement and receipt books, and the leases and conveyances of Christ Church property from 1546 onwards.

Published sources

Abbreviations and series

AgHistEW *Agrarian History of England and Wales* (General Editor: Joan Thirsk)

Miller, Edward (ed.), *Agrarian History of England and Wales*, vol. iii: *1348–1500* (Cambridge, 1991)

Thirsk, Joan (ed.), *Agrarian History of England and Wales*, vol. v (1): *Regional Farming Systems, 1640–1750* (Cambridge, 1984)

Thirsk, Joan (ed.), *Agrarian History of England and Wales*, vol. v (2): *1640–1750* (Cambridge, 1985)

Mingay, G. E. (ed.), *Agrarian History of England and Wales*, vol. vi: *1750–1850* (Cambridge, 1989)

Collins, E. J. T. (ed.), *Agrarian History of England and Wales*, vol. vii: *1850–1914*, 2 vols (Cambridge, 2000)

Whetham, Edith H. (ed.), *Agrarian History of England and Wales*, vol. viii: *1914–1939* (Cambridge, 1978)

HUO *History of the University of Oxford*

McConica, James, *History of the University of Oxford*, vol. iii: *The Collegiate University* (Oxford, 1986)

Tyacke, Nicholas, *History of the University of Oxford*, vol. iv: *The Seventeenth Century* (Oxford, 1997)

Sutherland, L., and Mitchell, L., *History of the University of Oxford*, vol. v: *The Eighteenth Century* (Oxford, 1986)

Brock, M. G., and Curthoys, M. C., *History of the University of Oxford*, vol. vi: *The Nineteenth Century, Part 1* (Oxford, 1997)

Harrison, Brian, *History of the University of Oxford*, vol. viii: *The Twentieth Century* (Oxford, 1994)

ODNB *Oxford Dictionary of National Biography*, ed. H. C. G. Matthew and B. Harrison (Oxford, 2004)

Pevsner, Nikolaus, *The Buildings of England* series

Tyack, Geoffrey, Bradley, Simon, and Pevsner, Nikolaus, *Berkshire* (London, 2010)

Hartwell, Clare et al., *Cheshire* (London, 2011)

Bettley, James, and Pevsner, Nikolaus, *Essex* (London, 2007)

Newman, John, *Kent: West and the Weald* (London, 2012)

Pickford, Chris, and Pevsner, Nikolaus, *Warwickshire* (London, 2016)

VCH *Victoria County Histories*

Baker, T. F. T. (ed.), *A History of Middlesex* [*VCH Middx*], vol. vi (London, 1980)

Baugh, G. C. (ed.), *A History of the County of Shropshire* [*VCH Salop*], vol. x (London, 1998)

Cockburn, J. S., and Baker, T. F. T. (eds.), *A History of the County of Middlesex* [*VCH Middx*], vol. iv (London, 1971)

Crossley, Alan (ed.), *A History of the County of Oxford* [*VCH Oxon*], vol. iv (London, 1979)

Crossley, Alan (ed.), *A History of the County of Oxford* [*VCH Oxon*], vol. xi (London, 1983)

Ditchfield, P. H., and Page, William (eds.), *A History of the County of Berkshire* [*VCH Berks*], vol. ii (London, 1907)

Ditchfield, P. H., and Page, William (eds.), *A History of the County of Berkshire* [*VCH Berks*], vol. iv (London, 1924)

Herbert, N. M. (ed.), *A History of the County of Gloucestershire* [*VCH Glos*], vol. vii (London, 1981)

Herbert, N. M. (ed.), *A History of the County of Gloucestershire* [*VCH Glos*], vol. ix (London, 2001)

Lee, J. M., and McKinley, R. A. (eds.), *A History of the County of Leicestershire* [*VCH Leics*], vol. v (London, 1964)

Lobel, Mary D. (ed.). *A History of the County of Oxford* [*VCH Oxon*], vol. vi (London, 1959)

Page, William (ed.), *A History of the County of Essex* [*VCH Essex*], vol. ii (London, 1907)

Page, William (ed.), *A History of the County of Oxford* [*VCH Oxon*], vol. ii (London, 1907)

Page, William (ed.), *The Victoria History of Hampshire and the Isle of Wight* [*VCH Hants*], vol. v (London, 1912)

Page, William (ed.), *The Victoria History of the County of York* [*VCH Yorks*], vol. iii (London, 1913)

Page, William (ed.), *The Victoria History of the County of York, North Riding*, [*VCH YorksNR*], vol. i (London, 1914)

Page, William (ed.), *A History of the County of Kent* [*VCH Kent*], vol. ii (London, 1926)

Page, William (ed.), *A History of the County of Buckingham* [*VCH Bucks*], vol. iv (London, 1927)

Page, William (ed.), *A History of the County of Sussex* [*VCH Sussex*], vol. ii (London, 1973)

Page, William (ed.), *A History of the County of Suffolk* [*VCH Suffolk*], vol. ii (London, 1975)

Powell, W. R. (ed.), *A History of the County of Essex* [*VCH Essex*], vol. iv (London, 1956)

Salzman, L. F. (ed.), *A History of the County of Warwick* [*VCH Warks*], vol. v (London, 1949)

Monographs and articles

Allen, Robert C., *Enclosure and the Yeoman* (Oxford, 1992)

Ashby, M. K., *The Changing English Village: A History of Bledington, Gloucestershire, in Its Setting, 1066–1914* (Kineton, 1974)

Bendall, Sarah, *Dictionary of Land Surveyors and Local Map-Makers*, 2 vols (London, 1997)

Bill, E. G. W., *Education at Christ Church, Oxford, 1660–1800* (Oxford, 1988)

Brittain-Catlin, Timothy, *The English Parsonage in the Early Nineteenth Century* (Reading, 2008)

Broad, John, 'Cattle plague in eighteenth-century England', *Agricultural History Review*, 31 (2) (1983), 104–15

Broad, John, *Transforming English Rural Society: The Verneys and the Claydons, 1660–1820* (Cambridge, 2004)

Broad, John, and Hoyle, Richard (eds.), *Bernwood: The Life and Afterlife of a Forest* (Preston, 1997)

Brod, Manfred, 'Marcham's misfortune: David Jones, vicar 1699–1724', *Coral Rag: The Marcham Society Journal*, i (2001)

Buckland, William, and Conybeare, William D., 'Observations on the south-western coal district of England', *Transactions of the Geological Society of London*, 2 (1) (London, 1824), 210–316

Catto, Jeremy, et al., *Unarmed Soldiery: Studies in the Early History of All Souls College*, The Chichele Lectures, 1993–1994 (Oxford, 1996)

Challis, C. E., *Currency and the Economy in Tudor and Early Stuart England* (London, 1989)

Chalklin, C. W., 'Urban housing estates in the eighteenth century', *Urban Studies*, 5 (1) (1968), 67–85

Charles-Edwards, Thomas, and Reid, Julian, *Corpus Christi College, Oxford: A History* (Oxford, 2017)

Clark, A. (ed.), *Life and Times of Anthony Wood, Antiquary, of Oxford, 1632–1695, Described by Himself*, 3 vols (Oxford, 1891–4)

Compton, H. J., *The Oxford Canal* (Newton Abbot, 1976)

Cross, F. L., and Livingstone, E. A., *Oxford Dictionary of the Christian Church* (Oxford, 2005)

Crossley, David, *Post-Medieval Archaeology in Britain* (Leicester, 1990)

Curthoys, Judith, '"To perfect the college…": the Christ Church almsmen 1546–1888', *Oxoniensia*, lx (1995), 379–95

Curthoys, Judith, *The Cardinal's College: Christ Church, Chapter and Verse* (London, 2012)

Curthoys, Judith, 'Enclosure and the changing landscape of Hillesden', *Records of Buckinghamshire*, 53 (2013), 181–200

Curthoys, Judith, 'Hythe Bridge Street, Park End Street, and their connecting streets: changing transport and changing architecture in the parish of St Thomas, Oxford', *Oxoniensia*, 82 (2017), 133–63

Curthoys, Judith, *The Stones of Christ Church: The Story of the Buildings of Christ Church, Oxford* (London, 2017)

Curthoys, Judith, *The King's Cathedral: The Ancient Heart of Christ Church, Oxford* (London, 2019)

Curtler, W. H. R., *The Enclosure and Redistribution of Our Land* (Oxford, 1920)

Darwall-Smith, Robin, *A History of University College, Oxford* (Oxford, 2008)

Denholm-Young, N., *Cartulary of the Medieval Archives of Christ Church* (Oxford, 1931)

Down, C. G. and Warrington, A. J., *The History of the Somerset Coalfield* (Newton Abbot, 1971)

Dunbabin, J. P. D., *Rural Discontent in Nineteenth-Century Britain* (London, 1974)

Dunbabin, J. P. D., 'Oxford and Cambridge college finances, 1871–1913', *Economic History Review*, xxviii (1975), 631–47

Dyos, H. T., 'The speculative builders and developers of Victorian London', *Victorian Studies*, 2 (1968), 641–90

Evans, Eric J., *The Contentious Tithe: The Tithe Problem and English Agriculture, 1750–1850* (London, 1976)

Evans, Eric J., *Tithes: Maps, Apportionments and the 1836 Act* (Chichester, 1993)

Fletcher, David H., *The Emergence of Estate Maps: Christ Church, Oxford, 1600–1840* (Oxford, 1995)

Flinn, Michael W., *The History of the British Coal Industry*, ii (Oxford, 1984)

Foster, Joseph, *Alumni Oxonienses*, 8 vols (London, 1888–91)

Frost, Richard, *Dr Robert South, D.D. 1634–1716* (Oxford, 1987)

Gay, E. F., 'The Midlands revolt and the inquisitions of depopulation of 1607', *Transactions of the Royal Historical Society*, xviii (NS) (1904)

Hall, David, *The Open Fields of England* (Oxford, 2014)

Harvey, P. D. A., *Manorial Records* (Gloucester, 1984)

Hibbert, C. (ed.), *Encyclopaedia of Oxford* (London, 1988)

Hill, Christopher, *Economic Problems of the Church: From Archbishop Whitgift to the Long Parliament* (London, 1971)

Hilton, R. H., *The Decline of Serfdom in Medieval England* (London, 1969)

Historic Manuscripts Commission, *Report on the Manuscripts of His Grace the Duke of Portland, KG. Preserved at Welbeck Abbey*, vii (1901)

Hoyle, Richard W. (ed.), *The Farmer in England, 1650–1980* (Farnham, 2013)

Hurst, Derek, *Sheep in the Cotswolds: The Medieval Wool Trade* (Stroud, 2005)

Jennings, Anthony, *The Old Rectory: The Story of the English Parsonage* (Durham, 2018)

Jones, John, *Balliol College: A History*, 2nd edn (Oxford, 2005)

Kain, Roger J. P., and Oliver, Richard R., *The Tithe Maps of England and Wales: A Cartographic Analysis and County-By-County Catalogue* (Cambridge, 1995)

Keene, Derek, Burns, Arthur, and Saint, Andrew (eds.), *St Paul's: The Cathedral Church Of London, 604–2004* (New Haven, CT, and London, 2004)

Kellett, J. R., *The Impact of Railways on Victorian Cities* (London, 1969)
Knowles, David, and Hadcock, R. Neville, *Medieval Religious Houses: England and Wales* (London, 1971)
Lane, Carolina, 'The development of pastures and meadows during the sixteenth and seventeenth centuries', *Agricultural History Review*, 28 (1) (1980), 18–30
Langlands, Alex, Ginn, Peter, and Goodman, Ruth, *Victorian Farm: Rediscovering Forgotten Skills* (London, 2008)
Le Neve, John, and Horn, Joyce M. (comp.), *Fasti ecclesiae anglicanae, 1541–1857*, viii: *Bristol, Gloucester, Oxford and Peterborough Dioceses* (London, 1996)
Leadam, I. S. (ed.), *The Domesday of Inclosures, 1517–18* (New York, 1971)
Martin, J. M., 'The social and economic origins of the Vale of Evesham market gardening industry', *Agricultural History Review*, 33 (1) (1985), 41–50
McClatchey, Diana, *Oxfordshire Clergy, 1777–1869: A Study of the Established Church and of the Role of Its Clergy in Local Society* (Oxford, 1960)
Miller, Celia (ed.), *Rain and Ruin: The Diary of an Oxfordshire Farmer, John Simpson Calvertt, 1875–1900* (Gloucester, 1983)
Morrison, K. A., and Minnis, J., *Carscapes: The Motor Car, Architecture and Landscape in England* (London, 2012)
Mullett, Charles F., 'The cattle distemper in mid-eighteenth-century England', *Agricultural History*, 20 (3) (1946)
Neeson, J. M., *Commoners: Common Right, Enclosure and Social Change in England, 1700–1820* (Cambridge, 1993)
Neild, Robert, *The Financial History of Trinity College, Cambridge* (Cambridge, 2008)
New, Elizabeth A., *Seals and Sealing Practices* (London, 2010)
Overton, Mark, *Agricultural Revolution in England: The Transformation of the Agrarian Economy, 1500–1850* (Cambridge, 1996)
Pearsall, Mark, 'The Land Tax, 1692–1963', *Magazine of the Friends of the National Archives*, 22 (3) (December 2011)
Port, M. H., *Six Hundred New Churches: A Study of the Church Building Commission, 1818–1856, and Its Church Building Activities* (1961)
Prior, M., *Fisher Row: Fishermen, Bargemen, and Canal Boatmen in Oxford* (Oxford, 1982)
Rackham, Oliver, *Trees and Woodland in the British Landscape: The Complete History of Britain's Trees, Woods and Hedgerows* (London, 1990)
Record Commission, *Valor ecclesiasticus*, vol. ii (London, 1814), 250–53
Reed, M., 'Enclosure in north Buckinghamshire, 1500–1750', *Agricultural History Review*, xxii (1984)
Report of the Royal Commission on Tithe Rentcharge in England and Wales (London, 1936)
Richardson, Walter C., *History of the Court of Augmentations, 1536–1554* (Baton Rouge, LA, 1961)
Rickard, R. L., *The Progress Notes of Warden Woodward round the Oxfordshire Estates of New College, Oxford, 1659–1675* (Oxford, 1949)
Royal Commission on the Historical Monuments of England, *An Inventory of Nonconformist Chapels and Meeting-Houses in Central England* (London, 1986)
Slinn, Sara, *The Education of the Anglican Clergy, 1780–1839* (Woodbridge, 2017)

Smith, Catherine, *Early Days: PGS c.1750–1870, the Penny Street School* (Portsmouth, *c.*2004)
Spence, Richard T., *Skipton Castle in the Great Civil War* (Skipton, 1991)
Stawell, Jessica, *Aldsworth, 1000–2000: The History of a Cotswold Village* (Cheltenham, 2002)
Stuart, Denis, *Manorial Records: An Introduction to their Transcription and Translation* (Chichester, 1992)
Tarlow, Sarah, *The Archaeology of Improvement in Britain, 1750–1850* (Cambridge, 2007)
Thirsk, Joan, *England's Agricultural Regions and Agrarian History, 1500–1750* (London, 1987)
Thirsk, Joan, *Alternative Agriculture: A History from the Black Death to the Present Day* (Oxford, 1997)
Thompson, F. M. L., *Landowners, Capitalists, and Entrepreneurs: Essays for Sir John Habakkuk* (Oxford, 1994)
Tiller, Kate (ed.), *Church and Chapel in Oxfordshire, 1851: The Return of the Census of Religious Worship* (Oxford, 1987)
Tindall, Gillian, *The Fields Beneath: The History of One London Village* (London, 1977)
Turner, Michael, *Enclosures in Britain, 1750–1830* (London, 1984)
Turner, Michael, and Mills, Dennis, *Land and Property: The English Land Tax, 1692–1832* (Gloucester, 1986)
Turner, M. E., Beckett, J. V., and Afton, B., *Agricultural Rent in England, 1690–1914* (Cambridge, 1997)
Twinch, Carol, *Tithe War, 1918–1939: The Countryside in Revolt* (Norwich, 2001)
Universities Commission, *Report of the Commissioners Appointed to Inquire into the Property and Income of the Universities of Oxford and Cambridge, and of the Colleges and Halls Therein* (London, 1874)
Venn, John, and Venn, J. A., *Alumni Cantabrigienses* (Cambridge, 1927)
Wade Martins, Susanna, *The English Model Farm: Building the Agricultural Ideal, 1700–1914* (Macclesfield, 2002)
Wade Martins, Susanna, *Farmers, Landlords and Landscapes: Rural Britain, 1720 to 1870* (Macclesfield, 2004)
Wadmore, J. F., 'Tonbridge priory', *Archaeologia Cantiana*, xiv (1882), 326–43
Wakeling, Edward (ed.), *Lewis Carroll's Diaries: The Private Journals of Charles Lutwidge Dodgson (Lewis Carroll)*, vol. vii (Luton, 2004)
Ward, G. R. M. (trans.), *The Foundation Statutes of Bishop Fox for Corpus Christi College in the University of Oxford, AD 1517* (London, 1843)
Washington, E. S., and Marsh, A. J., *Portsmouth Grammar School, 1732 to 1976* (Portsmouth, 1976)
Watson, Nigel, *Independent Vision: A History of the Portsmouth Grammar School* (London, 2008)
Whittle, Jane (ed.), *Landlords and Tenants in Britain, 1440–1660: Tawney's* Agrarian Problem *Revisited* (Woodbridge, 2013)
Whyte, William, *Unlocking the Church: The Lost Secret of Victorian Sacred Space* (Oxford, 2017)
Williams, Penry, *The Council in the Marches of Wales under Elizabeth I* (Cardiff, 1958)

Williamson, Tom, Liddiard, Robert, and Partida, Tracey, *Champion: The Making and Unmaking of the English Midland Landscape* (Liverpool, 2013)

Unpublished papers and dissertations

Benthall, Richard, 'The House's land', *Christ Church 1994* [annual report]

Bill, E. G. W., *Catalogue of Treasury Papers* (April 1955) [typescript]

Bowers, Roger, 'To Oxford from Osney: The Genesis of the Cathedral Church of Christ, and of its Grammar School and Adjunct Academy, 1539–1550', unpublished paper (2019)

Graham, M., 'The Suburbs of Victorian Oxford: Growth in a Pre-Industrial City', unpublished PhD thesis, University of Leicester (1985) [available on line at https//lra.le.ac.uk/handle/2381/8427]

Turnock, John Lawrence, 'The Endowed Grammar Schools of Shropshire, the Careswell Exhibitions and the Response of Local Communities to Educational Reform, 1860–1914', unpublished PhD thesis, University of Manchester, 1998

Index

All places are in Oxford unless otherwise stated. *Italic* page numbers refer to black and white illustrations; colour plates are indicated by 'Pl.'

A

Abbey Road 119, 120
Abbots Wood (Oxfordshire) 30, 37–8, 41–3, 214*n*65, 215*n*74–6, Pl.
Abbotsbury Abbey (Dorset) 194
Abingdon Abbey (Berkshire) 191, 192, 194, 196, 214*n*58
Ackton Hall Colliery (Yorkshire) 166, 167
Acton (Cheshire) 193
Acton Grange (Cheshire) 193
Adderbury (Oxfordshire) 169, 198
Adderley (Shropshire) 219*n*28
advowsons (clerical incumbencies)
  list of 70
  numbers of 44, 73, 216*n*1
Adwick (Yorkshire) 70, 224*n*27
agricultural depressions
  early 19th century 102
  late 19th century 42–3, 142, 145–57, 169, 171, 178, 234*n*33–4
  1930s 176–8
Agricultural Development Act (1939) 179
Agriculture Acts (1920; 1937) 173, 178–9
Aldington (Worcestershire) 201
Aldrich, Dean Henry 206
Aldsworth (Gloucestershire) 30, 70, 103, 147–8, 194, 213*n*46, 218*n*20, 235*n*51
All Souls College 21, 57, 213*n*48
  estate maps 76–7
Allen, Benjamin 161–2
Allestree, Richard 205
almshouse (Christ Church) 118, 135–6
Alperton (Middlesex) 128
Altham, Roger 18, 205
Alvanley (Cheshire) 62

Alvechurch (Worcestershire) 201
Alveley (Shropshire), Barrets Farm 101, *endpapers*
Amersham (Buckinghamshire), Dr Challoner's Grammar School 227*n*80
Amesbury Abbey (Wiltshire) 192
Andrewes, Henry 92
Andrews, Richard 33
Anne, Queen 218*n*23
 Queen Anne's Bounty 49, 50, 218*n*23, 218*n*26
Antinomians 59, 220*n*64
Anti-Tithe League 69–71
ap Mores, John 25
Arderne, Thomas 15, 210*n*42
Ardington (Berkshire) 53, 56, 57–8, 70, 95, 191, 218*n*20, 218*n*24, 219*n*51, 220*n*58
Armstrong, Henrietta 169–70
Arnold, Charles 104, 140
Arnold, Richard 111–12, 230*n*139
Arreton (Isle of Wight) 98, 195
Arundel, William 68–9, 222*n*109
Ashendon (Buckinghamshire) 70, 87–8, 192, 218*n*20
Ashton under Lyne (Lancashire), Reform Society 138
Asquith Commission (Royal Commission on Oxford and Cambridge Universities; 1922) 172
Astrop (Northamptonshire) 168, 197
Astwood (Buckinghamshire) 86
Atterbury, Dean Francis, bishop of Rochester 206
Auditor (of Christ Church) 11, 15–18
 stipend and salary 15–16, 16–18, 210*n*45
 see also Bedford, Samuel; King, John; King, Philip; Palmer family

B

Badby (Northamptonshire) 54, 55–56, 70, 107, 197
Badcock, Benjamin 110, 139
 maps 113, 139, Pl.
Badsey (Worcestershire) 70, 148, 202, 235*n*48
Bagot, Dean Lewis, bishop of St Asaph 82, 107, 206, 224*n*29, 229*n*122
bailiffs' book (Cardinal College) 5, *6*
bailiffs' books (Christ Church) 22
Balliol College 74, 145, 153, 185, 240*n*63
Ballowe, William 204
Balscott (Oxfordshire) 200
Bampton (Oxfordshire) 94
Banbury (Oxfordshire) 132, 198
Banbury Road 172
Banister, William 38–9, 215*n*79
Barber, William 37, 56–7, 215*n*72
Barkham family (East Walton) 78–9, 224*n*17
Barnes, Ralph 57
Barton (Lancashire) 50
Barton, Philip 205
Batey, Keith 205
Bath Abbey (Somerset) 24, 201
Batheaston (Somerset) 24, 70, 201, 211*n*12, 233*n*7
Bathurst, Henry 205
Batsford (Gloucestershire) 46, 70, 94, 194, 217*n*11
Bayham Abbey (Sussex) 1, 5, 189
Bayne, Thomas Vere 152–4, *154*
Beckley (Oxfordshire) 198
Bedells, Grafton 126, 127
Bedford (Bedfordshire) 136
Bedford, Samuel 16
Belsyre, Alexander 15, 204

benefactions *see* endowment (Christ Church)
Benson (Oxfordshire) 50, 70, 107–10, 198, 218*n*20, 219*n*28, 229*n*133
Benthall, Richard 185, 205
Bentham, Edward 205
Bernard, Daniel 204
Bernard, Thomas 204
Berrick (Oxfordshire) 107–10
Besselsleigh (Berkshire) 67
Bicester Abbey (Oxfordshire) 200
Bill, E. G. W. 204, 211*n*14, 223*n*13
Bimney (Northamptonshire) 197
Binsey (Oxfordshire) 37, 70, 110, 174, 198, 213*n*46, 218*n*20, 232*n*68, Pl.
Binsey Lane 171
Bishop, Henry 215*n*75
Bisley, Frances 35
Black Bourton (Oxfordshire) 70, 175, 198, 213*n*46
Black Death (1348–9) 32, 84, 225*n*42
Blacket family (West Smithfield) 132
Blackmore (Essex), Priory Church of St Laurence 189, Pl.
Blackthorn (Oxfordshire), Essex Farm 96–7, 198, 227*n*88
Blayney, Benjamin 135, 205, 232*n*67
Bledington (Gloucestershire) 68–9, 70, 106–7, 146, 194, 222*n*108–9, 225*n*52, 228*n*113, 234*n*34
Blomfield, Charles, bishop of London 141
Board of Agriculture, foundation 105, 229*n*117
Bobbington (Staffordshire) 101
Bodicote (Oxfordshire) 198
Bollington (Cheshire) 193
Bolton Priory (Yorkshire) 198, 202
Book of Evidences 75–6, *76*, 80, 180, 230*n*5
Bosanquet, Charles Ion Carr 180, 181–4, 205
Bosiat (Northamptonshire) *see* Bozeat
Bossom, Louisa 170
Bostock, Charles 94
Bostock, Joan 93–4, 192
Bostock Trust 96, 198
  Windsor houses 93–4, 132–4, *135*, 192, 232*n*61
Boston in Bramham (Yorkshire) 65
Botley (Oxfordshire) 198
Botley Road 118, 170
Boulter, Dean Hugh, archbishop of Armagh 96, 206
  bequest 96–7, 198
Bourne, Robert 46
Bourton-on-the-Water (Gloucestershire) 94, 96, 194
Bozeat (Northamptonshire) 88
Bradshaw, Dean William, bishop of Bristol 206
Bradwell Priory (Buckinghamshire) 189, Pl.
Bramham (Yorkshire) 65, 70, 202
Brampton Bierley (Yorkshire) 224*n*27
Braunston (Northamptonshire) 129
Brewer Street 170, 233*n*20
brewing 116, 119, 140
Bridgnorth (Shropshire) 228*n*98–9
Bridgwater (Somerset) 180
Briggs, Henry 167, 237*n*24, 237*n*34
Bristol 163
Brize Norton (Oxfordshire) 37, 70, 95, 110, 136, 147, 179, *182*, 187, 198, 218*n*24
  aerodrome 179
  Manor Farm 168
Broad Street 113
Brooks, John 18, 34, 161

Broughton (Yorkshire) 70
Brown, Cecil David 184
Brown Clee Hill (Shropshire) 101, 228*n*102
Bruton, Edward George 58, 134
Brymbo Steelworks (Denbighshire) 169
Buchan, John (*later* 1st Baron Tweedsmuir) 173
Buck, Samuel and Nathaniel, *Buck's Antiquities* 3
Buckland, William 165, *165*
Budworth (Cheshire) *see* Great Budworth
Bull, John 205
Bullock, Joseph 111
Burford (Oxfordshire) 234*n*34
Burges, John 223*n*11
Burton, Thomas 34, 205
Burton Dassett (Warwickshire), Marlborough Farm 179
Busby, Richard 192
Buscot (Berkshire) 191
Butcher Row 116
Butlers Marston (Warwickshire) 95, 106, 107, 112, 201
Butterton, Nicholas 86
Buttington (Montgomeryshire) 69
Button, Ralph 92, 205

C

Cadogan, Charles Cadogan, 2nd Baron 107
Cakebread, William 115
Calcetto Priory (Sussex) 189
Calvertt, John Simpson 146–7, 234*n*34, 234*n*40
Cambridge Camden Society 57
Camden, George Pratt, 2nd Marquess of 123
canals 116, 119, 128–9, 129–30, *130*, 135, 164, 237*n*22
Canterbury College 215*n*69
Canterbury Quadrangle 35, 215*n*69
Canwell Priory (Staffordshire) 189
car transport 118, 119–20
Cardinal College
  dissolution 7–8
  'feeder' grammar schools 1, 2, 97–8, 208*n*4
  foundation and construction 1, 5, 8, 234*n*34
  funding and finances 1–7, 10, 32, 189–90, 198, 208*n*3
  statutes 5, 7, 8, 11, 18, 141, 209*n*13
Careswell, Edward 99, 200, 228*n*98
Careswell Trust estate (Shropshire and Staffordshire) 59–60, 98–102, *100*, *101*, 200, 228*n*98, *endpapers*
Carew, Dean George 206
Carey Trust 156
Carfax tower 232*n*66
Carleton (Yorkshire) 70
Carleton, George 114
Cartwright, Sir John 33, 214*n*50
Cassington (Oxfordshire) 70, 173, 198
Castle, Field & Castle (estate agents) 69, 139
Castlemaine, Roger Palmer, 1st Earl of 212*n*21
Cathedral, Christ Church *see* Christ Church Cathedral
Cathedrals Act (1840) 141
cattle farming 47, 85, 97, 147, 214*n*64, 227–8*n*92
Cave, Anthony 65, 221*n*89
Caversfield (Buckinghamshire) 111, 230*n*140

Caversham (Oxfordshire) 49, 70, 95, 107, 140, 198, 227*n*84
Cecil, Robert (*later* 1st Earl of Salisbury) 22
Chaceley (Worcestershire) 202
Chadwick (Worcestershire) *105*, 112, 202, 214*n*62, 233*n*7
Chadwick, Dean Henry 206
Chalgrove (Oxfordshire) 46, 70, 198
Chaloner, Robert 94–5, 199, 227*n*80
Chamberlain, Neville 178
Chamberlaine, Timothy 114
Champneys, Basil 231*n*29
Chandlings Wood (Berkshire) 35, 36, *36*, 67, 191, 214*n*58, 214*n*64
Chandos, James Brydges, 1st Duke of 192
Chaplains' Quadrangle 16
Chapman, William 111
Chapple, William 102
Chapter Clerks 15, 18
  see also Brooks, John; Willis, John
Chapter House 8
Charing Cross, Euston and Hampstead Railway Company 126–7
Charles I, King 28, 212*n*32
Charles II, King 16, 38
  see also Restoration (1660–88)
Charlton (Wiltshire) 70, 95, 201, 218*n*24
Charlton, Andrew 99
Charter of Dotation (Christ Church) 9, *10*, 191
Charterhouse School (London) 97
Chatteris (Cambridgeshire), Holwood Farm 94, 193
Chawner, John 53
Cheshunt (Hertfordshire) 190
Cheyney Lane *see* Market Street
Chicksands Priory (Bedfordshire) 191
Chilmark (Wiltshire) 217*n*12
Chinnor (Oxfordshire) 217 *n*16
Chippenham (Wiltshire) 70, 201
Christ Church Cathedral 8–9
  Latin Chapel 95
  plate 16
  repair and restoration 151, 214*n*65, 235*n*57
Christ Church Meadow 37, 199
Christ Church Oxford Act (1867) 73, 142–5, *143*
Church Building Act (1818) 62
church construction, maintenance and restoration 56–65, 73
Church Cowley (Oxfordshire) *see* Cowley
Chute Forest (Wiltshire) 201
cider production 150, 162
Civil War, English 27–9, 38, 74, 87, 94, 95, 180, 223*n*1, 223*n*3
Claines (Worcestershire) 140, 202
Clanfield (Oxfordshire) 198
  Chestlion Farm 239*n*40
Clarendon Hotel 230*n*4
Clarke, William Wiseman 53, 219*n*39
Clattercote (Oxfordshire) 198
  Priory 198, 201
Clavering, Robert 205
Claydons, The (Buckinghamshire) 78, 86, 89, 192, 223*n*11
Clement VII, Pope 2
Clergy Residencies Repair Act (1776) 49, 55, 219*n*48
Clerke, Frances 91
Cleveland Commission 152–3, 157
Clifton (Oxfordshire) 33, 199, 213*n*46, 214*n*50
Clifton-on-Teme (Warwickshire) 202
climate change 187
Clive, Robert Clive, 1st Baron 228*n*99

coal mining 110, 158–67, 169, 228*n*102, 236–7, 238*n*8
Cochrane & Co. (mining company) 169
Coke, Thomas (*later* 1st Earl of Leicester) 229*n*134
Coldridge, John 102, 228*n*106–7
Colham (Middlesex) 197
College Wood *see* Abbots Wood
Collins, Judd 50
Collins, William 131
Committee for Establishing Baths and Wash-Houses 65, 221*n*93
Commonwealth of England 16, 29–30, 38, 74, 94
Conybeare, Dean John, bishop of Bristol 206
Conybeare, William Daniel 165
Cook, John 115
Cooper, Frank 170
Cooper, Dean Thomas, bishop of Winchester 206
Cople (Bedfordshire) 70, 191
Copp (Lancashire) 50, 62
copyhold (land tenure) 31–3, 78–80, 213*n*41
  enfranchisement and abolition 33, 80, 173–5
Copyhold Act (1894) 80, 173–4
Copyhold Commission 151, 157, 233*n*20
Corbett, Dean Richard, bishop of Norwich 206
Cork, Elizabeth, Countess of (*née* Clifford) 27–8
Cork, Richard Boyle, 2nd Earl of 27–8
Corn Laws, repeal (1846) 145
Corn Production Act (1917) 171, 177
Corn Rent Act (1576) 20–22, 34, 211*n*9
Cornish, Henry 205
Cornmarket 230*n*4
  Star Inn 114, 230*n*4
Cornwall, Duchy of 11, 159, 162–3, 163, 166, 192, 237*n*1
Corpus Christi College 5, 8, 76–7, 213*n*48
Cotton, Edward 94
Coventry (Warwickshire) 63, 116
Covered Market 134
Cowley (Oxfordshire) 57, 62, 70, 130–31, 198, 213*n*46, 218*n*20
  Church Cowley 30, 130, 168, 213*n*48
  St James School 179
  Temple Cowley 130
Cowley Road 172
Cox, Dean Richard 35, 191, 206, 214*n*58
Coxeter, Thomas 159, 161–2, 236*n*11
Crabtree, Richard 122
Cripley Road 119, 120
crocodile farming 240*n*64
Cromwell, Thomas 5
Croyden, George 205
Croydon (Surrey) 180
Cumberland, Henry Clifford, 5th Earl of 27
Cumnor (Berkshire) 191
Curtoppe, James 15, 210*n*42
Cutteslowe (Oxfordshire) 49–50, 97, 199

D

Dalbeney, Thomas 24–5
Daresbury (Cheshire) 70, 193, 213*n*43
Davenport, George 41
Daventry (Northamptonshire) 20, 33–4, 54, 70, 129, *130*, 136, 141, 170,

180, 187, 197–8, 213*n*46, 232*n*50
Priory 8, 189, 197, 198
public houses 173
see also Thrupp
Davis, Isaiah 92, 93
Davis, Richard (Little Compton tenant) 59
Davis, Richard (surveyor) 103, 107, 110, 128, 229*n*133, 231*n*47
maps *endpapers*, Pl.
Day, John 162
Day, Thomas 204
Dean (of Cardinal College) 5–6, 7, 209*n*13
stipend 4
Dean (of Christ Church)
list of deans 206
role and responsibilities 8–9, 11, 26, 43, 44–5, 102, 142–3
use of title 209*n*13
Dean (of King Henry VIII College) 8
Debenhams (department store) 173
Deddington (Oxfordshire) 26, 33, 35, 168, 175, 199, 213*n*46, 214*n*50, 239*n*57
Deeping St James (Lincolnshire) 196
Denton family (Hillesden) 86–7
depopulation 85, 89, 225*n*42, 226*n*55
depressions *see* agricultural depressions
Dewey, William 38–9
Digby, William 205
diocese of Oxford
creation 8, 9
diocesan seat 8, 9
dissolution of monasteries *see* monasteries
Ditton Priors (Shropshire) 228*n*101
Sydnall Farm 99–101, *101*
d'Ivry, Roger 215*n*80
Dixon, Eliza 232*n*53
Dodgson, Charles (Lewis Carroll) 153, 156, 213*n*43
Dodnash Priory (Suffolk) 189
d'Oilly family 39, 215*n*80
Dolben, John 205
Donnington (Shropshire) 228*n*98–9
Dorchester (Oxfordshire) 95, 218*n*24
Abbey 198, 199
Dorman-Smith, Sir Reginald 179
Dormer, John 114
Dorset, Robert 204, 215*n*70
Dorton (Buckinghamshire) 37, 70, 192, 218*n*20, *endpapers*
Down Ampney (Gloucestershire) 44, 70, 194
Drayton St Leonard (Oxfordshire) 50, 56, 70, 95, 199, 218*n*20, 218*n*24
Drury, Dean John 206
Dry Sandford (Berkshire) 84, 192, 225*n*37
Ducie, Thomas Reynolds-Moreton, 1st Earl of 107
Dugmore, John 110, 229*n*134
Duns Tew (Oxfordshire) 199
Duppa, Dean Brian, bishop of Winchester 206, 214*n*65

E

East Claydon (Buckinghamshire) 78, 89, 192, 223*n*11, 223*n*13
East Garston (Berkshire) 24, 70, 95, 106, 107, 192, 218*n*24
East Walton (Norfolk) *77*, 78–80, 82, 197, 213*n*46, 223*n*13–21
Easterton (Wiltshire) 201
Easthampstead (Berkshire) 70, 192
Easton Maudit (Northamptonshire) 70, 88–9, 198, 226*n*54

Ecclesiastical Commissioners 49, 72, 141, 221*n*82, 236*n*1
Estates Committee 141
Ecclesiastical Leases Acts (1571; 1572) 20, 119, 158
Edington Priory (Wiltshire) 200, 201
Education Act (1902) 221*n*88
Edward I, King 26
Eedes, Richard 204
Egerton, John 28
Elham (Kent) *176*, 177
Elizabeth I, Queen 17, 20, 21–2, 98, 210*n*36, Pl.
Ellerbeck (Yorkshire) 50, 175, 202, 213*n*46, 226*n*58, 239*n*57
Little Bridge Farm 179
Elm Hall 76, 134–5
Elsfield (Oxfordshire) 173, *174*, 199, 238*n*30, Pl.
Elstow Abbey (Bedfordshire) 198
Elton, Sir Abraham 160, 162
Emery, John 161–2
enclosure 33, 80, 81, 84–93, 103–12, 137, 225–6, 229
endowment (Christ Church)
foundation 9–11, *12–3*, 44, 84–93, 114, 115, 131, 191–203, 210*n*33, 213*n*46, 226*n*60
later benefactions and trusts 93–103, *96*, 121, 191–203, 226*n*67, 226*n*72, 227*n*81
Enstone (Oxfordshire) 146, 199, 234*n*34
Epwell (Oxfordshire) 199
Eton College (Berkshire) 20
Evans, Walter 91–2
Evenlode (Worcestershire) 59
Evesham (Worcestershire) 187, 235*n*48
Abbey 197, 201, 202
Ewelme (Oxfordshire) 107–10
Eynsham (Oxfordshire) 94, 199, 222*n*108, 226*n*72
Abbey 75, 195, 198, 200

F

Fanshawe, John (Treasurer) 205
Fanshawe, John (vicar of Frodsham) 61, 220*n*68, 220*n*71
Farleigh Priory (Wiltshire) 201
Farr, William 115
Fauconberg, Roger 222*n*107
Faussett, Godfrey 145, 152–4, *153*, 156, 205, 235*n*62
Featherstone (Yorkshire) 63–5, 70, 166–7, 169, 202, 214*n*62, 238*n*8
Felixstowe Priory (Suffolk) 189
Fell, Dean John, bishop of Oxford 37, 47, 67, 206
bequest 94, 96, 217*n*11, 219*n*46
trustees' purchases 192, 193, 194, 198
Fell, Dean Samuel 27, 40, 200, 204, 206, 214*n*65, 223*n*3
Fell Tower 151
Fenny Compton (Warwickshire) 135, 179, 201, 213*n*46
Fetyplace, Edward 5, 208*n*12
Field, Francis Hayward 147–8, 149, 235*n*51
Field & Castle (estate agents) *see* Castle, Field & Castle
Finance Act (1977) 178
Finance Committee (Christ Church) 144–5, 151–3, 185
Fire of London Disputes Act (1666) 131, 232*n*55
'First Fruits and Tenths' (ecclesiastical tax) 49, 218*n*23

First World War 127, 169–72, 175, 238*n*21–22
Fisher, Richard 216*n*91
Fisher Row (*formerly* Warham Bank) 114–15, 117, 140, 230*n*11, Pl.
Fleet Marston (Buckinghamshire) 192
Flitton (Bedfordshire) 70, 191
Flore (Northamptonshire) 70, 198
Forester, Paul 205
Fortescue, Sir John 22
Foulkes, Peter 56, 220*n*52
foundation endowment *see* endowment (Christ Church)
Fox, Richard, bishop of Winchester 5
Frampton, Robert, bishop of Gloucester 199, 226*n*72
Francis, Thomas 15, 210*n*42
Freckleton (Lancashire) 50
Freind, William Maximilian 46, 217*n*16
Frilford (Berkshire) 67, 222*n*104
Frodsham (Cheshire) 61–2, 70, 193, 213*n*43, 220*n*67–71

G

Gaisford, Dean Thomas 206
Gamon, Benjamin 115
Gardiner, Bernard 57
Gardiner, Richard 94, 194
Garford (Berkshire) 67, 222*n*104
Garsington (Oxfordshire) 37, 94–5, 199, 214*n*66, 227*n*79–80
Gastrell, Francis 205
General Enclosure Acts (1836; 1845) 106
George Street 76
Gilbert, John 205
Gilbert's Acts 219*n*48
Glasgow 172
Glaspole, Joseph 107
glebe land, definition of 44
Gloucester (Gloucestershire) 39
  St Oswald's Priory 202, 203
  St Peter's Abbey 194
Goodenough, Edmund 54
Goodwin, Dean Thomas, bishop of Bath and Wells 206
Goodwin, Dean William 206
Goosnargh (Lancashire) 50, 51, 196, 233*n*1
Grafton (Oxfordshire) 199
grain prices 20, 22, 89, 102, 145, 171, 173, 175–6, 177, 211*n*9
grammar schools 1, 2, 45, 65, 98
  Dr Challoner's Grammar School 227*n*80
  Ipswich School 98, 208*n*4, 208*n*9
  Portsmouth Grammar School 65, 98, 195, 228*n*96
Grand Junction Canal 128–9, *130*
Grand Union Canal 116
Gray, Francis Anthony 205
Great Bowden (Leicestershire) 24, *40*, 52–3, 70, 196, 211*n*18
Great Budworth (Cheshire) 66, 70, 193, 222*n*99
Great Fire of London (1666) 74, 131, 133, 222*n*98, 232*n*55
Great Hampton (Worcestershire) *see* Hampton
Great Linford (Buckinghamshire) 86
Great Quadrangle (Tom Quad) 74, 151, 214*n*65
  Fell Tower 151
  Mercury 94
  Wolsey Tower 151
Great Torrington (Devon) 30, 70, 110–11, 194, 211*n*9, 213*n*39, 229*n*135

Great Western Railway (GWR) 118, 173, Pl.
Greenhill (Middlesex) 128
Gregg, Thomas 110, 121, 163–4, 237*n*18
Gregory, Dean David 205, 206, 220*n*52
Gregory family (Astrop) 168
Grenville, Richard 87
Grey, Charles Grey, 2nd Earl 141
Guilsborough (Northamptonshire) 198
Guilsfield (Montgomeryshire) 25, 69, 197, 212*n*21
GWR *see* Great Western Railway

H

Hall (Christ Church), staircase 6, 16
Hall, Dean Charles Henry 206
Hall, John 220*n*67
Hambleton (Lancashire) 50
Hamel, Model Dwellings 117–18
Hammond, John 205
Hamond family (East Walton) 79–80
Hampden, Richard 91–3
Hampstead Norreys (Berkshire) 94, 192, 217*n*15
Hampton (Worcestershire) 70, 149, 202, 218*n*20
Hancock, Thomas 46, 217*n*12
Hannars, Richard 38, 215*n*72–3
Harbin, Henry 97
Harringworth (Northamptonshire) 70, 198
Harris, Hamlyn 55–6
Harrow (Middlesex) 65, 128–9, 170, 173, 197, 213*n*46, 231*n*47
Harrow Weald (Middlesex) 129
Hart, Benjamin 68–9
Haslewood, George 59–60
Hatton (Cheshire) 193
Hawkhurst (Kent) 53–4, 62, 70, 196, 218*n*20, 219*n*41, Pl.
Hawkins, John 68–9, 222*n*108
Hawksmoor, Nicholas 222*n*98
Hearne, Thomas 78, 97
Heaton, Dean Eric 206
Hedley, Richard 25
Helsthorpe (Buckinghamshire) 95, 110, 192
Hempton (Oxfordshire) 33, 199, 213*n*46, 214*n*50
Henry VIII, King 9, 10, 11, 226*n*60
  'First Fruits and Tenths' tax 49, 218*n*23
Hester, George Parsons 118
Heton, Martin 204
High Legh (Cheshire) 193
High Street (the High) 113, 115
Highley (Shropshire) 200
Hillesden (Buckinghamshire) 70, 86–7, 104, 173, 192, 225*n*46, Pl.
Hillier, Thomas 58
Hillingdon (Middlesex) 128, 197
Hinchliffe, John, bishop of Peterborough 107, 229*n*122
Hind, Richard 54
Hinde, Thomas 63, 166
Holford, Elizabeth, Lady 97
Holford Trust 97, 199
Holmes, Robert 205
Holwell, William 56, 220*n*52
Hook, Walter Farquhar 63, 64, 221*n*83
Hook Norton (Oxfordshire) 199
Hook Norton Ironstone Partnership 169
Horkesley Priory (Essex) 2, 189
horticulture 148–50, 180

Hospital of St John of Jerusalem (Knights Hospitaller) 194, 195, 198
Housing (Rural Workers) Act (1926) 239*n*53
Howley, William 205
Howson, John 204, 215*n*70
Hoyland (Yorkshire) 224*n*27
Hunslet (Yorkshire) 63
Hutchinson, George 168, 171, 177–8, 180, 205, 237–8*n*1
Hutton, Leonard 204
Hythe Bridge 116
Hythe Bridge Street 115, 116, 119, 230*n*11

I

Idbury (Oxfordshire) 199
Ilbury (Oxfordshire) 214*n*50
Iles, Thomas 204
Inclosure Act (1773) 105
Inclosure Consolidation Act (1801) 105–6
industrialisation 56, 62, 116, 118, 163, 167, 169
Inglaton, William 132
Inglesby, William 115
Ipswich (Suffolk) 1
  School 98, 208*n*4, 208*n*9
  St Peter's Priory 1, 3, 189
Iron Acton (Gloucestershire) 70, 194, 227*n*81
ironstone quarrying 169, 179
Ivychurch (Kent) 196
Ivychurch Priory (Wiltshire) 201

J

Jackson, Dean Cyril 205, 206
Jackson, William 205
Jackson's Oxford Journal 108, *109*
Jacobson, William 205
James I, King 212*n*21
James, Dean William, bishop of Durham 206
Jane, William 194, 227*n*81
Jeffreys, John 205
Jesus College 113, 140
Jones, David 66–7, 69, 222*n*98–9
Jones, Lang, Wootton & Sons (estate agents and auctioneers) 127
Jones, Roger 25
Judgson,William 50, 219*n*28

K

Keble, Thomas 215*n*74
Kennall, John 204
Kent, Henry Grey, 4th Earl of 191
Kentish Town (Middlesex) 49, 95, 119, 121–8, *125*, 129, 179, 197, 227*n*84, 230–31, Pl.
Kenton (Middlesex) 128, 129
Kersey, John 86
Kexby (Yorkshire) 189
Kidlington (Oxfordshire) 181, 183
Kildwick (Yorkshire) 70, 202, 233*n*7
King, James 18
King, John (auditor) 16
King, Dean John, bishop of London 16, 206, 215*n*71
King, Philip (auditor) 16, 215*n*71
King Henry VIII College 8, 11, 209*n*24
King's College (Cambridge) 1, 210*n*36
Kingsley (Cheshire) 61–2, 220*n*71
Kingston upon Thames (Surrey) 180
Kirkham (Lancashire) 26, 50, 70, 175, 196, 213*n*46
  parish 50, *51*, 62, 233*n*1
  parsonage 55
Kirton (Lincolnshire) 180, 196, 239*n*50

Knights Hospitaller *see* Hospital of St John of Jerusalem
Knutsford (Cheshire) 51, 193, 213*n*43

L

Lamb, Henry 69
Land Registration Act (2002) 175
Land Tax 140
Langbaine, Gerard the elder 27, 212*n*25
Langbaine, Gerard the younger 113
Lassells, Francis 90–91
Lathbury (Buckinghamshire) 47, 65, 70, 91–3, 192, 221*n*89
Launde Priory (*later* Abbey; Leicestershire) 51, 193
Lavendon Abbey (Buckinghamshire) 192, 198
Law of Property Act (1925) 174
Lawrence, C. W. 123
Lawrence, Guy 55
Lawrie, James 205
Leafield (Oxfordshire) 146
Lee, Matthew 95, 194
Lee Trust 95, 201, 202
Leeds (Yorkshire) 63–5, 202
Leppington (Yorkshire) 189
Lesnes Abbey (Kent) 3, 189, 208*n*8
Lew (Oxfordshire) 199
Lewis, Dean Christopher 206
Lewis, Timothy 236*n*17
Leyton (Essex) 194
Library (Christ Church) 46
Liddell, Dean Henry 71, 152, 154, 206
limestone quarrying 169
Lincoln College 212*n*32
Little Compton (Gloucestershire) 58–9, 65, 70, 95, 194, 218*n*24, 220*n*59
  parsonage 58, *60*
  St Denys's church 58–9, 220*n*65
  woods 30, 107
Little Hampton (Worcestershire) *see* Hampton
Littlemore Priory (Oxfordshire) 3, 8, 189
Littletons, The (Worcestershire) 54, 70, 95, 148, 202, 218*n*24
livestock diseases 97, 145, 227–8*n*92
Llanrhaeadr (Denbighshire) 218*n*24
Lloyd, Charles, bishop of Oxford 108
Lloyd, Thomas 99
LNWR *see* London and North Western Railway
Local Government Act (1888) 234*n*33
London
  canals 128–9
  Charterhouse 97, 131
  City 131–2, *133*, 180, 232*n*55
  Great Fire (1666) 74, 131, 133, 222*n*98, 232*n*55
  Greycoat Hospital 218*n*24
  Hampstead 126
  railways 123–4, 126–7, 129, 132
  Shadwell 28
  St Bride's 232*n*55
  St Mary Woolnoth 66, 222*n*98
  St Pancras 121, 127, 179, 231*n*29
  St Paul's Cathedral 28, 141, 211*n*3
  St Sepulchre's 131–2, *133*, 196
  Westminster School 20, 49, 65, 95, 98, 217*n*14
  see also Harrow; Kentish Town; Leyton; Wembley
London and North Western Railway (LNWR) 118, 129
Long, Samuel 50, 219*n*28
Long Compton (Warwickshire) 220*n*64

Long Marston (Hertfordshire) 50, 70, 195
Long Preston (Yorkshire) 27–8, 70, 202
Louis XIV, King of France 140
Louth (Lincolnshire) 234*n*34
Lowe, Dean John 206
Lower Swell (Gloucestershire) *see* Netherswell
Ludlow (Shropshire) 25
Lund (Lancashire) 50
Lyford (Berkshire) 192

M
Magdalen Bridge 114
Magdalen College 1, 147, 210*n*36
  Muniment Tower Pl.
Maiden Bradley (Wiltshire) 70, 201
Maids Moreton (Buckinghamshire) 30, 32–3, 175, 192, 213*n*46, 213*n*48, 214*n*49
main gate (Christ Church) 6, 16
Mainwaring, Robert 51
Manley (Cheshire) 193
manorial estates 7, 30–34, 78–9, 173–5, 213*n*38, 213*n*41, 213*n*46
map-making 76–8, 81, 99, 112, 138–9, 219*n*41
Marah, William Hennessey 58–9, 60, 65
Marcham (Berkshire) 54, 66–7, 69, 70, 192, 221*n*95, 222*n*104
market gardening 122, 148–50, 180
Market Harborough (Leicestershire) 24, 70, 196
  St Mary in Arden 49, 70, 212*n*9
Market Lavington (Wiltshire) 55, 70, 201
Market Street (*formerly* Cheyney Lane) 113, 140, 170
Markham, Dean William, archbishop of York 206, 217*n*16
marl mining 162, 236*n*17
Marlborough Road 118
Marshall, Dean Richard 206
Marthall (Cheshire) 193
Martock (Somerset) 158
Mary I, Queen 11, *14*, 93, 195
Masham, Samuel Lister, 1st Baron 167, 237*n*34
Massey, Dean John 206
Masters Garden (Christ Church) 238*n*1
Matthew, Dean Tobie, archbishop of York 204, 206
Meadow, Christ Church *see* Christ Church Meadow
Meadow Buildings 151, 209*n*18
Medley (Oxfordshire) 199
Meifod (Montgomeryshire) 24–5, 69, 71–2, 197, 212*n*21
Mere (Cheshire) 193
Merton College 76–7, 145, 176, 177, 178, 210*n*41, 221*n*89, 239*n*36
Merton Field 171
Merton Priory (Surrey) 158, 198, 201
Methodism 59, 63, 220*n*64
Metropolitan Railway (London) 124
Middle Claydon (Buckinghamshire) 86
Middle Littleton (Worcestershire) 202
Midland Railway 123–4, 126, 127
Midland Revolt (1607) 85, 226*n*55
Midsomer Norton (Somerset) 24, 70, 110, 158–66, *160*, 168, 201, 213*n*46, 236*n*11, 237*n*18
Milcombe (Oxfordshire) 199
Mill Street 118–19, 120
Mills, John 29–30, 38, 205, 213*n*37
mining and quarrying *see* coal; ironstone; limestone; marl

Mitford family 217*n*11
Mogg family (Somerset) 162, 163, 236*n*15
monasteries, suppression and dissolution 1–5, *2*, *4*, 10, 24, 189–90
Moore, Margaret 114
Moore, Roger 115
Mordaunt, Sir John 131
Morgan, William 121–2
Morison, Sir Richard 90, 200, 202, 203, 226*n*60
Morley, Dean George, bishop of Winchester 206
Morrell, James 81
Morrell's brewery 119
Morris, John 94, 192, 204, 217*n*15
Morris exhibitions 46, 94, 217*n*15, 226*n*70
Morrison, William (*later* 1st Viscount Dunrossil) 178–9

N

Napoleonic Wars 102, 103, 104, 138, 214*n*54
National Coal Board 165
National Society for Promoting the Education of the Poor 65
Netherswell (Gloucestershire) 70, 95, 147, 195, 218*n*24
New College 34, 176, 178, 212*n*32, 234*n*29, 239*n*36
New Inn Hall Street 76
New Windsor (Berkshire) *see* Windsor
Newdigate, Sir Richard 93
Newman, John Henry 57
Newnham (Northamptonshire) 70
Newport (Shropshire) 228*n*98–9
Newton (Cheshire) 193
Newton, Thomas 107–9
Nine Years' War 140
nonconformism 53, 59, 63, 69–71, 220*n*64
non-resident and absentee clergy 55, 56, 67–9, 141
Norley (Cheshire) 61–2, 220*n*71
North Kilvington (Yorkshire) 50, 90
North Littleton (Worcestershire) 70, 202
North Marston (Buckinghamshire) 192
North Nibley (Gloucestershire) 22–3, *23*, 70, 195
North Otterington (Yorkshire) 50, 67–8, 70, 90, 202, 222*n*106–7
Northallerton (Yorkshire) 50, 68, 90, 180, 202, 222*n*106, 226*n*58, 226*n*60
  Hospital of St James 90, 202, 226*n*60
  parish 50, 90–91
  School 68
Northampton Mercury (newspaper) 78
Northmoor (Oxfordshire) 94
Norton Abbey (Cheshire) 193, 200
Notgrove (Gloucestershire) 195
Notley Abbey (Buckinghamshire) 192, 195, 198, 201
Nuffield College 119
Nunhouse (Yorkshire) 50, 226*n*58
Nunnery Wood (Worcestershire) 41, 216*n*89

O

Odcombe (Somerset) 70, 201, 227*n*81
Offenham (Worcestershire) 70, 95, 110, 148, 149, 218*n*20, 218*n*24
  Hill Farm *149*, 150
Onslow, Arthur 135, 205, 232*n*67
Oriel College 212*n*32

Oseney Abbey (Oxfordshire) 39, 115, 191, 192, 195, 198, 199, 200, 213*n*48
  cartulary 75
  seat of bishops of Oxford 8
Osmotherly (Yorkshire) 50, 202, 226*n*58, 228*n*92
Osney Island 118
Otford Palace (Kent) 208*n*5
Ottery St Mary (Devon) 94, 102, 194, 227*n*74, 228*n*107
  Cadhay Farm 102
Over Tabley (Cheshire) 193
Overy (Oxfordshire) 199
Owen, David 72
Owen, Dean John 206, 213*n*37
Oxford (churches and parishes)
  All Saints 113
  St Aldate's 135–6, 140, 199
  St Ebbe's 199
  St Edward's 199
  St Frideswide's 62
  St George's 39, 114, 199, 215*n*80
  St Giles 199
  St John's 199
  St Martin's 134–5, 199, 232*n*66
  St Mary Magdalen 70, 199
  St Mary the Virgin 199
  St Michael's 76, 199
  St Peter in the East 200
  St Peter-le-Bailey 200
  St Thomas's 57, 62, 70, 115–21, *117*, *120*, 129, 140, 157, 169–70, 171, 200, 213*n*46, 218*n*20, 230*n*11, Pl.
Oxford Canal 116, 119, 129
Oxford Canal Company 135
Oxford Castle 77, 114, 215*n*80, Pl.
  gaol 66, 134, 136
  mill stream 115
  St George's church 39, 114, 199, 215*n*80
Oxford Mileways Act (1771) 113, 134
Oxford University Press 236*n*67
Oxpens 171

P

Pacey's Bridge 230*n*11
Paget, Dean Francis, bishop of Oxford 206
Palmer, James 212*n*21
Palmer, Roger (*later* 1st Earl of Castlemaine) 212*n*21
Palmer family (Christ Church auditors) 15–16, 32, 37, 215*n*71
Park End Street 116–17, *117*, 120, 170, 230*n*11
Parsonages Act (1838) 221*n*82
parsonages and vicarages, construction and maintenance 49, 52–6, 220*n*54, 221*n*82
Paul, Rachel 94, 199, 222*n*108
Paul, William, bishop of Oxford 94, 222*n*108
Paul exhibitions 94, 222*n*108
Paulinus of Theydon 39, 216*n*81
Paulton (Somerset) 158–60, 237*n*22, 237*n*28
Paver, William 166, 237*n*31
Paving Commission (Oxford) 134, 135, 140
Pearson, John, bishop of Chester, *Exposition on the Apostle's Creed* 45, 217*n*7
Pearson, John Loughborough 62
Peckwater Quadrangle 22, 191, 232*n*68
  Library 46
Peel, Sir Robert 141

Pembroke, Philip Herbert, 4th Earl of 212*n*21
Pembroke College 140, 155, 201, 236*n*67
Pembroke Street 169
Penrice, Sir Henry 68
Pension Fund (Christ Church) 151–2, 153, 156, 235*n*60, 236*n*68
Peover (Cheshire) 51, 193
Percy, Dean Martyn 206
Periam, George 47
Perry Wood (Worcestershire) 39–41, 216*n*84, 216*n*84–9, 216*n*89
Peterson, George 71
Petre, Sir William 194, 196, 198, 201
Phillips, Thomas, *William Buckland* *165*
Pickhaver, Ralph 204
Piercy, Thomas 42
Piers, Dean John, archbishop of York 206
Piers, William 204
Pinner (Middlesex) 128, 129
Pitchcott (Buckinghamshire) *183*, 192
Pitt, William, the Younger 139
plague 15
  Black Death (1348–9) 32, 84, 225*n*42
Plumpton (Lancashire) 62
Pocock, Edward 205
Pontypool (Monmouthshire) 163
Pope, Sir Thomas 197, 199, 200
Portsmouth (Hampshire) 98
  Grammar School 65, 98, 195, 228*n*96
Pott, Phineas 205
Potter, John (Treasurer) 205
Potter family (Oxford drapers) 169
Poughley Priory (Berkshire) 5, 189, 208*n*12
Powis, Edward Clive, 1st Earl of 228*n*99
Preston (Cheshire) 193
Preston (Middlesex) 128, 129
Price, Bartholomew 154, *155*, 236*n*67–8
Prideaux, Nicholas 158
Prideaux Place (Cornwall) 236*n*1
Pridham, Lawrence 110–11, 229*n*135
Probert, John 228*n*99
  survey of Careswell Trust estate 99–102, *100*, *101*, *endpapers*
Proctor, Henry 68–9
progresses and visitations 5, 8, 23–7, 30–31, 32–3, 34, 78, 80, 168, 180
Public Baths and Wash-Houses Act (1846) 221*n*93
public houses 112, 119, 127, 172–3, 180, 214*n*66
Pugin, A. W. N. 57
Purnell, John and Thomas 22–3
Purston Jaglin (Yorkshire) 63, 64, 166
Pusey, Edward Bouverie 63–4
Pynham (Sussex), Calcetto Priory 189
Pyrton (Oxfordshire) 70, 200

Q

Quakers 220*n*64
quarrying and mining *see* coal; ironstone; limestone; marl
Quatford (Shropshire) 59–60
  Hillhouse Farm 59–60, 101
Queen Street 116
Queen's College 27, 210*n*42, 227*n*79

R

Rackham, Oliver 214*n*54
rack-renting 40, 83, 139, 142, 150–51, 168, 234*n*41

Radcliffe, Anthony 191, 205
Radcliffe, Geoffrey 178
Radcot (Oxfordshire) 200
Radford (Somerset) 164, 237*n*24, 237*n*28, Pl.
Radipole (Dorset) 104
Radstock (Somerset) 158–9, 237*n*22–3
railways 118, 119, 120, 123–4, 129–31, 132, 148, 157, 232*n*53
Randolph, John 135, 232*n*67
Randolph, Thomas *17*
Rangeworthy (Gloucestershire) 195
Ravensthorpe (Northamptonshire) 70, 110, 198
Ravenstone Priory (Buckinghamshire) 189
Ravis, Dean Thomas, bishop of London 34, 206
Read, John 66, 221*n*95
receipt books 15, 22, 211*n*51
Redesdale, John Freeman-Mitford, 1st Baron 217*n*11
Redistribution of Seats Act (1885) 234*n*33
Rees-Mogg family (Somerset) 236*n*15
Reform Act (1832) 138, 234*n*33
Reform Act (1884) 234*n*33
refrigeration 148
renewable energy 187
Rent Restriction Act (1915) 172
Restoration (1660–88) 16, 33, 34, 47, 74, 94
Rewley Abbey 115
Rewley Road 230*n*11
railway station 118
Reynolds, Dean Edward, bishop of Norwich 206, 213*n*37
Ribby with Wrea (Lancashire) 50
Richardson, Hugh 205
Ridge, Hugh 158
Ridge, William 158
Ridgel, Thomas 87
Robotham, Robert 27
Rockingham, Charles Watson-Wentworth, 2nd Marquess of 81–2, 83, 224*n*24, 224*n*26
Roderick, Dorothy 227*n*81
Rodnight, Sarah 170
Rolle, John Rolle, 1st Baron 111
Romanby (Yorkshire) 50, 90
Romney Marsh (Kent) 169, 196, 238*n*5
Rose, William 129, 232*n*50
Rostherne (Cheshire) 28, 31, 51–2, 193, 212*n*30, 213*n*43, 219*n*35
Rothschild, Mayer Amschel, Baron de 192
Rowland-Steyner families (Worcester tenants) 39–41
Rowley, John 81, 82
Roxeth (Middlesex) 128, 129
Royal Agricultural Society Show (1950) 181, 183
Royal Commission on Agricultural Depression (1882) 234*n*33
Royal Commission on Oxford and Cambridge Universities (Asquith Commission; 1922) 172
Royal Oxford Hotel 230*n*11
Rudby (Yorkshire) 190
Rugby (Warwickshire) 116
Rumburgh Priory (Suffolk) 3–5, 189, 208*n*9
Runcorn (Cheshire) 70, 172, 193, 213*n*43
Ruskin, John 57
Russell, John Russell, 1st Earl 138
Russell, William 233*n*70

S

Sackville, Thomas (*later* 1st Earl of Dorset) 22
Salisbury Colliery (Somerset) 237*n*28
Salter, Edward 53–4
Sampson, Dean Thomas 37, 206
Sampson, William 237*n*18
Sancroft, William, archbishop of Canterbury 78, 224*n*15
Sandford (Berkshire) 84, 192
Sandwell Priory (Staffordshire) 190
Saunderton (Buckinghamshire) 192, 213*n*46
Savills (land agents) 187
schools, provision of 65, 97–8, 118, 221*n*88, 228*n*97–8
  see also grammar schools
Scott, Sir George Gilbert 62
seal and seal box (Christ Church) 6–7, *7*, 209*n*18, 209*n*20
Second World War 43, 178–80
Semley (Wiltshire) 56, 70, 201, 220*n*52, 227*n*83
Sevenoaks (Kent) 179–80
Severn Stoke (Worcestershire) 202
Shabbington (Buckinghamshire) 219*n*28
Shallcross, James 24–5
sheep farming 84, 85, 93, 110, 214*n*64, 226*n*56, 238*n*5
Sheering (Essex) 54, 70, 94, 179, 194, 219*n*46
Shelswell (Oxfordshire) 239*n*53
Shenton, William 52
Shifford (Oxfordshire) 94
Shifnal (Shropshire) 228*n*98–9
shipbuilding 34, 98, 214*n*54
Shippon (Berkshire) 11, 84, 192, 210*n*37, 225*n*37
Shipton-on-Cherwell (Oxfordshire) 200
Shirley, Walter Waddington 205
Shotover (Oxfordshire) 200
Shotteswell (Warwickshire) 201, 211*n*12
Shrewsbury (Shropshire)
  Red Lion 25
  School 228*n*97–8
Sibford Gower (Oxfordshire) 168, 200, 213*n*46
Siddall, Henry 204
Siddall, Thomas 204
SIGA rents 135, 140, 232*n*68
Silsoe (Bedfordshire) 191
Silverside, Giles 122
Silverside, Isaac 97
Simpson, Dean Cuthbert 206
Skene, William Baillie 156–7, 205, 210*n*41, 236*n*69
Skinner, Matthew 46–7, 54
Skipton (Yorkshire) 70, 202, 233*n*7
  Castle 27, *29*, 212*n*27
Slapton (Buckinghamshire) 70, 192, 227*n*81
Smallwell, Edward 46
Smalridge, Dean George, bishop of Bristol 206
Smelt, Thomas 68
Smith, Henry (Treasurer) 200, 205
Smith, Robert (of Market Harborough) 196
Smith, Robert Payne (Treasurer) *144*, 145, 205
Smith, Dean Samuel 205
Smith, William (founder Portsmouth Grammar School) 98, 195, 228*n*94
Smith, William 'Strata' (civil engineer) *164*, 165

Smith family (Great Torrington) 30, 213*n*39
Smith-Woolley & Co. (land agents) 180–81, 183, 187
Snape Priory (Suffolk) 190
Somerset Coal Canal 162, 163, 164, 165, 237*n*22
South, Robert 49, 95, 121, 197, 198, 218*n*24
  see also South Trust
South Brent (Devon) 194
South Hinksey (Berkshire) 130
South Littleton (Worcestershire) 54, 70, 95, 148, 202, 218*n*24
South Stoke (Oxfordshire) 15, 16, 37, 56–7, 70, 95, 104, 168, 200, 210*n*42, 213*n*46, 215*n*69, 215*n*71–3, 216*n*91, 218*n*24
  church 37, 57
  public house 172–3
  woods 30, 36, 37–8, 41–3, 214*n*65, 215*n*75, 218*n*24, Pl.
  see also Woodcote
South Trust 49, 73, 95, 169, 199, 218*n*24–5, 219*n*27, 219*n*51, 227*n*83
Southam (Warwickshire) 179
Southampton, Thomas Wriothesley, 1st Earl of 196, 197
Southwell, Sir Richard 197
Spalding (Lincolnshire) 180, 196
  Wragg Marsh Farm 180, *182*, 239*n*50, Pl.
Spelsbury (Oxfordshire) 70, 200, 239*n*57
Spencer, John 133–4, 232*n*61
Spenser, Johanne 25
Spenser, William 24–5
St Aldate's 37, 135–6, 140, 170
St Frideswide's Priory 1, 8, 189, 198, 199
  cartulary 75
St John's College 15, 118, 119
St Mary de Pré Priory (Hertfordshire) 189
St Oswald's Priory (Gloucestershire) 202, 203
St Tudy (Cornwall) 70, 94, 193
Stadhampton (Oxfordshire) 200
Standlake (Oxfordshire) 94, 200
Stansgate Priory (Essex) 190
Stanton St John (Oxfordshire) 97, 223*n*11
Stapleton, Elizabeth, Lady 108
Statute Law Revision Act (1948) 232*n*55
statutes (Cardinal College) 5, 7, 8, 11, 18, 141, 209*n*13
statutes (Christ Church) 11, 209*n*20, 210*n*39, 236*n*68
statutes (King Henry VIII College) 8, 11
Staunton-on-Wye (Herefordshire) 70, 195
Staverton (Northamptonshire) 47, *48*, 70, 218*n*19
steam engines 164, 237*n*23
Stebbing, Frank 167
Steyner family *see* Rowland-Steyner families
stocks and shares, investment in 83, 129, 140, 171, 181, 188, 225*n*33, 238*n*22
Stone, John 53
Stottesdon (Shropshire), Walkerslow Farm 101
Stratford, William 49–50, 159, 161, 205
Stratford Trust 49–50, 199, 218*n*26–7

Stratton Audley (Oxfordshire) 50, 70, 95, 104, 107, 111–12, 140, 180–81, 200, 213*n*46, 218*n*20, 218*n*24, 219*n*30, 229*n*136–7, 230*n*139–40, 230*n*143, 239*n*53, 239*n*57
Strong, Dean Thomas Banks, bishop of Ripon 206
Students (Christ Church)
  clerical incumbencies 45–52, 216*n*4, 217*n*13, 218*n*18–20
  and college governance 9, 14–15, 142–3, 145
  and college income 9, 22, 145, 152, 157
  definition 210*n*31, 216–7*n*6
  examinations 46, 217*n*6
  marriage prohibition 142, 216*n*4, 217*n*6
  numbers of 9
  ordination 45–6, 217*n*7, 217*n*10
  pensions 144, 235*n*60
  stipends 9, 15, 45, 142, 216*n*6
  teaching and research 9, 45, 217*n*7
Styrley, Robert 24, 211*n*18
Sudbury (Middlesex) 128, 129
Sudley (Cheshire) 193
Suffolk, Charles Brandon, 1st Duke of 208*n*12
Sumner, John Bird, archbishop of Canterbury 61, 220*n*70
Swan, Robert 51–2, 219*n*35
Swanton Novers (Norfolk) 30–31, 34, 35, 70, 175, 197, 213*n*46, 214*n*62
Swayne, John 114
Swerford (Oxfordshire) 200
Swing Riots (1830) 109
Swinton (Yorkshire) 81, 224*n*27
Swymmer, Anthony 162
Swymmer, Henry 159–62
Syddall, Thomas 31
Syresham (Northamptonshire) 89

T

Tanner, Thomas, bishop of St Asaph 78–80, 82, 205, 223*n*13–16, Pl.
Taswell, Joseph 162
Tatton (Cheshire) 193
Tawney, Edward 140
Taynton (Oxfordshire) 234*n*34
Temple Cowley (Oxfordshire) *see* Cowley
Temple Guiting (Gloucestershire) 70, 140–41, 195
terriers (estate documents) 42, *77*, 78, 79, 80–81, 83, 86, 107, 110, 223*n*12–13
Tetbury (Gloucestershire) 89–90, 195, 226*n*56–7
Tetsworth (Gloucestershire) 107
Tewkesbury Abbey (Gloucestershire) 194, 195
Thame Abbey (Oxfordshire) 192, 197, 198
Thelwall (Cheshire) 193
Theydon Mount (Essex) 216*n*81
Thimbleby (Yorkshire) 50
Thoby Priory (Essex) 2, 190, 208*n*4
Thomas, David, archdeacon of Montgomery 71–2
Thornbury (Gloucestershire) 55, 56, 70, 195, 220*n*52, 224*n*13
Thornmow (Devon) 94, 102, 227*n*74
Thornton, Richard 204
Thornton, Thomas 204, 215*n*70
Thornton-le-Beans (Yorkshire) 50, 90, 203
Thornton-le-Moor (Yorkshire) 50, 90, 203
Thornton-le-Street (Yorkshire) 50, 90, 203

Thorp (Yorkshire) 224*n*27
Thorp, Jennifer 239*n*36
Thrupp (Northamptonshire) 21, 130, 198
Thynne, Thomas (*later* 1st Viscount Weymouth) 94, 200, 227*n*77
Ticehurst (Sussex) 62
Tickford Priory (Buckinghamshire) 8, 190
Tiddington (Oxfordshire) 200
timber, income from 34–43, 171, 187, 214*n*54, 214*n*62, 216*n*83
Tincleton (Dorset) 194
Tiptree Priory (Essex) 2, 190
Tithe Act (1936) 178
tithe barns, demolition of 112, 230*n*144, 233*n*7
Tithe Commissioners 138, 139
tithe commutation 108–10, 137–9, 175–8, 222*n*114, 230*n*142, 233*n*7, 239*n*39, 239*n*43
tithe war (Wales; 1880s) 69–72, 177
Tolpuddle (Dorset) 24, 70, 194
Tom Quad *see* Great Quadrangle
Tonbridge (Kent) 2–3, 136, 180, 208*n*5
  Priory 1, 2–3, *3*, 190, 209*n*24
Tooker, Samuel 81
Tottie, John 205
Towers, Thomas 5
Treales (Lancashire) 50
Treasurer (of Christ Church)
  deputies 14–15, 204, 210*n*40
  list of Treasurers 204–5
  role and responsibilities 11–15, 26, 144–5, 187–8
  selection and appointment 144–5, 204, 236*n*69
Tresham, William 8, 209*n*26, 209*n*27
Trevor, Richard 205
Tring (Hertfordshire) 11, 14, 50, 70, 93, 195, 213*n*46
Trinity College (Cambridge) 229*n*122
  endowment 11
  estates 11, 210*n*35
  foundation 11
  scholarships 65, 217*n*14, 232*n*55
  statutes 210*n*39
Turkdean (Gloucestershire) 38–9, 70, 195, 213*n*46, 215*n*74, 215*n*79, 216*n*83, 233*n*7
  school 65, 213*n*46
Twyning (Gloucestershire) 70, 195, 222*n*109
Tyler, Thomas 161–2
Tymbigh, William 131
Tyringham, William 91, 226*n*61
Tysoe (Warwickshire) 201

U

Universities and Colleges Estates Acts (1858; 1860; 1880) 119, 134, 141–2, 156–7, 172, 191, 209*n*21, 223*n*6, 233*n*20
Universities and Colleges (Trusts) Act (1943) 181
University College 8, 210*n*41, 238*n*21–22, 238*n*27
Upperton, Clement 126, 127
Upton (Norfolk) 110, 197, 213*n*46, 229*n*134
Upton, Ambrose 205

V

Vale Royal Abbey (Cheshire) 26, 193, 196
Verney family (Claydon) 86, 89
Vernon family (Ardington) 58, 220*n*58
Vernon Studentships 219*n*35

vicarages *see* parsonages and vicarages
Vickers, Val 136
Villiers, Barbara (*later* Countess of Castlemaine) 212*n*21
visitations *see* progresses and visitations

W

Wake, Arthur 204
Waldegrave family (Radstock) 237*n*23
Wallingford (Berkshire) 78, 192
  Castle 15, *15*, 192, 215*n*73
  College of St Nicholas 15, 192
  Priory 5, 190
war memorials 171–2
Warham, William, archbishop of Canterbury 3, 208*n*5
Warham Bank *see* Fisher Row
Warneford, Samuel 58
  Ecclesiastical Charity 58–9
Warren, Sir John Borlase 111
Warton with Freckleton (Lancashire) 50
Warwick (Warwickshire), Collegiate Church of St Mary 200
Wastie, Sarah 57
Wath upon Dearne (Yorkshire) 70, 81–2, 83, 203, 224*n*24–30, Pl.
Weald (Oxfordshire) 200
Weeton (Lancashire) 50, 62
Welford, RAF (Berkshire) 208*n*12
Welsh Church Act (1914) 72
Welsh tithe war (1880s) 69–72, 177
Welshpool (Montgomeryshire) 25, 69, 197, 212*n*21
Welton (Somerset) 161, 237*n*24, 237*n*28
Wem (Shropshire) 228*n*98–9
Wembley (Middlesex) 128, 129, 136
Wendlebury (Oxfordshire) 70, 200
Wendling (Norfolk) 35, 180, 197, 213*n*46, 214*n*62
Wentnor (Shropshire) 70, 94, 200
Wentworth Woodhouse (Yorkshire) 81, 224*n*24, 224*n*27, Pl.
West, Francis 216*n*85
West, Richard 35
Westbury-on-Trym (Somerset), Holy Trinity Church 39
Westby with Plumptons (Lancashire) 62
Westfaling, Herbert 204
Westley, William 227*n*81
Westminster School (London) 20, 49, 65, 95, 98, 217*n*14
Weston, John 26, 204, 215*n*70
Westwell (Oxfordshire) 70, 168, 173, 174, 200, 213*n*46, 239*n*33
Wetwang (Yorkshire) 8, 190, 209*n*26
Weymouth, Thomas Thynne, 1st Viscount 94, 200, 227*n*77
Wheaton, John 102
Wheeler, John 38, 215*n*74
White, Dean Henry 206
White, Sir Thomas 232*n*55
Whitechapel (Lancashire) 50
Whitgift, John, archbishop of Canterbury 22
Whitmell, Edward 54
Whittingham (Lancashire) 196
Whitton (Cheshire) 193
Whitwood (Yorkshire) 62–3
Wickham, William 195
Wickhamford (Worcestershire) 70, 202
Wigginton (Hertfordshire) 11, 14, 50, 195
Wilbraham, George 61, 220*n*71
Wilkinson, Henry 205
Willen (Buckinghamshire) 70, 192

William III, King 140
Williams, Dean Alwyn, bishop of Winchester 206
Williams-Wynn, Sir Watkin 228*n*99
Willis, John 39, 74–5, 115, 131, 230*n*5
Willis, Thomas 75
Winchcombe Abbey (Gloucestershire) 194, 195, 199
Windsor (Berkshire)
  Bostock Trust houses 93–4, 132–4, *135*, 192, 232*n*61
  Dean and Chapter 102, 194, 209*n*24, 227*n*74
Winson (Gloucestershire) 195
Wolsey, Cardinal Thomas
  background and character 1
  dissolution of monasteries 1–5, *2*, *4*
  downfall and death 7, 98, 209*n*24
  foundation and construction of Cardinal College 1, 5, 8, 10, 97–8, 209*n*13
Wolsey Tower 151
Wood, Anthony 75
Wood, Thomas, bishop of Lichfield 94, 193
Wood, Thomas (surveyor) 42
Wood Norton (Norfolk) 46–7, 54, 70, 168, 180, 197, 213*n*46, Pl.
Woodcock, Henry 205
Woodcote (Oxfordshire), College Wood Farm *183*
Woodeaton (Oxfordshire) 173, 200
Woodhouse, Martha 61–2, 220*n*71
Woodhouse, Samuel 220*n*71
woods *see* timber
Woodside Ironworks (Worcestershire) 169
Woodson, John 114
Woodstock Road 172
Woodward, Michael 34
wool trade 84, 85, 93, 226*n*56, 238*n*5
Worcester (Worcestershire) 136, 173, 179, 202, 233*n*70, Pl.
  Frog Mill 202
  St Wultstan's Hospital 200, 202
  woods 39–41, 200, 216*n*84–9
Wortley (Yorkshire) 63–4
Worton (Oxfordshire) 200, 214*n*62
  Colliers Farm 37
Wotton Underwood (Buckinghamshire) 87
Wotton-under-Edge (Gloucestershire) 23, 70, 195, 213*n*46
Wren, Sir Christopher 222*n*98
Wriothesley, Thomas *see* Southampton, Thomas Wriothesley, 1st Earl of
Wroxton (Oxfordshire) 169, 179, 200
Wyck Rissington (Gloucestershire) 222*n*109
Wykes Priory (Essex) 190
Wyld Court (Berkshire) 94, 192, 217*n*15

Y
Yelverton, Sir Christopher 88–9, 226*n*54
Yelverton, Sir Henry (1566–1630) 115
Yelverton, Sir Henry (1633–70) 89
York (Yorkshire)
  Holy Trinity Priory 202
  St Mary's Abbey 3–5
Young, Frederick, map of Hawkhurst 219*n*41, Pl.
Young, William 81–2, 224*n*24, 224*n*28

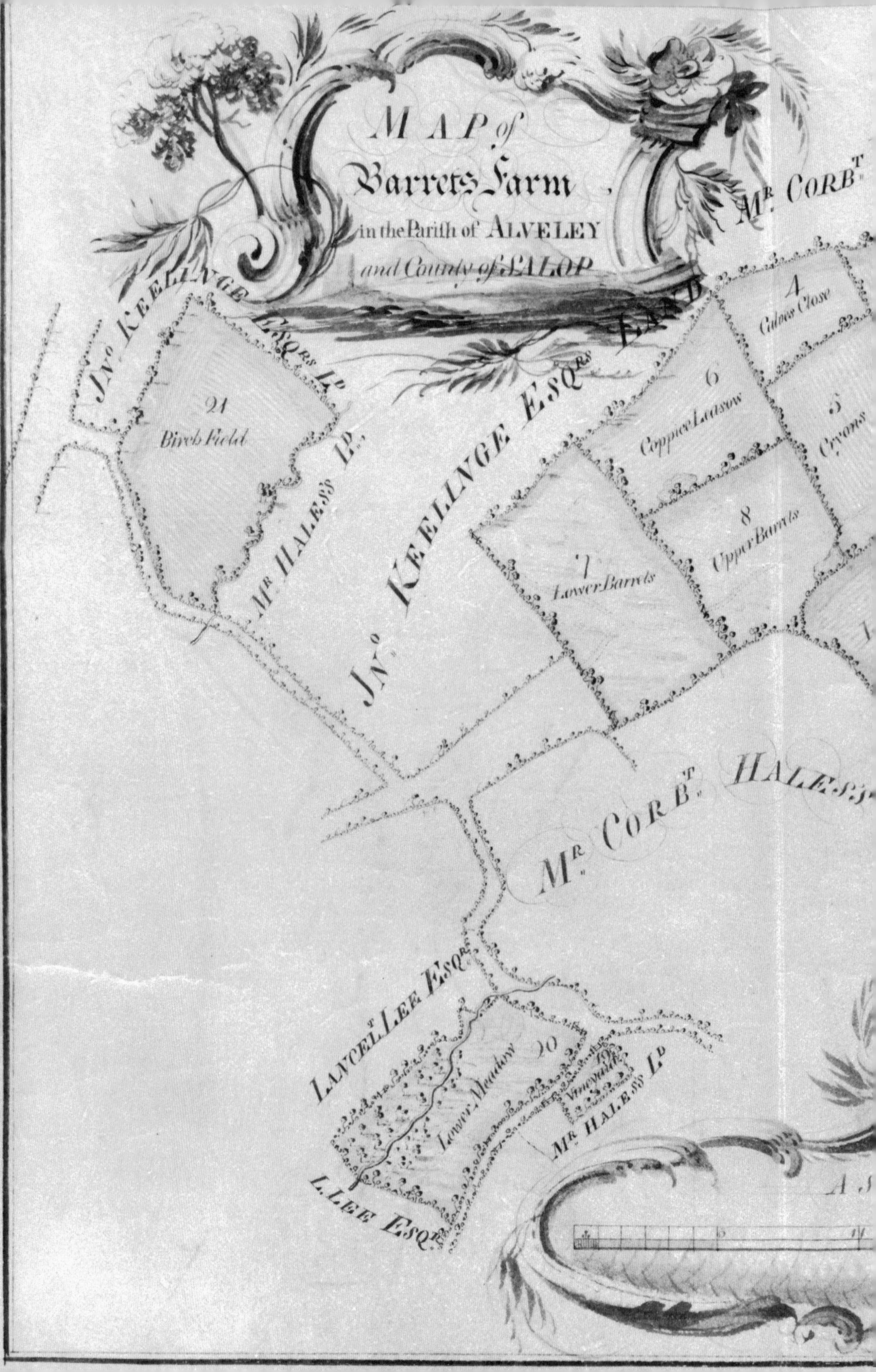
MAP of
Barrets Farm
in the Parish of ALVELEY
and County of SALOP
Mr. CORBt.
4
Calves Close
6
Coppice Leasow
5
Cryons
Jno KEELINGE ESQrs Ld
21
Birch Field
Mr HALES's Ld
Jno KEELINGE ESQrs LAND
7
Lower Barrets
8
Upper Barrets
Mr CORBt HALES's
LANCELt LEE ESQr
20
Lower Meadow
19
Vineyard
Mr HALES's Ld
L. LEE ESQr